The Yale Library of Military History

Donald Kagan and Frederick Kagan, Series Editors

War

by Land, Sea, and Air

Dwight Eisenhower and the Concept of Unified Command

DAVID JABLONSKY

Series Foreword by
DONALD KAGAN AND FREDERICK KAGAN

Yale

UNIVERSITY PRESS

New Haven and London

Published with assistance from the Kingsley Trust Association Publication Fund established by the Scroll and Key Society of Yale College.

Designed by James J. Johnson and set in Fairfield Medium type by Tseng Information Systems, Inc.

Printed in the United States of America by Sheridan Books, Ann Arbor, Michigan.

Library of Congress Cataloging-in-Publication Data

Jablonsky, David.

War by land, sea, and air : Dwight Eisenhower and the concept of unified command / David Jablonsky.

   p. cm. — (The Yale library of military history)

Includes bibliographical references and index.

ISBN 978-0-300-15389-7 (cloth : alk. paper) 1. Eisenhower, Dwight D. (Dwight David), 1890–1969—Military leadership. 2. Unified operations (Military science)—History—20th century. 3. Combined operations (Military science)—History—20th century. 4. Allied Forces—Organization. 5. World War, 1939–1945—Campaigns—Western Front. 6. North Atlantic Treaty Organization—Armed Forces—Organization. 7. United States—Armed Forces—Organization. 8. United States. Joint Chiefs of Staff—Chairmen—History—20th century. 9. United States—Military policy. 10. United States—History, Military—20th century. I. Title.

E836.J24 2010

973.921092—dc22

[B]

2009034628

A catalogue record for this book is available from the British Library.

This paper meets the requirements of ANSI/NISO z39.48-1992 (Permanence of Paper).

10 9 8 7 6 5 4 3 2 1

For Kyra and Dave with great love and pride

For, lo, the winter is past,
The rain is over and gone;
The flowers appear on the earth;
The time of the singing of birds is come,
And the voice of the turtle is heard in our land.
—Song of Solomon

Contents

Series Foreword

W AR HAS BEEN A SUBJECT of intense interest from the beginning of literature around the world. Whether it be in the earliest literary work in the Western tradition, Homer's *Iliad*, or the Rigvedic hymns of ancient India, people have always been fascinated by this dangerous and challenging phenomenon. Few can fail to be stirred by such questions as: How and why do wars come about? How and why do they end? Why did the winners win and the losers lose? How do leaders make life-and-death decisions? Why do combatants follow orders that put their lives at risk? How do individuals and societies behave in war, and how are they affected by it? Recent events have raised the study of war from one of intellectual interest to a matter of vital importance to America and the world. Ordinary citizens must understand war in order to choose their leaders wisely, and leaders must understand it if they are to prevent wars where possible and win them when necessary.

This series, therefore, seeks to present the keenest analyses of war in its different aspects, the sharpest evaluations of political and military decision making, and descriptive accounts of military activity that illuminate its human elements. It will do so drawing on the full range of military history from ancient times to the present and in every part of the globe in order to make available to the general public readable and accurate scholarly accounts of this most fascinating and dangerous of human activities.

In this important book David Jablonsky investigates General Eisenhower's contributions and the challenges he faced as a planner, commander chief of staff, and president in the development of a unified command system. Among the many biographies of General Eisenhower and military histories, this book is uniquely dedicated to the pursuit throughout his career of a structure for unified command.

This book is a study of Eisenhower's involvement in the evolution of unified command in American and Allied military forces. The author explains and analyzes the efforts Eisenhower made as an Army commander and as president to bring about an effective system. As a young infantry officer he began a serious study of unified command, continuing as a student at the Army's Command and General Staff School and then in his work as a staff officer working closely with Douglas MacArthur, when he was chief of staff and later as commander of the Philippine Army when MacArthur was creating that force.

Eisenhower served as chief of staff to the commander of one of the two field armies engaged in the Louisiana Maneuvers in 1941 and was called to the War Department following Pearl Harbor to help plan the relief of American forces in the Philippines. Soon he turned to working on plans for a combined command with the British and Dutch in the Pacific and then on the plans for the Allied command that would carry on the war in Europe. Chief of Staff George C. Marshall was so impressed by the work that he gave Eisenhower the command.

Eisenhower gained important, if painful, experience with the many military and diplomatic challenges of dealing with Allies as he tried to create a unified command in the campaigns in North Africa, Sicily, and Italy. At last, he undertook the overall command of the massive American and British forces in the campaign in northern Europe.

Soon after the end of the war, Eisenhower replaced Marshall as chief of staff and began arguing for a Department of Defense to unify the services and to establish a clear-cut chain of command. The new organization, however, did not meet his goals. Later, as the first commander of NATO forces, he battled with the various NATO countries to establish unified command. Again he had to struggle with parochial interests and was unable completely to achieve the goals he sought.

As president he worked hard to create a unified command system in the Department of Defense, achieving much but not all he would have liked. The system he achieved in 1958 remained in place until the 1980s, when the Goldwater-Nichols Act established a more clear-cut unified command than the American military had ever had in the past; subsequent events have suggested that there is still much work to be done.

Jablonsky's is a powerful work of scholarship. He has exhausted the published primary sources, not only the many memoirs of Eisenhower and others involved, but also the Eisenhower Papers and the vast array of government documents available, as well as some manuscript sources. At the same time he tells a fascinating story that reveals much about the character of General Eisenhower and brings to light the special experience and personal qualities he brought to his task. He has a wonderful eye for a quotation and the ability to present complicated material in a clear and understandable style. The human aspects of Eisenhower emerge clearly, and we come to know and understand him as an impressive, complex, and highly interesting person.

This book is not only valuable as a work about a significant historical figure and an important subject in military history. It also sheds light on continuing issues in the struggle to resolve such problems as the parochial interests of the military services, relationships with allies, and so produce a system of unified command that meets the needs of our time.

DONALD KAGAN AND FREDERICK KAGAN

Acknowledgments

To begin with, my thanks to General Edward C. Meyer (ret.), former US Army chief of staff, for his contributions to this book. Throughout his career, from combat duty in Korea and Vietnam to Defense reorganization in the final years of his service, General Meyer consistently carried out his duties in a manner reminiscent of Dwight Eisenhower.

I am also extremely grateful to Donald and Fredrick Kagan for their foreword and for their expert supervision and editing of the book. Thanks also to Yale University Press senior editor Christopher Rogers for his patience and guidance, to his assistant editor, Laura Davulis, for her direction of the entire project, and to manuscript editor Dan Heaton for his expert editing.

My appreciation also to Lieutenant General Richard G. Trefry (ret.), Major General William F. Burns (ret.), and Major General Robert H. Scales (ret.) for their support and advice.

Special thanks to five intrepid readers for their detailed comments and suggestions: Donald W. Boose Jr., Henry G. Gole, John Derek Hale, James S. McCallum, and John F. Troxell.

Thanks also for their outstanding institutional support to Thomas Branigar and the staff at the Eisenhower Library; David A. Keough and the staff at the US Army Military Institute; and Bohdan I. Kohutiak, the director at the US Army War College library, and his staff, particularly Kathy Hindman and Margaret D. Baumgardner.

My appreciation to the following for support and advice: John Bodin, Joseph R. Cerami, Edward C. Coffman, Leonard J. Fullenkamp, Brian Linn, Michael R. Matheny, John D. Murray, Edward Skender, and Lewis Sorley.

Finally, my love and enduring gratitude to Wiebke, as always the keeper of the gate, and to my daughter and her husband, to whom this book is dedicated.

Introduction:
The Past as Prologue

I want to reinstitute civilian control of the military!

SECRETARY OF DEFENSE DONALD RUMSFELD

I N OCTOBER 1999 General Pervez Musharraf installed himself as head of Pakistan after an army coup. The Clinton administration protested immediately. The general's response, as recounted by Dana Priest of the *Washington Post,* was not to the president, nor to Secretary of State Madeline K. Albright, Defense Secretary William S. Cohen, or even the US ambassador in Islamabad, but to the commander in chief (CINC) of US Central Command, General Anthony C. Zinni. "Tony," Musharraf began his phone call to Zinni, "I want to tell you what I'm doing."[1]

The incident illustrates that by the end of the twentieth century the CINCs of the regionally focused, unified combatant commands had become the modern equivalents of the Roman Empire's proconsuls: sometimes semiautonomous, well-funded implementers of foreign policy. One major cause was the rise of peacekeeping and nation-building missions in the wake of the Cold War, which impelled these commanders into larger diplomatic and political roles. By 1999 their resources and organization dwarfed the assets and influence of other agencies in the foreign policy structure, particularly the State Department, which as Priest noted, "was shriveling in size, stature, and spirit even as the military's role expanded."[2] Each CINC had a huge joint staff. Even Southern Command, focused on an area not normally ranked high on Washington's national security priorities, had a staff of more than one thousand, a higher number dealing with Latin America than the combined total of staff officers addressing that area in the departments of State, Treasury, Commerce, and Agriculture, as well as in the Pentagon in the Joint Staff and the Office of the Secretary of Defense. And when the CINCs traveled—usually in their own planes accompanied by large retinues of assistants and staff—they often were welcomed personally by heads of states and governments, overshadowing the US ambassadors to those countries.[3]

The rise of the CINCs reflects an evolving concept of unified command in the United States during the past century that began with unity of command. That principle focused, in theory, on the authority of a single commander to direct all forces employed in pursuit of a common purpose. In practice, however, despite increased Army-Navy interaction beginning early in the century, unity of command was limited to an individual service, and overall unity of effort between military departments was effected only by coordination through cooperation and common interests. This changed with World War II. That global conflict brought new command-and-control requirements focused on the synergistic nature of land, sea, and air warfare and the need for close combined operations with allies, particularly the British. The result was a concept of unified command at the theater strategic level that expanded the principles of unity of command and unity of effort to produce "a command with a broad continuing mission under a single commander and composed of significant assigned components of two or more Military Departments."[4]

Dwight David Eisenhower was instrumental in developing this concept. His first thirty years in the Army, from his entrance into West Point until Pearl Harbor, prepared him for change in this regard. Informal and formal education during this period inculcated new lessons concerning theater-level joint and combined unity of command and effort from the First World War. To this were added lessons concerning those principles at the national level derived from his experiences in the War Department concerning mobilization planning and in the Philippines in establishing the defense organization for the president of that country. Finally, Eisenhower's participation in the 1941 Louisiana Maneuvers provided him with invaluable lessons concerning the movement of large land forces and the need to use the full potential of air and sea power to support them.

For the first six months of World War II, Eisenhower was at the center of US-British negotiations concerning joint and combined organization for war. Working again in the War Department, he helped create in the Pacific the first unified and combined command and was a key staff participant in conferences and meetings that resulted in the almost informal, ad hoc establishment of the Joint Chiefs of Staff as an organizational basis for United States participation under the newly created Anglo-American Combined Chiefs of Staff. In this capacity, Eisenhower created the terms of reference for a European Theater unified command before being notified that he would command it.

From 1942 until the end of World War II, Eisenhower implemented his evolving concept of unified command with increasing success in the European Theater. His experiences as a unified and combined commander in North Africa, Sicily, Italy, and northwest Europe only strengthened his belief in the efficacy of the concept and the fact that war by separate land, sea, and air forces was no longer feasible. By 1945, however, it was clear to Eisenhower as well as to other leaders that in order for the unified theater organizations to work effectively in the postwar era of new and evolving concepts of warfare and national security, there must be changes at the national level, where the principles of unity of command and effort were being overwhelmed by the traditional tide of service parochialism. What was needed as part of a new national security state, he came to believe, was centralized unification of the services—in essence a third element of the unified command concept that would allow the other two elements, unity of effort and unity of command, to be fully realized in Washington.

After World War II, Eisenhower worked consistently with the Truman administration as Army chief of staff, acting chairman of the Joint Chiefs of Staff, and Supreme Allied Commander in Europe to further service unification at the national level and to improve the theater unified command organizations in the field. But implementation of the overall unified command concept was still problematic, as Eisenhower discovered during his subsequent eight-year tenure as president of the United States. Increasingly frustrated in his dealings with the Joint Chiefs of Staff concerning a "middle way" between security and solvency, he outlined proposals to Congress in spring 1958 for the reorganization of the Defense Department that focused on the nature and extent of authority by the CINCs of the multiservice combatant commands over their component commanders and by the president and secretary of defense over the CINCs.

The 1958 Defense Reorganization Act would fall short of fully realizing Eisenhower's goals. But almost a quarter of a century later, the Goldwater-Nichols Act, building on his concept, moved significantly in that direction for the Department of Defense. With the end of the Cold War and, a decade later, the 11 September 2001 terrorist attacks, the United States is faced today, as it was in 1945, with a drastically altered environment requiring new organization for national security. That organization clearly will have to include improvements in how the government coordinates all the elements of national power to prepare for complex contingencies ranging from postconflict stabilization operations to homeland security challenges.[5] In the first decade of the twenty-first century, Eisenhower's approach to unified command continues to provide a rich conceptual base as organizational reformers turn from the Defense Department to the entire US government. "The past is never dead," Gavin Stevens tells Temple Drake in William Faulkner's *Requiem for a Nun*. "It's not even past."[6]

PART ONE

Formative Years, 1903–1941

CHAPTER ONE

Reform and Education, 1903–1928

You could not possibly . . . explain the place satisfactorily to an outsider, any more than you could explain what went on inside yourself.

    JOHN P. MARQUAND, *MELVILLE GOODWIN, USA*

West Point and all it means is so deep inside you that you are not articulate about it. West Point did more for me than any other institution.

    DWIGHT D. EISENHOWER

In the fall of 1896, I entered the Lincoln School, little aware that I was starting on a road in formal education which would not terminate until 1929 when I finished courses at the Army's War College.

    DWIGHT D. EISENHOWER

DWIGHT EISENHOWER ARRIVED at the United States Military Academy at West Point, New York, in June 1911 after a three-day journey across half a continent from his hometown of Abilene, Kansas. The US Army at the time consisted of 4,388 officers and 70,250 enlisted men. Approximately a quarter of this force was stationed abroad on "foreign service" in American possessions ranging from the Philippines and Hawaii to the Panama Canal Zone and Puerto Rico. The remainder was scattered throughout the United States. The Military Academy appeared then much as it does today: a combination of monuments and gray, gothic buildings isolated on a sixteen thousand–acre reservation in the scenic highlands above the Hudson River. Eisenhower was one of 285 new cadets entering West Point in the class of 1915, and he was not alone in his trepidation as he moved up the hill from the railway station to his new home. "If any time had been provided to sit down and think for a moment," he recalled late in life, "most of . . . us would have taken the next train out."[1]

    West Point in 1911 had stagnated since the Civil War—a small, largely forgotten college with an overwhelmingly narrow professional focus hidden in the wilderness of the Hudson River Valley. The basic problem was that the majority of Academy officials was convinced that the pedagogic principles most effective in producing good military leaders had not changed in the century since Sylvanus Thayer, West Point's founder, had established his "system." The spirit of the institution at the start of the second decade of the twentieth century remained one of self-satisfied continuity, summed up by one superintendent, who, looking back on his tenure during that period, noted that he had "brought to West Point no arrogant project of drastic reform. . . . It goes forward on its majestic course from year to year . . . moving serenely under its traditions."[2] And General Henry (Hap) Arnold, who graduated four years before Eisenhower entered West Point, recalled more than forty years later that the corps had lived "in conformance with a code, and with daily routines which had not changed strikingly . . . since Grant was a cadet."[3]

There was very little impetus from outside the Academy to remedy this situation. A month before Eisenhower entered West Point, President William Howard Taft appointed Henry Stimson as secretary of war. Stimson was a skilled New York City trial lawyer who had run unsuccessfully for governor of the state the previous year. In future years he would continue his public service as secretary of state in the Hoover administration and in 1940 under Franklin Roosevelt once again in the important position of secretary of war. But in 1911 that office governed, in Stimson's judgment, "a profoundly peaceful army, in a nation which saw no reason to suppose that there was any probability of war for decades." As a consequence, he noted that year that the secretary of war was "by a good deal the least important officer in the Cabinet."[4] And yet the Army of 1911 was undergoing a long-delayed modernization; and in almost every issue brought before Stimson, the divide was between the officers who preferred the old system and those who were focused on the ideal of a modernized flexible force.

The initial catalyst for the change was the 1898 Spanish-American War, which had been a disaster for the War Department. More than two hundred thousand volunteers swarmed to the colors at the outbreak of that "splendid little war," straining the minuscule staffs and the lethargic routine of the twenty-five thousand–man Regular Army. The expanded ranks began training at hastily established camps in the South and were soon subject to a variety of debilitating medical epidemics. Adding to the picture of the Army's incompetence was the age and condition of the weaponry and equipment. And the problems of supply were particularly noticeable at Tampa, the Cuban Expedition's port of embarkation, where freight cars transporting food, ammunition, and equipment were backed up for weeks on railroad sidings. To make matters worse, the soldiers of that expeditionary force boarded obsolete vessels that were further delayed in the tropical heat for six days while the commanding general awaited orders from the War Department. "The soldiers are jammed together like animals on those fetid ships," Lieutenant Colonel Theodore Roosevelt complained. "We are in a sewer . . . stinking of rot and putrefaction."[5]

The result of what Henry Stimson termed the "absurd confusion" of the Spanish-American War was a pervasive sense of the War Department's incompetence and corruption.[6] The job of addressing these problems fell to Elihu Root, a New York City lawyer, a partner and mentor of Stimson, and as a result of an 1899 appointment by President William McKinley, the secretary of war in the immediate aftermath of the conflict with Spain. The department that Root inherited in 1899 was a mess. The war with Spain had demonstrated in dramatic fashion that the system was unable to mobilize, train, and deploy forces effectively into a combat theater, much less provide the troops with adequate supplies once deployed. The new secretary of war soon found himself confronted by what Stimson described as the "vast inertia of somnolent inbreeding"—an organization marked by dispersal of responsibility and accountability as well as by disintegration of authority.[7] At the top of the organizational hierarchy was the commanding general of the Army, a position created and continued more for administrative duties than for those of command. Since the Civil War, there had been a tendency on the part of officers occupying this ranking position in the Army to believe that they were independent of what they perceived as the "ignorant whims" of presidents and secretaries of war. That state of mind had led General Sherman, as commanding general in 1874, to move his headquarters from Washington's "wickedness" to St. Louis.[8]

In his reforms, as they emerged in the 1903 legislation, Root replaced the office of the commanding general of the Army with that of chief of staff to the president, charged with supervising all the troops of the line and the special staff and supply departments. To assist the chief of staff, the act created a general staff corps, a body of officers "entirely separate from and independent of the administrative staff."[9] The new title of the

Army's ranking officer was important. For by creating the position of chief of staff, Root was able in the regulations implementing the new law to make clear that command of the Army rested ultimately with the president in his constitutional capacity as commander in chief—a relationship he believed had never been clearly established with the position of commanding general. "When an officer is appointed to the position of 'Commanding General of the Army,'" Root concluded, "he naturally expects to command, himself, with a high degree of independence. . . . The title of Chief of Staff, on the other hand, denotes a duty to advise, inform, and assist a superior officer who has command, and to represent him, acting in his name and by his authority in carrying out his policies and securing the execution of his commands."[10]

The other major reform effort in 1903 concerned relations between the services. Historically, when US Army and Navy units had operated together, the arrangements for unity of effort were ad hoc in nature. The joint overseas operations required by the war with Spain, however, demonstrated that such arrangements were not enough. During that conflict, there were massive interservice problems. At one juncture during joint operations against Santiago in the Cuban campaign, relations between the two services became so rancorous that the Army commander would not allow the Navy representative to sign the official document of Spanish surrender. These problems were duly reported back home, further encouraging the demands for reform of the military.[11]

At the same time, the American victory against Spain significantly extended the dimensions of US national defense with the acquisition of overseas possessions ranging from Puerto Rico and Guam to the Hawaiian Islands and the Philippines. The increase in American security concerns fed the already considerable reform focus on joint Army-Navy operations in both peace and war. As a consequence, the service secretaries issued a joint order on 17 July 1903 creating a Joint Board of the Army and the Navy with the mission "to hold stated sessions and such extraordinary sessions as shall appear advisable for the purpose of conferring upon, discussing and reaching common conclusions regarding all matters calling for the cooperation of the two services."[12] But it was Elihu Root who publicly addressed the underlying rationale for the new organization in his annual report at the end of the year. "If the two forces are ever to be called upon to cooperate," he wrote, "the time to determine what each shall do, and the time for each to learn what the other can do, is before the exigency arises."[13]

This rationale caused the two service staffs, supported by planners from their war colleges, to cooperate in producing a set of "Rules for Naval Convoy of Military Expeditions" for the Joint Board in November 1905. The Board's revisions were approved the next year by both service secretaries and the president and issued as Army and Navy General Orders—the first set of published regulations concerning the conduct of joint operations. The 1906 "Rules," however, did not settle the question of who was to command joint forces ashore. The Marine position by 1909 was that the senior line officer would command regardless of service. War Department regulations, on the other hand, specifically prohibited the command of Army troops by Marines except on direct presidential order. The Joint Board agreed with the War Department and in October 1910 ruled that when the services engaged on land "in a common enterprise," the senior Army officer of the line "should command the whole and have authority to issue such orders to the officers in command of the naval and marine detachments while on shore as may be necessary for the success of the enterprise engaged upon."[14] Interservice cooperation would not be enough, the board concluded; divided responsibility was simply an invitation to fail.

The Joint Board finding was approved by both service secretaries and the president but failed to pass legislative scrutiny in a Congress sympathetic to the Marine Corps. By 1913 the Navy had reversed its position. Both British and American history, the Navy's General Board pointed out, demonstrated that it was not "either necessary or advisable to make any change in the cooperation principle which now obtains in joint operations on shore. . . . The present procedure, cooperation between the land and sea forces, with its limits as to authority and command not too well-defined, may not be ideal; but it . . . worked well in the past and promises to work well in the future."[15]

The issue returned in more substantial form in spring 1915, a few months before Eisenhower's graduation from West Point. In March, Major-General William H. Carter, previously a key military adviser to Secretary Root and now the commanding general of the Hawaiian Department, proposed the establishment of a unified command in Hawaii. If an emergency should occur that isolated the islands, General Carter argued, there was a need for a single authority to control all military and naval forces ashore and that part of the fleet, both surface ships and submarines, necessary to stop enemy landings. Martial law would also have to be established in these circumstances, an impossibility under the principle of cooperation. For General Carter, the logical choice to head the unified command in an emergency should come from the Army, and he recommended that the appropriate regulations be published by both services, providing for unity of command in Hawaii. The defense of the island, he concluded, should not be a function of "the state of mind or courtesy which may prevail between the superior officers."[16]

The Joint Board met in October 1915 to decide on the Carter proposal and on the larger issue of whether to vest command on shore to an Army officer over Navy and Marine officers of higher rank. Marine Colonel John A. Lejeune argued that general officers from the Army were not necessarily better qualified to command large bodies of mixed forces than those of the Navy and Marines. Nor, he pointed out, should Army officers senior to those in other services command in every case. "It is, I believe an incontestable fact that troops of the Marine Corps, grade for grade, are as a rule as well-qualified for command on shore as are officers of the Army."[17] The Navy agreed, arguing that it was impossible to establish rules that would allow one service to command the other in its own element. Generally, then, cooperation should be the governing basis for joint unity of effort.

These issues had little impact on the United States Military Academy. West Point remained committed during Eisenhower's student years to a prescribed engineering curriculum that not even the advent of World War I could alter. During the first year of that conflict, which was Eisenhower's last at the Academy, there was no attempt to apply the lessons of the war to the curriculum. Even as the implications of trench warfare began to emerge, the Department of Military Art continued to emphasize cavalry tactics and student visits to Civil War battlefields.[18] It was true, of course, that Eisenhower and his classmates were thoroughly conversant with the concept of unity of command on which Root and his reformers were basing their calls for change in Army structure and joint procedures. But in the West Point program that concept was couched only in terms of Army forces, far removed from a larger focus that could engender joint unity of effort.

Nevertheless, West Point had a broader influence that would affect how Eisenhower during his long public career would deal with many of the issues underlying the Root reforms. The Military Academy preached a corporate ideal to Eisenhower and his classmates far removed from the popular American vision of rugged individualism that had been the influential hallmark of their formative years. The officers who emerged in the class of 1915 for the most part scorned individual genius as superfluous, if not dangerous. Teamwork as part of a smoothly functioning machine was the ideal for modern war, which, as the German General Staff was even then demonstrating, had become rationalized and routinized—a structure in which any officer could replace any other in the performance of duties.

Nowhere was the efficacy of this approach more in evidence for the young Eisenhower than on the football field, whether in his capacity as a gifted player until a career-ending injury or thereafter as a coach. In coaching at the Academy and in the early part of his active service he would hone all the traits that would serve him so well: organizational ability, competitiveness and energy, powers of concentration, and skill in obtaining the best out of available talent with enthusiasm and optimism. These characteristics would later influence his outlook on unity in joint and combined operations. When he was supreme commander during World War II, his private conversations with key subordinates from all services and Allied nations, as well as his orders of the day, were studded with football slang ranging from "pull an end run" and "hit the line" to "get that ball across the goal line."[19] "I believe that football," he wrote much later in life, "perhaps more than any other sport, tends to instill in men the feeling that victory comes through hard—almost slavish—work, team play, self-confidence, and an enthusiasm that amounts to dedication."[20]

Thoroughly imbued with this corporate ideal, Eisenhower graduated in June 1915 from West Point and was assigned to the 19th Infantry at Fort Sam Houston in San Antonio, Texas. On 1 July 1916 he married Mamie Geneva Doud, and the same day was promoted to first lieutenant. The slow-paced, leisurely life quickened after the American entry into World War I in April 1917. The next month, Eisenhower was promoted to captain with less than two years service, an unheard-of progression in peacetime. In September his first son, Doud Dwight, was born, and Eisenhower began training officers at Fort Oglethorpe, Georgia. Thereafter, he served briefly at Fort Leavenworth, Kansas, and Camp Meade, Maryland, before moving in March 1918 to Camp Colt, Pennsylvania. There he established and assumed command of the largest tank-training center in the United States. Eisenhower remained at Camp Colt for the duration of the war, seething in a frustration only compounded by the declaration of an armistice with Germany a week before he was to sail to Europe. "I suppose we'll spend the rest of our lives explaining why we didn't get into this war."[21]

In another important wartime development, the Allies moved toward greater unity with the creation in fall 1917 of the Supreme War Council because of the Italian defeat at Caporetto and the withdrawal of Russia from the war. The Council consisted of the premier and one other minister from Italy, Great Britain, and France, with sporadic American representation. Each of the four powers also provided an army officer with an appropriate staff as its permanent military representative. Their purpose was to add multinational considerations to strategic issues and policies on a continuing basis and to review operational plans submitted by the national army commanders in the field. These military representatives submitted their conclusions and recommendations as "joint notes" to the Supreme War Council.[22]

At its inception, the powers of the Supreme War Council were advisory. There was no unity of command or effort, and the inter-Allied reserve was little more than symbolic. Only with the March 1918 Ludendorff offensive did the Allies finally achieve real unity of military control. On 26 March, French and British leaders gave Marshal Ferdinand Foch coordinating authority over both Allied armies. On 3 April the Allied leaders met again in increasingly desperate circumstances and agreed that Foch should be the generalissimo exercising the "strategic direction of military operations."[23] This was considerable power even though commanders of the national armies retained tactical control of their forces as well as the right to appeal to their respective governments concerning any controversial decision. The positive turn of events in the field after the Foch appointment further emphasized the value of a united command but also somewhat obscured the potential and value of the Supreme War Council as a decisional organization at the highest political level of grand strategy.

After the war both services worked together from May to July 1919 to reorganize the Joint Board in response to public and congressional pressures for more centralized defense unity. Despite the reorganization, however, the new board remained structurally unable to resolve issues not amenable to compromise—an advisory body of officers with no executive functions, whose conclusions obtained official force only with the approval of both service secretaries. The result was a board generally perceived as a means of reaching joint action and procedure agreements that were necessary for coordination sufficient for the two services to operate autonomously on major issues. In fact, Army and Navy spokesmen testifying in the interwar years at congressional hearings on the advisability of placing the two services under a single department often cited the existence of the Joint Board as proof that sufficient coordination had been established.[24]

That type of rationale did little to stem the spate of post–World War I proposals to place the military services under a single Department of Defense. The impetus toward "unification" generally stemmed from a perceived need for comprehensive administrative reorganization in the executive branch and from the movement for increased autonomy for the Army's Air Service. In January 1922 the Joint Committee on the Reorganization of Government proposed a general restructuring plan based on the "single-purpose" principle, which included unifying the two existing military departments into a Department of Defense headed by a single civilian cabinet secretary who would be supported by undersecretaries of the Army, Navy, and National Resources. In 1923 President Harding indicated that he favored a single defense department. But it was not until the following year that the joint committee began hearings. At that time, the service secretaries, supported by their key military subordinates, rejected the president's recommendation and opposed unification of their departments. By the time the committee made its final recommendation to Congress in June 1924, the primary report focused on civilian agencies and made no reference to the unification of the War and Navy departments.[25]

Given this generally restrictive outlook, the new Joint Board was no more successful than its pre-1914 predecessor with the concept of unified command in operations. Instead, the board deliberately rejected the principles of unity of command and unity of effort, substituting a limited variant to be used when the mission fell within the "paramount interest" of one military department, with that service temporarily exercising operational control over the forces of the other. "The Committee is of the opinion," the board concluded, "that in joint Army and Navy operations the paramount interest in one or the other branch of the National forces will be evident, and in such cases intelligent and hearty cooperation . . .

will give as effective results as would be obtained by the assignment of a commander for the joint operation, which assignment might cause jealousy and dissatisfaction."[26]

A major consideration of Joint Board members during these five years was the austerity of the postwar environment. The demobilization rush after World War I dwarfed even the massive process after the Civil War. Within six months of the armistice, 2,608,218 enlisted men and 128,436 officers were discharged. Eisenhower was initially caught up in this effort at Camp Colt. After a temporary assignment at Fort Benning and a special mission to help move an experimental Army convoy across the United States in the summer of 1919, he arrived back at Camp Meade. There, in addition to other duties, he coached the post football team from 1919 to 1921. More important, it was at Camp Meade that he began a lifelong friendship with George Patton and, through him at a dinner party in fall 1919, with Major General Fox Conner. Conner, an 1898 West Point graduate, was a tall, robust, soft-spoken and wealthy Mississippian who had been General John J. Pershing's operations officer in France, where he was generally acknowledged to have been the intellectual force of the AEF.[27]

Conner was impressed by Eisenhower and used his influence to have him assigned in 1922 as his executive officer in the Panama Canal Zone, where the general had taken command of the 20th Infantry Brigade. By that time, Eisenhower had been first demoted from lieutenant colonel to captain then shortly thereafter promoted to major, a rank at which he would remain for sixteen years. Of vastly more importance for the thirty-year-old officer was the death of his cherished three-year-old son in January 1921. In 1922, when he joined General Conner in Panama, both he and Mamie were inconsolable—the beginning of a lifetime of grieving for a loss from which Eisenhower never fully recovered. In that year Congress directed that the active Army strength would not exceed 12,000 commissioned officers and 125,000 enlisted men, legislation that relegated the United States to seventeenth place among nations with standing armies.[28]

Eisenhower served under General Conner from January 1922 to September 1924 at Camp Gaillard, a jungle post in the Canal Zone approximately halfway between the coasts. The time with Conner, he recalled near the end of his life, was "a sort of graduate school in military affairs."[29] Many of the lessons concerned unity of command and unity of effort at the highest level, particularly in terms of controlling large forces. Conner often spoke with enthusiasm of Colonel George Marshall as "nothing short of a genius," who as the operations officer (G3) of the AEF's First Army had moved 500,000 soldiers and 2,700 guns from the Saint-Mihiel area to the Argonne in two weeks with complete security. "You and Marshall are a lot alike," he once observed to Eisenhower. "I've noticed time and again that you attack problems in the same way."[30] In all this, the general's emphasis was invariably on the lessons of the Great War. He had been a firsthand witness to the cost for the Allies of divided command for much of the war, particularly when Marshal Foch was not provided with sufficient power in keeping with his position of supreme commander. Conner's message to Eisenhower was unequivocal. Versailles ensured another war with Germany, which would result in victory for the Western nations only if they fought as a coalition under a unified command. "When we go into that war it will be in company with allies," he elaborated. "Systems of single command will have to be worked out. We must not accept the 'co-ordination' concept under which Foch was compelled to work."[31]

After leaving Panama, Eisenhower and his family, which now included a second son, John Doud, had brief tours at Camp Meade and the Army recruiting station at Fort Logan, Colorado. In the meantime, General Conner arranged for him to transfer temporarily to the Adjutant General Corps—a branch with two open billets in the Command and General Staff School class of 1926. In April 1925 Eisenhower received his orders for the school with an August reporting date. "I was ready to fly," he recalled, "—and needed no airplane."[32]

At Fort Leavenworth, the Command and General Staff School emphasized thinking under stress without encouraging much independent thought. It was a world in which there was only one correct solution for any problem, an environment, as Eisenhower observed, in which "ideas and principles" enunciated by any instructor had been "carefully scrutinized by the higher authorities of the school to insure that he does not deviate from the accepted teachings."[33] Those teachings were primarily centered on the unity of tactical command at corps level and below. The focus was understandable. The basic assumption for staff training and education was that warfare involved larger forces than ever before, rendering it increasingly difficult for a commander without a well-trained staff to exercise unity of command over combat, combat support, and combat service support troops. Given this tactical emphasis, very little attention was given by the school to unity of effort in the form of coalition warfare and Army air command and control, much less to joint operations with the Navy.

Nevertheless, at a more basic level concerning unity of effort, the Leavenworth emphasis on producing a smooth-functioning tactical war machine did reinforce the value of teamwork for Eisenhower and his classmates. On 11 September 1925 the commandant of the Command and General Staff School, Brigadier General Edward King—also known as "Big Hearted Eddie"—presented the opening lecture to the class on the subject of command unity. The presentation was laced with sports metaphors and analysis that surely must have resonated with Eisenhower. "A football team composed of individuals of medium ability, indoctrinated in team work and led by a real leader," General King concluded, "will beat a team of hastily assembled stars, all wanting to carry the ball individually and in eleven different directions."[34] The conference system used in the Leavenworth curriculum also added to the emphasis on teamwork. For most instruction, Eisenhower and his colleagues were divided into committees of up to ten members apiece. Each committee prepared a report on some aspect of the issue or problem. Each member of the committee contributed to the report, which was gathered together by the committee head and presented to the class.[35]

The concept of teamwork extended only so far for Eisenhower when it came to study methods. Instead of the normal study group or committee which typically might involve as many as six or eight students, he and his friend from the days at Fort Sam Houston, Major Leonard (Gee) Gerow, worked in the third-floor dormer apartment in Eisenhower's quarters, converting it into a study festooned with maps and filled with books and staff studies. At the end of the ten-month course, Eisenhower graduated first in the class of 245 students. It was a considerable achievement for an officer who had not attended his service school and who had graduated in the middle of his West Point class—a tribute, in short, to his postgraduate schooling under Fox Conner.[36]

In August 1926 Eisenhower reported to the 24th Infantry Regiment at Fort Benning, where he served a brief tour as a battalion commander as well as assistant post executive officer. In January 1927, at the request of General Pershing, who was acting on a Fox Conner recommendation, Eisenhower joined the Office of the American Battle Monuments Commission in Washington. The commission, headed by Pershing, had been created by Congress to establish and maintain cemeteries and erect monuments honoring the almost 120,000 Americans who had died in action or from other causes in the Great War and were interred in Europe.

Upon completion of the project, Eisenhower entered the US Army War College at Washington Barracks near Buzzard Point in Southwest Washington as a member of the class of 1928. Much of that curriculum focused on industrial mobilization planning. The joint instruction centered on the principles for the coordination of forces contained in the new Joint Board guidelines, the 1927 *Joint Action of the Army and the Navy* (*JAAN*). The first principle was mutual cooperation to be used in instances when the mission could be accepted by relatively independent action of the deployed forces as approved by both departments in their independent war plans. The second was the limited variant of unity of command and effort, in which the commander of the service not having "paramount interest" was required to execute the mission assigned by the commander of the service that did. "In executing such a mission," the *JAAN* elaborated, "the subordinate status does not yield the actual command of his forces. He shall, however, be held responsible . . . for the proper subordination of his activities to those of the commander having paramount interest." The final principle was the hierarchical subordination of all component forces under one commander, a combination of complete unity of command and effort that would be adopted if the president in his capacity as commander in chief so directed. "Where the magnitude and character of the operations warrant," the directive added, "a commander exercising unity of command shall have a headquarters separate and distinct from those of the commanders of the forces of the two services and shall deal with those forces as coordinate elements of his command."[37] The student investigating committee, in its report to the class, did not select one principle above the others, merely observing that all would require "joint training and close liaison between the two services."[38]

Eisenhower personally worked on two committees that dealt directly with unity of command and effort. In one concerned with the Western Front strategy of the First World War, he was the lone member of the subcommittee charged with examining in detail the evolution of command organizations. "Upon the failure to create unity of command," he wrote of the 21 March 1918 German offensive, "the plan for defense on the Western

Front collapsed. . . . The greatest risk of the Allies was taken when they failed to provide for a Supreme Commander of all the forces on the Western Front." In the future, Eisenhower concluded, "some central authority should always be constituted to coordinate the efforts of all forces in any particular theater of operations."[39]

Reform and Experience, 1929–1941

The War Department moves in mysterious ways, its blunders to perform.

DWIGHT D. EISENHOWER

They can't even agree upon a football game, and you gentlemen know it. Only a few years ago the heads of the Army and naval districts in Hawaii . . . did not even speak to each other. They would not recognize the other on the street, and I am told if it was known one was going to a social gathering the other made a point to stay away. Then talk to me about cooperation and coordination. That could not have happened had they been under one department head.

JOHN NANCE GARNER, SPEAKER OF THE HOUSE, 1932

A FTER THE ARMY WAR COLLEGE, Eisenhower returned to the Battle Monuments Commission in order to revise his guidebook, this time to be based on his personal examination of the battle and burial areas. Mamie insisted that he take the assignment despite his protestations: "I'm an Army officer not a doggone Baedeker."[1] The family moved to Paris for fourteen months—time that Eisenhower used to walk the battlefields and examine in detail the killing grounds of the First World War, still fresh in their depressing desolation a decade after the Armistice. From this experience, he emerged with a deeper understanding of the theater strategic and operational conduct of the Great War, not to mention a visceral appreciation of a conflict that had lasted 1,563 days and caused the death of some ten million soldiers and the wounding of twenty million more. "Fox Conner must be wrong," he concluded. "Men can't be that crazy so soon again."[2]

The Eisenhowers arrived back in the United States in September 1929, a month before the financial panic that would usher in the Great Depression. Soon they were settled in Washington as Eisenhower began his new assignment at the War Department. The nation's capital at the time was, in John Dos Passos's description, "a drowsy sun parlor," a sprawling, slow-moving, almost languid southern city, not yet surrounded by suburbs.

It was a middle-class town with a middle-class government staffed by employees of modest incomes and ambitions, many since the McKinley administration. It was also a town in which people routinely bought used rather than new Chevrolets; a town in which Raleigh Haberdasher on F Street could suggest in an advertisement that a man with an office job really should have more than one suit. And, above all, it was a town of limited centralized function, in which the national government was primarily concerned with handling mail, regulating immigration, collecting tariffs, and enforcing Prohibition. "If the Federal Government should go out of existence," Calvin Coolidge commented, "the common run of people would not detect the difference in the affairs of their daily life for a considerable length of time."[3] Only after the onset of the Depression did the US government begin systematically to affect the daily lives of its citizens in the form of support to farmers, regulation of markets, mediation of labor disputes, and aid to the aged and infirm.

The focus of the government during Eisenhower's tour in the War Department from 1929 to 1935 remained traditionally inward in response to the overwhelmingly domestic economic threat. As a result, the principal agencies for the foreign component of national security—the departments of State, War, and the Navy—were housed together unceremoniously in what later would become the Old Executive Office Building and, in 2002, the Eisenhower Executive Office Building. The military staffs, in turn, were scattered throughout the World War I "tempos," the temporary buildings on Constitution Avenue that had been constructed in 1917 and were still being used in the Eisenhower administration in the 1950s. The Department of the Treasury, in contrast, was housed by itself in ornate space almost equivalent to the State-War-Navy Building, while other agencies concerned with the domestic component of national security—Commerce, Labor, Agriculture, and Justice—occupied the grand neoclassical structures along 14th Street and Constitution.

In early November 1929 Major Eisenhower began work in the State-War-Navy Building as the assistant to Major General George Van Horn Moseley, a 1899 West Point graduate who had been Pershing's principal logistician in Europe. Moseley was the military adviser to Assistant Secretary of War for Procurement Frederick H. Payne, an austere, self-made millionaire from New England who had close links to both President Herbert Hoover and to Patrick J. Hurley, the secretary of war. The primary function of Payne's office had ironic overtones: develop a plan whereby a peacetime economy, already collapsing on all sides, could be mobilized in the event of war. For Eisenhower, who spearheaded this effort, it meant planning for expansion of plants in a time of mass closures of factories; preparing for matériel shortages at a time when no one could afford the goods already stockpiled in enormous quantities; anticipating a manpower crisis in a time of widespread unemployment; and drafting appropriate legislation that would drastically expand government expenditures and deficit spending, just as the Hoover administration was concentrating its efforts on cost cutting in order to balance the budget.

Eisenhower was sent into a hostile environment to survey America's military-industrial potential, traveling in mufti on extensive trips, making numerous visits to factories and plants, and meeting with prominent businessmen. On one of these trips, he met Bernard Baruch, the head of the War Industries Board in the First World War, who believed that in the next war it would be necessary to freeze prices, wages, and costs of matériel in order to avoid inflation, a staple of all past conflicts. A war dependent on industrial and social mobilization, Baruch maintained, could not be conducted through the normal peacetime governmental agencies and procedures. When war broke out, so would competition between departments of government, which in turn would interfere with maximum industrial production. For their part, the military services, citing the generally satisfactory history of Army-Navy cooperation, denied that this would occur in their departments. But Eisenhower had to work with his naval counterparts on these issues at the Army and Navy Munitions Board and considered this to be "convenient reasoning and foolishness. Even during a war against a common enemy, armies and navies of the same nation have often delighted in warring against each other for guns, men—and applause."[4]

The Munitions Board was designed to plan jointly for mobilization, having been created in 1922 based on the lessons arising from American lack of industrial preparedness for the First World War. But as Eisenhower noted, the board seldom met, and when it did, it accomplished nothing of significance because the Navy, which expected to fight the next war with the existing fleet, was simply not interested in such a concept. "Neither the Army-Navy Munitions Board nor its subsidiary committees have been particularly active during the last nine years," he observed in 1931, "nor have they always been able to settle controversial questions placed before them."[5]

None of this discouraged Eisenhower from attempting to further unity of effort in the form of joint service planning. Whether in the articles and speeches he wrote for Secretary Payne or in his role as the chief drafter of the official procurement and mobilization report for the War Policies Commission, a basic theme was always joint cooperation. The War Department could present a general mobilization proposal to the president, he emphasized, but "if the broad plan so presented were objected to in principle *by the Navy* . . . the whole plan would be absolutely worthless."[6] With this in mind, Eisenhower often kept his counterparts in the Navy Department informed of mobilization planning projects he initiated with the Army General Staff. It was a process that he perceived in a more inclusive definition of jointness as a means to guard against what he termed in a speech written for Secretary Payne the "spirit of bureaucracy." This was particularly important, he elaborated, because "the development of adequate war plans in the larger sense demands real cooperation. We must attain unity of effort—no other way can we progress. . . . When we are settling one of our own problems, or when we are dealing with the Navy and other departments, let us remember that we are all in the service of the United States."[7]

These types of efforts were given a boost with the arrival of Douglas MacArthur in the fall of 1930. At the age of fifty, the youngest chief of staff in US Army history, MacArthur was an old friend of General Moseley and was, as Eisenhower happily noted, "receptive to the ideas we had been advocating."[8] In 1932 the new Army chief of staff began employing Eisenhower on various projects outside the purview of Secretary Payne's office. "This year I wrote the Annual Report of the C. of S. and edited the reports of the Sec. War and the A.S.W.," he confided in his diary that November.[9] And in February 1933, when MacArthur formalized the arrangement by transferring Eisenhower within the War Department to his office, the new "military secretary" noted: "My work will apparently be little different from that I have been performing for him for two years but he alone will be my boss."[10]

Less than a month after Eisenhower assumed his new position, Franklin Roosevelt was inaugurated as president. It was during this period that Eisenhower consolidated his concept of the president as an activist commander in chief. Already in his mobilization planning efforts, he had reiterated his belief that "Congress should empower the President to make, in war, such readjustments in, and additions to, the Executive

Departments of the Government as are necessary to assure adequate control of all National resources."[11] The advent of the New Deal simply confirmed Eisenhower's tendency to extend his perception of the president's centralized command role to the domestic, peacetime assault on the Depression. "For two years I have been called 'Dictator Ike' because I believe that virtual dictatorship must be exercised by our President," he wrote in his diary just before Roosevelt's 4 March 1933 inauguration. "Things are not going to take an upturn until more power is centered in one man's hands."[12] Within a few months, Eisenhower became exasperated with the New Deal. "My God," a diary entry in June 1933 exploded, "but we have a lot of theorists and academicians in the administration." Nevertheless, his image of the president at the peak of a national chain of command remained as solidly embedded for the domestic struggle as it did for war. "I believe that unity of action is essential to success in the current struggle. . . . We *must* conform to the President's program regardless of consequences."[13]

MacArthur's reign as chief of staff was also marked by an attempt to settle some outstanding joint issues. In February 1933, just as he welcomed Eisenhower officially to his staff, MacArthur submitted to the Joint Board a twenty-four-page list of proposed changes to the 1927 *Joint Action of the Army and Navy* (*JAAN*) document. The proposals dealt with many of the issues addressed the following year by the congressionally mandated "Baker Board," named for its chairman, former Secretary of War Newton B. Baker. At one juncture, the board considered and promptly rejected a proposal for the unification of the services. "It is far better that (the Army and the Navy) should be free to concentrate on their normal and customary missions," the board concluded, "rather than to adopt a system based upon occasional and short-lived joint operations, especially since these can be met by the adoption of principles insuring coordinated actions."[14]

In September 1935 the service secretaries approved a new *JAAN* that incorporated the Army changes and other extensive revisions of the earlier document. Nevertheless, there was no alteration from the 1927 manual in the choices for coordination and operations: mutual cooperation, full unity of command, and the limited unity of command embodied in paramount interest. The continued inclusion of limited unity of command masked the need for hard choices between the other two options. For although both the Army and the Navy accepted the concept, this did not solve the problem of determining which service had paramount interest in exercising unity of command. In Hawaii, for instance, major forces of both services were involved in the protection of Pearl Harbor. This left the Army responsible for the defense of Oahu; but that mission did not confer, from the Navy's perspective, the right of the Army commander to control the fleet that was based there. And in fact the Navy maintained that the requirements of the fleet should dominate the mission of base defense, since the fleet would have the task of conducting offensive operations against the enemy.[15]

This stalemate ended in June 1938, when General Malin Craig, the Army chief of staff, submitted in response to a Navy proposal a complete revision of the 1935 *JAAN* chapter on the "Coordination of Operations of the Army and the Navy." In the new draft adopted shortly after the Munich Conference that fall, the principle of paramount interest was eliminated, leaving the coordination of joint operations normally to be accomplished by mutual cooperation. This did not preclude the principle of full unity of command if the president so directed, or if the service secretaries so specified in a joint agreement, or if the field commanders in a given situation could agree on the need for a unified command and on the service that should exercise that command. In practice, however, the two services were unable to agree before the Second World War on any single situation that would justify a unified command. At different times, there were attempts to create a single commander for Hawaii, the Philippines, and Panama. But the arguments for mutual cooperation always prevailed; and the American high command at the time of the attack on Pearl Harbor consisted of two virtually autonomous services that lacked any extensive or well-integrated coordinative structure.[16]

Many of these developments occurred during the years when Eisenhower served under MacArthur. It was not an easy task working for this flamboyant and egocentric personality. As chief of staff, MacArthur worked in a huge office behind a massive desk in the State-War-Navy Building, separated from Eisenhower's tiny office only by a slatted door that did not reach the floor and through which he could summon his assistant merely by raising his voice. The new chief maintained an unusual routine that included two- to four-hour absences from his office during the day, usually compensated for by work well into the evening. As a consequence, Eisenhower recalled, "my hours became picturesque."[17] Of these and other inconveniences, he observed, the egocentric general appeared completely unaware: "MacArthur could never see another sun, or even a moon for that matter, in the heavens as long as he was the sun."[18] In this regard, Eisenhower never ceased to be amazed by the chief of staff's habit of referring to himself in the third person and by his disregard for the traditional line between military and political matters. "If General MacArthur ever recognized the existence of that line," he recalled in his memoirs, "he usually chose to ignore it."[19]

And yet the major and the general had a great deal in common and genuinely liked and respected each other. Certainly, Eisenhower, who spent eleven of his thirty-seven years in the Army working directly for both General MacArthur and General Marshall, was closer personally to MacArthur. Both men were Academy graduates and fanatically partisan followers of West Point football. They often exchanged jokes. And Eisenhower and Mamie enjoyed frequent social contact with MacArthur and, in the Philippines, with his new wife, Jean Faircloth. For Eisenhower, MacArthur was "decisive, personable," and possessed of "amazingly comprehensive and largely accurate" knowledge. "My God, but he was smart," he recalled. "He did have a hell of an intellect."[20] All in all, looking back from the vantage of his Second World War responsibilities, Eisenhower was "deeply grateful" for the experience of working under MacArthur. "Hostility between us has been exaggerated," he observed. "After all, there must be a strong tie for two men to work so closely for seven years."[21]

The seven years included four in the Philippines. In 1935 General MacArthur's tour as chief of staff ended. That year Congress passed the Tydings-McDuffie Act, creating a ten-year commonwealth status for the Philippine Islands that would lead to independence in 1946. To prepare for this, Manuel Quezon, the president-elect of the commonwealth, requested that the United States dispatch a military mission to establish a system for national defense, and that General MacArthur head the mission as military adviser to the new government. MacArthur accepted after insisting that the Philippine legislature stipulate that the American adviser be designated a field marshal in the country's army. At the same time, he pressed strongly for his military assistant to accompany him. Eisenhower was "not ecstatic about the prospect."[22] But in the end, the forty-five-year-old major acknowledged that he was in no position to argue with the chief of staff, who had not even offered a fixed period for the assignment.

Eisenhower arrived in the Philippines with MacArthur in October

1935 and departed in mid-December 1939, three months after the beginning of the war in Europe that General Conner had predicted fifteen years earlier. In 1936 he was promoted to lieutenant colonel, the rank he had previously held almost two decades before. And in 1937, with MacArthur's retirement from active American service, Eisenhower became the senior US Army officer in the mission. During this period, much of what he attempted in terms of the defense of the Philippines was maddeningly and depressingly futile. But the experience in the commonwealth further reinforced Eisenhower's thoughts on unity of command and effort at the highest level. By 1939 he had become convinced that at the national level, "clear cut administration through established channels of communication and authority must be relied upon . . . to achieve . . . unity of purpose and effort." The focus of this organization, Eisenhower wrote in his final personal observations for President Quezon, should be the secretary of national defense, the key link in a political-military chain of command that must be rigidly enforced. "To the Secretary," he emphasized, "should be delegated, by his Excellency, every vestige of authority and responsibility that is possible under a liberal interpretation of the law. . . . The single avenue of communication from his Excellency to the Army should be through the Secretary of National Defense."[23]

In December 1939 the Eisenhowers sailed from Manila. The destination was San Francisco and from there to duty at Fort Lewis, Washington. By that time, as war preparations became more urgent, the Army leadership was beginning to deal with command unity problems at the highest level. In July 1940 the War Department tried out the standard doctrine since the First World War on wartime operations. In accordance with that doctrine, a field headquarters nucleus would be activated during wartime under the commanding general, field forces, a position to be filled by General George C. Marshall, Army chief of staff since July 1939. The new chief was a 1902 graduate of the Virginia Military Institute and known as an aloof and self-contained officer of fierce integrity who insisted on the highest standards of conduct, efficiency, and dedication. During the First World War, as the chief of operations in the US First Army, he had emerged as an early advocate of unified command in field operations. He and a few other officers at the time argued that given the complexity of modern war, a single commander with final decision-making authority was required. Without that single focal point, intricate military movements could not be planned and implemented, and vast numbers of men, weapons, and equipment could not be allocated quickly.[24]

It quickly became apparent to Marshall that the field headquarters concept was unworkable. In the event of war, according to the doctrine, the chief of staff would deploy overseas as the expeditionary force commander while using the expanded field headquarters as his operational base. But the major problems in establishing a relationship between that organization and the War Department General Staff had not diminished in the intervening two decades. Of more importance by 1940 was the realization that the impending war would be fought on a global basis rather than in one theater. It would therefore be impracticable for a single overall commander to take the field in one theater while maintaining responsibility for operations in several others. The only solution was for the direction of all Army operations to emanate from Washington. This would require more efficient organization within the War Department in order to work effectively. Already, on the eve of the Second World War, it was estimated that at least sixty-one officers had the right of direct access to the chief of staff. For George Marshall, organizational reform was in the air.[25]

The other impetus for American organizational reform came from the British. The "United States–British Staff Conversations" took place in Washington from 29 January to 29 March 1941. Although the entire conference, known as "ABC-1," was primarily focused on formulating Allied strategy, it did consider organizational arrangements for the two countries should the United States enter the war.

In the early drafts of ABC-1 documents, the British used the term "United States Chiefs of Staff" extensively to indicate an American counterpart to the British chiefs of staff. But such a designation did not appear in the final ABC-1 report, which referred throughout the document to the US Army chief of staff and US chief of naval operations. The distinction highlighted the institutional differences between the two countries less than a year before Pearl Harbor. In Britain, there was a corporate high command designated as the Chiefs of Staff Committee. In the United States, the powers of high command were to be found in individuals—in the president as commander in chief and in his primary professional subordinates, the two service chiefs. There was, however, no final institutional form for these relationships, a fact that became more and more apparent to the leadership and staff of both American services as they became familiar with the forms and procedures of the British structure. One result was that the American service secretaries and their chiefs met informally with the British delegation to discuss how the British system might apply in the United States. Another result was that the conference final report called for the two nations to "collaborate continuously" and recommended that action be initiated immediately by both governments to address the issue of the higher direction of the war should America enter the conflict.[26]

In June 1941 the General Board of the Navy issued a most revolutionary proposal, a draft plan for the "Command Organization of the United States Armed Forces" that recommended the establishment of a joint general staff from both services; the appointment of a single chief of staff from either service, responsible directly to the president; and the creation of unified commands in every theater and in all coastal defense areas. In July, General Leonard Gerow, in his capacity as director of the War Plans Division, recommended that General Marshall adopt the plan provided it proved acceptable to the president and the two service departments. But the Roosevelt administration was in the midst of a delicate balancing act in the summer of 1941. In that period of increasing crisis, there was still a large measure of public and congressional opinion that would have reacted with suspicion at the very least to any attempts to strengthen the structure of the US high command when the primary rationale for that move was to help prepare for war.[27]

In the meantime, Eisenhower was passing rapidly through ever more challenging assignments in keeping with General Marshall's almost Darwinian philosophy. Eisenhower served from January to November 1940 at Fort Lewis as battalion commander and regimental executive officer in the 15th Regiment, General Marshall's old unit, which had returned from China in 1938. As the regiment maneuvered throughout 1940 from the outlying areas of Washington State to the Monterey Peninsula in California, Eisenhower was ecstatic to be once again with troops "after eight years of desk and staff duty in the rarefied atmosphere of military planning and pleading."[28] In November 1940 he managed to stave off a bid to join Gerow in War Plans Division, reminding his old friend that he had had only six months of troop duty since 1922, a fact that had often "been thrown in my teeth."[29] That month he became the chief of staff of the 3rd Division at Fort Lewis, the parent unit of the 15th Regiment. Four months later, in March 1941, he was promoted to colonel and assumed duties as chief of staff of IX Corps with responsibilities for Army units in the entire northwestern United States. In June, Lieutenant General Walter Krueger, the commanding general of the Third Army, wrote General Marshall, requesting that Colonel Eisenhower be assigned as the Third Army Chief of Staff. Marshall agreed to the assignment. On 1 July the Eisenhowers arrived at Fort Sam Houston, the location of the Third Army Headquarters and the site of their wedding exactly twenty-five years earlier.

General Krueger was, in Eisenhower's admiring description, a "hard-bitten" soldier, up from the ranks, who had fought with distinction in the Spanish-American War, the Philippine Insurrection, and the First World War. Most important for the new Third Army chief of staff, the sixty-year-old Krueger was a leader who through more than forty years of service "had kept pace with every military change."[30] In August and September 1941 the two worked well together in the Louisiana Maneuvers, the largest exercise conducted by the US Army before America's entrance into the Second World War. The exercise called for the Third Army, with 240,000 men, twice the size of Grant's largest army in the Civil War, to "invade" Louisiana and attack General Ben Lear's Second Army of 180,000 men. Eisenhower considered the whole enterprise "a vast laboratory experiment," particularly since not one of the officers on the active list had commanded a unit as large as a division in the First World War and since staff officers who had worked above regimental level had largely left the service. The results for him of the "grand maneuver" were "incalculable," providing lessons and experiences that he "appreciated more and more as subsequent months rolled by." In a short period, the exercise developed among younger leaders skill and practice in the handling of large field forces; accelerated the process of eliminating unfit officers; and, absolutely key from Eisenhower's perspective, "accustomed the troops to mass teamwork."[31]

In a broader sense, the maneuvers pointed out to Eisenhower the problems of military preparedness in a time when business as usual was the attitude in much of America. During the exercise, he was shocked to learn that the legislation to extend the Selective Service had passed by only a single vote in Congress. And throughout the maneuvers, the Detroit assembly lines continued the unabated production of new cars even as many of the troops in the exercise were forced to use mock tanks and weapons—and in the case of one cavalry unit, to rent horses. At the operational level, the maneuvers resulted in an overwhelming victory for Krueger's Third Army and a personal triumph for his chief of staff. Soon Eisenhower, who had been identified in a news photograph caption early in the exercise as "Lt. Col. D. D. Ersenbeing," was well on his way to larger and more accurate recognition.[32] In late September 1941 he was promoted to brigadier general, and on 12 December, five days after the Japanese attack at Pearl Harbor, he was notified in a telephone call from Washington that the chief of staff had requested that he "hop a plane and get up here right away."[33] On 14 December 1941 Brigadier General Eisenhower reported to General Marshall's office in the Old Munitions Building.

PART TWO

Wartime Unified Command, 1941–1942

CHAPTER THREE

Beginnings of Combined and Joint Command, December 1941–January 1942

Washington in Wartime has been variously described in numbers of pungent epigrams, all signifying chaos.

DWIGHT D. EISENHOWER

You must have some inkling of the real pressure under which I am now working. The days are too short. I rarely leave this rabid room in the daylight.

DWIGHT D. EISENHOWER

EISENHOWER SERVED HIS second tour in the War Department from December 1941 to June 1942. It was a period of great intellectual growth in which his theoretical concepts concerning unity of command and unity of effort at the highest political and military levels were honed in the reality of his first encounters with the complexities of establishing and dealing with unified Allied commands. His stated qualifications for these challenges were "those of the average hard-working Army officer of my age," certainly a self-effacing analysis of stunning inaccuracy.[1] For in fact the fifty-two–year-old brigadier general was supremely well qualified for the job. There were, of course, the years of self discipline and study. Added to this was an icy intelligence and driving ambition, all hidden behind the open manner and infectious grin that a British counterpart would later estimate as "worth an army corps in any campaign."[2] When Eisenhower's diaries were published, one reviewer commented on his "closed, calculating quality" and continued: "Few who watched him carefully indulged the fantasy that he was a genial, open, barefoot boy from Abilene who just happened to be in the right place when lightning struck."[3]

The nation's capital to which Eisenhower returned in December 1941 was in the process of transforming from a sleepy southern city to a boom town, full of lobbyists and contractors, and short of living space. Much of the city's focus during this period was on the circumstances surrounding the Japanese attack at Pearl Harbor. Given the military reverses in the first six months after that disaster, there was a great deal of concern about the American command structure, particularly in terms of unity of command and effort. For most observers, Pearl Harbor appeared to be an object lesson in what could happen at the top level of the armed forces absent such unity. In February 1942 Wendell Wilkie, the 1940 Republican presidential candidate, had endorsed the concept of supreme allied commander in a speech at Boston. And in the following months, at least seven bills before Congress focused on the establishment of a unified Department of National Defense under a single secretary.[4]

On Sunday morning, 14 December 1941, Eisenhower went directly from Union Station to the War Department for the initial interview with the chief of staff. Although it was the fourth time Eisenhower had met Marshall, it was the first time he had talked to him for more than two minutes. Marshall was typically blunt and direct in his assignment of the newly arrived brigadier general as deputy chief for the Pacific and the Far East in the War Plans Division. "Eisenhower, the Department is filled with able men who analyze their problems well but feel compelled to always bring them to me for formal solution," the chief of staff stated. "I must have assistants who will solve their own problems and tell me what they have done."[5] Eisenhower thrived under this kind of guidance throughout ever more challenging missions assigned to him by his new boss. Each one was a test for a new assignment, the successful accomplishment of which was rarely acknowledged by Marshall. "The nearest that he ever came to saying [anything I would call] complimentary directly to my face," Eisenhower remembered, "was 'You are not doing badly so far.'"[6] That, of course, coming from the chief of staff, was enough. "If he hadn't delivered," Marshall commented later of Eisenhower, "he wouldn't have moved up."[7]

Eisenhower found Marshall, ten years his senior, to be "remote and austere." At the same time, he came to have "unlimited admiration and respect" and even "affection" for the chief of staff, who, like Fox Conner, was both a teacher and a boss to him and, like Eisenhower, was a firm believer in professional performance based on teamwork. Eisenhower toiled long hours during what he termed "the frantic tumultuous months" he was assigned to the War Department.[8] Eighteen-hour days were broken only by a brief lunch in his office of coffee and a hot dog. "I am fast becoming an appendage to my desk," he wrote, "and I don't like it."[9] Added to this was the fact that in his capacity as deputy for the Pacific and Far East, Eisenhower had to monitor the defeat and capture of both the American garrison in the Philippines, which included many close friends, and the Philippine force, which he had been instrumental in building. These developments were not helped by accusations from MacArthur that the Philippine Islands were being deliberately sacrificed by the War Department. "MacArthur has started a flood of communications," Eisenhower noted in his diary in late January 1942, "that seem to indicate a refusal on his part to look facts in the face, an old trait."[10]

By the end of the Washington tour, Eisenhower was ready for the next assignment. "In a day or so I'll be leaving," he wrote on 19 June 1942 with palpable relief. "This has been a tough, intensive grind."[11] The "grind" began immediately for the new War Plans Division deputy as he attempted to deal with the fast-moving, mostly disastrous post–Pearl Harbor events in the Far East and the Pacific. In addition, he was heavily involved in preparations for the oddly named Anglo-American Arcadia Conference, which took place in Washington from 22 December 1941 to 14 January 1942. The British delegation consisted of Prime Minister Winston Churchill, the Chiefs of Staff Committee, and the minister of supply, Lord Beaverbrook. As both prime minister and the newly created minister of defence, Churchill was responsible to the War Cabinet and had assumed the supervision and direction of the Chiefs of Staff Committee. "Thus for the first time," he wrote in his Second World War memoirs, "the Chiefs of Staff Committee assumed its due and proper place in direct daily contact with the executive Head of the Government, and in accord with him had full control over the conduct of the war and the armed forces."[12]

The British chiefs of staff were headed by Field Marshal Sir John Dill, recently relieved by Churchill as chief of the Imperial General Staff and representing his replacement in that position, General Sir Alan Brooke. Dill was tall and sinewy, with alert eyes and a long-boned face. He was possessed of great warmth and charm and, like Marshall, was frank and self-disciplined. The two men would remain close friends until Dill's death in late 1944—a relationship demonstrated by Marshall's arrangements for the British officer to be interred in Arlington National Cemetery. Accompanying Dill was Admiral of the Fleet Sir Dudley Pound, First Sea Lord since 1939. Pound was an old seadog who had commanded a battleship at the 1916 battle of Jutland and was at sixty-four years beginning to show his age with a noticeable limp and an inclination to nap through those parts of the conference not concerned with the Royal Navy. Finally, there was Air Chief Marshal Sir Charles Portal, head of the Royal Air Force since October 1940. He was an Oxford graduate and at forty-eight the youngest of the military advisers. In argument, Portal was even-tempered and unruffled, and this, combined with great attention to detail and what Marshall called "the best mind of the lot," earned him the respect of all the Americans at the conference.[13]

The American military delegation was not as clearly defined. Only Marshall was really a chief of staff, and his dominant position was generally equivalent to the British chief of the Imperial Staff. The Navy had double representation. Six days before the conference, the president appointed Admiral Ernest J. King to be commander in chief, US Fleet, and in an executive order moved the post to Washington with the duties of planning and directing the actual operations of the Navy's combat forces. King was a strong-willed former submariner, carrier commander, and naval aviator, known for his irascibility. "He is the most even-tempered man in the Navy," one of his daughters said of King. "He is always in a rage."[14] The assignment left the chief of naval operations charged only with the mission of professional administration of the Navy. That position was occupied by Admiral Harold R. Stark, "a nice old lady" in Eisenhower's estimation, who would remain as chief until March 1942, when he was reassigned to London and King assumed both positions.[15] The American air representation presented a more fundamental problem. The Royal Air Force was an autonomous service, coequal with the British Army and the Royal Navy. But at the time of the Arcadia Conference, the Army Air Forces, as the name implied, were just one of several arms and services of the US Army. Marshall's solution was to make General Henry A. (Hap) Arnold, the chief of the Army Air Forces since 1938, his deputy chief of staff for air as well. Arnold, a friend of Marshall's since their initial 1914 meeting in the Philippines, would remain a member of the American Joint Chiefs without any formal authorization throughout the war.[16]

On the evening of 23 December 1941, the Arcadia Conference opened with a plenary meeting in the White House of the two sides, the president and the prime minister in attendance. Eisenhower described himself as one of the "unimportant" staff officers at the conference, participating in some of the subordinate working-level meetings.[17] In actuality, he was heavily involved in the adoption by both the British and Americans of the concept of unified command at the theater level and its associated structure, an accomplishment that Marshall would later consider a major contribution to the final victory. In fact, the chief of staff was more concerned at the end of 1941 with organization than with strategy, which had been generally resolved. The most immediate problem was in the Pacific. The major grand strategic assumption before Pearl Harbor was that it would be possible to hold the Aleutian and Hawaiian Islands, Samoa, Fiji, the Solomon Islands, the East Indies, Singapore, Malaya, and the maritime Siberian provinces. During the Arcadia Conference, it became increasingly evident that the Japanese could not be contained in this manner, that they might sweep over the East Indies southward to Australia and through Burma westward into India and even the Middle East. As a consequence, the Allies hastily established a new theater of war known as the American, British, Dutch, Australia (ABDA) Area, which stretched in a confusing manner from the Bay of Bengal to Australasia.[18]

On 24 December 1941, his tenth day in the new job, Eisenhower prepared a memorandum for the chief of staff concerning unity of command and effort in the ABDA area, emphasizing that "the strength of the allied defenses in the entire theater would be greatly increased through single, intelligent command." That notwithstanding, he narrowed the focus to "*local areas* only" in order to persuade the British to accept incrementally the concept of unity of command.[19] This was too constrained for what Marshall had in mind. On Christmas Day he proposed a unified command for the Pacific theater reflecting his strong belief that "the most important consideration is unity of command." Only a commander responsible for the entire area, the Army chief of staff asserted, could decide the question of allocating forces. The various issues that were now being considered were "mere details" which would continuously recur unless settled in a broader fashion. "I am convinced that there must be one man in command of the entire theater—air, ground, and ships," Marshall emphasized. "We cannot manage by cooperation. Human frailties are such that there would be emphatic unwillingness to place portions of troops under another service. If we make a plan for unified command now, it will solve nine-tenths of our troubles."[20]

Marshall spoke without notes and with an emotion that made a lasting impression on those present as he broadened the subject to a necessity for a single commander in each theater operating under instructions from a combined organization in Washington. "We had to come to this in the First World War," he concluded, "but it was not until 1918 that it was accomplished, and much valuable time, blood and treasure had been needlessly sacrificed. If we could decide on a unified command now, it would be a great advance over what was accomplished during the World War."[21]

The British were clearly reluctant to discuss the issue without talking to Churchill. Air Marshal Portal argued that everything would proceed smoothly once allocation decisions had been made and a directive issued. Marshall strongly disagreed. The chiefs of both countries could concur on allocations, he countered, but there would still be no achievement of unity of command and effort. At the heart of the matter was the fact that at the time of the Arcadia Conference, the British had already been waging war for more than two years by managing their campaigns in each theater through a committee of commanders from the three services, none of whom was provided full authority or responsibility for the total operation. In each theater, the commanders in chief worked by mutual cooperation under tight supervisory control from the British chiefs of staff and the prime minister in London. In this manner, interservice problems were usually avoided in theater. But this advantage was more than offset by the inherent problems that beset committees attempting to operate in crisis situations.

These types of differences were reflected in some animosity on both sides, usually hidden behind a professional military veneer. For the Americans, the normally better-prepared and organized British counterparts could at times appear to alternate between pomposity and condescension. "Our people," Marshall conceded after the war, "were always ready to find Albion perfidious."[22] Eisenhower recalled Fox Conner's warning about the difficulties of working with allies and kept many of his prejudices to himself. Generally, the British officers liked him, finding the deputy chief of the War Plans Division to be fair-minded and objective. But Eisenhower's diary betrayed his frustrations. "The conversations with the British grow wearisome," he noted during the conference. "They're difficult to talk to, apparently afraid someone is trying to tell them what to do and how to do it. Their practice of war is dilatory."[23] And somewhat later, as the Allies worked out the boundaries of the ABDA command, the Dutch and Australians joined the British as the object of an outburst that Eisenhower confined to his note pad: "But what a job to work with the

Allies!! There's a lot of big talk and desk hammering around this place — but very few doers!"[24]

The British, on the other hand, were appalled at what they perceived as disorganization at the highest level of the American political-military structure. Even the president, they noted, had no secretariat; and the two services acted as if they were independent powers, often pursuing contradictory courses. Moreover, at the initial military meeting, there was no formal agenda and nobody had been designated to take minutes. "There are no regular meetings of their Chiefs of Staff," Field Marshal Dill wrote General Brooke shortly after the New Year, "and if they do meet there is no secretariat to record their proceedings. They have no joint planners and executive planning staff. . . . Then there is the great difficulty of getting the stuff over to the President. He just sees the Chief of Staff at odd times, and again no record. . . . The whole organization belongs to the days of George Washington."[25]

The Christmas Day meeting ended with the successful British postponement of the issues of unity of command and effort. Marshall realized that he had not prepared the ground sufficiently for such a sweeping proposal and assigned Eisenhower the task of preparing a letter of instruction that "could serve as a concrete suggestion" for establishing a unified command in the Southwestern Theater. The letter, to an as yet undetermined Pacific-area supreme commander, would outline his mission, define his authority, and guarantee each nation's control over issues concerned with national sovereignty. Eisenhower drafted a directive that placed limitations on the Pacific supreme commander as severe as those under which Marshal Foch had initially operated in 1918. "The purpose of these rigid restrictions," Eisenhower noted, "was to convince the other members of the conference that no real risk would be involved to the interests of any of the associated powers while on the other hand great profits would result."[26]

The day after Christmas, Marshall outlined the Eisenhower draft directive to Secretary of War Stimson and informed him of his willingness, if the British agreed, to give the Pacific command to General Sir Archibald P. Wavell, currently the commander in chief of the United Kingdom forces in India. On the morning of 27 December, Marshall, along with Stimson and Arnold, secured the president's support for the Eisenhower draft at a bedside conference in the White House. With his position now fortified, Marshall resumed his overtures to the British chiefs on the afternoon of 27 December, just as the news began to filter back that General Mac-Arthur had declared Manila an open city in order to spare it as Japanese forces poured into Luzon. The chief of staff pointed out the safeguards that Eisenhower had written into the draft. The restrictions were drastic, he conceded; but given the dispersed nature of Allied forces throughout the Pacific, "if the supreme commander ended up with no more authority than to tell Washington what he wanted, such a situation was better than nothing, and an improvement over the present situation."[27]

Suddenly, in an unexpected shift, the British chiefs ceased to resist the concept of unified command and began to criticize the Eisenhower draft for excessively restricting the supreme commander. Marshall quickly agreed, and Admiral Stark, seeing the British beginning to yield, declared that the establishment of the principle of unified command was the key, and that the draft could always be revised as necessary. The meeting ended with an agreement to prepare a new directive for approval by the two civilian leaders. It was a welcome outcome. In the end, Marshall recalled proudly, "the chief of the Naval planners rushed to the door to shake hands with me and put his arm around me, which surprised me."[28]

That evening at the White House, however, Churchill, accompanied by Lord Beaverbrook, argued against the concept. Unity of command could work, he told Roosevelt and Harry Hopkins, the president's confidant and close friend, when there was a continuous line of battle, as there had been in the First World War from the Vosges to the Channel. But in the Far East, some of the Allied forces were separated from each other by a thousand miles or more. The armies, navies, and air forces of the four countries, the prime minister stated, should therefore operate separately, with each service commander reporting into a Supreme War Council in Washington. At some point in the evening, Beaverbrook slipped Hopkins a note indicating that despite his performance, Churchill was open to further argument on the subject. As a consequence, Hopkins arranged for a meeting between Marshall and Churchill—an example of the extraordinary influence wielded by this fragile éminence grise of the White House in his informal, extraofficial capacity to bring about agreements that might have stalled indefinitely or failed.[29]

The meeting took place the next morning in the prime minister's White House bedroom. The Army chief of staff walked back and forth as he made his arguments. Churchill responded belligerently. It was difficult, he argued, to expect the Navy to place its ships under an Army commander, and in any event, what could an Army officer know about handling ships? Marshall exploded. "What the devil does a naval officer know about handling a tank?" he demanded. The purpose was to get unified control of the armed forces, not to enlist sailors as tank drivers. "I told him," Marshall recalled, "I was not interested in Drake and Frobisher, but I was interested in having a united front against Japan."[30]

Marshall was not optimistic about the outcome of the meeting. But on 28 December, after further talks with Roosevelt, Churchill cabled the War Cabinet in London to emphasize that the "question of unity of command has assumed urgent form," and to point out that Marshall, who "has evidently gone far into detailed scheme and has a draft letter of instruction," had pleaded the case "with great conviction."[31] The next day, the prime minister cabled London that subject to the approval of the War Cabinet, he had accepted the proposal, "most strongly endorsed by General Marshall," that "unity of command shall be established in Southwestern Pacific." The proposal was, he was convinced, "a war winner." The offer to Wavell, Churchill understood, was one that only the highest sense of duty could induce the British general to accept, since "it was almost certain that he would have to bear a load of defeat in a scene of confusion."[32]

On the morning of 2 January 1942, Eisenhower's revised letter of instruction was sent to General Wavell, providing somewhat more authority for the new commander than had the original draft. He was authorized to coordinate in the ABDA Theater "the strategic operations of all organized land, sea and air forces." To this end, he could dispose of reinforcements, require necessary reports from subordinate commanders, control all communiqués concerning the forces under his command, and organize task forces for specific missions. At the same time, however, the ABDA commander was forbidden to interfere administratively or with communication between the national contingents and their governments. And he was specifically directed not to alter the organization at the tactical level of the national forces in his command. Most important, the 2 January letter stipulated that should any national force commander consider that an order from the supreme commander might threaten his country's national interest, "such commander is, before obeying the order, authorized, upon instant notification to the Supreme Commander of his intention, to appeal to his own government."[33] That day, Japanese forces occupied Manila, and MacArthur began his retreat down the Bataan Peninsula to the island fortress of Corregidor. "Unity of command in ABDA area seems assured," a tired Eisenhower noted on his writing pad that evening. "Good start!—but what an effort. Talk-talk-talk."[34]

The British agreement to a unified ABDA command opened up a broader issue concerned with arrangements for responsibility and control of the entire war under the principles of unity of command and effort. Churchill's dispatch on the subject to the War Cabinet stated that Wavell, as the supreme commander of ABDA, would receive his orders from "an appropriate joint body who will be responsible to me as Minister of Defence and to the President, who is also Commander-in-Chief of all United States forces."[35] Hopkins had suggested the wording to the prime minister. "It seemed to me so essential to get the unity of command through in the South West Pacific," he wrote, "that rather than try to define what the 'appropriate body' would be, I urged both the Prime Minister and the President to send it along and decide the make-up . . . later."[36]

The urgency of the situation in ABDA, however, would not allow for much postponement of decisions on issues such as overall command composition. Already on 30 December, Hopkins noted that the "suggestion of 'an appropriate joint body' has kicked up a hell of a row. . . . It now develops that everybody and his grandmother wants to be on the joint body."[37] The vehicle for such participation at the ABC-1 conference in March 1941 had been a Supreme War Council, primarily oriented on Anglo-American collaboration. But after June 1941 there would have to be Russian representation under the concept; and after Pearl Harbor, as the ABDA deliberations indicated, there were Dutch, Australian, and New Zealand interests, as well as the larger question of China. The Supreme War Council, in effect, would be an unwieldy, impractical agency for immediate political and military direction. Moreover, the basic fact by early 1942 was that the United States and Great Britain were the only two major powers actively engaged in hostilities with all the Axis countries. In addition, both the Soviet Union and China were geographically isolated, while the exterior positions of America and Britain held out the potential for initiative and decision at that particular time in the war. All this caused the two countries to view the war as a global whole, which in turn drew them toward a joint Anglo-American direction of the conflict rather than toward some enlarged organization for supreme Allied control. It would be "utterly impracticable," Marshall pointed out, to have such a combined command post "changed into a Congress of nations."[38]

The president was heavily involved in the various joint command studies between the two countries. On New Year's Day he and the prime minister approved a combined organization to supervise the ABDA Command. Under this agreement, the ABC-1 design was modified to place the primary focus on a committee composed of the chiefs of staffs from the two nations, from which Wavell would receive his direction and to which he would report. These Combined Chiefs of Staff would sit in Washington, where a permanent Joint Staff Mission under Field Marshal Dill would represent the British chiefs.

The ABDA prototype featured heavily in the subsequent discussions toward the end of the Arcadia Conference. On 13 January 1942 the chiefs from both nations considered a paper submitted by the British on "Post Arcadia Collaboration." Admiral Pound opened the meeting with a statement indicating that the combined body already agreed upon for the direction of the Pacific unified command "would be suitable not only for ABDA, but for all other operational matters as well."[39] The statement was the first official declaration in favor of a permanent, combined strategic body with unlimited military jurisdiction for any area under Anglo-American responsibility. The US response indicated that the Americans had moved well beyond the cautious approach so evident in ABC-1, and particularly beyond the general assumption of those conversations that any organization established would serve as a type of joint secretariat acting as a liaison between the British chiefs in London and their American counterparts in Washington. For Marshall in the wake of Pearl Harbor, the traditional concept of liaison was simply not adequate to deal with the new circumstances; and in accepting the British proposal, he emphasized that there could be no question "of having any duplication of the Combined Chiefs of Staff organization in Washington and London."[40] The consultations that would occur in Washington between the US high command and the British Joint Mission representing the British chiefs would be decisive.

At a final meeting on the afternoon of 14 January, the British and American chiefs approved the revised collaboration paper and agreed to submit it to their national leaders. The opening paragraph summed up almost casually the genesis of coordinated effort and direction under a unique binational high command on a scale and to a degree unmatched in the history of modern war: "In order to provide for the continuation of the necessary machinery to effect collaboration between the United Nations after departure from Washington of the British Chiefs of Staff, the Combined Chiefs of Staff (formerly designated as 'Joint Chiefs of Staff') propose the broad principles and basic organization herein outlined." The paper marked the first appearance of the title "Combined Chiefs of Staff (CCS)," defined as "the British Chiefs of Staff (or in their absence from Washington, their duly accredited representatives), and the United States opposite numbers of the British Chiefs of Staff." The paper also went on to define the Combined Staff Planners, the combined version of the US Joint Planning Committee, and the Combined Secretariat—all with assigned general missions. Finally the Combined Chiefs addressed the two basic terms associated with unity of command and effort. "To avoid confusion," they concluded, "we suggest that hereafter the word 'Joint' be applied to Inter-Service collaboration of one Nation, and the word 'Combined' to collaboration between two or more of the United Nations."[41]

Ultimately, the Combined Chiefs organization was a reflection of the committee and secretariat system that had been refined and perfected by the British over the years. At the top together were the president and the prime minister, served by the Combined Chiefs of Staff in a relationship that was virtually identical with that of the British chiefs to Churchill in the United Kingdom. The combined organization, in short, was recognition that issues concerned with global war direction would involve a continuous process of compromises that would also ensure the safeguarding of vital national interests. From the American viewpoint, the committee system was not the most efficient mechanism for military decisions in terms of unity of command. But given the complex business of combined direction in a global war, the system appeared to be the best arrangement that could be devised. As for the British, even General Brooke, who initially wrote of "the false arrangements made in Washington," concluded in the end that the Combined Chiefs of Staff organization was "the most efficient that had ever been evolved for strategy and effort of two allies."[42] And Churchill was even moved to postulate that "future historians" might well perceive the Combined Chiefs as the "most valuable and lasting result" of the Arcadia Conference.[43] His physician, however, who accompanied the prime minister on all his travels, viewed the result differently. "The Americans have got their way," he recorded in his diary, "and the war will be run from Washington."[44]

CHAPTER FOUR

Unified European Theater Command, February–June 1942

My gang and I never get home. We sleep here and our food is sent in. They hit us with directives and queries late in the afternoon and we're expected to have a full set of plans at the White House by nine the next morning.

DWIGHT D. EISENHOWER

Looks like WPD has to kick everybody in the pants.

DWIGHT D. EISENHOWER

THE UNITED STATES Joint Chiefs of Staff came into existence in an even more unplanned fashion than the Combined Chiefs of Staff. Stark, King, Marshall, and Arnold had been in attendance on 21 December 1941 at the White House meeting preceding the arrival of the British contingent at the Arcadia Conference. They were present at all subsequent sessions of that conference and at the first meeting of the Combined Chiefs on 23 January 1942. Soon it became more logical and convenient to refer to the American group as the United States Chiefs of Staff, or, in keeping with the agreed definition, as the Joint United States Chiefs of Staff. "It would be difficult," Lawrence Legere concludes of this reactive genesis, "to imagine anything less the result of considered study of organizational problems."[1]

The Joint Chiefs met every Tuesday at the Public Health Building located directly across Constitution Avenue from the War Department. On Friday afternoons in the same building, the US Joint Chiefs joined with members of the British Joint Mission headed by Field Marshal Dill for meetings of the Combined Chiefs of Staff. By the middle of March, both the Joint Chiefs of Staff, which had met five times, and the Combined Chiefs, with eleven sessions completed, were deeply engaged in the day-to-day management of the war.[2]

That month, the 77th Congress, like most legislative sessions since the 1918 armistice, was considering several bills to establish some form of a Department of National Defense with a single secretary. Roosevelt, however, was satisfied with the evolving Joint Chiefs of Staff system that held the service chiefs directly responsible to him for strategic and operational matters. At a press conference, the president attacked an earlier *New York Times* editorial entitled "Unity of Command," labeling as "completely false" the paper's contention that the services had no joint staff. And when Admiral King and other advisers persisted in attempts to obtain official authorization for the Joint Chiefs, Roosevelt replied that more specific legalization "would provide no benefits and might in some way impair flexibility of operations."[3] The president, of course, was referring to his flexibility.

At the same time, there were important changes within the service departments. In January 1942, Marshall selected Major General Joseph T. McNarney, Eisenhower's West Point classmate and an old friend, to reorganize the War Department. McNarney was the ideal man for the job, Eisenhower noted, "possessed of an analytical mind and a certain ruthlessness in execution which was absolutely necessary to uproot entrenched bureaucracy and streamline and simplify procedures."[4]

And on 9 March the president relieved Admiral Stark of the duties of Chief of Naval Operations that he had discharged since August 1939. A few days later, Admiral King assumed those duties in addition to those he already performed as commander in chief of the US fleet. The new arrangement affected both of the evolving high-level organizations. Stark's departure reduced the size of the Joint Chiefs and left Marshall as the senior and presiding officer. In terms of the Combined Chiefs, King now exercised supreme authority both in command of the fleets and of the offices and bureaus within the Navy Department and was thus a more balanced counterpart for Admiral Pound.

On 16 February, Eisenhower became chief of War Plans Division. Gerow, relieved to be off to command a division, left his old friend with a wry benediction: "Well I got Pearl Harbor on the book; lost the Philippine Islands, Singapore, Sumatra. . . . Let's see what you can do."[5] By that time, the president and the secretary of war had approved many of Marshall's detailed directives. "We are faced with a big reorganization of the War Department," Eisenhower noted in his diary. "The general staff is all to be cut down, except the War Plans Division, which now has all joint and combined work (a terrible job), all plans, and all operations so far as active theaters are concerned. We need help."[6] That help came when Marshall's reorganization went into effect on 9 March. On that day, Eisenhower took over the Operations Division (OPD), the newly created organization more broadly focused and larger than the War Plans Division that it replaced.

The principal emphasis of Marshall's reorganization was decentralization, achieved, ironically, by the consolidation of all departmental agencies into three major commands. The combat components were placed into the first two commands, the Army Ground Forces and the Army Air Forces. The bureaus and special staff were consolidated into the third command, the Services of Supply, later renamed the Army Service Force. Each of these principal commands had its own headquarter staff and its own commanding general who within his command responsibilities made policy and implemented programs. Equally significant, the majority of the planning and operational functions ultimately came to reside in the Operations Division, described by Eisenhower as "the Chief of Staff's personal command post."[7] In that structure, theaters of operations throughout the world were linked by direct communication with OPD. That division would consider any requests coming from those theaters and establish requirements and priorities in light of decisions by the Joint and Combined Chiefs concerning the relative emphasis to be given each theater. The three Army commands would receive the requirements established in OPD and fill them, necessarily creating their own policies in the day-to-day performance of the required tasks.[8]

During Eisenhower's tenure as the head of OPD, it was necessary for that agency to be more involved initially in the process while the theaters and services located and trained their own staffs. This meant that Eisenhower and his officers, as Marshall's strategic planning staff in his capacity as Army chief of staff as well as his membership in both the Joint and Combined Chiefs, helped establish strategic and military policy that, once approved, provided overall guidelines for Army activities in the theaters of operations. As a consequence, OPD became the only Army agency that could issue Army directives for implementing joint and combined decisions. The new arrangements also meant that OPD became the essential conduit between the theater commanders and the chief of staff, representing the views and requirements of those commanders to Marshall and in turn conveying his direction and advice to them. "You

gentlemen are not my staff officers," Marshall advised Eisenhower and his
subordinates in the Operations Division. "You are the representatives of
those theater commanders and you'd better satisfy *them*."[9]

The major impact of all this for the chief of staff was twofold in terms
of unity of command and effort. The reorganization freed him considerably from day-to-day details, allowing him to devote a greater amount of
time to the broader strategy and policy of the Joint and Combined Chiefs
of Staff. Equally important, the new arrangements clarified Marshall's relationship with his civilian superiors. For the secretary of war, the chief of
staff was designated his immediate adviser on all military matters. Secretary Stimson, in turn, would prescribe the functions, duties, and powers
of the Army forces and the War Department agencies and issue detailed
administrative orders on matters ranging from personnel to property.
But to the executive order of 28 February outlining these changes, the
president inserted an important caveat. "Such duties by the Secretary
of War," he ordered, "are to be performed subject always to the exercise
by the President directly through the Chief of Staff of his functions as
Commander-in-Chief in relation to strategy, tactics, and operations."[10]
This addition, as Ray Cline points out, placed Marshall at "the pinnacle
of power."[11]

Given these arrangements, it was natural that Operations Division
under Eisenhower in the spring of 1942 would increase in size and importance. Another result was that as Marshall established his control and
direction of American combat forces throughout the world, OPD became
the equivalent of a field headquarters for a global battleground organized
into theaters of war and theaters of operations, in which those forces were
specifically engaged against the enemy within the theaters of war. As a
consequence, Eisenhower and his OPD staff worked in an environment
almost as tense and dramatic as that of an actual field headquarters, and
sometimes more so because of the instantaneous and constant knowledge of what was happening in all theaters. During this period, it was not
uncommon for the OPD chief, fortified by vitamin pills and Philip Morris
cigarettes, to work until ten or eleven P.M. and then return to the office
a few hours later to finish off a project. His position was "a slave seat" at
best, Eisenhower wrote to General Krueger. "I have never left the office in
daylight and Sunday and all holidays are exactly the same."[12] He pushed
his staff, expanded to more than one hundred officers, equally hard. One
visitor, who had worked under Eisenhower at Fort Lewis, was struck by

the frenzied activity of the Operations Division—"the sense of urgency, of hurry, as though all could tell of deep, dark secrets." At the center of the maelstrom was the OPD chief: "His methods had not changed from those I had been familiar with. . . . Every problem was carefully analyzed. There was the same extraordinary ability to place his finger at once on the crucial fact in any problem or the weak point in any proposition. There was the same ability to arrive at quick and confident decisions. And the same charming manner and unfailing good temper."[13]

The tour in OPD was an invaluable experience for Eisenhower. His knowledge of the workings of that department, of course, would be of great help when he eventually became an Allied supreme commander. Most important, the assignment helped him to forge his relationship with Marshall and other high-level political and military leaders with whom he came increasingly into contact. At one point, for instance, President Quezon suggested that if the United States removed its troops from the Philippines and granted independence to the islands, he would attempt to persuade the Japanese to remove their troops. It was Eisenhower's task to prepare the resolute presidential messages to both Quezon and Mac-Arthur on the sensitive subject, which concluded that the "duty and necessity of resisting Japanese aggression to the last transcends the importance of any other obligations now facing us in the Philippines."[14] That evening, after confiding in his diary the frustration at the "long, difficult, and irritating" task of drafting the presidential replies to the two leaders ("Both are babies"), Eisenhower casually noted: "Tonight at 6:45 I saw the president and got his approval to sending the messages."[15] Typically, his first appearance in the White House Usher's Log for that visit read "P. D. Eisenhower."[16] In a similar example, Eisenhower prepared a memorandum on 19 March from Secretary Stimson to the president with an attached "former Naval person" Roosevelt-to-Churchill message on the status of unity of command in China that demonstrated the combination of Eisenhower's sophisticated knowledge, ease, and fluency in preparing communications between two national leaders. The president dispatched the message on 20 March exactly as Eisenhower had drafted it; and the prime minister later reprinted it in his Second World War memoirs.[17]

The message to Churchill also demonstrated Eisenhower's increased involvement at the highest level of considerations concerning unity of command and effort, as the deterioration continued of the strategic situation that had caused the creation of the ABDA command and the provision for its control by a combined unified organization. On 22 February, Eisenhower noted in typically understated form in his diary that "ABDA is disintegrating."[18] By that time, Singapore had fallen, MacArthur was holed up on Bataan, Rangoon was weakening in Burma, parts of Sumatra had fallen, Borneo had been captured, and the Japanese were poised to assault Java. It was obvious that the capitulation of Java would split the ABDA area in half, necessitating a revised command arrangement. On 23 February the Combined Chiefs of Staff ordered General Wavell to dissolve his headquarters and pass command from the British to the Dutch. That same day, the Combined Chiefs also approved a British proposal for a general division of command responsibility between a Pacific area under American control and an Indian Ocean area under British control. The American approach was expanded by the president to his chiefs and service secretaries in a meeting on 7 March in which he proposed the division of the world into three general areas, with the United States given responsibility for the Pacific, the United Kingdom for the Far and Middle East, and both nations for Europe and the Atlantic.[19]

On 8 March, Eisenhower prepared a study for Marshall based on Roosevelt's guidance, which "after approval by the President is to be presented to the Combined Chiefs of Staff." For the new areas in which either country was assigned separate strategic responsibility, "the Joint Chiefs of Staff of the government shall exercise jurisdiction over all matters of minor strategy and all operations." This would not diminish the role of the Combined Chiefs, Eisenhower emphasized, which in all areas would "exercise general jurisdiction over grand strategy and over such related factors as are necessary for proper implementation, including the allocation of war material." As for the European and Atlantic area of Anglo-American responsibility—an area, Eisenhower underscored, in which "the major effort . . . must be made"—the Combined Chiefs would exercise "direct supervision over both grand and minor strategy."[20] Marshall made only one major change to the study, substituting *theater* for *area* throughout the paper before circulating it among the American Joint Chiefs. That day, expressing his concern over "the complexity of the present operational command setup," Roosevelt forwarded the Eisenhower proposals to Churchill, who accepted them informally on 18 March.[21] Although there was never any formal approval of this division of the world in keeping with the concept of unity of command, the Allies acted for the remainder of the war as if there had been.

Eisenhower's 8 March study also called for the Joint Chiefs to assign "sub-area commands" in the Pacific. Marshall had been initially in favor of one unified command under MacArthur, whose "dominating character," he told Stimson in February, "is needed down there to make the Navy keep up their job in spite of rows which we shall have between them."[22] In the intervening weeks as he dealt with Admiral King's increasing intransigence on the issue, the Army chief of staff came to see that a division of responsibility in the Pacific was necessary if MacArthur were to retain command of a substantial part of that theater of war. As a consequence, even while Eisenhower's 8 March study was being used as the president's proposal for global division, Marshall directed his OPD chief to prepare a memorandum to the Joint Chiefs that accepted the Navy's concept of a twofold division of the Pacific, but not King's specific geographic delineation.

At a Joint Chiefs meeting on 9 March, Marshall was apparently either convinced by King's firm defense of the Navy solution or unwilling to move toward a deadlock that might require presidential intervention. In any event, he did not insist on the adoption of the Eisenhower proposals, but only that the Philippines be included in the Army theater of operations for "psychological reasons."[23] The result was the division of the Pacific into two theaters of operations: the Southwest Pacific Area (SWPA) consisting of New Guinea, Australia, the Philippines, the Solomons, the Bismarck Archipelago, and the Netherlands Indies except Sumatra, under the supreme command of General MacArthur; and the Pacific Ocean Area (POA) that included the rest of the Pacific under the supreme command of Admiral Chester W. Nimitz.

The next day, Eisenhower's father died. For the busy OPD chief, there seemed to be "no time to indulge even the deepest and most sacred emotions." On 11 March, the day MacArthur escaped from the Philippines, Eisenhower left work early at 7:30 P.M. after noting simply in his diary: "I haven't the heart to go on tonight." And on 12 March, the day of the funeral, he closeted himself in his office, shutting off all business and visitors for thirty minutes of meditation.[24]

Throughout the remainder of March, Eisenhower and his OPD staff worked with Admiral Turner and his war plans staff to establish the directives for the supreme commanders of the two Pacific theaters. These documents, issued on 30 March for both commanders, reflected a new procedure that had evolved from the Army-Navy struggle in the Pacific as part of the evolving procedures of the Joint Chiefs of Staff. Under this system, the JCS would designate a chief of the service with the most responsibilities in a given theater as an "executive agent," who, acting on directives from the chiefs, would generate orders and supervise the unified command. In the Pacific, General Marshall was the executive agent for SWPA, Admiral King for the PAO. "All instructions to you," the directives concluded to the two area commanders in terms of their respective service chiefs, "will be issued by or through him."[25]

In the field under these arrangements, the unified commanders exercised operational control over the land, sea, and air component commands assigned to the theater, with the parent service still preserving and guarding direct administrative and support links to those components. The Joint Chiefs provided a great deal of leeway to the theater commanders, allowing them to prepare the detailed operational plans in informal liaison with the planners from the two service departments as well as from the subordinate Joint Chiefs committee system, termed the Joint Staff, consisting of officers from both services. In this capacity, the Joint Staff was restricted to the joint aspects of service plans, connecting the Army and the Navy horizontally without being involved in details of service planning that provided vertical staff direction.

Eisenhower's efforts concerning the issue of unified command in the Pacific were typical of his busy and often frustrating schedule dealing with the Navy on joint problems. On 16 December 1941, two days after his arrival at the War Plans Division and under the immediate post–Pearl Harbor pressure for unity of command and effort, he worked on negotiations between the two services to create unified command structures in Hawaii under the Navy, in Panama under the Army, and in the Antilles and Atlantic approaches under the Navy. In February, however, as the Navy moved in a bid for dominance over the American coastline, joint relations began to be more acrimonious. "We're telling them what is plain fact," Eisenhower noted, "defense of continental United States is Army responsibility, and many forces assisting should be under our command. What a gang to work with. . . . Fox Connor was right about allies. He could well have included the navy."[26] By that time, the principal problem from Eisenhower's perspective was Admiral King, whom he recognized as a fighter, but also as "an arbitrary stubborn type, with not too much brains and a tendency toward bullying his juniors."[27]

On 20 March, Eisenhower provided a typical menu of joint command issues for Marshall to raise with King. Foremost was the need for joint agreement "on the theater in which the first principal combat of the war must be fought."[28] On 25 March he followed up with a thousand-word memorandum to Marshall that incorporated much of his thinking since January on conducting a global war. Aside from protecting the American homeland, he argued, the "immediately important tasks" involved the security of England, the retention of the Soviet Union as an ally in the war, and the defense of the Middle East. Given these considerations, the principal target for the first major Allied offensive should be Germany, "to be attacked through western Europe," an objective "toward which we can all begin turning our coordinated and intensive effort."[29] At lunch in the White House that day, Marshall presented Eisenhower's arguments for a cross-Channel attack to the president, Hopkins, the other chiefs, and the service secretaries. Roosevelt approved and instructed the Army chief of staff to work out the details, a mission immediately turned over to OPD. Eisenhower returned an extensive proposal on 1 April to Marshall, who received the president's strong endorsement of the paper the next day, as well as an order to go to London to obtain support from the British for the rapid buildup of US forces and equipment in Britain, code name BOLERO, in support of a spring 1943 invasion of France known as ROUNDUP.

There were three important consequences of Eisenhower's increasing interaction with Marshall in the winter and spring of 1942. The first was that on 27 March, Eisenhower received word that he was to be promoted to major general. "This should assure that when I finally get back to troops," he noted in his diary, "I'll get a division."[30] The second was that the chief of staff recognized the growing expertise of his OPD chief in the complex business of unified and combined command by having him in May begin the process of drafting directives for the future American commander in a European Theater of Operations (ETO). The third consequence was that in writing these directives, Eisenhower was not to consider restrictions on the authority of the commander as he had in his earlier proposal at the Arcadia Conference for the ABDA commander. On 11 May he sent a written analysis to Marshall of an organizational chart drafted by General McNarney for a possible BOLERO chain of command, emphasizing that the theater commander must enjoy Marshall's full confidence. In this way, that commander could ensure that all planning in England for all services "*must* be cleared through him; otherwise his position will be intolerable." The theater commander, he added, "should be allowed to carry *out his task with minimum interference from this end.*"[31]

The next day, Eisenhower forwarded to Marshall his first attempt at a directive for a European theater commander that incorporated his thoughts from the 11 May critique, concluding that "absolute unity of command should be exercised by the Theater Commander to be designated."[32] In the meantime, he was encountering interservice problems over landing craft, a major item in the BOLERO buildup and therefore an important issue for the Navy, which controlled the production and allocation of all such craft even as the first tug of the Pacific theater was beginning to be felt. At a 6 May meeting of a BOLERO subcommittee, Eisenhower set out a series of questions—"on which I begged the answers last February"—concerning all aspects of landing craft production, use, types, and accountability. The answers were still not sufficient. "How in hell can we win this war," he wrote in his diary that evening even as he noted the surrender of Corregidor, "unless we can crack some heads?"[33] On one front with the Navy, however, he was more successful. During this period, Marshall sent Eisenhower to see the chief of naval operations on an important matter. King hardly looked up from his desk and gave only one word in reply: "No." Eisenhower responded by telling the admiral that he was not giving the Army chief of staff's suggestion the proper consideration, adding that King's attitude did "not do much to assure co-operation between the two services." King's reaction was surprisingly mild, and in the ensuing conversation with Eisenhower, he admitted that "one of the things I continually search myself for is to see whether I am acting according to logic or merely out of blind loyalties of 40 years in the Navy." It was a turning point for Eisenhower. "From that time on," he recalled, "I had a friend in the Navy."[34]

In terms of unity of command, however, there were more immediate problems for Eisenhower within his own service. The Army headquarters in London had been established before Pearl Harbor under Major General James E. Chaney as the US Special Observation Group, with the primary mission of compiling and forwarding back to the US the lessons learned by the British Army as the war unfolded. Since the January dispatch of an American division to Northern Ireland, Chaney's headquarters had become US Army Forces, British Isles (USAFBI), charged with operating as a theater command in preparation for ROUNDUP, the planned May 1943 invasion of France. From Eisenhower's perspective and based on

Marshall's observation from his trip to England, the London headquarters was not making any progress in preparation for BOLERO, and he was left with "an uneasy feeling that either we do not understand our commanding general in England or they don't understand us."[35] As a result, the OPD chief began a twelve-day trip to England on 23 May, in which his worst fears were confirmed about Chaney and his personnel, who worked eight-hour, five-day weeks in mufti, with no sense of urgency, and were not even perceived by the British as an American theater headquarters. "They were definitely in a back eddy," Eisenhower observed, "from which they could scarcely emerge except through a return to the United States."[36]

In England, Eisenhower met three senior British officers who would play major roles in his future conduct of the war. The first was Vice Admiral Lord Louis Mountbatten, related to the royal family and at the age of thirty-eight a genuine war hero, whose flagship had been sunk under him by the Germans in 1941. He was the chief of Combined Operations and impressed Eisenhower with his open and friendly manner, his knowledge and concern about the issue of landing craft, and his already proven ability to create a cohesive joint staff. The second was Lieutenant General Bernard Law Montgomery, who had commanded the Third Division in France in 1940 and the II Corps at Dunkirk. At their only meeting, Montgomery ordered Eisenhower to extinguish his ever-present cigarette, an act that infuriated the American general, who nevertheless described the British general in his trip report as "a decisive type who appears to be extremely energetic and professionally able."[37] Finally, there was General Sir Alan Brooke, chief of the Imperial Staff and Marshall's counterpart in the British Chiefs of Staff. Brooke was a devoted and expert ornithologist as well as an artillery officer with extensive combat experience, who from their first meeting in May 1942 invariably treated Eisenhower with patronizing condescension that bordered on disdain. "As Supreme Commander," he wrote later of Eisenhower, "what he may have lacked in military ability he greatly made up for by the charm of his personality."[38] Eisenhower's normal practice in his memoranda for record of trips and conferences was to say something nice about those with whom he consulted, or not mention them. In this context, as Stephen Ambrose points out, "he seldom mentioned Brooke."[39]

On 28 May, Eisenhower met with Brooke and the other British Chiefs to discuss the overall command organization of ROUNDUP. The British submitted organization charts that essentially incorporated their committee system, with command lines leading from the Combined Chiefs to the combined commanders in chief of the land, air, and sea forces of both nations, each of whom would control separate national forces for his respective service. In response, Eisenhower stated that the American organization was suited to a unified command of all services and that in principle the United States believed that "single command was essential and that committee command could not conduct a major battle."[40]

The next day, Eisenhower met alone with Brooke and offered his own modification of the British diagram as a "tentative suggestion only." In this approach, the supreme commander would take directions from the Combined Chiefs of Staff and be supported by a combined British and American staff composed of all services. The supreme commander would directly operate through the commander of all naval forces (primarily British); the commander of air striking forces (all US and British strategic air forces); the US Army commander (US ground and air support forces); and the British Army commander. The advantages of this approach, Eisenhower noted on the diagram, were that American air support would be kept under US Army command; strategic air forces would be combined under a single commander; and the ground forces of the two countries would be territorially divided, with the respective commanders reporting directly to the supreme commander. The discussions were inconclusive. But for the American general about to return to the United States, it was "quite apparent that the question of high command is the one that is bothering the British very much and some agreement, in principle, will have to be reached at an early date in order that they will go ahead wholeheartedly to succeeding steps."[41]

On 8 June, after his return from England, Eisenhower finished a revision of his draft 12 May directive to the US commander in chief of the European theater that reflected not only his recent experiences abroad but those since rejoining the War Department six months before. The directive was a quantum leap from the flaccid one that he had prepared for the ABDA command and a marked improvement over the one he had helped draft for MacArthur. Unified authority fairly bristled from the paper. Given the distance between Europe and the United States, Eisenhower stipulated, it was essential that "absolute unity of command should be exercised by the Theater Commander," who was charged "with the strategical, tactical, territorial, and administrative duties" under the strategic direction of the Combined Chiefs.[42]

The same day, Eisenhower brought the directive to Marshall, requesting that the chief of staff read it carefully, since it was likely to become an important document in terms of the further conduct of the war. "I certainly do want to read it," Marshall replied. "You may be the man that executes it."[43] Three days later on 11 June, Marshall confirmed the appointment. "The Chief of Staff says I'm the guy," Eisenhower noted in his diary. "Now we really go to work."[44] Part of that work was to ensure that Admiral King understood the concept of unity of command that Eisenhower had written into what had become a directive for his own authority and operations. He discovered that he need not have worried. The naval leader emphasized that what Eisenhower was embarking upon was "the first deliberate attempt by the American fighting services to set up a unified command in the field for a campaign of indefinite length." Moreover, Eisenhower recalled, "he said that he wanted no foolish talk about my authority depending upon 'co-operation and paramount interest.' He insisted that there should be a single responsibility and authority and he cordially invited me to communicate with him at any time I thought there might be intentional or unintentional violation of this concept by the Navy."[45]

Eisenhower's appointment on 11 June to head the European theater came at the end of what Forrest Pogue calls a "remarkably casual" process.[46] There was, however, nothing casual in Eisenhower's reaction to the formal announcement. On his way out of the Munitions Building that day, the preoccupied theater commander encountered an old friend who asked how things were going. "Brother," Eisenhower replied. "What do you think they've done to me now?" He shook his head. "They're sending me over to command the whole shebang!"[47] On 22 June he met with Roosevelt, Churchill, and Hopkins at the White House. The next day in a driving rain, Eisenhower departed from Bolling Field. There was no delegation to see him off and no fanfare when he arrived in Britain.

PART THREE

Wartime Unity of Command and Effort, 1942–1945

CHAPTER FIVE

Unity in Theory:
London, June–November 1942

To Ike, the principle of unity of command is almost holy.

CAPTAIN HARRY C. BUTCHER, USNR

I learned one lesson through all these many months and many experiences. It is that in war there is scarcely any difficulty that a good resounding victory will not cure—temporarily.

DWIGHT D. EISENHOWER

O N 24 JUNE 1942 Eisenhower assumed command of the 53,390 officers and men of the European Theater of Operations, US Army (ETOUSA), with the mission to prepare for American participation in a cross-Channel invasion of France (SLEDGEHAMMER) later in the year.[1] The new commander was somewhat overwhelmed by his position; hardly surprising for someone so little removed in time from the rank of lieutenant colonel and still awed sufficiently by the authorities with whom he was dealing to be delighted by autographed photographs from Roosevelt, Marshall, and King. This did not go unnoticed by his British colleagues, one of whom was struck by Eisenhower's "rather naïve wonder at attaining the high position in which he [finds] himself."[2] Added to this was the strain caused by the talks with the British on SLEDGE-HAMMER, which had stalled by midsummer over "the same problems," he wrote Fox Conner, "that you faced twenty-five years ago."[3] He was smoking four packs of cigarettes a day and had begun to turn down dinners that involved British officers, since custom dictated that smoking was not permitted until the formal toasts to the king were made at the end of the meal. "This life has much resemblance to the OPD one," he wrote Mamie in early August.[4]

The strain was not eased by the arrival in London on 18 July of the Joint

Chiefs of Staff and Harry Hopkins, dispatched by the president to settle the question of Allied operations for the remainder of the year. Eisenhower did not take part in the final negotiations on 22 July that resulted in the decision to end SLEDGEHAMMER and accept the British proposal for the Allied invasion of North Africa (TORCH). In return, the British agreed to a cross-Channel invasion in 1943 (ROUNDUP) and to allow an American to command the Allied Expeditionary Force in North Africa, the latter concession primarily due to residual French bitterness toward the United Kingdom. Both General Marshall and Admiral King supported Eisenhower for the position, and when the question was raised at the 25 July Combined Chiefs of Staff meeting on the last day of the Joint Chiefs trip to London, King was typically blunt: "Well you've got him right here. Why not put it under Eisenhower?"[5] The new commander was formally confirmed by the president two weeks later. In August, Eisenhower could still protest in a letter to Fox Conner that he was "too simple-minded . . . to attempt to be clever."[6] But both Conner and the Army chief of staff knew better. For Marshall, Eisenhower was the logical choice to command the North African invasion because of his intelligent and orderly mind, his administrative experience, and, above all, his ability to get along with others and make them work together.

But as Marshall also realized, these leadership characteristics required a different style for Eisenhower's chief of staff if they were to result in effective implementation. As a result, but only after much procrastination, the Army chief reluctantly acceded to Eisenhower's persistent requests and on 30 June released Brigadier General Walter Bedell Smith from his duties in Washington, where he had served since 1941, first as secretary of the General Staff in the War Department and later as secretary to the Combined Chiefs of Staff. Smith, an expert in high-level staff work, was well acquainted with the officers of both the US and British chiefs of staff. He had risen through the ranks, initially in the National Guard and then in the Regular Army, serving under Marshall in earlier years at Fort Benning, Georgia. His ferocious temper, due in part to painful intestinal disorders and often vented "on friend and foe alike," was legendary. All this was matched by a face normally set in a grim, determined manner that General Hastings L. Ismay, Churchill's chief staff officer, likened to that of a bulldog.[7]

The reaction of some to Smith's personality was captured by Captain Harry C. Butcher, Eisenhower's naval aide and confidant, who characterized the new chief of staff as "a neurotic with an aching ulcer."[8] Behind the tough, brusque manner, however, was a skilled negotiator who was held in genuinely high esteem as a consummate professional by the majority of the American, British, and French political and military leadership. Moreover, Smith's mastery of administrative detail, combined with his intractable demands for immediate results, allowed him to slash through red tape when time or the dead hand of tradition threatened to block progress. Above all, he zealously guarded Eisenhower's time by controlling all correspondence as well as direct contacts with the Allied commander by staff and visitors.

Smith's addition to the Allied headquarters was a significant benefit for a commander who had been attempting to break new ground in terms of unity of command and effort since his arrival in London. Eisenhower's efforts were not helped by the fact that the organizations to which he reported were new and still evolving. The Combined Chiefs of Staff in Washington consisted of the unprecedented mix of the British Chiefs (represented by their mission in the United States) and the American Joint Chiefs. The Joint Chiefs of Staff, in turn, had emerged in the spring as the agency for directing the entire American military effort with no formal charter, executive order, or even a letter—only Roosevelt's very loose warranty in April to create a counterpart of the British Chiefs of Staff. In the end, its existence depended on the confidence of the president.

As a result, Marshall lobbied throughout the spring of 1942 to create a position for an officer not involved in either service department who could be a source of information on joint issues to help decision making at the White House. As a representative of the president, this officer could act as a moderator in debates by the Joint Chiefs, particularly since they lacked a mechanism to decide on issues with seemingly irreconcilable service differences. At the same time, he could help keep track of decision papers sent to the White House, a serious problem that had arisen because of a lack of an orderly system. Equally important, the Army chief wanted a disinterested person as chairman over the Joint Chiefs. Since the departure of Admiral Stark, he had acted in the awkward capacity of presiding over discussions with King and Arnold in which he was also a key participant. Finally, Marshall believed that the new position would be an appropriate and timely response to those advocating a single military department.[9]

The Army chief of staff was unsuccessful in convincing the president and Admiral King of the need for the new position until later that spring, when it was announced that Admiral William D. Leahy would be returning from his assignment as ambassador to Vichy France. Leahy was a man of recognized integrity and had served previously in his capacity of chief of naval operations as an intimate adviser to the president, whom he had known since Roosevelt's service as assistant secretary of the Navy in the First World War. On 20 July 1942 the admiral assumed duties as chief of staff to the commander in chief of the Army and Navy of the United States. At the same time, he became the fourth member of the Joint Chiefs and assumed chairmanship in his first appearance at the twenty-sixth meeting of that organization on 28 July. Leahy had no command authority in this unprecedented position; but he soon proved invaluable as the daily conduit of presidential decisions, intent, and requirements to the Joint Chiefs and of that organization's recommendations, advice, and options to Roosevelt. The chiefs could still consult directly with the president, but the new arrangement avoided the necessity of such meetings on a frequent basis for the routine exchange of information and direction. At one point, Marshall mentioned to his British counterpart that he often did not see Roosevelt for a month or six weeks. Brooke could hardly believe it. "I was fortunate," he noted enviously in his diary, "if I did not see Winston for six hours."[10]

These unprecedented developments in Washington were matched in the field with the unequivocal combined nature of Eisenhower's chain of command, a development that he had helped initiate while at OPD when the Combined Chiefs of Staff had divided the world into three theaters. It had been decided at the time that since the predominant forces in the Pacific were American, the commander in that area would report through the Joint Chiefs of Staff to the Combined Chiefs. In a similar manner, because of British predominance in the Middle East and Southwest Asia, the commanders in those theaters would report through the British Chiefs to the Combined Chiefs. Only in the European Theater was the commander of allied forces required to report directly to the Combined Chiefs of Staff. In issuing their directives to the supreme commanders in all theaters, the Combined Chiefs normally acted through the chiefs of staff of the country that provided the commander. The American Chiefs made the head of the service that supplied the commander their executive agent for this task. As a consequence, the directives from both the Combined Chiefs and the Joint Chiefs were formally communicated by

Marshall to Eisenhower, who sent his messages to the Combined Chiefs by the same channel.[11]

The combination of command chain and procedures had important implications for Eisenhower. The fact that he worked directly for the Combined Chiefs allowed him to deal more effectively with the British prime minister, who, by background and inclination, tended to dip down to the operational and even the tactical levels of war. Using this organizational anchor, Eisenhower would not provide Churchill with any information, recommendations, or requests that had not already been given to his combined military superiors. "I try to satisfy his extraordinary impatience and his desire for personal news," he assured Marshall, "but I am not . . . allowing anything to interfere with my clean cut line of subordination to the Combined Chiefs of Staff."[12] Throughout the war it was to be a struggle, which Eisenhower proudly considered himself to have won by sticking to the principle of unity of command and the concomitant lines of authority that supported it. "Some of the questions in which I found myself, at various periods of the war, opposed to the Prime Minister were among the most critical I faced," he recalled in his war memoirs, "but as long as I was acting within the limits of my combined directive he had no authority to intervene except by persuasion or by complete destruction of the Allied concept."[13]

The procedural focus on Marshall in the US and Allied chains of command was also an important aspect of Eisenhower's efforts at command unity in the new and complex environment in which he was operating. As a protégé of Marshall's in the theater of primary focus, he adopted early on a relaxed approach in his correspondence with the Army chief, writing long, often chatty letters concerning his problems. "I try to write General Marshall about once every ten days, along general conversational lines," he wrote to an old friend, "in the hope that these letters will supplement daily situation reports and reviews furnished to the Combined Chiefs of Staff, so that he may have a very accurate picture of conditions and probable developments."[14] Initially in the early uncertain days of the North African campaign, Eisenhower's letters were full of flattery and reflected his need for guidance and reassurance from the chief of staff. As he developed as theater commander, however, the letters began to reflect a more mature relationship. Throughout the period, Marshall replied with letters of encouragement and, conscious of Eisenhower's great respect for him, normally prefaced any opinions he offered with statements such as "don't let me influence your judgment" and "don't let this worry you." At the same time, he carefully noted Eisenhower's requirements and passed on segments of the letters to the War Department staff, to Stimson, and even to the president.[15]

As the planning proceeded in the late summer and fall of 1942, Eisenhower had to deal with two more urgent concerns directly associated with his unique assignment. To begin with, he needed to create an integrated staff. The new commander had no illusions about the difficulties in forming such an organization when he established his Allied Force Headquarters (AFHQ) in August at Norfolk House on London's St. James's Square. The cramped location itself was unsatisfactory, since he wanted the combined staff not only to work together but to "live together like a football team."[16] The new commander, in fact, regarded Anglo-American cooperation, in General Ismay's words, "almost as a religion" and insisted on combined staffs at all levels—a stark contrast to Marshal Foch's exclusion of foreigners from his staff after he was appointed supreme commander of the Western Front in 1918.[17] In the early days at AFHQ, Eisenhower noted, basic differences in national characteristics and training caused staff officers from the two countries to conduct their business "in the attitude of a bulldog meeting a tomcat."[18] There was, he acknowledged to Marshall, a general American antipathy toward the British that had its roots "as far back as when we read our little red school history books."[19] Added to this was an American perception of once again coming to the rescue—a new twist to an old refrain from the previous conflict, when the AEF had been referred to as "After England Fails." Moreover, British behavior often seemed supercilious to Americans, resulting in what appeared to be condescending and patronizing attitudes. British descriptions of the US soldiers as "our Italians" did nothing to mitigate this perception.[20]

At the staff level, stereotypes of one military by the other did not long survive the combined meetings and conferences. For US officers, the British generally turned out to be informal rather than stuffy, and in fact the initial American impression was often that their counterparts were flippant. British staff officers, on the other hand, expected the Americans to be candid, rugged individualists but were often left with impressions of ponderous formality. In terms of staff work, the British officer generally focused on thorough planning and meticulous execution of directives. In meetings, they tended to argue their cases on merits in a patient and logical manner, normally seeking to avoid unsubstantiated assertions. In contrast, the American staff officers were normally impatient with detailed planning, believing that deficiencies in organization and administration would be overcome by improvisation once operations began.

At the same time, those American officers who had served in Washington had little joint experience and were in fact accustomed to a fight for existence between the services, often played out before a Congress not particularly interested in closely reasoned military arguments. As a consequence, while the British staff used representatives from all three services to plan joint operations, the US staff was accustomed to a procedure whereby each service created its own plans and then attempted to gain acceptance from the other services. For Eisenhower, this single-service approach had been a source of frustration since his duty in OPD. At one point during the planning for TORCH, he cabled Marshall to ask King to assign two of the Navy's most capable officers to assist his joint and combined staff. When the officers arrived and were asked by the planners to help answer a myriad of operational questions, their response, as reported to the infuriated Allied commander, was that they were there only to listen.[21]

Despite these problems, Eisenhower and Smith used the time in London to enforce unity of effort throughout the Allied staff, to include the different service representatives from both nations. The supreme commander's fanaticism on Anglo-American solidarity was the driving force. "In the organization, operation, and composition of my staff," he recalled, "we proceeded as though all its members belonged to a single nation."[22] This approach paid immediate dividends. "In most offices" of AFHQ by the fall, Stephen Ambrose noted, "the co-operation was so complete that British officers joined their American opposite numbers for a coffee break in the morning, while the Americans joined the British for tea in the afternoon."[23] In the meantime, Eisenhower's irascible chief of staff used the US staff system as the basic foundation to probe and attempt new combinations in the unprecedented joint and combined environment. From this, Smith forged a unified staff with established procedures for synthesizing the views from the various AFHQ staff divisions, while eliminating the bias that normally accompanied such specialization. All this produced a flow of digested information and advice to Eisenhower, who, after making the required decisions, turned them back to Smith to coordinate policy execution within the staff and with subordinate commanders.[24]

In actuality, AFHQ was an ad hoc affair that established as a consequence an important, flexible organizational trend for the future. Throughout the rest of the war, the structure and personnel of the Allied organization would remain fluid depending on the demands of overall coalition strategy. But the essential foundation remained the principles of unity of command and unity of effort. And the basic leadership nucleus remained that of Eisenhower and Smith, both devoted to those principles. It was an accomplishment of which the supreme commander was justifiably proud, noting to Marshall on the eve of the North African invasion that "we have established a pattern for Combined Staff operation that might well serve as a rough model when expeditions of this nature are undertaken in the future." There were many things, he concluded, working in favor of the Allies:

> The greatest single feature, of course, was the fact that there was one responsible head. The next thing was that the British government made absolutely certain that commanders and staff officers, detailed to the expedition, had no mental reservations about their degree of responsibility to the Supreme Commander. The third feature was that throughout the preparatory period the Combined Chiefs of Staff, on both sides of the water, preserved the attitude that they had placed responsibility on one individual and refused to interfere in matters properly pertaining to him.[25]

Eisenhower's emphasis on a single responsible authority recognized by the Combined Chiefs was a reminder of his second major task concerned with establishing unified command lines to complement the integrated headquarters staff that he was building. During the summer of 1942 old Army friends repeatedly warned him that the conception of Allied unity, which was the foundation of the unified and combined command scheme, was impractical and impossible. "I was regaled with tales of allied failure," he recalled, "starting with the Greeks, five hundred years before Christ, and coming down through the ages of allied generals to the bitter French-British recriminations of 1940."[26]

To these pessimistic predictions were added the complex amphibious nature of three widely separated, simultaneous assaults, particularly in light of not only the failure of the Gallipoli campaign in the previous war but the more recent experience of 19 August with the disastrous cross-Channel operation at Dieppe. Finally, there was a fundamental Allied disagreement on the landings. The British and Eisenhower wanted a series of amphibious assaults to the east to allow the speedy seizure of Tunis, the primary port for reinforcing the German Afrika Korps, then engaged with Commonwealth forces advancing from Egypt. Eisenhower was overruled by the American Joint Chiefs, who had decided on an additional landing at Casablanca—"the only instance," he later noted, "when any part of one of our proposed operational plans was changed by intervention of higher authority."[27] The primary concern in Washington was that the Allies establish a presence in Morocco to discourage Spain from entering the war as a German ally or from allowing Germany to use Spain as a launching point for attacks on the Allied rear in North Africa. But the Casablanca option also meant that there would be no quick capture of Tunis. Instead, the Allies were to seize nine objectives on an almost one thousand–mile coastal front from Casablanca, the capital of French Morocco, to the other two port cities of Oran and Algiers.[28]

For these and countless other reasons, the entire preinvasion period was one of "strained anxiety" for the supreme commander as he attempted to establish unified lines of authority. In early August, Eisenhower proposed that he should have four principal subordinate commands: Allied Air, Allied Navy, British Army, and US Army. "Alliances in the past," he warned, "have often done no more than to name the common foe, and 'unity of command' has been a pious aspiration thinly disguising the national jealousies, ambitions and recriminations of high-ranking officers, unwilling to subordinate themselves or their forces to a commander of different nationality or different service."[29] The British rejection of the proposal seemed to confirm his point, highlighting differences in both the joint and combined arenas. One issue was the degree of control that the Allied commander was to be given over troops of nationality other than his own. Another was the degree of operational control that he could exercise over the land, sea, and air forces in his theater. Eisenhower, however, was not deterred by these differences, as Butcher noted in his diary: "Ike said that long as he is to be C-in-C . . . he will have the kind of organization *he* wants."[30]

Nevertheless, Eisenhower soon came to the realization that time limitations, coupled with the complexity of tasks and missions to be accomplished, precluded the immediate establishment of a completely clear-cut command organization. There would be no unified air command, for instance, because of resistance by air force leaders from both nations due to the geographically dispersed nature of the Allied operations. Eisenhower was successful, however, in creating a separate US western Air Command and placing it as well as the Eastern Air Command of the RAF under his direct operational control.[31] On the other hand, the Allies did designate a single Allied naval commander of the Expeditionary Force, Admiral Sir Andrew Browne Cunningham, "a real sea dog" in Eisenhower's estimation and destined to be one of his closest and most enthusiastic collaborators in joint and combined operations. But even then, as Cunningham noted, the "chain of command was always a little nebulous," primarily because of Admiral King's reluctance to place American ships under British command.[32] A compromise was reached whereby the US Western Naval Task Force was to be released at a certain longitude from the commander in chief, Atlantic Fleet, to Eisenhower's direct control. In any event, both men proceeded as if there were clearly defined command lines. "So far as Cunningham and myself are concerned," Eisenhower reported to Marshall, "we are prepared to accept anything that is workable and go at it."[33] But the overall result, as the ubiquitous Butcher observed, was that the supreme commander was dealing with two air and two naval commanders as well as two ground commanders—an organization much different from that envisaged in August: "It looks as if he will be trying to do a circus stunt of riding about six horses at the same time."[34]

Despite these difficulties, the new organization was an important step in the US effort, under way since the Arcadia Conference, to move the command structure away from the British committee system, in which each service commander in chief served as a coequal in theater, cooperating with the other commanders, but responsible only to his respective chief in London. In September, Eisenhower optimistically reported to Washington his impression that in the shift toward a more unified command the British were willing to place in his hands "the maximum degree of exclusive authority and responsibility that is feasible in an operation involving troops of two nationalities."[35] But a problem was already developing that would become the most serious threat in the preinvasion period to the American unity of command efforts. The issue was grounded in the basic difference between the way the British and American chiefs dealt with their respective field commanders. The approach of the Joint Chiefs was to give a commander a mission, provide him with a definite size force, and then interfere as little as possible in his execution of the order. In contrast, as Eisenhower observed, the British military leadership in London maintained close daily contact with their commanders and insisted on being constantly informed on details concerning strength, plans, and situation: "It was always a shock to me raised in the tradition of the American services to find that the British Chiefs regularly queried their commanders in the field concerning tactical plans."[36]

Eisenhower received a greater shock on 10 October, when he was provided a copy of a draft directive from the British Chiefs to Lieutenant General Kenneth A. N. Anderson, the leader of the newly created British First Army, who was to command the postinvasion drive from the west on Tunis. The directive was essentially a copy of the British government's instructions to Sir Douglas Haig in 1918, which greatly diminished Marshal Foch's power as Allied commander over British forces by reserving all tactical control over those forces to the British commander, who could appeal to his government if he considered that his forces might be "imperiled" by Allied direction.

Eisenhower responded the same day to General Ismay, examining the directive in detail. He had no doubt that as fighting developed in the new theater, British and American units would be imperiled. But the emphasis on the remedy in the draft undercut the basic principle of unity of command. Instead, such a directive "should be deliberately written so as to emphasize the purpose of the UK and the US to unify the Allied Force and to centralize responsibility for its operation, and . . . any authorization for departing from normal channels of command and communication should be made specifically dependent upon the arise of extraordinary and grave circumstances." In closing, Eisenhower was at his best—conciliatory, impersonal, and objective, yet firmly passionate about unity of command and unity of effort in joint and combined operations. "I believe that this directive," he wrote, "should be written in the form of a short statement of principles, emphasizing unity of the whole . . . and while I believe that the British Chiefs of Staff probably see this matter exactly as I do, I think the wording of their directive is such as to weaken rather than to support the spirit that should be developed and sustained among all ranks participating in this great enterprise."[37]

The British response granted Eisenhower far greater authority than had been provided to Foch. "You will carry out any orders issued by him," the revised directive informed Anderson concerning the Allied Commander-in-Chief. The British general did have the right, "in the unlikely event" of receiving an order that he considered would "give rise to a grave and exceptional situation," to appeal to the War Office, but only if he did not squander an opportunity or endanger any part of the Allied effort while appealing and only if he first informed Eisenhower.[38] For the Allied commander, the new directive was "now worded most satisfactorily," with its emphasis on unity and subordination of national forces to a combined unified command, while the so-called "escape" clause was applicable only to the most unusual circumstances and, in any event, ringed by caveats that further emphasized command unity.[39] Most important, he had established a new concept for Allied operations that was far removed from the rudimentary overtures of unified command that he and the Army chief of staff had made almost a year before at the Arcadia Conference. "From the day I came over here," an elated Eisenhower wrote Marshall on 20 October, "I have dinned into the British the fact that you considered unity of command to exist only when the commander of an Allied Force had the same authority . . . with respect to all troops involved, as he had to those of his own nationality. I am now benefiting from this crusade."[40]

CHAPTER SIX

Testing the Theory:
North Africa, November 1942–May 1943

Like the American troops and their officers, he had much to learn. The education began in Tunisia; it was long, painful, and expensive.

STEPHEN AMBROSE

Within the African theater one of the greatest products of the victory was the progress achieved in the welding of Allied unity and the establishment of a command team that was already showing the effects of a growing confidence and trust among its members.

DWIGHT D. EISENHOWER

O N MONDAY, 2 NOVEMBER 1942, Eisenhower and his party left for an airfield near Bournemouth to begin the flight to the TORCH command post at Gibraltar. The invasion of North Africa began on 8 November with three major amphibious assaults under command of American officers. The Western Task Force under Major General George S. Patton sailed directly from the United States to land on the Atlantic coast of French Morocco. The Center Task Force, sailing from the United Kingdom and composed of American and British troops under Major General Lloyd Fredendall, landed at Oran in western Algeria. The Eastern Assault Force, under the command of Major General Charles Ryder, a West Point classmate of Eisenhower's, landed with primarily American troops at Algiers in central Algeria and subsequent to the amphibious assault turned over operations to the Eastern Task Force under the dour Scotsman General Kenneth Anderson, whose code name was GROUCH. As commander in chief, Allied Expeditionary Force, Eisenhower was directed to "command all forces assigned to Operation TORCH under the principle of unity of command."[1]

In practice, Eisenhower exercised direct command over the task force leaders and over the British and American units that would be formed after the landings. He also directly commanded the land-based air assets through the US Western Air Command (Twelfth Air Force) under Brigadier James H. Doolittle and the British Eastern Air Command under Air Marshal Sir William L. Welsh. In addition, he exercised indirect command through Admiral Cunningham, the British naval commander in chief, over the senior naval commanders of both countries. After the amphibious assaults, the naval task forces were to disperse, but Eisenhower was to have control as supreme commander over subsequent naval operations through Admiral Cunningham. As the news trickled in of the landings, Eisenhower recorded in his diary his sense of the historical significance of this unified structure. "What soldier ever took the trouble to contemplate the possibility of holding . . . an allied command of ground, air and naval forces?" he wrote. "Normally we pity the soldiers of history that had to work with Allies. But we don't now." The final results of TORCH were not known, he acknowledged, but all the elements of his command were "working together beautifully and harmoniously. That's something."[2]

Eisenhower's optimism was soon dampened. It was true, of course, that the minimum TORCH objective of seizing the main ports between Casablanca and Algiers had been achieved relatively quickly. Nevertheless, the broader aim was to use these ports as bases to move General Anderson's British forces eastward for eventual linkup with General Sir Harold Alexander's British desert forces moving westward in pursuit of Rommel's Afrika Korps after the October British victory at El Alamein. The key to this strategy was the capture of the Tunisian posts of Bizerte and Tunis, a goal that for Eisenhower "guided every move we made — military, economic, political."[3]

Almost immediately, however, problems with unity of command began to intrude. Eisenhower had planned that Anderson's British forces would have the primary mission of taking Tunisia, with US forces securing the rear in occupation status as insurance against any German attack through Spain into Morocco. But because of the swift German moves toward Tunis and Bizerte, the supreme commander decided to hurry the movement of American troops to the east as reinforcements for the British. The problem was that no plans had been developed for how US units were to be integrated into British organizations, or for how the logistics and transportation requirements of the American forces were to be met as they raced eastward. One result was that Eisenhower was reduced to ad hoc orders concerning organization and unity of command that, he recalled after the war, "were not clearly understood nor vigorously executed."[4]

There was an even more fundamental problem for the supreme commander. Because of a lack of complete structural planning for unified command, the direction of joint and combined naval and air assets at the beginning of the campaign was haphazard at best. There was little allocation of Allied planes for reconnaissance or for assaults on Axis transports bringing enemy forces by sea. Moreover, strategic bombers were not initially available for attacks on the Italian and German forces in Tunis and Bizerte because of assaults ordered against Italy and other targets outside North Africa. Finally, naval forces did not launch any attacks on enemy convoys for a period of three weeks, and during the entire month of November, the Allies failed to sink even one Axis ship moving toward Tunis.

These developments were all set against the backdrop of continuing political problems with the French authorities in North Africa whose forces resisted the initial TORCH landings. "I am so impatient to get eastward and seize the ground in the Tunisian area," an irritated Eisenhower cabled Marshall on 9 November, "that I find myself getting absolutely furious with these stupid Frogs."[5] The key to the problem was the diminutive, moonfaced French Admiral Jean François Darlan, commander of the Vichy French Armed Forces, who after his capture in Algiers agreed at noon on 10 November to an armistice and signed an order for all French forces in North Africa to stop fighting. On 13 November, the day the British Eighth Army captured the Mediterranean port of Tobruk, Eisenhower flew to Algiers and signed a formal agreement with the admiral by which the French under Darlan would maintain administrative control of North Africa, while the Allies would have regional military rights and jurisdiction.

News of the agreement with a former high Vichy official of demonstrated pro-Fascist political leanings touched off a firestorm of Allied protest that would distract Eisenhower from his unified command responsibilities for almost two months. The supreme commander defended his actions in terms of securing the Allied rear during the race toward Tunisia and thereby causing the fighting to cease in Oran and Casablanca as well as persuading the French at Dakar, on the west coast of Africa, to join the Allies. But Eisenhower's primary objective was not realized by the agreement, for Darlan was not able to convince the French Army in Tunis to resist the German forces. "They don't seem to know which side of the bread is buttered," the Allied commander commented as the French forces withdrew from the port city.[6] The result was strategic failure for TORCH. On 30 November, German counterattacks stopped Anderson's First Army short of the city. "It is obvious," Butcher recorded in his diary, "we have lost the race for Tunis."[7]

Many of these types of problems, Eisenhower realized, came from attempting to run a unified joint and combined command in North Africa from Gibraltar. As a consequence, he originally planned to relocate to Algiers as early as 10 or 11 November. The move was postponed because the undersea cable from Great Britain to Gibraltar provided better communication to the Combined Chiefs than he would receive in Algiers. With the emerging furor over the Darlan affair, however, this advantage began to lose its luster. "I've been pounded all week from the rear," Eisenhower noted on 21 November. "Sometimes it seems that none of us in the field can do anything to the satisfaction of Washington and London."[8]

On 23 November the supreme commander flew to the Maison Blanche airfield in Algiers and drove to the Hôtel St. Georges, on a hill overlooking the city where AFHQ forward had been established. Almost immediately, he acquired a severe head cold that would linger for months, leaving him in a "general below-par physical condition," not helped by constant smoking, long hours of work, and many sleepless nights due to Luftwaffe attacks.[9] Added to this were staff problems that would plague AFHQ even after Bedell Smith's arrival from London on 11 December. Before he left Gibraltar, Eisenhower had considered placing an arbitrary limit of 150 officers on the Allied staff, noting the need to be "perfectly ruthless in cutting out useless positions" in order to devise the most effective organization of minimum size.[10] But within weeks of the move, AFHQ had expanded to 300 officers, with nearly 400 offices scattered through eleven buildings as Smith began to plan for future campaigns, all the while managing current operations. By the beginning of the New Year, the American staff alone in the Allied headquarters numbered more than 1,400.[11]

At the same time, Eisenhower was grappling with problems concerned with the unified direction of air support. Even before he moved his headquarters to Algiers, he was under increasing pressure from General Arnold to create a theater air force headquarters controlling all US forces based in Europe and Africa. "If our airplanes are sprinkled from hell to breakfast in small gobs here, in small gobs there," he pointed out, "Germany will be able to secure superiority of the air anyway she elects."[12] To head this command, Arnold recommended Major General Carl "Tooey" Spaatz, the commander of the Eighth Air Force in England and a 1914 West Point graduate who had marched behind Eisenhower in parade formation. Both airmen were motivated in part by greater confidence in strategic bombing than in direct air support; moreover, under a more unified command they could shift planes from the Twelfth Air Force in North Africa to the Eighth Air Force in the United Kingdom. Eisenhower wanted to maintain control of US air assets in both areas, but for just the opposite reason. For the supreme commander, a more unified air structure would facilitate obtaining air reinforcements from Britain. Such a command was "a necessary development," he concluded, that could best be implemented after the completion of the Tunisian campaign.[13]

The air command-and-control issue assumed fresh urgency on 27 November with the visit to AFHQ of Air Marshal Sir Arthur William Tedder, the air officer commanding-in-chief for the Middle East. Tedder was a tall, slim, taciturn man, given to incessant pipe smoking; he was as dedicated as Eisenhower to Anglo-American solidarity. The success of Alexander's forces in the Western Desert, particularly that of the Eighth Army, owed a great deal to his outstanding organizational capability and the fact that, unlike many of his RAF colleagues, who were devoted to the panacea of strategic bombing, he also understood the value of close air support of the infantry. He looked upon the Air Force, one Luftwaffe intelligence assessment reported, as a "spearhead artillery"; he was a leader who "provided for air support for the advance of even the smallest Army units."[14]

In this first meeting in Algiers with Eisenhower, Cunningham, and Air Marshal Welsh, commander of RAF units in Tunisia, Tedder was "deeply disturbed" by what he saw and heard. The communications for the air forces were practically nonexistent except for the archaic French telephone system. The airfields were inadequate, with congestion and lack of dispersal that were "almost unbelievable." Finally, there was no semblance of a combined headquarters in terms of air operations. Air Marshal Welsh and his headquarters were located some miles outside Algiers. And General Doolittle and the US Twelfth Air Force Headquarters, situated in town apart from AFHQ, were, in Tedder's estimate, "running a separate war."[15] This perception was reinforced on the day of his visit when the US

Air Force refused assistance to General Anderson's First Army operations in the north despite Eisenhower's assurance that the US air was to be under Welsh's operational control. In his final private interview with the supreme commander, Tedder presented his observation and recommendations in a typically open and candid manner.

Eisenhower immediately began to act on Tedder's recommendations while seeking a temporary assignment for the air marshal that would allow him two weeks to study the overall air situation and provide advice. The British Chiefs had been in close communication with Tedder, however, and were doubtful about his usefulness in a purely advisory capacity. Instead, they suggested that he create an air command arrangement similar to that of Cunningham's naval structure by establishing an advanced headquarters in Algiers; there he would command and coordinate all TORCH air force activity in Algeria and Tunisia under Eisenhower's supreme command. At the same time, Tedder would continue to be responsible to the British Chiefs for Middle East air operations, particularly those concerned with the Eighth Army, and for cooperating with Eisenhower in air operations over the rest of the Mediterranean. Eisenhower was tactful in declining the offer on 3 December. "I do not . . . see how he could well serve as commander in two separate theaters, which are under separate ground commanders and in both of which special tactical problems exist at this moment."[16] His air problem, he emphasized, was "immediate and critical," requiring a "stop gap" arrangement to meet an "emergency."[17]

A Mediterranean unified air command, Eisenhower informed Marshall on 29 December, presented too many complications at the time. But he had become convinced that there must be a single air command for TORCH in Northwest Africa. On 5 January 1943, acting under the authority of the Combined Chiefs, General Spaatz assumed command of Allied Air Force, consisting of both the British Eastern Air Command and the US Twelfth Air Force. For the present, bombing operations in Northwest Africa and in the Mediterranean would be based on cooperation between commands—a goal that was, Eisenhower rationalized, "easier to accomplish . . . than is the more intricate one of assuring a complete unification of air effort within this new and sprawling theater."[18] In its brief life, the new command would begin to group air units from both countries, regardless of nationality, according to their functions and tactical requirements.

Eisenhower was less successful with the organization of his ground troops, primarily because of the "pell mell race to Tunisia."[19] The spearhead of that race was General Anderson's force of three infantry brigades and one tank brigade, optimistically referred to as the British First Army. This force quickly outran its air and logistic support and by 3 December was stalled before Tunis in the face of German counterattacks even as Nazi troops from Italy and Sicily began to pour into Tunisia. Attempts to reinforce Anderson resulted in the piecemeal use of American units, which were intermingled in British formations. The mixture caused additional logistical and command unity problems because of differences in organization, doctrine, equipment, and training. For the increasingly frustrated supreme commander, the campaign was a far cry from the paper exercises that he had enjoyed so much at the Army schools in the 1920s. "I think the best way to describe our operations to date," he wrote an old friend in the War Department, "is that they have violated every recognized principle of war, are in conflict with all operational and logistic methods laid down in text-books and will be condemned, in their entirety, by all Leavenworth and War College classes for the next twenty-five years."[20]

The resumption of Anderson's attack to the east was scheduled for 9 December, but the British commander was worried about the strength of his force and soon reported that the offensive would have to be put off for a week or ten days. Eisenhower was under increased pressure from the Combined Chiefs, concerned that further postponement of the Allied offensive might result in a prolonged battle of attrition. And although Churchill cabled that he was "filled with admiration" for Eisenhower's conduct of the campaign thus far, the prime minister's message also exhorted the supreme commander to "go for the swine in front with a blithe heart."[21] But by this time, Eisenhower had managed to move only 31,000 of the 150,000 troops under his command to the front and, "like a caged tiger," in Butcher's estimation, had acquiesced in total frustration to his field commander. "This has been a hard day," he wrote Mamie on 16 December. "An Allied C in C takes a forceful pounding, every day, but some are worse than others."[22]

One problem was the inefficient functioning of the AFHQ staff, which even after Smith's arrival from London on 11 December heaped on the supreme commander too many issues that could and should have been decided or settled at lower levels. "The odd thing about it," Eisenhower noted in his diary, "is that most of these subordinates don't even realize that they are simply pouring their burdens upon the next superior."[23] The more basic problem, however, was that the duties of a unified and combined commander added a unique political-economic dimension: he was responsible for managing and nurturing a coalition, maintaining civil stability, and coordinating the land, sea, and air elements of the theater strategic campaign, even as he attempted to focus on the tactical ground battle. "Politics, economy, fighting—all were inextricably mixed up and confused one with the other," Eisenhower recalled after the war.[24] And once again, there was no familiar professional anchor for the experience. "This unique type of command," he observed at the time, "carries with it a lot of things that were never included in our text books. . . . I think sometimes that I am a cross between a one-time soldier, a pseudo-statesman, a jack-legged politician and a crooked diplomat. I walk a soapy tight-rope in a rain storm with a blazing furnace on one side and a pack of ravenous tigers on the other."[25]

Eisenhower's principal aide in attempting to keep his balance on the "soapy tight-rope" was Robert Murphy, the State Department representative in Algeria since the Franco-German armistice in 1940. Murphy was a tall, handsome, somewhat heavyset man of great charm and self-confidence who was a special adviser to Eisenhower before the invasion, and thereafter the head of the Civil Affairs Section in AFHQ. Marshall strongly advised Eisenhower to begin to acquire other State Department assistance in solving some of his political and economic problems and to plan for the transition of much of his responsibility for civil affairs directly to Murphy as soon as the military situation would permit. The beleaguered supreme commander was happy to comply. "The sooner I can get rid of all these questions that are outside the military in scope," he responded to the Chief of Staff, "the happier I will be. Sometimes I think I live 10 years each week, of which at least nine are absorbed in political and economic matters."[26]

The reality, however, was that because of the unique structure of his unified command, Eisenhower could not just focus on the military aspects of the theater campaign. The Allied commander in chief's headquarters was the clearing house for policy implementation in North Africa by a variety of American and British agencies. In particular, both the US State Department and the British Foreign Office were dependent on the supreme commander for their policies in theater. In addition, there were problems associated with the dual chain of command. In his

capacity as Allied commander, Eisenhower was responsible through the
Combined Chiefs to Churchill and Roosevelt. As commander in chief
of US forces in North Africa, he answered to the president, who occasionally sent him direct instructions on political issues with information
copies to the British prime minister. Churchill nearly always concurred
for the sake of Allied harmony. But in order to ensure that British views
were adequately presented, he dispatched Harold Macmillan, the par-
liamentary undersecretary of state for colonies, to be minister resident
at AFHQ, emphasizing somewhat disingenuously that he was "to be in
the same relation to you as Murphy, who I presume reports on political
matters direct to the President as Macmillan will to me. Although *not*
formally a member of your staff he fully accepts your supreme authority
throughout the theater and has *no* thought but to be of service to you. I
hope he and Murphy will work together so that you can relieve yourself
of the burden of local politics."[27]

The result was a constant stream of directives and advice to Eisenhower from the Combined Chiefs, the Joint Chiefs, the Foreign Office,
and the State Department, as well as from the two Allied leaders. Marshall
understood that this institutional spigot to his protégé could not simply
be turned off and that a coalition supreme commander could never escape completely into the purely military aspects of the theater campaign.
With the completion of the Darlan negotiations, the chief of staff assured
Eisenhower in early December that he had not only his complete confidence but his "deep sympathy in conducting a battle, organizing a fair
sixth slice of a continent, and at the same time being involved in the most
complicated and highly supervised negotiations of history."[28] Nevertheless, there were limits to his patience, particularly when, after two post-
ponements, Anderson scheduled a new offensive to resume shortly before
Christmas. On 22 December an increasingly concerned Marshall cabled
Eisenhower: "I think you should delegate your international diplomatic
problems to your subordinates and give your complete attention to the
battle in Tunisia."[29]

The message was not lost on Eisenhower. That day he set out on a
thirty-hour drive to the front, arriving at Anderson's headquarters on 24
December. There he confirmed that incessant winter rains had transformed the terrain into a quagmire that made any decisive attack impossible for at least two months, when the rain would end. Eisenhower
understood that the failure to trap Rommel's rump army in Libya be-

tween Anderson's First Army and Montgomery's Eighth Army meant that German forces could fall back on interior lines in Tunisia and that the campaign would be one of attrition. It was a "bitter decision"—"the severest disappointment I have suffered to date," he reported to the Combined Chiefs.[30]

To add to Eisenhower's troubles, the French forces refused to serve under Anderson, at one point even recommending that a French general assume command of all Allied forces at the front. On 1 January 1943, Eisenhower solved the problem temporarily by assuming direct command of military operations on the entire front. To facilitate that control, he established an advance command post at Constantine, the ancient Numidian capital, four hundred miles east of Algiers. In charge of this headquarters would be Major General Lucian K. Truscott Jr., a fiery cavalryman who had worked for Eisenhower at Fort Lewis in 1940 and who was to represent him in directing General Anderson's British First Army to the north and General Fredendall's II US Corps spread thinly in the south as well as General Alphonse Juin's French Army detachment, poorly equipped and still demoralized from the events of 1940, situated between the British and American forces. "With Ike in 'personal command' of the front and riding British, French and American forces," Butcher noted, "he will have his hands full helping to dope out the grand strategy of the war at Casablanca."[31]

The naval aide was referring to the upcoming summit of Allied leaders, scheduled for 14–23 January at Anfa near Casablanca. He was also vastly overemphasizing Eisenhower's role in the conference. The supreme commander visited the summit for only one day, 15 January, after a dangerous trip from Algiers over the Atlas Mountains in a B-17 that lost two engines en route. Added to this experience were the relentless effects of a two-month battle with colds and flu, the disappointing results of the Tunisian campaign, and security concerns in terms of the Allied leaders in his theater. All this took a toll on Eisenhower's performances in conferences with Roosevelt, Churchill, and the Combined Chiefs. "Ike seems jittery," Roosevelt commented to Harry Hopkins after a personal meeting, in which Eisenhower, in response to a presidential query, blurted out 15 May as his estimate for completion of the Tunisian campaign. The prediction, it turned out, was remarkably accurate, a "miraculous guess"; but at the time Roosevelt held the opinion that he could not promote the supreme commander "until there was some darn good reason for doing it." While

Eisenhower had performed well, the president informed Marshall, "he hasn't knocked the Germans out of Tunisia."[32]

In the meantime, the British dominated the summit. One important reason was that the Joint Chiefs were split in their approaches to the British proposal to continue in the Mediterranean against Sicily within the overall grand strategic objective of defeating Germany first. For Marshall, the proposal meant the death of ROUNDUP, his preferred option of a 1943 cross-Channel invasion, already badly singed by the flames of TORCH. King and Arnold, however, were attracted by the possibility of a quick victory in the Mediterranean, King by the prospect of enlarged operations in the Pacific theater and Arnold in hopes of air assets for the strategic bombing of the German heartland. Another incentive, as Eisenhower realized, was that ROUNDUP as originally conceived could not be staged in 1943, because the earlier estimates of required strength had been too low and because inaction in 1943 "could not be tolerated" by the "big bosses."[33] The United States simply had no other viable strategic alternative to Churchill's "soft underbelly."

British dominance at the conference was also buoyed by superior staff preparation and organization. For support, they anchored off Casablanca a six thousand–ton ship that had been converted into a reference library, served by a staff of clerks who provided facts and statistics to bolster detailed British proposals. The American delegation, by contrast, was supported by a single logistician and tended toward generalities and broad observations. The result was that most of the memoranda written at Casablanca were the product of the British staff with, as Tedder condescendingly observed, "a little assistance from the Americans." One key OPD planner was more direct. "We lost our shirts," he commented in terms of the British delegation's dominance. "They swarmed down upon us like locusts, with a plentiful supply of planners and various other assistants, with prepared plans to insure that they not only accomplished their purpose but did so in stride and with fair promise of continuing in the role of directing strategy the whole course of this war. . . . From a worm's eye viewpoint it was apparent that we were confronted by generations and generations of experience in committee work, in diplomacy, and in rationalizing points of view."[34]

In addition to their efforts in the realm of grand strategy, the British were equally successful at Casablanca in persuading the Americans to accept a new Allied command arrangement, in which Eisenhower as the commander in chief, Allied Forces, would have three principal subordinates. Tedder would command a single Mediterranean air force that included subordinate commands for Northwest Africa, the Middle East, and Malta. Cunningham was to change his designation from commander in chief, Naval Expeditionary Force, to commander in chief, Mediterranean, with power over all Royal Navy units in that area, as well as US Naval Forces, Northwest Africa, the newly created American naval command in the western Mediterranean. And once the Eighth Army entered Tunisia, Alexander would assume two roles, one as Eisenhower's deputy commander in chief, Allied Forces, the other as commander of the newly formed 18th Army Group, which was to include the British First Army under Anderson and the British Eighth Army under Montgomery, as well as the French and American land forces in Tunisia. The new structure would be implemented in mid-February and remain in effect for HUSKY, the Allied invasion of Sicily.[35]

Marshall was pleased with the new arrangements, which he considered to represent "tremendous British concessions."[36] Britain had the dominant forces, and the battle on Eisenhower's front was proceeding slowly at the same time Montgomery was driving into Tunisia. It was thus natural for the British public, the Army chief believed, to expect Alexander or Montgomery to be put in overall command, particularly because Eisenhower held only a three-star rank. But Brooke had something more in mind in proposing the new command structure to Churchill who successfully presented it to Roosevelt. First, it would allow the continuation of AFHQ, which impressed the chief of the Imperial General Staff as a smoothly functioning organization. Second, he believed that in terms of the ground command, Eisenhower had "neither the tactical nor strategical experience required for such a task." By bringing Alexander from the Middle East to serve as deputy to Eisenhower, Brooke correctly noted in his diary, "we were carrying out a move which could not help flattering and pleasing the Americans in so far as we were placing our senior and experienced commander to function under their commander who had no war experience." Finally, all this fed into a larger agenda for Brooke that supported his country's way of conducting theater war. "We were pushing Eisenhower up into the stratosphere and rarefied atmosphere of a Supreme Commander," he noted, "where he would be free to devote his time to the political and inter-allied problems, whilst we inserted under him . . . our own commanders to deal with the military situations and to restore the necessary drive and co-ordination which had been so seriously lacking."[37]

From this perspective, the new arrangements were designed to perpetuate the British committee system of day–to-day command: a triumvirate of British subordinates cooperated with one another at the operational level as semi-independent, coequal commanders in chief who responded to the Combined Chiefs of Staff through the supreme commander, essentially acting as a go-between in his capacity as the chairman of the committee at the theater strategic level. In his war memoirs, Eisenhower recalled the new command structure as "extraordinarily pleasing" because it meant "complete unity of command"—an "exceptionally gratifying experience in the unification of thought and action in an allied command."[38] But if he held such views as the Casablanca conference came to a close, they were quickly dispelled by two memoranda from the Combined Chiefs that attempted, as Butcher noted, "to issue directions as to how and what his subordinates were to do."[39]

As a consequence, Eisenhower dispatched a cable to Marshall on 8 February, outlining his philosophy for dealing with what he considered an intrusion into his unified command by the memoranda. The first Combined Chiefs document, dated 20 January, dealt with the organization of the new air command, stipulating that the organization of that command must "be left to the decision of the Air Commander-in-Chief."[40] This was the equivalent of a red flag to Eisenhower, who believed that both planning and organization must be under the control of the unified commander. It was nothing more, he wrote Marshall, than "the British tendency toward reaching down into a theater and attempting to compel an organization along the lines to which they are accustomed. . . . As far as I am concerned, no attention will be paid to such observations. It is my responsibility to organize to win battles."[41]

The second memorandum, dated 23 January, directed Alexander to take over planning details of the organization for HUSKY, authorizing him to "*cooperate*" with Tedder and Cunningham in executing the project.[42] For Eisenhower, this was nothing more than a return to the problems that had beset the creation of Wavell's ABDA command a year earlier at the Arcadia Conference. "Coordination," not "cooperation," was what was required in terms of the interaction of land, sea, and air elements, and Eisenhower believed passionately that it was something only a commander in chief of a unified command could direct. He was not averse to having a deputy commander for ground operations and in fact had considered Patton for that role. But concerned that Alexander's second role as his overall deputy commander in chief, Allied Forces, "would imply an influence in Naval and Air matters," the supreme commander emphasized that Alexander's primary mission as 18th Army group commander would be to command, and even then only those troops in contact with the enemy.[43] Responsibility for the organization and control of the remaining ground elements, such as theater strategic reserves and rear area support echelons, would remain with the unified commander as part of his coordinative functions with all the services. All this would not preclude his land, sea, and air deputies from settling broad problems under his direction, he wrote Marshall, "but it seems impossible for the British to grasp the utter simplicity of the system that we employ."[44]

Eisenhower hastened to assure the chief of staff that he saw nothing vicious or even deliberate in the British action, which simply reflected their own doctrine and training. "But when two governments accept the principle of unified command . . . in a particular theater," he added, "I . . . believe that they must leave him a considerable freedom in organizing his own forces as he sees fit." This was as close to a mild reproof to his mentor as Eisenhower would come in terms of the interference in his command by the Combined Chiefs organization, half of which, after all, consisted of Marshall and the other Joint Chiefs of Staff. "I have grasped your idea," he reminded the Army chief in this regard, "and . . . I will be constantly on my guard to prevent any important military venture depending for its control and direction upon the 'committee' system of command."[45]

Despite these tribulations, Eisenhower was awarded a fourth star on 11 February, the twelfth officer in the history of the US Army, beginning with Ulysses S. Grant, to attain the rank of full general. Sixteen months earlier he had been a colonel, and he still retained the permanent Regular Army rank of lieutenant colonel. The promotion was a political necessity in order to make him an equivalent rank to his British deputies. It was certainly not a reward for progress in Tunisia, where the Germans had launched a limited offensive focused primarily on the underequipped French. In response, Eisenhower ordered the French to subordinate themselves to Anderson while at the same time allowing them to save face by emphasizing that the British general operated under him as supreme commander. The French did not object because the need for unity of command, as Eisenhower noted, "had become too obvious." Two days later, he placed all Allied forces on the Tunisian front under Anderson's command as part of the First Army—a move that included a composite French and US Corps as well as the thirty-two thousand soldiers in Fredendall's US II Corps.[46]

A major problem in Tunisia was that Eisenhower was attempting to act as supreme commander from his headquarters in Algiers as well as tactical field commander through his command post at Constantine, far to the east. The result, as Carlo D'Este points out, "was that he did neither particularly well."[47] In Algiers, he was increasingly involved in planning for HUSKY, tentatively scheduled for mid-June and an operation that he believed was going to be "difficult and hazardous."[48] But he also spent a great deal of time in relatively unimportant meetings and in hosting visitors—tasks that if properly delegated would have allowed him more time to focus on the battle front. The consequences were paradoxical for a man devoted to the sanctity of unity of command and the chain of command. For in hurried visits to the front during this period, Eisenhower often issued ambiguous directions, interfered with his tactical commanders, and generally produced a tangled command structure, which he complained in early February had become "too complicated to be placed on paper."[49] By that time, mixed units were the norm across much of the 250-mile front. "The generals of three nations had borrowed, divided, and commanded one another's troops," one officer observed, "until the troops were never quite certain who was commanding them."[50]

The denouement occurred on 14 February, when Rommel launched an offensive in the south against the US II Corps. When the German offensive culminated a week later, the battle of the Kasserine Pass, as it became known, had resulted in five thousand American casualties and the destruction of hundreds of US tanks and other weapons and equipment. During the last phase of that battle, Alexander arrived to establish the 18th Army Group, from which he would exercise tactical command of the land battle on Eisenhower's behalf with the First Army in the north and the Eighth Army entering Tunisia in the south. It was a much needed change to the chain of command.

Alexander was Britain's youngest general and a favorite of Churchill, who admired his "easy smiling grace and contagious confidence."[51] He was also familiar with defeat and withdrawal. He had been a junior officer in the Irish Guards during the 1914 retreat from Mons; an acting brigade commander trying to stop the flood of German troops in the March

1918 Ludendorff offensive; the commander of the rear guard at Dunkirk in 1940; and, most recently, the commander dispatched by Churchill to Burma to extricate British forces after the Japanese invasion. As a consequence, during his tour of the US II Corps on 19 February, Alexander recognized the telltale signs of troop demoralization and lack of control at the higher echelons of command. Many of the problems were due to the incompetence of Fredendall, the II Corps commander so concerned about his own security that he used two hundred engineers for three weeks to build his own underground command post. "I'm sure you must have better men than that" was Alexander's scathing observation to Eisenhower, who placed George Patton in command of the corps on 5 March.[52] In view of the situation, Alexander tersely informed Eisenhower, he was assuming overall command of the front immediately. He was more specific in a cable to Brooke. "The general situation is far from satisfactory," he wrote. "British, American and French units are all mixed up on the front, especially in the south. Formations have been split up. There is no policy and no plan of campaign. The air is much the same. This is the result of no firm direction or centralized control from above.[53]

The Kasserine battle left the supreme commander's morale, in Patton's description, "as low as whale tracks on the bottom of the sea."[54] Nevertheless, he was heartened by Alexander's efforts to get the "front tidied up once and for all" and reported to Marshall that because of the new command organization, he expected his burdens "to be much lightened."[55] They were, and for a month after Kasserine, he allowed Alexander to direct the impending campaign without interference. The 18th Army Group headquarters quickly became a British organization, structured along British lines and primarily manned by British staff officers fresh from Cairo, with a few token American and French liaison officers. It was the antithesis of Eisenhower's combined AFHQ, and in the wake of Kasserine, it gave the impression of professionals dispatched just in time to teach amateurs their job. In all this, the supreme commander's passive approach seemed to fulfill Brooke's structural goal at Casablanca of semi-independent British deputies operating as a cooperating committee.

The situation began to change in the spring as the supreme commander recovered his health. "I have caught up with myself," he reported to Marshall on 3 March, "and have things on a fairly even keel."[56] The primary catalyst for a more active role as unified commander was Alexander's order for the final offensive, which envisioned the employment of American units in a support role as Montgomery and Anderson joined forces for a final assault. Eisenhower was shocked into action, requesting on 23 March that Alexander "make a real effort to use the II US Corps right up to the bitter end of the campaign."[57] This effort was unsuccessful, but he was further galvanized by a message from Marshall at the end of the month that emphasized the Army chief's opposition to Alexander's plan and noted that Eisenhower's reports on the matter had "aroused a fear in my mind that in this vital matter you might give way too much . . . with unfortunate results as to national prestige."[58]

As a consequence, the supreme commander, in a meeting on 14 April, ordered Alexander to move II Corps to the north coast of Tunisia, with Bizerte as the objective. The ground commander resisted, pointing out the difficulties in marching the corps across Anderson's supply lines, in establishing a new front, and in providing logistical support to that new front. Moreover, he added, there was the problem of the US fighting performance at Kasserine. Eisenhower kept his temper and insisted that Alexander obey his orders, outlining the need to consider American political sensibilities if there were to be "a sustained and energetic United States effort"—an explanation so basic to coalition warfare as to demonstrate how ill suited Alexander would have been as a supreme combined commander.[59]

By 25 March, Montgomery's Eighth Army was poised to penetrate Rommel's Mareth Line in southern Tunisia, the last obstacle to a linkup under 18th Army Group. For Eisenhower the accelerating pace of events was matched by a whirlwind of conferences in the field and in his headquarters. "I have no thought," he wrote Mamie at the time, "except crawling off in a corner and keeping still in every language known to man."[60] On 7 April the Allied forces linked up as the Germans retreated northward along the Tunisian coast toward Bizerte and Tunis. The final assault that began on 5 May resulted in the capture of Bizerte by II Corps just as Anderson's main effort arrived in Tunis. On 13 May, two days before the date Eisenhower had predicted to the president for the German collapse, Tunisia fell to the Allies—"one continent . . . redeemed," in Churchill's description.[61] A week later, *Ikus Africanus,* as some of his classmates had begun to refer to him, resplendent in riding breeches and knee boots and holding a swagger stick, reviewed the victory parade in Tunis for more than two hours. Just behind him on the reviewing stand were Alexander, Cunningham, and Tedder.[62]

The position of honor for his subordinates was indicative of the relationship that Eisenhower had established with them despite the command arrangements that had emerged from the Casablanca Conference. Those arrangements theoretically pushed him up and out of the unified action with a system in which the combined-service commanders in chief operated as a committee of equals, each potentially reporting to the Combined Chiefs. But for Eisenhower, the British committee system was simply inadequate for the demands of modern conflict, and he maintained his insistence throughout the North African campaign that final authority remained with him. Nevertheless, except for his confrontation with Alexander over the use of II Corps, he never attempted an open exercise of his power—a move that might have proved divisive. Instead, he was confident that his three British commanders in chief would accept his authority as final, particularly because of the lack of unanimity they had already demonstrated in the interservice disputes that invariably arose. To this end, he maintained close contacts with Tedder and Cunningham, co-locating their headquarters with his own in the Hôtel St. Georges. In addition, despite his stipulation that Alexander command only those ground forces actually in combat, Eisenhower maintained a close liaison with the British general through personal visits, telephone calls, and messages, in addition to the exchange of staff officers and other personal representatives.

Equally important, Eisenhower further involved his subordinates in developing with Smith a viable, vertically integrated Allied command and staff structure during the campaign. Once plans had been formulated, they were given to Cunningham, Tedder, and Alexander; they offered advice on them to Eisenhower, who, assisted by his staff, facilitated the working out of differences at the highest level. In the beginning, the air and naval commanders had been concerned about placing senior officers from their services on the AFHQ staff. But these assignments did not diminish the prerogatives of the commanders in chief as principal advisers to Eisenhower and in fact did much to improve interservice coordination. In reality, as Smith pointed out, the ever-expanding AFHQ carried out integration more completely than purely American commands that often paid lip service to the principles of unity of command and effort. The result was a sense of cooperation of the staff that prevented officers from viewing problems and issues strictly on national lines. How far the organization had come was demonstrated at the mid-May TRIDENT Conference in Washington. At Arcadia and at Casablanca, the higher authorities had made decisions on all details of TORCH and the North African campaign. But at TRIDENT, in a vote of confidence for the team of Eisenhower and Smith, the Combined Chiefs argued that the Mediterranean command-and-staff structure should be given control of decision making after the beginning of the invasion of Sicily.[63]

In January 1943 there had been many doubts as to the control Eisenhower exercised over the theater, particularly concerning his attempts to command directly the tactical American, French, and British units that made up his land force. By the end of the campaign, he was working through his own modified approach to unity of command, dealing directly and effectively with single component commanders for land, sea, and air, a far cry from the beginning of TORCH, when he had directed six subordinate commands. He had, in effect, created the organization for unified command that the Combined Chiefs of Staff had denied him in a formal directive. It had been an extremely difficult learning experience for the Supreme Commander. But he had emerged with more confidence, not hesitating to defend his prerogatives as a unified commander. Most important, Eisenhower had honed his skills in conducting coalition warfare despite some hard tests of Anglo-American cooperation. If the coalition could survive the initial and struggling stages of that union with all its inherent disappointments, frustrations, and recriminations, it seemed certain to Eisenhower that it could remain effective as the conflict moved to other theaters. "There is one thing . . . that we are doing in which we improve every day," he wrote to an old friend toward the end of the Tunisian campaign. "We are establishing a pattern for complete unity in Allied effort—ground, air, navy—that will stand the Allied Nations in good stead throughout the remainder of the war."[64]

CHAPTER SEVEN

Unity in Practice:
Sicily and Italy, May–December 1943

I have gotten so that my chief ambition in this war is finally to get to a place where the next operation does not have to be amphibious, with all the inflexibility and delay that are characteristic of such operations.

DWIGHT D. EISENHOWER

I do not see how war can be conducted if every act of the Allied Commander in Chief must be referred back to the home government for advance approval.

DWIGHT D. EISENHOWER

MAY TO DECEMBER 1943 was a time in which Dwight Eisenhower continued to learn by hard experience the complexities of a unified command structure in a joint and combined environment. There were still problems remaining from the Casablanca Conference command arrangements in terms of coordinating land, sea, and air forces through his three British deputies. These problems were compounded as the buildup for the cross-Channel invasion (OVERLORD) began to be given priority over Eisenhower's Mediterranean command. That priority was not always self-evident, however, since it was not until the Teheran Conference at the end of this period that agreement on the Allied strategic pattern in Europe was complete. Until that time the British and American political and military leaders at the highest levels attempted to use the unified command structures that were developing in the United Kingdom and the Mediterranean as tools to adjust in their favor the unresolved strategic pattern for defeating Germany. Eisenhower was at the center of these contradictory efforts, often buffeted not only by Churchill, Roosevelt, and the Combined Chiefs but by his own mentor, George Marshall, as well. All of this contributed to his strategic experience in using the unified command structure—experience that would make him uniquely qualified to take command of OVERLORD. Ironically, however, as the period came to an end, it was the global unified command structure that would play the major role in Eisenhower's last leadership assignment of the war.

Preparation in the spring for the invasion of Sicily (HUSKY) did not begin auspiciously. There were major differences among the AFHQ planners and the three British subordinate major commanders over the number, location, and size of landing objectives in Sicily. Montgomery advocated through Alexander a compact, powerful landing, and Tedder and Cunningham proposed numerous, dispersed landings to capture as many Axis airfields as possible on the first day. Throughout the spring, Eisenhower failed to resolve these arguments, causing Churchill to rail at the absence in Algiers of "directing mind and will power" and Montgomery to compare the Allied headquarters in that city to "an orchestra playing without a conductor."[1] By 29 April, after a meeting in which the Allied commander was still not able to resolve the planning differences, even Admiral Cunningham, normally one of Eisenhower's staunchest supporters, noted that there was no fixed plan "two months off D-Day and the commanders all at sixes and sevens."[2]

The details of HUSKY remained undecided until 2 May, when Montgomery arrived in Algiers to make the case for his plan. "I expect I am a bit unpopular up here," was his understated greeting at Maison Blanche airport to Bedell Smith, who could not have agreed more. "General," the acerbic Smith retorted, "to serve under you would be a great privilege for anyone, to serve along side you wouldn't be too bad. But . . . to serve over you is hell."[3] Nevertheless, the British commander soon enlisted the AFHQ chief of staff to his cause, and when Eisenhower's three subordinate commanders in chief arrived the next day, they accepted Smith's presentation of Montgomery's plan for concentrating the HUSKY assault on the southeastern part of Sicily.

The HUSKY decisions were made in a grand strategic vacuum because of the unresolved Anglo-American differences on how best to defeat Germany. The British favored major offensives into Italy and other areas of the Mediterranean after HUSKY and the indefinite postponement of the cross-Channel assault into France. The Americans were willing to plan further operations in the theater if HUSKY went well. But such operations, as Marshall informed Eisenhower in late April, "are not in keeping with my idea of what our strategy should be. The decisive effort must be made against the Continent from the United Kingdom."[4] The Allied attempt at grand strategic resolution occurred at the second political-military summit of 1943, the 12–25 May TRIDENT Conference in Washington. The result was strategic impasse and compromise. From their deliberations in the Federal Reserve Building, the Combined Chiefs directed Eisenhower to eliminate Italy from the war immediately but provided no more troops to the theater commander; in fact, they scheduled for November the transfer of seven of his divisions to the United Kingdom, where the troop buildup for OVERLORD was to continue. The British, in turn, accepted a target date for that operation of either 1 May or 1 June 1944.

In late May, Churchill and Marshall flew to Algiers to flesh out the vague agreement at TRIDENT to continue operations in the Mediterranean until Italy was out of the war. Eisenhower's natural tendency to adjust and compromise was reinforced by the contrary pressures exerted on him as he hosted the five-day conference, at times acting almost as a mediator between the British and American high commands. This meant withstanding the considerable and unrelenting influence exerted by Churchill throughout the conference. "The PM recited his story three different times in three different ways last night," Eisenhower recorded on 30 May.[5] Later that day, Brooke observed a "very sleepy Eisenhower" emerging from a meeting with the British leader. "I smiled at his distress having suffered from this type of treatment [from Churchill] repeatedly."[6] In the end, the decision on further Mediterranean operations was postponed until the outcome of HUSKY was certain.

On 6 July, Eisenhower departed Algiers for Tunis. The next day, he visited his two new advance command posts at Carthage and at Amilcar on the Bay of Tunis. On 8 July he flew to Malta. On 10 July at 2:30 A.M., fourteen hundred warships and troop transports disgorged eleven hundred landing craft and the 160,000 men that made up the seven Allied divisions onto the beaches of southeastern Sicily. The initial news came to the supreme commander at his Malta headquarters via a BBC report from "General Eisenhower." "Thank God—," Eisenhower responded, "*he* ought to know."[7]

Although the Sicilian landings were successful, the entire assault was hardly a model of joint operations. Unlike in TORCH, Eisenhower did not have direct control of operations and attempted with little success to coordinate the different services. The Allied Air Force initially focused on deep inland targets, leaving the air above the assault beaches without a protective umbrella of fighters. This allowed the Luftwaffe to attack the incoming ships at will, causing high naval losses until Tedder could switch some air assets to the beaches. And on the night of 11 July, when reinforcing airborne units en route to their drop zones on the island were shot up by Allied naval gunners, there were strong recriminations among ground, naval, and air commanders.

From a unified command perspective, the situation did not improve after the landings during the campaign that lasted until mid-August. After the war, Eisenhower asserted that in Sicily "we were wise . . . to proceed methodically to the conquest of an island in which the defending strength was approximately 350,000."[8] But the fact remained that the Axis force consisted of only 60,000 German troops and a large contingent of relatively demoralized Italians. In effect, this German Army Corps, lacking air and naval support, was able to delay two Allied armies of 480,000 troops for thirty-eight days before escaping on 17 August across the Straits of Messina to the Italian boot with the majority of its weapons and vehicles. During this period, the supreme commander did not effectively concentrate his superior Allied air and naval forces to prevent the evacuation of enemy forces across the straits or to destroy the Axis ferries, which carried out their tasks in daylight. All in all, most military historians agree with Carlo D'Este that it was not an impressive performance: "Eisenhower played no role, made no important decisions, and had virtually no impact on Operation Husky."[9]

One reason was that Eisenhower simply did not have time in the busy summer of 1943 to focus fully on the Sicilian campaign. Already on 17 July the supreme commander had met with his deputies in Algiers to examine various post-HUSKY options to take Italy out of the war. But there were still too many imponderables, not the least of which was grand strategic direction. In mid-August, the third Anglo-American summit of the year (QUADRANT) was held in Quebec City to settle that question. The conference marked great progress by the American staff in preparing and presenting the United States' grand strategic case. The conferees agreed that the cross-Channel operation was to be the principal Allied effort under an American commander, with a target date of 1 May 1944. There was also agreement that the combined bomber offensive (POINTBLANK) would remain the top priority and was to be executed in preparation for OVERLORD from all suitable bases, to include those in Italy and other areas of the Mediterranean. There were, however, still compromises concerning the two theaters. The Mediterranean issue was not permanently settled; and Eisenhower was left with a vague directive to fight a war in Italy with no clear-cut strategic goal and only with assets already available to him, many of which were due to be sent to England later in the year.[10]

In the meantime, the supreme commander continued the planning process, a demonstration in itself that he and his theater staff were increasingly influential in the planning and conduct of operations. As the tempo of these operations increased and events began to outrun plans, Eisenhower's staff found itself more involved in operational functions rendered in an earlier period only in Washington. On 16 August, the day before the Allies entered Messina, Eisenhower confirmed the final plans for the British Eighth Army to cross the straits to the Italian toe (BAY-TOWN) in early September and for the US Fifth Army to land twenty-five miles south of Naples a few days later at the Gulf of Salerno (AVA-LANCHE). Eisenhower's role in the process was much more active than it had been in the planning for HUSKY. He began by merging US air assets in the Mediterranean under Spaatz, who would continue to operate as Tedder's deputy commander in chief of all British and American air forces in that theater. "Strategic and tactical operations in the air force merge so frequently into one problem," he wrote Marshall, "that it is impossible to coordinate those operations during periods of intensive fighting except through one headquarters."[11]

The plan for AVALANCHE called for the destruction of enemy airfields and the interdiction of Axis lines of communication by heavy bombers in order to isolate the Salerno beaches. Thus, as Tedder recorded, it was a "shock" when after much resistance by Eisenhower from mid-July to mid-August, the Combined Chiefs ordered the supreme commander on 17 August to return three B-24 Liberator groups borrowed from the Britain-based Eighth Air Force. Eisenhower immediately appealed to Marshall. "If our present heavy bombing strength should suffer this reduction we would be skating on very thin ice in AVALANCHE," he wrote. "That operation, if successful, will provide to the Allied air forces most favorable bases for the continuation of the air offensive against Europe; but to have a fair chance to win those bases, we need this strength at this time." On 19 August, Arnold upheld the order, pointing out that the three heavy bomber groups would provide the Eighth Air Force with another long-range striking force "which might well account for an aircraft factory each week." That type of result, the USAAF chief concluded, using Eisenhower's own inter-heater argument against him, would help the forces in the Mediter-ranean as much as those in England.[12]

The decision reduced the Mediterranean bomber fleet to four B-17 Fortress groups and two B-24 groups—a sharp reminder to Eisenhower that as preparations for OVERLORD proceeded, he no longer commanded the primary theater, as he had since the fall of 1942. That day he informed the Combined Chiefs of his determination to go ahead with AVALANCHE despite the risks, which he proceeded to outline in detail, using joint lessons from the Sicilian campaign. Tedder was equally direct with the British Chiefs, explaining how AVALANCHE would differ from HUSKY. Salerno would not succeed without numerical and operational air superi-ority, which had been difficult to achieve so far from Allied bases. Already, the rapid reinforcement of German divisions in Italy demonstrated the critical role of air in delaying enemy concentrations for at least two weeks after the landings. "There is a tendency to consider the Italian chicken as being already in the pot," the air chief marshal concluded, "whereas in fact it is not yet hatched."[13]

The planning process was further complicated for Eisenhower by de-velopments in Italy. On 25 July, Italian authorities arrested Mussolini and replaced him with Marshal Pietro Badoglio, former chief of the Italian General Staff. The next day, Roosevelt advised Churchill that any armis-tice terms should be "as close as possible to unconditional surrender." And with the memories still fresh of Eisenhower's deal with Admiral Dar-lan in the early stages of TORCH, the president stated his preference early to the British leader: "In no event should our officers in the field fix any general terms without your approval and mine."[14] This left Eisenhower in a "dilemma," as he wrote Marshall on 29 July, in the absence of "some di-rective that will allow me to act promptly and quickly in the event that an authoritative representative of the Italian government should ask me for a military armistice."[15] And even when such communications did arrive, Harold Macmillan noted, there was no hard guidance and authority, only "contradictory and conflicting" instructions: "Poor Eisenhower is getting pretty harassed. Telegrams (private, personal and most immediate) pour in upon him from the following sources: (i) Combined Chiefs of Staff (Washington), his official masters. (ii) General Marshall, Chief of U.S. Army, his immediate superior. (iii) The President. (iv) The Secretary of State. (v) Our Prime Minister (direct). (vi) Our Prime Minister (through me). (vii) The Foreign Secretary (through me)."[16]

In mid-August, Eisenhower was given authority to soften armistice terms in proportion to the amount of assistance the Italians would provide the Allies. But there was still political sensitivity to the matter, and his authority went no further. As he continued his preparations for the Salerno landings with limited forces and resources against a foe that was much stronger than originally calculated, Eisenhower was increasingly more willing to make concessions than were the Combined Chiefs of Staff or the heads of state. "The risks attendant on AVALANCHE which have been pointed to you and which we are perfectly prepared to accept," he informed Washington, "will be minimized to a large extent if we are able to secure Italian assistance just prior to and during the critical period of the actual landing. Even passive resistance will greatly increase our chances of success."[17] On 29 August the president relented and provided authorization through the JCS for Eisenhower to proceed with the surrender negotiations on the basis of military terms. The Italian armistice was signed on 3 September, the day two British divisions successfully crossed the Straits of Messina and, meeting only light resistance, began to move north up the toe of Italy. On 8 September at 6:30 P.M., Eisenhower announced the armistice through Radio Algiers. After waiting ten minutes for Badoglio's proclamation, he ordered the station to issue the Italian leader's statement. At 7:45 P.M., acting on direct orders from the king, Badoglio proclaimed the armistice; and a few hours later in the early morning of 9 September, the Allied landings began on the beachheads in Salerno Bay.[18]

The Germans anticipated amphibious operations within the range of Allied land-based air and had prepared mobile defenses in and around Salerno. These defenses held until reinforcements arrived, and on 12 September the Germans counterattacked, threatening in the next few days to drive the Sixth Army into the sea. Nevertheless, Eisenhower remained optimistic. Recalling the divided command arrangements for HUSKY, he insisted that his deputies be co-located with him at his advanced Amilcar command post. "We meet daily," he informed Marshall on 13 September, "and it is astonishing how much we can get done to keep our staffs operating at full tilt to execute needed projects." The result was a command structure altered for quick decisions and rapid action that could swiftly concentrate enormous joint power at the critical location, proving for the supreme commander once again "that the greatest value of any of the three services is ordinarily realized only when it is utilized in close coordination with the other two."[19]

To this end, Eisenhower had Tedder use all strategic as well as tactical air assets over the beachhead. On 15 September both air forces made a supreme effort, "working overtime" in the battle area, with the strategic bombers alone conducting seven hundred sorties in a twenty-four-hour period. Thereafter, as Allied tactical squadrons were able to establish themselves in southern Italy within operational range of Salerno, the strategic forces returned to their normal role of disrupting the German lines of communication. At the same time, Cunningham's naval forces used more than eleven thousand tons of shells on the beachhead—the equivalent of seventy-two thousand 105mm field artillery howitzer high-explosive projectiles. The joint air and naval blitz had, in Tedder's description, an "electric effect" upon Allied troops that soon resulted in consolidation of the landing sites. "The three Commanders in Chief are doing everything that men can do," Eisenhower reported to the Combined Chiefs on 14 September.[20] Two days later, he outlined how operations in the theater had been carried out "through combinations of the Three Services," based on "a teamwork and a mutual understanding that, in my own opinion are becoming very effective."[21]

Incredibly, Eisenhower found a chance to reflect on these and broader lessons of Allied command in advice he transmitted to Admiral Louis Mountbatten as the battle of Salerno reached its climax. At QUADRANT, the Allied leaders had created a new Southeast Asia Command to be headquartered in New Delhi and commanded by Mountbatten, with whom Eisenhower had formed a firm friendship from their first meeting in spring 1942. In early September, the new commander wrote Eisenhower for advice "on the duties and tribulations with which a Supreme Allied commander is faced" and "on the pitfalls to avoid and the line you consider one should take up."[22] In his reply of 14 September, Eisenhower addressed his theory and practice of command forged after almost a year in the unique circumstances of his combined environment. Ostensibly, he noted, the basis of Allied unity of command was to be found in the directives of the Combined Chiefs of Staff. In reality, the "true basis" for Allied unity was the mutual respect and cooperation that formed the framework for the interaction of the senior officers assigned to an Allied theater. In such circumstances, he concluded, it would never be possible to solve completely the complexities of establishing unity of command and effort in any Allied structure: "This problem involves the human equation and must be met day by day."[23]

He was not trying to portray the position of an Allied commander in chief, Eisenhower advised Mountbatten, as if commanding a battle fleet or a destroyer flotilla. On the other hand, he emphasized, that position was in no sense of the word a figurehead or a nonentity. "He is in a very definite sense the Chairman of the Board, a Chairman that has very definite executive responsibilities." As such, the position was not to be viewed according to the British system of command, which was essentially unworkable when sizable numbers of troops from both countries were placed together in one theater to achieve a common goal. Under one configuration that might emerge from that system, there could be six commanders in chief reporting to the Combined Chiefs. Who, then, Eisenhower asked, would carry out all the tasks apart from the actual ongoing military operations? And who would have the authoritative voice in dealing with the Combined Chiefs of Staff? "The point I make," he concluded to Mountbatten, "is that while the set-up may be somewhat artificial, and not always so clean-cut as you might desire, your personality and good sense *must* make it work. Otherwise *Allied* action in any theater will be impossible."[24]

In the meantime, differences between the United Kingdom and the United States on the agreed strategic pattern to emerge from the Quebec Conference were becoming more apparent, as each party used divergent proposals for the command arrangements of the European and Mediterranean areas to influence the outcome in its favor. On the British side, there was the assumption since QUADRANT that Marshall would become supreme commander of OVERLORD and that Eisenhower would turn over the Mediterranean to a British commander. As a result, on 3 November the British Chiefs proposed a unified command for the entire Mediterranean theater under the commander in chief, Allied Forces. The British commanders in Cairo would continue to be responsible to the British Chiefs for the operation and administration of the Middle East base and for those parts of the current Middle East Command located in Africa, Asia, and the Levant. In Washington, Field Marshal Dill explained that the arrangement would allow for more flexibility in Mediterranean operations and place the additional Middle East forces under the Combined

Chiefs. Eisenhower agreed, pointing out on 7 November that the proposal was "a logical centralization of operational responsibility."[25]

But Marshall argued strongly within the JCS for rejection of the proposal. The United Kingdom, he reasoned, wanted a unified Mediterranean command structure in order to provide impetus for operations the British would like to undertake in the eastern Mediterranean. The Combined Chiefs of Staff controlled resource allocation in Eisenhower's Allied theater. From the perspective of the British Chiefs, Marshall explained, resources currently under Eisenhower's control would be more accessible for their purposes under a unified Mediterranean command, particularly since the British would undoubtedly soon insist on being the executive agent for that area as US troop strength in the Mediterranean diminished. Instead, he argued, the Joint Chiefs should propose that a supreme commander be designated for the entire scope of Anglo-American operations against Germany in northwestern Europe and the Mediterranean. On 9 November the JCS decided to address both the British and American command proposals at the next summit in Cairo (SEXTANT).[26]

Marshall's proposal reflected another strategic aspect of the command problem, that of finding a replacement for the Army chief of staff if he took command of OVERLORD, without disrupting the command and staff structure he had help create in Washington and London. A major issue was that as the OVERLORD commander, Marshall would have to leave the Combined Chiefs of Staff. This would mean the absence of the strongest, most effective advocate of the cross-Channel operation in that body just as the British appeared to be wavering in the commitment to OVERLORD. The American Chiefs believed that Marshall was indispensable and could not be spared as a member and as their acknowledged leader. First and foremost, they did not want to lose the continuity of Marshall's strategic vision and concepts that he had upheld in joint and Allied counsels. This meant trying to keep the lead in the conduct of global war centered in the joint and combined mechanisms that had evolved in Washington under his direction. The alternative without the Army chief's guiding hand was a shift to the type of virtually independent super commands that Pershing and Foch had established in World War I. "We have the winning combination here in Washington," King concluded. "Why break it up?"[27]

Ultimately, it would be the president's decision, but he kept his own counsel during this period even as some objections to the possible transfer of the Army chief began to arise. At one juncture, General Pershing entered the fray, protesting to the president that any transfer of Marshall to "a tactical command" in a limited area "would be a fundamental and very grave error. . . . I know of no one at all comparable to replace him as Chief of Staff." In reply, Roosevelt explained to the former AEF commander that it was only fair to give Marshall a chance in the field. "The best way I can express it," he concluded, "is to tell you that I want George to be the Pershing of the Second World War—and he cannot be that if we keep him here."[28]

Nevertheless, the issue of the OVERLORD command was still unsettled when the president and the Joint Chiefs departed for the Cairo Conference. On 19 November, in a meeting of the Joint Chiefs with the president, Admiral Leahy suggested that the decision concerning unified command of the Mediterranean be postponed until after settlement of the overall command problem. But Marshall had changed his mind on the need for such a command and argued that accepting the British proposal would be "logical and show good faith." The president concurred. The United States would agree to a unified command in the Mediterranean and take up the question of an overall supreme commander separately.[29]

The command issue disappeared during the Teheran Conference when Stalin settled the grand strategic dispute on the Mediterranean versus OVERLORD by insisting on May 1944 as the latest date for a cross-Channel attack. The decision to give top priority to OVERLORD caused Roosevelt to drop the proposals for an overall commander in the West with a seat on the CCS. There would be one commander for OVERLORD, he informed Stalin on 30 November, another for the Mediterranean, and a temporary one for the recently agreed-upon invasion of southern France. These decisions led invariably to structural command problems that caused the president to choose Eisenhower over Marshall to command OVERLORD. Without an overall command in the West, Roosevelt agreed with his Joint Chiefs that command of the cross-Channel operation would be a demotion for Marshall. Moreover, that command would create a certain amount of structural awkwardness, since Marshall would take orders from the Combined Chiefs, an organization that would include Arnold and Eisenhower, two of his handpicked subordinates. Most important, from the president's perspective, Marshall would not be available to press the American strategic agenda in that combined body. Nor would he be available to handle the sensitive problems concerning relations with the Pacific theater and with Congress. It was therefore no exaggeration when Roosevelt explained his decision to Marshall: "I feel I could not sleep at night with you out of the country."[30]

But if Marshall was too important to spare, it was also true that despite his superb leadership abilities, he lacked Eisenhower's patience in working smoothly and effectively with Allied prima donnas in a combined environment. Nor did the chief of staff have Eisenhower's experience in commanding complex joint and combined amphibious operations acquired in a difficult apprenticeship that had lasted more than a year. Even Brooke, normally scathing in his criticism of Eisenhower's professional ability, acknowledged these facts. "The selection of Eisenhower instead of Marshall was a good one," he wrote. "Eisenhower had now had a certain amount of experience as a commander and was beginning to find his feet. The combination of Eisenhower and Bedell Smith had much to be said for it."[31]

In essence, then, it was Eisenhower's devotion to the principles of unity of command and effort as much as Marshall's indispensability that caused Roosevelt to appoint him as supreme commander for OVERLORD. Certainly, it was more important than the Allied leader's generalship up to then, which as Stephen Ambrose points out, had been "cautious and hesitant."[32] After all, OVERLORD was going to be a joint and combined amphibious operation. And in TORCH, HUSKY, and AVALANCHE, Eisenhower had demonstrated that he could create and run an integrated staff from all services and from both countries and successfully command their combined forces. It was a unique achievement of teamwork, nicely summed up in an appreciation by Cunningham when he left the Mediterranean in mid-October to become first lord of the Admiralty and a member of the Combined Chiefs. "I do not believe," the British admiral concluded, "that any other man than yourself could have done it."[33] Roosevelt saw the appointment of the supreme commander in a similar light. Later in the war, James Roosevelt queried his father on the decision. "Eisenhower is the best politician among the military men," the president replied. "He is a natural leader who can convince other men to follow him, and this is what we need in his position more than any other quality."[34]

CHAPTER EIGHT

The Lessons of Unity Applied: London, January–May 1944

I agree with you thoroughly on the necessity for preventing higher authority from dictating details of our organization in order that we may apply the experience that we have gained in the Mediterranean.

DWIGHT D. EISENHOWER

Here we are . . . on the eve of a great battle, to deliver to you the various plans made by the different Force Commanders. . . . I consider it to be the duty of anyone who sees a flaw in the plan not to hesitate to say so. I have no sympathy with anyone, whatever his station, who will not brook criticism. We are here to get the best possible results and you must make a really co-operative effort.

DWIGHT D. EISENHOWER

THE LESSONS AND EXPERIENCES of unified and combined command from the North African and Italian campaigns formed the basis for Eisenhower's plans and conduct of the war in Europe from January 1944 to May 1945. Command and control of air assets remained a major issue from the earlier Allied amphibious operations, an issue that the supreme commander was determined to solve for OVER-LORD. This was complicated by unique targeting problems in northwest Europe that had not existed in the Mediterranean landings. At the same time, despite agreement on OVERLORD, there were lingering Anglo-American differences on the role of Allied operations in the Mediter-ranean. The issues stemmed from different national outlooks on grand strategy that finally had to be resolved if Eisenhower was to maintain unity of command and unity of effort in northwest Europe. Finally the issue of overall ground command reemerged as cover for British efforts to alter that theater's campaign strategy. During these challenges, Eisenhower was buffeted by attempts to influence him from the very highest political and military levels of both countries. In the end he maintained the unity of his supreme command by relying on the trust established with his American and British superiors and subordinates since the spring of 1942 that he was ultimately devoted to a combined as well as unified effort to win the war in Europe.

In late December 1943 Marshall began to urge Eisenhower to return to the United States for a visit and rest before assuming his duties as supreme commander in the United Kingdom. On 29 December, Eisenhower cabled that such a visit was then impossible, but that he might be able to arrange it in February or early March. In his firm yet avuncular reply that day, the Army chief of staff left no doubt as to what he expected of his protégé. "You will be under terrific strain from now on," he reminded Eisenhower. "I am interested that you are fully prepared to bear the strain and I am not interested in the usual rejoinder that you can take it. It is of vast importance that you be fresh mentally and you certainly will not be if you go straight from one great problem to another. Now come on home and see your wife and trust somebody else for twenty minutes in England."[1]

Before departing North Africa, Eisenhower reviewed the status of his new command. Early on in the planning for the cross-Channel operation, the British had reverted to their traditional argument for a committee type of joint command, in which no service had overall control. Already in the summer of 1942, the Joint Chiefs of Staff had described the British proposals for the OVERLORD command structure as "destructive in efficiency in that none of them provide for an absolute unity of command by the Supreme Commander over all elements land, air and naval."[2] By November 1943 there were compromises. The combined planners agreed that whoever the supreme commander would be, he would employ the air and naval forces to influence the course of the OVERLORD assault and battle just as Eisenhower had done in terms of Alexander's ground forces. And after discussing the issue with the Allied naval and air commands in London that month, the planners issued a directive to the British 21st Army Group that gave the commander of that organization joint responsibility for planning the assault with the commanders in chief of those combined services for OVERLORD.

There were good reasons for the British to be given the lead. First, the initial Allied assaults would be made from the United Kingdom. More important, the British had both an Army Group and Army headquarters organized and thus available to begin cross-Channel planning when the

Allied concept emerged. In the coming months when the decision was made to enlarge the assault area and to land two armies instead of two corps, the 21st Army Group commander was tasked to command land operations. Although this made him de facto commander of the ground forces in the assault, he was never given the title of ground commander that Alexander had received in North Africa and Italy. The tenure for his position was not stipulated. But what was clear was that the arrangement could be changed anytime the supreme commander so desired.[3]

This was not enough for Bedell Smith, who urged Eisenhower to take command of the ground battle the day after the landing, reminding the supreme commander that when Alexander had ground command in the previous theater, his Army Group headquarters had tended to bypass and overshadow AFHQ. Already conscious of Fleet Street's tendency to elevate some British leaders, Smith tried to persuade Eisenhower to work against the impression that the British commanders in chief exerted control over planning and the conduct of the cross-Channel operation. "I kept arguing with him on the question and pushing him to take over," Smith recalled after the war. "I wanted to handle [OVERLORD] like a river crossing."[4] But Eisenhower, as he wrote Marshall in mid-December 1943, was satisfied with one initial ground commander given potential communication problems from SHAEF and the narrowness of the assault area; he expected that commander would be Alexander.

A few days later, however, after consultations with Eisenhower and others, Churchill decided that Montgomery would become the senior ground commander, while Alexander would remain in the Mediterranean in the same relationship to the new supreme commander in that theater as he had once had with Eisenhower. Montgomery was thus to have operational control of all land forces, including the First US Army under General Omar Bradley, until force buildups allowed a new American Army group equal both operationally and administratively to the British 21st Army Group, which would continue under Montgomery's command. At that time, Eisenhower noted in agreement, "I would deal personally with each of the Army Group Commanders."[5]

There were other changes in Eisenhower's organization, equally beyond his control. Tedder was to be his deputy for the entire command. To replace him, Air Chief Marshal Sir Trafford Leigh-Mallory had been appointed commander in chief, Allied Expeditionary Air Force. He was the object of intense dislike and distrust by American and British airmen alike and was generally regarded as the wrong choice for the position. The strategic air forces were controlled by the Combined Chiefs of Staff and consisted of the British Bomber Command under Air Chief Marshal Sir Arthur Harris and the US Strategic Air Force in Europe under Tooey Spaatz. The Allied naval commander was Admiral Sir Bertram Ramsay, an expert on amphibious operations who had returned from retirement to orchestrate the Dunkirk naval evacuation and then to serve as Cunningham's principal planner for TORCH. Under him, Rear Admiral Alan G. Kirk was commander of US naval forces for the cross-Channel attack and would turn over operational control of those forces to Ramsey on 1 April. Finally, Montgomery was promoted on Christmas Eve 1943 and became head of the British 21st Army Group as well as acting commander of Allied ground troops until some indefinite time after the invasion.[6]

The air arrangements particularly disturbed Eisenhower, who registered his objections with Marshall before departing for the United States. He had been assured that Tedder would continue to be his overall air commander. Instead, the British air marshal was to be an officer without portfolio as the deputy supreme commander. While acknowledging the rights of the Combined Chiefs in such matters, Eisenhower deplored "this tendency to freeze organizations so that a commander may not . . . use trusted and superior subordinates in their proper spheres." It was essential that the air command have a few senior officers that were experienced in the air support of ground troops—a technique that was not widely understood. "Otherwise," he reminded Marshall, "a commander is forever fighting with those air officers who, regardless of the ground situation, want to send big bombers on missions that have nothing to do with the critical effort." There was also evidence that the Combined Chiefs were directing the details of tactical air force organization by insisting on the establishment of two tactical air forces for the OVERLORD assault—an "unthinkable" development on the crowded beachheads that could adversely affect the unity of the command and "tie the hands" of the Allied staff. The idea was not to repeat the mistakes concerning organization and unity of command from earlier operations in North Africa and the Mediterranean.[7]

On the last day of 1943 Eisenhower conferred with Churchill at Marrakech. The next day he left Morocco and his Mediterranean command, flying to the Azores, then to Canada and on to Washington. He arrived on 2 January in such secrecy that Secretary Stimson learned of his presence only when notified hastily by the Army chief of staff that Sunday afternoon as Eisenhower's plane landed. The return trip was by air via the Azores to Prestwick, Scotland, and then from Glasgow by rail to London, where he arrived late on 15 January with security provided by a thick yellow fog. On 16 January 1944 Eisenhower established his Supreme Headquarters, Allied Expeditionary Force (SHAEF).

The location of SHAEF in and near London complicated Eisenhower's efforts to maintain the unity of his command in his dealings with the Combined Chiefs of Staff, since he could not avoid frequent personal meetings with the principal British leaders, including his occasional attendance at meetings of the British Chiefs of Staff. Moreover, the supreme commander lunched weekly with Churchill, and even after the transfer of his main headquarters to France, the prime minister and Brooke called him regularly by telephone in addition to visiting him on a fairly frequent basis. At the same time, as the invasion grew imminent, the British preferred to transfer an increasing number of Combined Chiefs functions to London. All this was somewhat balanced by Marshall's position as the prime conduit for orders to Eisenhower from the Combined Chiefs, which allowed the Army chief of staff to keep the US viewpoint constantly before the supreme commander. Eisenhower appreciated this and worked hard to reassure his mentor. "The upshot of all this," he wrote, "is that . . . the US Joint Chiefs of Staff can be certain that I will under no circumstances . . . keep officials on this side of the water better acquainted with any problems and more accurately informed as to the situation than I will do with respect to the US Chiefs of Staff."[8]

These countervailing influences in the Combined Chiefs of Staff also affected Eisenhower's charter as unified and combined commander. On 5 January 1944 the British Chiefs of Staff submitted a draft directive outlining the duties of the subordinate commanders in chief. Opposition quickly developed, particularly concerning a detailed listing of the powers of the ground force commander, which the Americans believed could later embarrass the supreme commander. The counterproposal recommended that these particular parts of the draft directive be confined to a listing of the land forces to be placed at Eisenhower's disposal, leaving him free to issue such directives to his army group commanders as he believed necessary. The British Chiefs agreed to accommodate the proposal, allowing the supreme commander to develop his control over the forces provided him and to command unhampered by restrictions. The major command question left unanswered by the Combined Chiefs concerned the control of the strategic air forces in Europe, which they agreed to defer for later resolution.

Other issues could not be deferred, particularly those concerning the specifics of the supreme commander's task in Europe. The British proposal appeared straightforward: "You will enter the Continent of Europe and undertake operations to secure lodgments from which further offensive action can be aimed at the heart of Europe." But for the JCS, the wording was symptomatic of the continued differences in strategic outlook that had emerged, beginning with the invasion of North Africa. From this perspective, the proposal implied that the British might attempt to limit operations to establishing a beachhead and conducting a holding action while primary operations were conducted elsewhere. Instead, the American Chiefs proposed a more positive, expansive approach: "You shall enter the Continent . . . and undertake operations striking at the heart of Germany and destroy her forces." For the British, this version was unrealistic in its excessive boldness, particularly since the available forty-division Allied force was certainly insufficient to overwhelm the German Army.[9]

The final compromise version retained the US goal while enlarging the scope of operations to other nations: "You will enter the Continent of Europe and, in conjunction with the other United Nations, undertake operations aimed at the heart of Germany and the destruction of her armed forces." The revised draft was accepted by the Combined Chiefs of Staff on 11 February and the final directive issued the next day. The document designated Eisenhower as supreme commander, Allied Expeditionary Force (SCAEF), responsible to the Combined Chiefs but authorized direct communication to both the American and British Chiefs. Moreover, as supreme Allied commander, Eisenhower was given the all important power to coordinate the requirements for UK and US forces placed under him. The target date for the cross-Channel attack was May 1944, and the Allied commander in chief of the Mediterranean Theater was directed to conduct operations in the south of France "about the same time as OVERLORD," scope and timing to be decided by the Combined Chiefs.[10]

In assuming formal command after nearly a month of serving as supreme commander, Eisenhower had good reasons for being pleased with the Combined Chiefs directive. Now he had a directive that was far superior in terms of unity of command than what had emerged from the Casablanca Conference little more than a year before. Its broad terms allowed him great latitude in exercising command and in formulating the operational details of his campaigns against Germany, using the greatest Allied force in history.

Eisenhower would need his commitment to Allied unity in dealing with the question of strategic air forces, the most pressing issue facing him in terms of the unity of his new command. In 1943 the US strategic air forces had been sent to the United Kingdom to participate in the combined bomber offensive against Germany (POINTBLANK). In January of that year the American bombers were placed with RAF Bomber Command under the strategic direction of Air Chief Marshal Charles Portal, acting as the executive agent for the Combined Chiefs. In the fall the JCS unsuccessfully proposed consolidation of the American and British strategic air forces under the supreme commander. The subject was raised again at the Cairo Conference. At the end of that summit the US Chiefs established the US Strategic Air Force in Europe under Spaatz, who was given operational control of the Eighth Air Force in the United Kingdom and the Fifteenth Air Force in the Mediterranean. Despite Eisenhower's role as the American European Theater commander, however, these forces were beyond his initial control because of the January 1943 Combined Chiefs directive. Moreover, the commanders of both strategic commands were dedicated air power advocates who believed that their service alone could win the war. Harris was focused on using RAF Bomber Command to bring about German surrender through terror bombing of German cities. And Spaatz envisioned using the Eighth Air Force to compel German capitulation by selectively destroying key industries, particularly oil production facilities.

On 12 February, Eisenhower presented a plan to support OVERLORD by destroying the railroad infrastructure in France, the Low Countries, and western Germany. The key to the proposal, he informed Marshall, was to "fix our recommended dates for the passage of command over Strategical Air Forces to this Headquarters." This "Transportation Plan," he argued, would have two important results. It would render the movement of German reserves and reinforcements extremely difficult once OVERLORD had begun. It would also reinforce the objectives of POINT-BLANK, particularly the strategic bombing of industrial complexes producing fighter aircraft and refined petroleum. At the same time, given the few months remaining before OVERLORD, long-range strategic bombing inside Germany would be unlikely to have any favorable effect on the invasion battlefield.

There were immediate objections from the two bomber commanders, who were soon supported by Churchill, Brooke, Portal, and Arnold. Part of the reaction was due to a reluctance to give Leigh-Mallory full control over the strategic bombing assets. But the fundamental issue was whether OVERLORD or POINTBLANK would have priority in the use of heavy bombers—in other words, a matter of command structure. The major activity in Bomber Command, Tedder noted in this regard, was "a series of adjustments to the records of their post bombing statistics, with the evident intention of demonstrating that they are quite unequipped and untrained to do anything except mass fire-raising on very large targets."[11]

The issue was raised again by Churchill in a meeting with Eisenhower on the night of 28 February. There could be no question, he asserted, of handing the British Bomber, Fighter, or Coastal commands "as a whole" over to Eisenhower, since those commands had other functions to perform for Portal. The prime minister was willing, however, to have the Combined Chiefs assign forces from those commands as the need arose. Eisenhower, in Tedder's description, objected to submitting his plans to the Combined Chiefs and "demurred at anything short of complete operational control of the whole of Bomber Command and the American Strategic Forces." The US Chiefs, with the largest air force in the United Kingdom, he emphasized, were willing to put all that force at the disposal of the supreme commander. If the British held out their vital striking force, he would not be able to face the JCS. He did not care if Churchill wished to hold Coastal Command under separate control, but if the British insisted on a less than all-out effort for OVERLORD with Bomber Command, he would "simply have to go home."[12]

On 9 March, Portal and Tedder produced a draft agreement on the use of the strategic air forces. Under this arrangement, the deputy supreme commander was to "supervise all air operations under the control of OVERLORD."[13] As a compromise, Eisenhower formally accepted the concept of Combined Chiefs intervention if that body believed there was a need to impose additional tasks on the bomber forces as a result of any perception by the British Chiefs that the requirements for the security of the British Isles were not being fully met. In any event, Eisenhower and Portal as the respective executive agents of the Combined Chiefs for the execution of OVERLORD and POINTBLANK were to approve the air plans created for OVERLORD. At that point, "the responsibility for supervision of air operations out of England of all the forces engaged in the programme including US Strategic and British Bomber Command together with any other air forces that might be available should pass to the Supreme Commander." Those strategic forces not used in support of the cross-Channel operation would be used in accordance with the coordination between Portal and Eisenhower. The compromise draft ended by stipulating that the directive for the employment of strategic bombing assets would be revised once the Allies were "established" on the Continent.[14]

On 14 April the Combined Chiefs passed the direction of the US and UK strategic air forces assigned to the Combined Bomber Offensive and the cross-Channel operation on to Eisenhower. After that date, the strategic bombers were to be available to the supreme commander upon call for direct support of land and naval operations when needed. "This was a role for which they had not previously been normally used," he noted, "but the SALERNO campaign had afforded convincing evidence of their effectiveness for the purpose."[15] In the end, the command structure consisted of Harris and Spaatz, who reported independently with their bomber commands to SHAEF, and Leigh-Mallory, who commanded the tactical forces that constituted the Allied Expeditionary Air Force (AEAF). The AEAF's main headquarters was at Stanmore, where Tedder coordinated the efforts of the three separate commands, just as Eisenhower had desired in the first place.

With the passage of the bomber commands to Eisenhower, Tedder defined the primary mission for the US Strategic Air Forces as the destruction of the German Air Force, with a secondary mission of bombing the enemy infrastructure system in accordance with the Transportation Plan. RAF Bomber Command was to continue its primary mission of disorganizing German industry. There was still, however, the problem of agreement on the infrastructure targets to be bombed in occupied countries. At one point the British War Cabinet took "a grave and on the whole an adverse view" of the proposal, citing the possible thousands of French casualties.[16] On 28 April, Eisenhower informed Churchill that he was willing to accept the "handicap" of postponing some targets with the greatest risk to civilians until a later stage of the operation, but he had altered the plan as far as possible without vitiating its value. If, as the prime minister and his cabinet had proposed, the attacks on railway centers were to be limited further, "such a modification would emasculate the whole plan." The concept for OVERLORD "was based on the assumption that our overwhelming Air Power would be able to prepare the way for the assault," he warned in conclusion. "If its hands are to be tied, the perils of an already hazardous undertaking will be greatly enhanced."[17] For Eisenhower, the hard joint and combined lessons from his experience in the Mediterranean left him no choice. "I have stuck to my guns," he wrote Marshall on 29 April, "because there is no other way in which this tremendous air force can help us, during the preparatory period, to get ashore and stay there."[18]

The War Cabinet considered Eisenhower's arguments on the night of 2 May. Churchill reminded the members of Eisenhower's onerous responsibility and recommended that care be taken not to add unnecessarily to the supreme commander's burdens. He was loath to interfere in military operations on political grounds, the prime minister concluded, but he had not fully realized that the use of air power before OVERLORD would assume so cruel and remorseless a form. The cabinet remained split and decided on an appeal to Roosevelt for a decision. On 7 May, Churchill wrote to ask the president to intervene, citing the number of French civilians already killed in the raids of the previous three weeks on rail centers in France. Roosevelt replied: "I am not prepared to impose from this distance any restriction on military action by the responsible commanders that in their opinion might militate against the success of 'Overlord' or cause additional loss of life to our Allied forces of invasion." The reply, as Churchill noted, was "decisive."[19]

By D-Day in the occupied countries, approximately seventy-one thousand tons of bombs had been dropped on rail centers, forty-four hundred tons on bridges, and eight hundred tons on open lines. In addition, the tactical air force had swooped on trains, convoys, and anything else that moved. There was a precipitous drop in railway traffic in the month leading up to the invasion and no evidence of an increase in pro-German sentiment on the part of the population. And despite American fears that US strategic forces would execute the majority of the transportation attacks, Bomber Command in this period struck a greater number of targets and dropped a larger tonnage of bombs than the US Eighth Air Force. The key to all this was the achievement of air supremacy over the invasion area and, indeed, over France. On D-Day this state of affairs limited German air to fewer than one hundred sorties against the Allied invasion force.

Later that month, John Eisenhower rode in a car with the supreme commander through a mass of vehicles lined up on the Normandy beachhead. "You'd never get away with this if you didn't have air supremacy," he remarked, leaning over his father's shoulder. "If I didn't have air supremacy," Eisenhower snorted impatiently, "I wouldn't be here."[20]

The supreme commander had set the stage for this accomplishment over a five-month period in which he brought the final strands of his unified command together. From April to September the US Strategic Air Forces and RAF Bomber Command reported to his headquarters independently, as did Leigh-Mallory, who commanded the tactical forces that made up the Allied Expeditionary Air Force. At Eisenhower's direction, Tedder coordinated the efforts of these three separate commands toward one goal: the successful implementation of OVERLORD. To his subordinates the supreme commander continually emphasized in this regard that "when a battle needs the last ounce of available force, the commander must not be in the position of depending upon request and negotiation to get it."[21] In his report to the Combined Chiefs and in his after-action report of the campaign, he returned again and again to the preparatory efforts of the joint air forces, "a belief in the effectiveness of which was the very cornerstone of the original invasion concept." And more specifically, there was his "conviction" that without the specific mission of "a prolonged campaign against the transportation systems of northwest Europe, the venture could not have logically been undertaken."[22] Most historians agree. Eisenhower's insistence on his unified command prerogative concerning the Transportation Plan, Stephen Ambrose points out, "was perhaps his greatest single contribution to the success of OVERLORD."[23]

The second major challenge to the unity of Eisenhower's command played itself out almost simultaneously with the strategic air forces issue in the most irritating, if not the most significant problem of the planning for the cross-Channel operation. The debate centered on ANVIL, the invasion of southern France, first as that operation affected OVERLORD and then as it affected the Italian campaign. It involved and in fact exacerbated Anglo-American strains and suspicions concerning the role of the Mediterranean Theater despite the acceptance of both Allies of northwest Europe as the primary theater. Ultimately, it became a matter of the relationship between both theaters and the calculated relationship of means and ends as the debate became increasingly focused on the problem of landing craft. Whatever the case, Eisenhower realized, without resolution of ANVIL, there could be no final resolution of the unified direction of the invasion and subsequent theater campaign.

At the Teheran (EUREKA) Conference, Stalin had urged a strong landing in southern France in conjunction with OVERLORD. Upon returning to Cairo, the Combined Chiefs on 6 December 1943 sent a directive to Eisenhower ordering him to prepare an outline for such an attack with two divisions. In addition to this plan, there was general agreement by early January that the size of the cross-Channel assault must be increased from three divisions to five seaborne and three airborne divisions, with two immediate follow-on seaborne divisions—all deployed on a broader front. The problem then became one of sufficient landing craft. They could not be easily diverted from the Pacific, and Southeast Asia had been stripped of all such transportation. This left the Mediterranean as the most likely source.[24]

Eisenhower's problems were compounded by other developments in that theater. General Sir Henry M. Wilson had replaced him as Allied commander in chief, Mediterranean, and on 7 January the Combined Chiefs passed the executive direction of that theater to the United Kingdom. This new structure allowed Churchill more freedom of action; and with a more direct role in determining the conduct of the Italian campaign, he resolved to break the stalemate. At an Allied meeting at Marrakech on 7–8 January, he confirmed an earlier decision to launch an amphibious operation at Anzio (SHINGLE) in order to move past the right flank of the German Winter and Gustav lines, thus forcing those troops facing the Allied Fifth Army to fall back. On 22 January, Allied forces landed successfully at Anzio. The Germans were able to contain the landing on the beachhead, however, and at the same time prevent any advance by the Fifth Army at the Gustav Line. There would be no immediate link-up of the two forces for a drive on Rome. "I had hoped that we were hurling a wildcat on the shore," Churchill wrote, "but all we got was a stranded whale."[25]

The day after the Anzio invasion, Eisenhower submitted his recommendation to the Combined Chiefs. The assault forces must be five divisions for OVERLORD, he confirmed. That operation marked "the crisis of the European war. . . . We cannot afford to fail." But ANVIL would make "an important contribution" to OVERLORD by containing German forces in southern France, where in any event US and French forces were available. As a consequence, he concluded, the two operations "must be viewed as one whole."[26] In reply, the British Chiefs recommended a broader OVERLORD assault front, a three- to four-month postponement of that operation, and a nearly simultaneous ANVIL if a two-division assault could be mounted in southern France. On 31 January the JCS agreed that OVERLORD should have a broader front and be postponed until 1 June. In terms of ANVIL, the American Joint Chiefs delegated their authority to Eisenhower, who would represent them in conferences with the British Chiefs.[27]

On 6 February, Eisenhower turned to his mentor for advice as he outlined both sides of the debate. "I am particularly anxious to have your personal views," he wrote Marshall, "because I feel that as long as you and I are in complete coordination as to purpose that you in Washington and I here can do a great deal toward achieving the best overall results."[28] Marshall's reply was hardly comforting. He found it strategically curious that the Americans and the British Chiefs at that stage of the planning appeared to have completely reversed themselves, with the Americans becoming "Mediterraneanites" and the British "heavily pro-OVERLORD." The root of the problem, Marshall emphasized, had to do with landing craft availability, which was all complicated by "a battle of numbers." In that regard, he noted that the British and American planners in Washington agreed that there was sufficient lift for a seven-division OVERLORD (five assault, two follow-up) and a two-division ANVIL. The British planners in London apparently did not agree with the figures. "OVERLORD of course is paramount," the Army chief of staff added, "and it must be launched on a reasonably secure basis of which you are the best judge." Nevertheless, with ANVIL, there would be eight or nine divisions that because of inadequate port facilities could not be employed in either northwest France or Italy. Could Eisenhower afford to lose this type of pressure? "I will use my influence here to agree with your desires," Marshall concluded. "I merely wish to be certain that localitis is not developing and that the pressures on you have not warped your judgment."[29]

Stung by Marshall's cable, Eisenhower traced in his reply his attempts to keep ANVIL intact even while trying to find the strength for OVERLORD. It was true, he acknowledged, that in order to achieve unity of purpose and effort he had at times modified somewhat his concepts of the campaign, but that was inevitable in combined Allied operations. Nevertheless, he assured the Army chief, he had never hesitated to convey his own personal convictions. "I merely recognize that OVERLORD, which has been supported by the US Chiefs of Staff," he reminded Marshall, "represents a crisis in the European War. Real success should do much to hasten the end of the conflict but a reverse will have opposite repercussions from which we would recover with the utmost difficulty."[30]

The somewhat defensive reply reassured Marshall, and on 11 February the JCS gave Eisenhower the authority to determine the fate of ANVIL. A week later, supported by joint staff technical advisers from Washington, Eisenhower submitted a plan based on the acceptance of a number of expedients in the assault and buildup for OVERLORD in an effort to preserve the strength in the Mediterranean for a two-division ANVIL. The British Chiefs responded that the allocation of landing craft in the proposal would skimp both operations. Moreover, the "shadow of ANVIL" was "cramping" General Wilson, already forced to use every possible resource in his theater for the campaign in Italy. Consequently, their recommendation was to cancel ANVIL and concentrate all efforts on "bleeding and burning German divisions" in Italy.[31] On 21 February, Montgomery joined the chorus, recommending "very strongly" against the southern operation. "Let us have two really good major campaigns—one in Italy and one in OVERLORD," he concluded.[32]

There was swift reaction in Washington, where after a special meeting with the JCS, the president directed Eisenhower to tell the British that there could be no abandonment of ANVIL without consultation with the Soviet Union. Eisenhower used this directive to work on a compromise with the British Chiefs that gave the Italian campaign "over riding priority over all existing and future operations in the Mediterranean," with first call on resources in that theater. Plans were to be drawn up, however, for other amphibious operations in the Mediterranean to support OVERLORD, with first consideration to ANVIL. There would be a review of the compromise on 20 March in terms of the Italian situation. On 24 February both heads of state and the Combined Chiefs accepted the compromise.[33]

On 22 March, with Marshall's concurrence, Eisenhower notified the British Chiefs of his opinion that ANVIL as an operation to be conducted simultaneously with OVERLORD was "no longer a possibility."[34] The British leaders accepted the conclusion, but the JCS insisted in reply that ANVIL only be delayed, not abandoned. Once the principal forces of the Fifth Army and those on the Anzio bridgehead had been joined, the Americans proposed, ANVIL should have priority over a continuing full offensive in Italy, with a target date for a two-division assault in southern France of 10 July. Moreover, if the British would make plans and preparation for this target date, the Joint Chiefs indicated their willingness to direct to the Mediterranean landing craft programmed to leave for the Pacific.

On 18 April the Joint Chiefs accepted the British compromise, which deployed resources to Wilson for an all-out offensive in Italy. Within this priority, the British commander in chief was directed to prepare plans for both ANVIL and the exploitation of Italy. But this compromise did not survive the fall of Rome and the drive of the Allied armies into northern Italy.

With the issue at a standstill, Churchill, as he had before TORCH, communicated directly with Roosevelt. He could not help Eisenhower, the prime minister informed the president, if it meant the complete ruin "of all our great affairs in the Mediterranean, and we take it hard that this should be demanded of us." The supreme commander, he implied, was being small-minded at a time when operations should be based on the largest considerations possible. ANVIL was a "bleak and sterile" operation that he found difficult to believe could have any impact on OVERLORD in the coming summer and fall. Roosevelt, however, had already accepted the JCS position, and in a message that crossed Churchill's, he supported Eisenhower's views in favor of ANVIL as early as possible. That operation had been agreed to at Teheran as part of a larger plan, he noted; and since that plan was going well, nothing need change, particularly since there were also more complex domestic considerations involved. "For purely political reasons over here," the president explained, "I should never survive even a slight setback in OVERLORD if it were known that fairly large forces had been diverted to the Balkans."[35]

The prime minister made a final effort on 9 August with the supreme commander to cancel ANVIL, now renamed DRAGOON by him on the basis of the British having been "dragooned" into the operation. At one point, Churchill even asserted that he might have to go to the king and "lay down the mantle of my high offices."[36] For Eisenhower, as he rejected Churchill's entreaties, it was one of the most trying sessions of the war. "I have never seen him so obviously stirred, upset, and even despondent," he wrote Marshall.[37] In the end, the prime minister finally gave in. On 10 August the British Chiefs of Staff directed Wilson to carry out DRAGOON on 15 August as planned.

It was the last gasp of the peripheral strategy. Italy, like China-Burma-India, would be a holding theater, a development that Churchill still bitterly regretted in 1953.[38] Nevertheless, the prime minister personally witnessed the DRAGOON operation and thereafter "adopted" it, complimenting Eisenhower in a cable on "the perfect precision" of the landing and "the intimate collaboration of British American forces and organizations."[39] It was almost too much for the supreme commander. "When I think of all the fighting and mental anguish I went through in order to preserve that operation," he wrote to Marshall of Churchill's cable, "I don't know whether to sit down and laugh or to cry."[40] That day, Eisenhower replied to Churchill: "I am delighted to note . . . that you have personally and legally adopted the DRAGOON. I am sure that he will grow fat and prosperous under your watchfulness."[41]

CHAPTER NINE

The Lessons of Unity Vindicated: Normandy to the Elbe, June 1944–May 1945

It is a bad thing to keep changing organizations just for the sake of change.

DWIGHT D. EISENHOWER

I feel that I learned many, many things during the war and if I had to do the whole thing over again there are many arrangements I would alter and revise. I would never, however, in such a command as we had in Europe appoint a so-called ground "Commander in Chief."

DWIGHT D. EISENHOWER

No more let us falter! From Malta to Yalta! Let nobody alter!

WINSTON S. CHURCHILL

O N D-DAY, EVEN General Morgan, who had been involved in every aspect of the OVERLORD planning, was "astounded at the . . . vastness of the operation" that integrated land, sea, and air forces into the largest joint and combined operation in history.[1] Participating in the invasion were eleven thousand airplanes, seven thousand ships, and four thousand landing craft carrying two hundred thousand soldiers and twenty thousand vehicles—all attacking fortified beaches over a fifty-mile front. On the American beaches alone, the plan was to land the equivalent of two hundred trainloads of troops, followed in the next two weeks by twice as many soldiers as there had been in the 1939 US Army. In order to deal with such immense and complex problems, one early iteration of the operational order for just the First US Army contained more words than *Gone with the Wind*.

For such an enterprise, Eisenhower had to settle major issues as he coordinated the efforts of the three services in moving the invasion force with supplies across the Channel and in providing each division after landing with the requisite daily requirement of seven hundred tons of supply a day. But much of the detailed responsibility by necessity had to be spread along the various chains of command. The process required a fine touch of decentralization within the unity of his command, one that Churchill appreciated as he dealt with Eisenhower during the preparation and conduct of OVERLORD. "He observed everything with a vigilant eye," the prime minister wrote of the supreme commander, "and no one knew better than he how to stand close to a tremendous event without impairing the authority he had delegated to others."[2]

The command and staff structures for OVERLORD remained in place for almost three months after the invasion. During that time, however, the British mounted their most serious challenge to Eisenhower's concept of unified command. The cause was the supreme commander's so-called broad-front strategy for moving on the Rhine and industrial base of Germany. The British proposed what they considered a more powerful "single thrust" on the northern axis to Berlin. When they were unable to persuade Eisenhower to change his broad-front strategy, they attempted to achieve the objectives of the single-thrust approach by altering SHAEF's unified command structure. The Combined Chiefs of Staff as an organization were not a party to the dispute, which was fundamentally about theater campaign strategy. They had already directed the overall objectives and general shape of the campaign and determined the necessary forces. The theater strategic alternatives remained with Eisenhower as theater commander, particularly since the Combined Chiefs had already provided enough troops to support either the single-thrust or the broad-front strategy.[3]

On 25 July, Eisenhower announced that Bradley would assume command on 1 August of the 12th Army Group, consisting of Patton's new Third Army and the existing First Army under Lieutenant General Courtney Hodges. Eisenhower would not take command of the new US army group and Montgomery's 21st Army Group until 1 September. Until then Montgomery would continue to direct the overall land battle, providing general directives to Bradley. The constriction of the initial beachhead and area of operation, he informed Marshall, required one man on the spot to be responsible for coordination, and that was Montgomery with his experience and seniority. The British commander was thus placed in temporary charge of ground operations, "but always under plans of campaign approved by me."[4]

The differences in strategic approach emerged in late August as the Allies successfully drove to the Seine, pouring through World War I battlefields and moving miles at the cost of a tiny percentage of the casualties that had been required for an earlier generation to gain yards. At that point, there was no coherent enemy force between the Seine and the German border. Eisenhower's decision on 19 August to cross the river in strength on the run was thus a natural reaction. But those efforts required an amount of supply that far outstripped planned capabilities. The problem was compounded by increased transport problems as the Allied lines of communications extended rapidly eastward. Moreover, part of that advance was through that section of France where the destroyed railroad infrastructure reflected not only the success of the Transportation Plan but also major problems for using that means of supply transport. At the same time, air supply was inadequate, particularly since many of the cargo aircraft were held in readiness for airborne operations that never occurred because of the rapid Allied advance. As a consequence, Eisenhower's decision to cross the Seine was very similar to his decision in November 1942 to race into Tunisia without waiting to build up supply bases and lines of communication. The results were also similar. For as in Tunisia, when the Allied forces in 1944 finally had to halt to straighten out the logistics problem and wait for supplies, they were still confronted by an active, undefeated enemy with a major battle looming in the future.[5]

On 23 August, Eisenhower visited Montgomery's headquarters at the British commander's request to discuss future operations. Montgomery began by insisting that Eisenhower leave land operations in his hands. The supreme commander "should not descend into the land battle and become a ground C-in-C," but instead "must sit on a very lofty perch in order to be able to take a detached view of the whole intricate problem—which involves land, sea, air, civil control, political problems, etc." He felt so strongly about this issue, Montgomery added, that he would gladly serve under Bradley to appease American public opinion. It was a dramatic offer that was politically not feasible, and Eisenhower refused by reiterating his intention to take control of both Allied army groups on 1 September. But the command structure was not the real issue, as Eisenhower realized when Montgomery turned to theater strategic matters, strongly criticizing the broad-front approach while presenting his single-thrust plan for his 21st Army Group to move northward, reinforced by Hodges's First Army and the First Allied Airborne Army. Further supplies to Patton's Third Army, he insisted, should be cut off to allow all available resources to go to his army group and Hodges's army.[6]

These differences formed the backdrop for a series of miscommunications and misunderstandings between Eisenhower and Montgomery that reached their initial climax in mid-October 1944. On 1 September the supreme commander's operational headquarters opened officially on the Continent. That day, Eisenhower assumed active command of two army groups, each consisting of two armies; one Allied airborne army; the naval units attached to the theater; and both the Allied tactical and strategic air forces. The newly established First Allied Airborne Army was a result of the supreme commander's requirement after Normandy for a suitable joint planning agency to coordinate operations of the parachute and glider units under ground command with the aircraft used for troop carriers, escorts, and resupply of those units under air force command. Under the new structure, Montgomery gave up responsibility for coordination between his 21st Army Group, consisting of the First Canadian Army and the Second British Army, and Bradley's forces. Bradley, in turn, assumed command of the newly formed 12th Army Group consisting of the First, Third, and Ninth US Armies. On 15 September, Eisenhower also assumed command of General Jacob Devers's Southern Group of Armies or 6th Army Group, the DRAGOON force consisting of the First French and the Seventh US Armies previously under AFHQ control.[7]

On 10 September, Eisenhower met with Montgomery at the 21st Army Group headquarters. In the week prior, despite increasing supply problems, the Allied forces had moved forward to within fifty miles of the Rhine. Both army group commanders were anxious to reinforce success and were demanding more supplies for further advance. At the 10 September meeting, Eisenhower agreed that Montgomery could use a key component of the strategic reserve, the First Allied Airborne Army, to launch an operation designed to move Allied forces over the lower Rhine. If MARKET GARDEN, as the operation was designated, was successful, the Allies would cut the land exit of German troops in western Holland, outflank the West Wall, capture the Ruhr, and most important, in terms of theater strategy, position the British Army Group for a drive along the north German plain toward Berlin. Nevertheless, Eisenhower was care-

ful to dampen the British commander's expectations in such a case for a
completely narrow front approach. Even if MARKET GARDEN succeeded
and all energies and resources were subsequently focused on the German
capital, Eisenhower informed Montgomery on 15 September, the Allies
must still be prepared to "direct forces of both Army Groups on Berlin."
It was his desire, he concluded, "to move on Berlin by the most direct and
expeditious route, with combined US-British forces . . . all in one coordinated, concerted operation."[8]

This touched off an exchange of messages that clearly demonstrated
the inability of the two men to understand each other. A meeting was
plainly in order. But when Eisenhower held a conference at Versailles
with his commanders on 22 September, Montgomery, then preoccupied
with his direction of MARKET GARDEN, sent his chief of staff. Predictably, the outcome of the conference was a compromise that pleased no
one. The top priority was to seize Antwerp and then attack toward the
Ruhr from the north. Patton's Third Army was to take no more aggressive
action until the requirements of the main effort in the north were met. At
the same time, however, Patton would not be stripped of all maintenance
and supplies, and Montgomery would not get control of the First Army,
only permission in emergencies to communicate directly with Hodges.
Bradley, who wanted a large offensive against the Ruhr on a three hundred–mile central front, had to settle for a lesser support role. But even
in support, to Montgomery's consternation, the American general was
directed to attack toward Bonn and Cologne and use any opportunities
to attack the Ruhr from the south.[9]

These developments, added to the unsuccessful end of MARKET GAR-
DEN on 27 September, left Montgomery frustrated and isolated in his
tactical headquarters. By early October it was obvious that there were
problems with the compromise of the 22 September Versailles conference. Antwerp was still closed, and Patton continued unauthorized advances. Most important, the failure of MARKET GARDEN was conclusive
for Eisenhower in terms of the narrow-thrust strategy: "What this action
proved was that the idea of 'one full blooded thrust' to Berlin was silly."[10]
For Montgomery, the problems were the result of a leadership process in
which a theater strategy, regardless of whether it was right or wrong, was
not directed down the chain of command. "We did not advance to the
Rhine on a *broad* front," he observed; "we advanced to the Rhine on several fronts, which were un-coordinated."[11] As a remedy to this situation,

Montgomery returned to the theater command structure. On 10 October, in a letter to Smith, the British leader proposed that he become the overall ground commander for the theater, with command over the 12th as well as the 21st Army Group. By trying to move simultaneously on the Ruhr, the Saar, and the Frankfurt area, he argued, the Allies were unlikely to reach any of the objectives. "All our troubles can be traced to the fact that there is no one commander in charge of the land battle," Montgomery concluded. "The supreme commander runs it himself from SHAEF by means of long telegrams. SHAEF is not an operational headquarters and never can be."[12]

The letter arrived at a low point for Eisenhower. He had accepted the Arnhem operation and now, as even Brooke admitted, "nobly took all the blame on himself."[13] His cautious approach to Montgomery and Bradley had allowed them essentially to choose their operational priorities. And Bradley and Patton were so discouraged by Eisenhower's actions that, in Patton's description, both generals were ready "to go to China and serve under Admiral Nimitz."[14] Finally, Marshall as well as Brooke and Ramsey were upset at the failure to open Antwerp. As a consequence, Eisenhower's patience with Montgomery reached its limit with the British commander's indictment of his unified command structure as a means to get his way on a narrow-thrust theater strategy. The type of command arrangement desired by Montgomery, Eisenhower noted, would have placed him "in a position to draw at will, in support of his own ideas, upon the strength of the entire command."[15]

The result was a harsh letter dispatched to Montgomery on 13 October only after Smith and Marshall, who was touring the theater, urged Eisenhower to send it. In the letter, he asserted his authority as supreme commander in terms of his two years of experience in dealing with the ground commander issue. Concerning the structure of command, he conceded that "a single *battlefield* commander" was necessary to accomplish one major task on the field of conflict. This arrangement worked up through the organization of armies and army groups. But when the theater stretched from Switzerland to the North Sea, one man could not "stay so close to the day by day movement of divisions and corps that he can keep a 'battle grip' upon the *overall* situation and direct it intelligently." It was, instead, a matter of breaking up the "*wide* front" of the campaign area into one primary and any number of secondary areas of operations. In addressing those areas, only the overall commander, "in this case myself," could adjust the larger boundaries, shift priorities for supplies and reinforcements, and allocate air, ground, and airborne support. These types of broad decisions, Eisenhower emphasized, could not be made by a general involved in the detailed day-by-day direction of combat at the tactical level of war. There were limitations even to the powers of the supreme commander, he reminded Montgomery, "and if you, as the senior commander in this Theater of one of the great Allies feel that my conceptions and directives are such as to endanger the success of operations, it is our duty to refer the matter to higher authority for any action they may choose to take, however drastic."[16]

On 16 October, Montgomery replied emphatically: "You will hear *no* more on the subject of command from me." He had given Eisenhower his view, he pointed out, "and you have given your answer. I and all of us here will weigh in one hundred per cent to do what you want and we will pull it through without a doubt." The message closed: "Your very devoted and loyal subordinate."[17] Nevertheless, the question of unity of command and its relation to theater strategy reemerged in November when the rapid advances of late summer and early fall were replaced by static battles near the Franco-German border reminiscent of World War I. The French campaign had been successfully concluded, but it had exceeded the requirements established in the OVERLORD plan. By late fall it was evident that SHAEF lacked the overwhelming manpower and material superiority necessary for a rapid continuation of the broad-front strategy. At the same time, the Germans were reconstituting a new strategic reserve in the west. From Brooke's perception, the entire situation was a prescription for disaster. "Ike is incapable of running a land battle," he noted in his diary on 29 November, "and it is all dependent on how well Monty can handle him."[18]

Montgomery, however, was no more successful in this endeavor than he had been in October. At a meeting at Maastricht on 7 December, in what he later described as playing a "lone hand" against Eisenhower, as well as Tedder and Bradley, who also attended the meeting, the British commander recapitulated what he considered had been agreed upon at a meeting in late November: the favoring of the narrow-thrust strategy and applicable command arrangements. Eisenhower and his companions were unmoved, maintaining that the broad-front winter offensive on both sides of the Ardennes was in fact working. In the end, the British lost the strategic debate. The Allied advance would be on a broad front to the

Rhine, clearing all enemy forces west of the river. Montgomery reflected that he had made telling arguments that "caused Eisenhower to wobble," but thought his efforts had been undone by Tedder and Bradley, who accompanied the supreme commander in his three-hour drive back to Luxembourg. "I can do no more myself," he wrote Brooke. "If we want the war to end within any reasonable period you have to get Eisenhower's hand taken off the land battle. I regret to say that in my opinion he just doesn't know what he is doing."[19]

On 16 December the situation was altered when German forces began a major counteroffensive in the Ardennes, designed to regain Antwerp and divide American and British forces. After determining that the offensive was not a spoiling attack, Eisenhower took charge of the battle. At a meeting with his three army group commanders at Verdun on 19 December, he set the tone by depicting the current situation "as one of opportunity . . . and not of disaster. There will be only cheerful faces at the conference table."[20] In quick succession, Eisenhower halted the southern offense, ordered Patton to attack north against the German flank, and committed the two airborne divisions that constituted his only reserve. On 20 December the president nominated the supreme commander to the newly established five-star rank of general of the Army. That day, over Bradley's objection, Eisenhower gave Montgomery command of the US First and Ninth armies north of the Bulge—the essence of what the field marshal had requested at the end of November.[21]

When Eisenhower visited Montgomery three days after Christmas, the British leader used the new arrangements to reopen the demand for a permanent revision of the unified command structure. The issue centered on whether in a new offensive to cross the Rhine, Montgomery would be given general coordinating powers to synchronize his operations with those of the American northern armies—an arrangement to which Eisenhower was ready to agree. The alternate was to grant Montgomery his wish to have complete operational direction of the entire assault. The confused meeting was a study in miscommunication. Montgomery believed that he had been successful in making his points concerning the command structure. And Eisenhower left the conference convinced that Montgomery had agreed to counterattack on New Year's Day 1945.[22]

The extent of the misunderstandings was revealed on 29 December when Montgomery followed his normal practice by emphasizing in a letter to Eisenhower what he believed had taken place in the previous day's meeting. To begin with, the counterattack would not begin until 3 January. Added to this unwelcome news was guidance on the command arrangements, startling in its arrogance. Recalling Bradley's earlier opposition to the field marshal's exercising operational control of the American 12th Army Group, Montgomery advised Eisenhower to be "very firm on the subject" and to avoid "any loosely worded statement." It would, therefore, not be enough to merely use the word *co-ordination*. Instead, one commander "must have powers to direct and control the operations," something that Eisenhower could not possibly do himself. Accordingly, Eisenhower's directive should read: "From now onwards full operational direction, control, and co-ordination of these operations is vested in C-in-C. 21st Army Group subject to such instructions as may be issued by the Supreme Commander from time to time." This would ensure that "all available offensive power" would be assigned for a full-scale northern assault on the Ruhr under "a sound set-up for command." If Eisenhower did not comply with these basic conditions, Montgomery concluded, "then we will fail again."[23]

The arrival of Montgomery's message at SHAEF coincided with a time of severe strain in Anglo-American relations. The British press had consistently criticized Eisenhower during the German Ardennes offensive, often recommending that Montgomery be given operational control of the entire campaign. The American press, particularly the McCormick-Patterson and Hearst newspapers, had reacted in chauvinistic kind, accusing Montgomery of intriguing for command. The Joint Chiefs were also irritated. Marshall viewed Eisenhower's earlier placement of American forces under Montgomery as a necessary but temporary expedient, but he feared that the pressure of events might cause the supreme commander to yield to British demands concerning a single ground commander. "My feeling is this," he wrote Eisenhower on 30 December: "under no circumstances make any concessions of any kind whatsoever." The chief of staff assured his protégé that he was not assuming such a concession would be made. But he wanted to ensure that Eisenhower understood the attitude of the American establishment, which would react to such an action with "terrific resentment." Marshall concluded the message with encouragement for the New Year. "You are doing a fine job and go and give them hell."[24]

The cable from Marshall stiffened Eisenhower's resolve. On the last day of 1944 he sent Montgomery a message that was unequivocal in its assertion of authority. "In the matter of command," he began, "I do not agree that one Army Group Commander should fight his own battle and give orders to another Army Group commander." Moreover, the current post-Ardennes plan called for making the main effort in the north and as a consequence for placing a complete American army under Montgomery's command. These would have been difficult decisions to make if he had not had personal confidence in the British commander. Montgomery's "frank and friendly" advice was always appreciated, Eisenhower emphasized, "but in your latest letter you disturb me by predictions of 'failure' unless your exact opinions in the matter of giving you command over Bradley are met in detail. I assure you that in this matter I can go no further." For his part, the supreme commander concluded, he would deplore the development of such an "unbridgeable gulf of convictions" that they would have to present their difference to the Combined Chiefs. "The confusion and debate that would follow would certainly damage the good will and devotion to a common cause that have made this Allied Force unique in history. *As ever, your friend.*"[25]

Montgomery, who was warned by his chief of staff that Eisenhower was "het up" over his letter, dispatched two letters of graceful submission to the supreme commander's authority, one before and one after the actual receipt of Eisenhower's forceful message. "You have stated your views and I have stated mine," the field marshal wrote in his first letter. "We will now go with your proposals."[26] To the chief of the Imperial General Staff, he was more direct. "I am now going to withdraw from the contest," he informed Brooke. "It is clear to me that we have got all we can and that we shall get no more."[27]

The rest of the British leadership, however, was not so ready to yield. For the British Chiefs, the Ardennes had demonstrated the danger of a broad-front campaign, and in early January they requested that the Combined Chiefs review the theater strategy at the forthcoming Malta and Yalta conferences. In particular, the review would focus on the case of strengthening the northern front and settling the command arrangements whereby one man should be directly responsible to the supreme commander for all ground forces employed in the main thrust. For Eisenhower, on the other hand, the failure of the German counterattack had demonstrated that even an overwhelming assault on too narrow a front could be not only contained but pushed back. In any event, as he wrote Marshall, he welcomed the review because the issues at stake were so important that the greatest possible degree of conviction concerning the theater strategy should be pursued.

At the same time, Eisenhower began to address in detail the British return to the issue of a ground commander. What he was giving Montgomery, he emphasized, already involved "all that one man can handle as a *battle* commander."[28] In effect, then, the Army group commander

> is the highest ground commander who has a logical function separate from that of the Theater Commander and who, at the same time, can be sufficiently freed from broad strategic, logistic and civil problems to give his entire attention to the battle. The next higher commander above the Army Group Commander, by whatever name he is called, such as Supreme or Theater Commander, necessarily controls broad strategy and commands air and sea forces, and therefore is the only one in position to bring additional strength to bear to influence the action. When the ground front is such that configuration and extent permit close battle supervision by a single Army Group Commander, then this officer is also known as the Ground Commander of the entire force. But when there is more than one Army Group in a single Theater, there cannot logically be an overall "ground commander" separate from the Theater or Supreme Commander.[29]

The meeting of the Combined Chiefs of Staff at Malta focused primarily on theater strategy and command arrangements and was therefore acrimonious—a "terrible meeting," in Marshall's assessment. At one point, Brooke expressed the concern of the British Chiefs about the influence of Bradley and Patton on Eisenhower. "Well Brooke," was Marshall's quick retort, "they are not nearly as much worried as the American Chiefs of Staff are about the immediate pressures . . . of Mr. Churchill on General Eisenhower. The President practically never sees Eisenhower, never writes to him—that is my advice because he is an Allied commander— and we are deeply concerned by the pressures of the Prime Minister and of the . . . British Chiefs of Staff, so I think your worries are on the wrong foot."[30]

More specifically, the British were concerned with the wording of Eisenhower's 20 January strategic assessment to the Combined Chiefs, which implied that there would be no crossing of the Rhine in the north until all the area west of the river, both north and south, had been cleared.[31] Smith, acting for Eisenhower at Malta, brokered compromise wording between the supreme commander back at SHAEF and the British Chiefs. "I will seize the Rhine crossings in the north just as soon as this is a feasible operation and without waiting to close the Rhine throughout its length," Eisenhower cabled his chief of staff. To this, however, he added a caveat that bothered the deeply suspicious British leaders: "I will advance across the Rhine in the north with maximum strength and complete determination immediately the situation in the south allows me to collect necessary forces and do this without incurring unreasonable risks."[32]

Because of American domestic sensitivities, the subject of overall ground commander was never formally considered at Malta, only secretly discussed in closed session by the Combined Chiefs without recorded minutes and with no other officers present. At Yalta on 2 February, however, Churchill's associated proposal for Alexander to replace Tedder was discussed by Roosevelt and Churchill, with Marshall and Brooke in attendance. The president and the chief of staff considered that politically in America it might appear that Alexander was being brought in to help Eisenhower after the Ardennes setback. Nevertheless, they were willing to accept the change in about six weeks' time after further Allied offensive operations had overshadowed the memory of the December German counterattacks.[33]

Eisenhower learned of these developments on 11 February. The next day, he summarized his thoughts on the matter in an unusually direct cable to Brooke. It was important, he began, that Alexander understand the command structure in order that he would not feel later that "his great qualities as a soldier" had been ignored or that he had been badly used. This was the segue into the supreme commander's principal message to Brooke. Within this structure, he asserted, "there can be no question whatsoever of placing between me and my Army Group Commanders any intermediary headquarters either official or unofficial in character." And should the press attempt to interpret Alexander's appointment as such a move, he would be forced immediately "to make a formal announcement setting forth the facts."[34]

Churchill was predictably upset with the message to Brooke. On 22 February he reminded Eisenhower that an eventual switch of deputies had been agreed upon at Yalta. "If however I am to gather from your letter that the British Deputy to the Supreme Commander would not be concerned with military matters except in an informal way, and would be principally responsible for dealing with the supplies of food and setting up a decent living standard in liberated and conquered territories," the Prime Minister wrote, "I must say quite frankly that I consider this would be a waste of Field Marshal Alexander's military gifts and experience." In reply, as was his custom, Eisenhower attempted to mollify the British statesman. But there was no disguising his unyielding resolve on the subject as he explained his position. The tendency of the press to give its own interpretation of "the delicate question of command," he insisted, might compel public announcements that could hurt Alexander's feelings. "So long as you understand my attitude and intent in this matter," he concluded, "I will not mention the subject further."[35] Eisenhower repeated these views when Churchill made one more attempt on 5 March in a visit to SHAEF. A few days later, the prime minister ruled that the entire matter should be dropped, in effect ending British attempts to change theater strategy by altering the unified command structure.[36]

By that time Eisenhower was thoroughly in control of a unified command that was defeating German forces all along the approaches to the Rhine from the North Sea to Switzerland, eliminating the Colmar pocket, capturing the Roer dams, and penetrating the West Wall. As the Allied forces in Europe swept eastward, the JCS Special Committee for Reorganization and National Defense, formed the previous year, finished its deliberations. On 11 April the four-man board published its report, much of it based on interviews conducted in November and December 1944 with fifty-six high-ranking US Army and Navy officers in all theaters of operation. Eisenhower's interview had occurred on 1 November. The principles and attitudes that made Allied joint unified operations so successful, he stated, could "serve democratic nations with equally brilliant results in time of peace." As a consequence, he recommended service unification and the establishment of a chief of staff position to "promote efficiency in combat operations." There was a need for integrated planning and budgetary processes encompassing all the services, and he was emphatic that the Army Air Force should evolve into an independent, coequal service in order to reflect the lesson then emerging from the war that "no great victory is possible without air superiority."[37]

Many of the other officers interviewed were in general agreement. With the exception of its chairman, the committee was in favor of a single-department system of organization for the US Armed Forces. That view, the report began, was supported by "Generals of the Army MacArthur and Eisenhower, Fleet Admiral Nimitz, [and] Admiral Halsey," as well as a "great majority of the Army officers and almost exactly half of the Navy officers." To head the single department, the committee recommended a secretary of the armed forces who reported directly to the president and whose responsibilities would include budget preparation and general administration. Under the secretary would be a commander of the armed forces, in charge of the three services operating as coequal operating arms. This officer would also act as chief of staff to the president and would be in charge of strategic planning and direction of military operations under unified commands in the field. The service chiefs would provide advice to the president on broad issues of general strategy and the budget, but they would not have any operational authority, which would be reserved for the commander of the armed forces.[38]

The committee chairman, Admiral James Richardson, submitted a dissenting minority report representing the Navy position that the Joint Chiefs should continue to operate as a coordinating entity and that the current departmental system, with the exception, if necessary, of the addition of a separate air force, should not change. The Joint Chiefs were unable to agree on the results. King assailed the majority report, blocked an Air Force attempt to publish the entire document, and claimed that the views of Nimitz and Halsey had not been reported correctly. At the same time, he dispatched the admiral who had sided with the two Army members of the committee in the majority to report to sea duty in the Pacific Theater. The entire disagreement ended participation by the JCS as a corporate body in the unification debate.[39]

The day after the submission of the Richardson Committee report, Roosevelt died of a cerebral hemorrhage, a further shock for Eisenhower, who had spent 12 April visiting the horrors of a German concentration camp at Ohrdruf Nord near Gotha. The Army had never anticipated that FDR, an assistant Navy secretary in World War I, would exert any pressure for unification. "At least, Mr. President," Marshall once asked in exasperation, "stop speaking of the Army as 'they' and the Navy as 'us.'"[40] The new commander in chief, Harry S. Truman, had a different attitude on the issue. In 1905 he had begun a thirty-five-year Army affiliation by joining the Missouri National Guard. All this was reinforced by his experience during World War II as chairman of the Senate Special Committee to Investigate the National Defense Program, which left him appalled by the "waste and inefficiency existing as a result of the operation of two separate and uncoordinated military departments."[41] By August 1944 he was arguing for a consolidation "under one tent" of the Army and the Navy, "ending the present jangles and jumbles." Heavily influenced by the ongoing, congressionally mandated hearings of the Army Pearl Harbor Board, Truman stressed that such a catastrophe would not happen under unification, "for instead of two sets of orders from Washington, one order will go out from a single secretary to one supreme head in each theater of operations."[42]

In the meantime, in the closing days of April and early May, Allied forces delivered the final joint and combined blows against Germany. "You would be proud of the Army you have produced," Eisenhower reported to Marshall on 15 April. "In the first place, the US ground and air forces are a unit; they both participate in the same battle all the way down the line from me to the lowest private. . . . I know of one or two Major Generals in the Air Force that one of my Army Commanders would accept as Division Commanders today."[43] The German surrender took place in the War Room of SHAEF at Reims. In the aftermath of the ceremony, Eisenhower quietly watched and listened as his subordinates proposed draft victory messages, each more grandiloquent than the last. Finally, the supreme commander stopped the proceedings and dictated the last message of the European war: "The mission of this Allied force was fulfilled at 0241, local time, May 7th, 1945."[44] Eisenhower was only a little less prosaic two months later as he dissolved SHAEF in his last message to all members of the Allied Expeditionary Force: "Combined Command terminates at midnight tonight, 13 July 1945, and brings to a close one of the greatest and most successful campaigns ever fought."[45]

Eisenhower could have added "unique" to his understated description, for there was no other commander on either side in World War II who had more multifaceted unified and combined command experiences. Until that conflict, no American had ever been in charge of a large unified command consisting of armies, navies, and air forces; and none had ever directed an Allied Command. There were, of course, unified operations in other theaters of the global conflict. But they were less complex—in the Central Pacific because the forces were primarily naval, and in the Southwest Pacific, the Middle East, and Southwest Asia because there were much smaller forces. Moreover, such commands were almost entirely peculiar to the Allies. The Russians, Germans, and Italians were dominated by army ground troops in the European and African theaters, and there were no efforts to organize these forces under unified commands. "The campaigns in the Mediterranean and in Europe had no prior parallel in the history of warfare," Eisenhower rightly observed after the war.[46]

Also unique were the pressures on Eisenhower as the supreme commander. Above him were the heads of government of the United States and the United Kingdom and their chiefs of staff—closely aligned against a common threat and yet at odds over grand theater strategies in the European Theater of war. As the ranking Allied leader, Eisenhower was often caught in the middle of opposing positions, usually delivered by Churchill and Marshall, on issues at the highest level of political-military affairs. This interaction was complicated from below by his British component commanders, who had to be weaned from their cooperative command system to a more unified one. It would be hard to imagine anyone more suitable to act in this environment than Eisenhower in his capacity as a broker among competing national, strategic, and personal sensitivities and tendencies.

This role often meant compromises. At times, particularly concerning the reconciliation of strategic and operational courses of action, the outcome could appear ambiguous. But the supreme commander never yielded on the matter of overall ground command and never shifted from the fundamental broad-front strategy that called for the Allies to advance in tandem. "I did everything that was humanely possible to support Montgomery's attack," he recalled after the war, "but never for one instant at the cost of complete inaction throughout the remainder of the front."[47] What animated Eisenhower was a goal from which he never deviated, what he correctly referred to in a 1948 letter to Churchill as "the miracle of Allied cooperation."[48] He achieved this goal, first because he would let nothing interfere with the cooperation and teamwork he demanded to preserve the integrity and unity of the Allied command and thereby the successful implementation of the coalition decisions. Second, there was his massive political discretion—an unparalleled fusion of empathy and diplomacy. Third, he used to great effect his charisma based on a unique combination of personal charm and a feel for the right touch at the right moment. Eisenhower, in short, inspired trust with a studious moderation based on common sense, decency, and a dislike of extremes, combined with a simple, self-effacing approach to problems that was, in Bedell Smith's description, "completely frank, completely honest, very human and considerate."[49]

There was an important collateral lesson from his efforts that became more urgent for Eisenhower even as he assumed his primary postwar duty in Europe as the commander in chief, US Forces of Occupation, Germany. He had, after all, just been through an experiment for more than two years in which officers from both the United States and the United Kingdom had dropped their service loyalties and national prejudices to work successfully under a unified command. Consequently, he was increasingly insistent through the summer in correspondence with Marshall, congressional committees, and friends that the US military establishment must move quickly toward unity of command and effort. "Integration of the means for waging war is vitally essential," he wrote at one point. "There is no such thing as *separate* land, sea and air war. We have proved over and over again in Africa and Europe, that through real integration, forces of the . . . services multiply rather than merely add their separate tactical effects." But integration, he warned, required the inculcation in each service of "unification in thought, purpose and training."[50] Moreover, this type of unified command at the theater level could work, Eisenhower reminded Marshall in the fall, less than a month before he would replace his mentor as chief of staff, only "through unification at the very top," at the national level under a single Cabinet-level department.[51] At that level, this third component of his concept of overall unified command, he believed, would ensure that the other two components, unity of effort and unity of command, permeated the structure from Washington down to the theaters of war and operations.

PART FOUR

Peacetime Unification, 1945–1950

CHAPTER TEN

Unified Command in Washington, June 1945–July 1946

I think that all of us, during the war, clearly understood that a period of bewilderment, misunderstanding, and probably some bungling would follow upon the conclusion of hostilities.

DWIGHT D. EISENHOWER

I, for one, am unwilling to have the Chief of the Army Air forces pass on the question of whether or not the Navy should have funds for building and maintaining a balanced fleet. One might just as well ask a committee composed of a Protestant, a Catholic, and a Jew to save our national souls by recommending a national church and creed.

FLEET ADMIRAL WILLIAM F. HALSEY JR.

Washington seemed little bothered about the long-term future. Present pressures preoccupied most legislators and government officials. . . . But of the future piled high with threats to our victory and to our continuing security, there seemed to be little thought.

DWIGHT D. EISENHOWER

IN THE CLOSING MONTHS of Eisenhower's occupation duties in Europe, the unification issue reemerged on the national agenda, beginning a struggle on his part to establish the concept of unified command at the highest level of government that would preoccupy him until the final years of his presidency. In the wake of World War II, the issue took on more prominence and urgency due to the rapidly evolving concept of what constituted American national security. While fighting that conflict and making preparations for the peace, US leaders had expanded the concept and used its terminology for the first time to explain America's relationship to the world. The background for this change involved the experience and understanding by these leaders of the massive technological and political transformations set in train by the war. The

European-centered international system had ceased to exist even as the United States emerged as a hegemonic power that appeared to demand a global role. "The world," Assistant Secretary of War John J. McCloy reported as early as the fall of 1945, after a global inspection trip, "looks to the United States as the one stable country to ensure the security of the world."[1]

At the same time, the linkage of national security to the primary core national interest of survival had grown stronger. For most of US history, the physical security of the continental United States had not been in jeopardy. But by 1945, with the advent of the long-range bomber, the atomic bomb, and the expectation of what the ballistic missile would accomplish, this invulnerability was rapidly diminishing. Given these changes, there was a general perception that the future would not allow time to mobilize, that preparation would have to become something permanent. For the first time, American leaders would have to deal with the essential paradox of national security faced by the Roman Empire and other great powers in the intervening centuries: *Si vis pacem, para bellum* — If you want peace, prepare for war. This, as Hanson Baldwin noted at the time, would require changes in American domestic institutions as radical as those in the strategic environment, since "total war means total effort, and the peacetime preparations for it must be as comprehensive . . . as the execution of it. Consequently the effects of total war transcend the period of hostilities; they wrench and distort and twist the body politic and the body economic not only *after* a war (as we are now seeing) but *prior* to war (as we shall soon see)."[2]

Allied to the concept of preparedness was the emerging idea that national security required all elements of national power, not just military, to be in place in peace as well as in war. "We are in a different league now," *Life* magazine proclaimed in 1945. "How large the subject of security has grown, larger than a combined Army and Navy."[3] And a year later, this sentiment was echoed by a key architect of the emerging institutional changes in Washington, who observed that most policymakers dealing with national security believed "that foreign policy, military and domestic economic resources should be closely tied together."[4] This linkage of national security with so many interdependent factors, whether political and economic or psychological and military, also led to a more expansive concept, with the subjective boundaries of security pushed out farther into the world, encompassing more geography and thereby more issues and problems. In this context, developments anywhere could be perceived to have an automatic and direct impact on US core interests. In 1948 President Truman applied to the entire world the words used in earlier times with regard to the Western Hemisphere: "The loss of independence by any nation adds directly to the insecurity of the United States and all free nations."[5] By that time, the emerging global aspects of that concept were also oriented increasingly on the Soviet threat. In that context, it soon became difficult to question the need for a national security establishment focused on a virtual state of war in peace with a nation that became the all-consuming focus of US national security. "The capabilities, declarations, and actions that comprised US national security policy made sense only with reference to the Soviet threat," Colin Gray has observed. "That threat, as variously defined over the years, was not a factor helping to define the purposes of US policy, grand strategy, and military strategy. It was *the* factor."[6]

There was in all this a kind of adverse synergism. On the one hand, the perception of Soviet intentions affected the manner in which US governmental elites defined national security. On the other hand, the increasingly broader concept of America's security had an effect on the interpretation of the intentions and capabilities of the Soviet Union. At the same time, the very ambiguity of the new term *national security* helped create a means for politicians and officials to bridge the gap between domestic and foreign policy. For politicians focused primarily on domestic audiences, the juxtaposition of godless, totalitarian communism with the promotion of US values was invaluable. For executive branch officials, the geopolitical linkage of Soviet moves to American and allied physical security was equally beneficial. "Our national security can only be assured on a very broad and comprehensive front," Secretary of the Navy James V. Forrestal argued in front of a Senate committee hearing on the unification of the services in 1945. "I like your words 'national security,'" one senator replied.[7] The result was a concept of national security that fundamentally revised America's perception of its relationship to the rest of the world. "The nation was to be permanently prepared," Daniel Yergin has observed. "America's interests and responsibilities were unrestricted and global. National security became a guiding rule. . . . It lay at the heart of a new and sometimes intoxicating vision."[8]

At the time, Forrestal was already a key figure in the looming issue of service unification. A man of immense drive and tension, this son of Irish immigrants, with his trademark boxer's nose, had been a highly success-ful, tough, and aggressive Wall Street financier before being appointed by President Roosevelt in 1940 to be the undersecretary of the Navy. In this capacity Forrestal was instrumental in enlarging the US fleet as part of the two-ocean strategy. In 1944, after the death of Navy Secretary Frank Knox, Roosevelt named Forrestal to fill that position. That year, after a conference at Eisenhower's headquarters "somewhere in France," the new secretary of the Navy announced that he was "tremendously impressed with the spirit and cooperation which the Supreme Commander has fos-tered among the British, the Americans and their Allies."[9] In the coming years, Forrestal would emerge as the strongest opponent of Eisenhower's approach to the postwar unified command of the armed forces. This did not diminish, however, the strong admiration and respect each had for the other.

The other important figure for Eisenhower with regard to the unifica-tion issue was President Truman. The two men first met on 18 June 1945, when Truman officially welcomed Eisenhower back to the United States by sending the presidential plane, the Douglas C-54 known as the *Sacred Cow,* to Bermuda for the supreme commander to use on the last leg of his trip from Europe. Part of the mutual rapport between the two men had to do with their similar backgrounds and outlooks. Both came from pioneer stock of small farmers and merchants, and they had grown up in locations less than 150 miles apart. Eisenhower's older brother Arthur had even roomed in the same Kansas City boarding house as Truman in 1905. Equally important, both men believed in an international role for the United States based on an expanded concept of American national secu-rity. One consequence was that they were firmly committed to the Army's framework of consolidation and centralization for shaping the nature of the evolving national security state, and to the belief that, as Truman expressed it, "the Commander in Chief ought to have a co-ordinated and co-operative defense department that would work in peace and war."[10]

Forrestal was not optimistic concerning this type of pressure for unifi-cation. As a consequence, he called on Ferdinand Eberstadt, a pioneer in Wall Street mutual fund activities, a former chairman of the Army-Navy Munitions Board, and a close friend of many years, to chair a committee on unification and postwar organization for national security. The Eber-stadt Report, which was published in September 1945, found no evidence that unification would improve US national security. At the outset, the report emphasized the necessity for unified command in the field, but it also cautioned "that there are positive dangers in organizing the highest level strategic planning under a unified command."[11] The solution was to establish the proper lines of coordination within the current system, not to indulge in such "dangerous experiments" as unification. From this perspective, there was no need for a secretary of defense, only the existing departments of War and the Navy, supplemented by a Department of the Air Force. These departments were to continue to be separately administered by cabinet-level secretaries. The efforts of the separate organizations would come together through a combination of interservice and interagency boards and committees, working in adversarial collaboration in keeping with Eberstadt's belief in the corporate neocapitalist structures that were part of his Progressive and New Era organizational experience: "Separate departments provide a greater representation of specialized knowledge, they provide a greater aggregation of experienced judgment and ensure representation of varying viewpoints."[12]

The service positions on unification were officially drawn in September and October 1945 because of the inability of the joint planning machinery to address the first major issue of the postwar era: the determination of the size, composition, and deployment of the armed forces. On 16 October the JCS forwarded the Richardson Committee report to the president with the differing individual views of the four chiefs. What victory all this constituted for the opponents of unification was diminished the next day when the Senate Committee on Military Affairs opened hearings on two bills to establish a single Department of Armed Forces. All the ranking military and civilian leaders from the recent war were expected to testify. These committee proceedings, Marshall advised Eisenhower earlier in the month, would be of the "greatest importance" to the Army, so much so that he had convened a high-level board to put together a full Army plan.[13]

On 10 November, Eisenhower flew to the United States to testify, expecting to be away from his duties at his Frankfurt headquarters for only a few days, but glad to leave even temporarily his occupation duties with their "unholy mixture of irritations, frustrations and bewildering conflicts."[14] Once again, however, his "personal crystal ball was cracked." In Washington, Truman asked him to replace Marshall as chief of staff of the Army. Eisenhower was bent on imminent retirement and recommended Omar Bradley instead. But the president had just appointed General

Bradley as head of the Veterans Bureau and asked Eisenhower to become Army chief until Bradley was available, which he estimated would be in two years. On those conditions, Eisenhower accepted.[15]

In the meantime, the Senate Military Affairs Committee had begun hearings on 17 October concerning the two unification bills. Both pieces of legislation proposed the establishment of a single military department and a separate air force and provided broad authority for the president and the overall secretary to create a detailed defense structure. The bills had been sponsored by members of the Military Affairs Committee and reflected the general sympathy of most in that body with some form of unification. The committee was in fact dominated by Army partisans, just as Navy partisans dominated the House and Senate Naval Affairs committees, and Forrestal considered it "a highly prejudiced body which had reached a conclusion in advance."[16] In any event, the details of the bills were largely ignored as the military and civilian leaders of World War II testified for two months in a Senate hearing room normally crowded with observers and reporters. That conflict had ended only a few months earlier, and the leaders were still at the height of their prestige and popularity as they began what the *New York Times* characterized as "a brass-knuckle fight to the finish."[17]

The War Department members were primarily concerned with demonstrating that the status quo was not acceptable in the postwar era and that an Army plan for unification of the armed forces into a single department would be a major step in rectifying that situation. As a consequence, General Marshall headed a parade of Army witnesses arguing for change. The chief of staff was particularly adamant about the JCS. "Even under the stress of war," he argued, "agreement has been reached in the Joint Chiefs of Staff at times only by numerous compromises and after long delays. . . . Committees at best are cumbersome agencies, especially when the membership owes loyalty and advancement to chiefs installed in completely separate governmental departments." The JCS should be continued, he concluded, but only as a group "divorced from administrative and operating responsibilities" of the services and focused primarily on providing advice to the president concerning broad issues that affected policy, strategy and the military budget.[18]

There was no disagreement between the two services on the need for unified command at the theater level. Forrestal emphasized this in his initial testimony even as he outlined the recommendations of the Eberstadt Report and argued for the status quo at the highest level of military direction. But the War Department's point, as newly appointed Secretary of War Robert Patterson explained to the committee, was that unified command was largely limited to the overseas theaters, with no overall unitary direction except by recourse to the president as commander in chief. Patterson had won a Silver Star as an infantryman in World War I, had served as a federal judge, and during the next conflict had been Stimson's undersecretary of war. Based on his experience in the last position, he had become a true believer in unification at the highest level. "I submit that the considerations that led us, under spur of necessity, to set up unity of command in the field," he testified, "point by every element of logic to the establishment of unity of authority at headquarters in Washington."[19]

The principal focus of Navy attention was on the proposed organizational structure outlined by Lieutenant General J. Lawton Collins to the Military Affairs Committee on 30 October. Collins had served as a division commander in the Pacific, where he had earned the nickname "Lightning Joe" from his command of the 25th ("Tropic Lightning") Division and his leadership style on Guadalcanal. Subsequently in the European Theater, he served with distinction as a corps commander under Eisenhower. Now, armed with a broad organizational chart, he had the unenviable job of acting as the spokesman for a board of senior Army officers established on 29 September to create an answer to the Eberstadt Report that would combine where possible Marshall's viewpoints with both the majority and minority reports of the Richardson Committee. The Collins Plan, as it became known, lacked much specificity since it was expected that details would emerge after an agreement in principle to some form of unification. In the meantime, Collins maintained, the plan was "an appropriate outline for a gradual evolution of a sound Department of the Armed Forces."[20]

In those areas where the proposal was specific, it was controversial. At the outset, the plan established a single Department of Armed Forces under a cabinet-level secretary and a separate Air Force. The secretaries of the three services were not accorded cabinet status, thus reducing the services to components of the new department. At the same time, Collins assured the committee that there was no intention in the plan to merge the services, which would be guaranteed "adequate autonomy" within the jurisdiction of the new department. Under this structure, he reassured the Navy, it would not lose the Marine Corps or its fleet air force. All land-based aircraft, however, including those belonging to the Navy, would go to the separate Air Force.[21]

As for the JCS, the plan would add a fifth member, the chief of staff of the armed forces, to the wartime composition of three service chiefs and the chief of staff to the president, a position still occupied by Admiral Leahy. To ensure that "no one arm or service" would "swallow up another" or dominate the "military thought" of the entire department, Collins recommended that the chief of staff to the president and the new chief of staff of the armed services not be selected from the same service at the same time. This new organization, renamed the US Chiefs of Staff in the plan, was to be legitimized by law and focused on recommendations concerning military policy, strategy, and budgets. The service chiefs would have control of their departmental budgets, routing their fiscal recommendations through the secretary of the armed forces, who would be required to pass them "without modification" to the president.[22]

The most controversial aspect of the Collins Plan concerned the establishment of a chief of staff of the armed forces. The Richardson Committee had recommended the creation of a commander of the armed forces and a general staff sufficient to support him. The new plan proposed the title "chief of staff" as a substitute for "commander." The holder of this position was to be the "the principal military adviser" to the secretary, and to emphasize the position's power even further, Collins described it as being more important than the chief of staff to the president. As if to confirm this, the organizational chart showed a chain of command from the secretary through the chief of staff of the armed forces to the chiefs of the Army, Navy, and Air Force, as well as to the theater commanders, thus implying that the new chief alone would direct operations in the field. All in all, the Collins Plan appeared in effect to have removed the civilian secretary from any significant influence not only on matters concerning appropriations in the unified department but on those concerning military strategy.[23]

All this was contradicted, however, in Collins's testimony. The chief, he emphasized, would not have a large staff, and the individual service chiefs would continue their wartime role of acting for the JCS as "executive agents" in the field, carrying out the directives of the Joint Chiefs with their own services operational staffs. As for civilian control of the military, Collins insisted that would lie "squarely in the hands of the

President, with the Secretary of the Armed Forces handling the major issues for him, based on the recommendations to him by the Joint Chiefs of Staff."[24] These efforts notwithstanding, there was no denying that the chief of staff of the armed forces was depicted on the Collins Plan chart as the only military man reporting to the secretary. "The point is that no matter what the chart looks like," Assistant War Secretary John J. McCloy testified somewhat defensively in the wake of Collins's appearance, "the fact is a good Secretary of the Armed Forces not only can but will reach down into all of the departments and divisions as he sees fit. . . . The chart of a regiment which shows lines moving through lieutenant colonels and majors does not preclude the colonel from maintaining contact with his captains."[25]

Eisenhower was well aware of the controversy concerning the Collins Plan when he appeared before the Senate Military Affairs Committee on Friday, 16 November. The five-star general declined a seat and stood throughout the hearing, which lasted from 10 to 11:25 A.M. He had only recently returned from a tumultuous welcome in Boston, and was arguably the most popular, if not the most famous, witness. At the outset of his prepared testimony, Eisenhower disclaimed familiarity with the details of the Army's plans and proposals on unification. He was only appearing before the committee, he insisted three days before becoming chief of staff of the Army, as "a soldier from the field," not as a representative of the War Department. Eisenhower's purpose in this somewhat disingenuous approach was quickly apparent, as he reminded the committee that in the field he had just commanded a force of five million, of which there had been more than three million men and women of the United States Army, Navy, and Air Force. "I therefore prefer to speak to you," he emphasized, "as one who had been privileged to know such a singular experience, and I should like to speak also as one who has experienced with them the successful conclusion of a great enterprise based on unity of command."[26]

That unity had not been easy to achieve. It was not until the North African campaign, Eisenhower explained, that the "first large scale example of unified command" had emerged. It was at that time "a new device," and there were many difficulties that remained to be overcome. By the time of the assault on Sicily, unified command had been achieved "by learning as we went—the hard way." Further problems with this type of command were met and surmounted in the Mediterranean and Europe. But the process had been lengthy and had taken place while lives were at stake. "In my opinion," Eisenhower summed up his major point, "these difficulties grew directly from the traditional separation of the Army and Navy, which is the inevitable outcome of the present organization of our military departments. Separation at the top necessarily fosters separation all along the line."[27]

Eisenhower summarized his case in the prepared statement by reminding the committee of the changing nature of national security, something he had experienced first as chief of OPD and then as a field commander. In the new era, the transformation from peace to war would be swifter than ever before. Unity of direction in Washington during peacetime would preclude entering a war as the US had done at Pearl Harbor. "It is in time of peace that this Nation must produce a balanced, adequate measure of our land, sea, and air power lest we lose the peace we have so dearly bought." This, in turn, necessitated what he called "perfected teamwork," a combination of joint training, indoctrination, and years of peacetime association that could be directed only by a single authority. Unification at the top, Eisenhower emphasized, would demonstrate to the members of all services the "essential truth" that "there is no such thing as a separate land, sea, or air war; therefore we must now recognize this fact by establishing a single department of the armed forces to govern us all."[28]

Afterward, there were specific questions on the Collins Plan, particularly concerning what Secretary Patterson called the "bogy" of civil-military relations in the form of the new position of chief of staff of the armed forces. Eisenhower worked hard to defuse the issue. The chief of staff, he asserted, should be removed from the chain of command between the secretary and the military heads of the services. Otherwise it would imply that the chiefs of the major forces could not deal directly with the secretary. The intent of the Collins Plan was to make the chief of staff an "adviser" to the civilian secretary, he pointed out, noting that "by drawing him as he appears on the chart, it looks like he is the fabulous man on horseback that we are always talking about." He would also not object to the placement of civilian assistant secretaries over each service, he added, emphasizing that the War Department would accept such a change. "Not only do I believe that there is nothing in this organization that tends to weaken civilian control of the armed forces in this country," Eisenhower concluded, "but I assure you, sir, if I found a single officer in the Army who advocated such a radical revolution in our traditions and thoughts, I would do my best to have him taken out of the Army to-morrow." [29]

Eisenhower had presented the most effective testimony in the packed Senate chamber, and his appearance essentially ended War Department participation. The next day, Admiral Chester W. Nimitz was the first of a series of additional Navy witnesses. Like Eisenhower, Nimitz had been born in Texas and had ended up in the service academy that was not his first choice. And like Eisenhower, Nimitz had been catapulted by World War II to high levels of command that would soon include the position of service chief. The admiral had long been a strong advocate of unifica-tion and had so testified in the field to the Richardson Committee the previous year. This was not, however, a sustainable position for a new chief of naval operations in the fall of 1945. "I now believe that the theo-retical advantages of such a merger are unobtainable," he explained to the Senate committee, "whereas the disadvantages are so serious that it is not acceptable." He made no apology for his change of opinion, Nimitz added, "since it represents my conviction based on additional experience and further study of the proposal and its current implications." [30]

On 17 December 1945 the Senate Committee on Military Affairs re-cessed its hearings without resolution of the unification issue. By that time, Eisenhower had officially assumed his duties as chief of staff. The unification issue took on new energy on 19 December when the president sent a special message to Congress, stating that "there is enough evidence now at hand to demonstrate beyond question the need for a unified de-partment." Truman's proposal called for a single Department of National Defense headed by a civilian, cabinet-level secretary, assisted by a civilian undersecretary, several assistant secretaries for functional areas, and an overall chief of staff. Under them were three coordinated land, sea, and air "branches," each headed by a military "commander" and a civilian as-sistant secretary. The chief of staff and the commanders of the three co-ordinate branches of the department would constitute an advisory body to the secretary of national defense and the president. The war years, the president reminded Congress, had demonstrated "that there must be unified direction of land, sea and air forces at home as well as in all the other parts of the world" where US forces were serving. "But we never had comparable unified direction in Washington," the president emphasized. "And even in the field, our unity of operations was greatly impaired by the differences . . . that stemmed from the division of leadership in Washington."[31]

The congressional response to the president's message was predictable. One member of the Senate Military Affairs Committee referred to the "unanswerable logic" of Truman's recommendation. On the other hand, the longtime chairman of the House Naval Affairs Committee, Congressman Carl Vinson of Georgia, known not always affectionately as "Uncle Carl," called the proposal "military power politics" designed to "sink the Navy." Vinson had entered Congress in 1914, the year before Eisenhower graduated from West Point. He had opposed unification as early as 1925, when he was a member of the Morrow Board, and again in 1932, when he was one of the leaders in the floor fight to eliminate the unification title from the Economy Act. Now in the wake of the president's message, he concluded that "the very phraseology of the scheme smacks of the Germany of the Kaiser and of Hitler, of Japanese militarism."[32] In the meantime, the Senate Military Affairs Committee had discontinued its hearings while appointing a subcommittee to work out a unification bill acceptable to the War and Navy departments.

These proceedings continued to preoccupy Eisenhower. In late November he summarized his philosophy on unification in a candid, unguarded reply to his old friend Everett "Swede" Hazlett, with whom he had corresponded since their departures from Abilene for their respective service academies, and with whom he could always "open up." Hazlett was nearing the end of his Navy career and had written to express his fears that a "swallowing up" of his service would occur with unification and to complain of a report that Eisenhower had proposed one uniform for all services. It was "self-evident," Hazlett concluded, "that it would be the Army uniform." The new Army chief of staff quickly dismissed the first point as undesirable from all perspectives: "One brother does not devour another; a guard on a football team is equally important with the tackle!" As for a single uniform, he considered it impracticable and probably unwise, but if one were adopted, it "could be blue, green, olive drab or a skyblue pink." The key to unification, Eisenhower emphasized, was to "understand that war has become a triphibious affair, and unless one laboriously picks out special circumstances, land, sea and air in varying ratio are employed in every operation of war."[33]

Gradually, the public controversy began to diminish. Forrestal reacted to the president's message by issuing a memorandum to all Navy Department personnel, advising them that they were expected "to refrain from opposition . . . in their public utterances" because of the president's pro-unification stance.[34] Eisenhower was ready to follow that lead. In a step reminiscent of his wartime efforts to keep Anglo-American relations on track, he ordered Army personnel, when discussing the issue of unification, to "avoid giving the appearance of criticizing a sister service," urging instead that "complete impartiality be maintained."[35] Forrestal found Eisenhower with his warmth and charm much easier to work with than the aloof Marshall, and he admired the way the new chief of staff attempted to work out joint issues. "Eisenhower is a good practical Dutchman and so is Nimitz," he observed, "and between them I believe we will make progress."[36]

That progress was almost immediately evident in the field of joint education. In his first few months in Washington, Eisenhower provided the primary vision and energy behind the creation of the National War College. He was heavily involved in the development of the mission, scope, and curriculum of the institution; it was his decision not to reopen the Army War College but instead to turn the building that had previously housed the school over to the National War College. Eisenhower was similarly involved in converting the old Army Industrial College to the Industrial College of the Armed Forces. And in the winter of 1946 he convinced Nimitz that there was "a distinct joint necessity" for a midlevel staff college for all the services. The chief of naval operations proposed that the school be named the "Army Navy Staff College." But for Eisenhower, the concept of jointness was too important to be subsumed in the unification issue. "Due to the added emphasis on air warfare," he replied, "I consider a name such as 'Armed Forces College' most appropriate since it is applicable regardless of whether or not there is an autonomous Air Force."[37] The opening of the Armed Forces Staff College in June at Norfolk, Virginia, the Industrial College of the Armed Forces in April, and the National War College in September marked the creation of three new joint institutions within one year of the end of the war, a testimony to Eisenhower's persistence and dedication to joint education.

Absent the discipline of unification, however, the two service chiefs were generally less successful in other coordination efforts, particularly in their attempts to resolve the two most intractable of joint issues concerned with service roles and missions. The Air Force wanted control over all land-based aircraft. The Navy's contention was that in order to have full command of the sea, it needed to control land-based aircraft for shipping protection, long-range over-water reconnaissance, and anti-submarine operations. The Navy also insisted on organizing the Marine Corps into divisions of combined arms responsible for the amphibious phase of landing operations, since an amphibious assault did not lose its naval character until the beachhead was secured and protracted warfare had begun. The Army, on the other hand, insisted that the Marines should have smaller, lightly armed units limited in combat to those minor shore operations of interest only to the Navy or necessary to augment the Army.

On 20 February a JCS planning committee submitted to the Joint Chiefs a roles and missions statement reflecting deep fundamental disagreements. In his reply on 6 March to the committee report, Nimitz renewed the Navy position on each point, pointing out that the current joint doctrine, the *Joint Action of the Army and the Navy (JAAN)*, approved in 1935 with subsequent changes, was still adequate as a statement of functions and as a broad mission outline for the services. This set off an exchange of memoranda labeled the 1478 series in the JCS communication scheme.[38]

On 15 March, Eisenhower rejected Nimitz's arguments in a memorandum to the JCS, unusually harsh and nonconciliatory in its astonishment, almost incredulity, at the Navy positions. For the use of the prewar *JAAN* as an argument for the status quo, the Army chief's contempt was palpable even in the bureaucratic jargon of the document. "Our problem should be solved on the basis of what is best for national security," he wrote, "not by reference to documents, agreements and laws, many of which are either outmoded by modern developments or were instituted under emergency conditions." In the future, "the accomplishment of practically every major operation of war will involve the roles of two or all three components, coordinated under the principle of unified command."[39]

After a further exchange of equally harsh opinions, Nimitz closed out the JCS 1478 series with a final memorandum that essentially restated earlier Navy views on the functions of the services. By that time the issue of roles and missions had been taken in essence from the military and was caught up in new unification legislation. On 9 April 1946, after nine drafts and three months of conferences and meetings with cabinet members, "unification" experts, and even the president, a Senate Military Affairs subcommittee introduced a new unification bill, S. 2044.

Under normal conditions, the unification bill would have moved quickly through Congress. The legislation was supported by a large majority of the Senate Military Affairs Committee, including the chairman and the second- and third-ranking majority members, as well as the ranking minority member, and was favorably reported to the Senate. Conditions, however, were not normal as the 79th Congress approached its end. Unification involved both military departments, and most members of Congress considered that the Senate Naval Affairs Committee should also provide advice on the subject. This was certainly Forrestal's position. He had already approached Carl Vinson, the chairman of the House Naval Affairs Committee, the previous fall concerning the possibility of developing and publicizing the Navy fears and objections within a forum that was both sympathetic and legitimate. Thus, despite the Military Affairs Committee's favorable recommendation and the president's personal endorsement, opposition by the Naval Affairs Committee prevented the congressional allies of the War Department from creating a floor majority in the Senate to support their stand and even from more explicitly calling for a formal vote on their reported legislation. The result was that on 30 April the Senate Naval Affairs Committee began its own unification proceedings, ostensibly on S. 2044.[40]

On 1 May, Forrestal began his presentation by associating himself and his department with the president's basic objective, which he defined in terms reminiscent of the Eberstadt Report as "an integrated military-diplomatic relations, industrial-economic organization which will meet the security needs of the nation."[41] On 3 May the chief of naval operations repeated many of the arguments concerning roles and missions that he had made in his memoranda to the JCS during the previous two months. General Alexander A. Vandegrift, the commandant of the Marine Corps, renewed the attack on 6 May. Vandegrift, who had commanded the Marines at Guadalcanal and received a Congressional Medal of Honor for his efforts, was not one to mince words. For some time he had been aware "that the very existence of the Marine Corps stood as a continuing affront" to the Army staff. "The bended knee is not a tradition of our corps," he concluded. "If the Marine as a fighting man has not made a case for himself after 170 years of service, he must go. But I think you will agree with me that he has earned the right to depart with dignity and honor, not by subjugation to the status of uselessness and servility planned for him by the War Department."[42]

On 9 May an infuriated Eisenhower reacted from China, where he was meeting with Marshall as part of an inspection trip in the Far East. He warned that under no circumstances should the Army dignify the attack by impugning the commandant's motives or by resorting to "profitless argument." Instead, the War Department should provide figures on the countless division-size Army landings in the war in both Europe and the Pacific: "Not one failure," he cabled. "Cite those against Sicily made in storm, that at Salerno against stiff opposition and those in Normandy under extremely difficult conditions of tides, weather, artificial obstacles and on Omaha beach against severe opposition."[43]

In the meantime, President Truman held a White House conference attended by the two service secretaries, Leahy, Spaatz, Nimitz, and, because of Eisenhower's absence, his deputy, General Thomas Handy. Truman opened the meeting by stating his intent to end the "acrimonious" interservice disagreements and then asked Leahy for his views as the chief of staff to the president. The admiral replied that he believed a solution could be worked out provided the proposed bill eliminated the single, supreme chief of staff of common defense as the principal military adviser and allowed the JCS to continue as the highest source of military advice for the president. His wartime experience, Leahy continued, had convinced him that the idea of a single chief was "dangerous," and that if he had so desired, he could have secured a great deal of power for himself during the war. Truman replied that he had also come to oppose the contentious position because "it was too much along the lines of the 'man on horseback' philosophy." When queried, Patterson stated that he still favored a single department with a single secretary and a single chief of staff. But in terms of the single chief, he admitted that he was not prepared to "jump into the ditch and die for the idea."[44]

Neither was Eisenhower. Although the Army leader had consistently supported the idea of a single chief of staff to advise the secretary and the president and believed that such a position would ultimately be necessary for the efficient functioning of the military, he still took a pragmatic view of the entire unification process as an evolutionary one. The fears expressed concerning the single chief were "unwarranted," Eisenhower pointed out, but that position was not "so important that we should

hold out for this feature to the point of wrecking any chance for unification."[45]

On 24 May, Eisenhower returned to Washington, where he was soon
involved in the negotiations between the two departments. In the end
there was agreement in accordance with the major War Department
concession to follow the Navy lead in formalizing the current JCS organization without a single, overall chief of staff or chairman. But there
remained fundamental disagreements concerning the issues of a single
civilian secretary and a single department, as well as the status of both
naval aviation and the Marine Corps.

On 15 June, Truman dispatched a joint letter to the secretaries of war
and the Navy. The president was unequivocal in his support for creating
a coordinate Air Force and for giving the Air Force the land-based aircraft for over-water reconnaissance, antisubmarine warfare, and shipping
protection. But he was also firm in his support of the Navy's position
that the Marine Corps should be responsible for tactics, techniques, and
equipment used by all landing forces involved in amphibious operations.
Truman was more ambiguous on the remaining issue of a single military
department, emphasizing that while there was "no desire to affect adversely the integrity of any of the services," they should "perform their
separate functions under the unifying direction, authority, and control of
the Secretary of National Defense."[46]

On 17 June, Patterson promised in an official reply his own and the
War Department's "wholehearted support" for the president's decision.[47]
On 24 June, Forrestal responded to the president in a letter that para-
phrased Truman's key objectives to reflect the Navy's "understanding" of
the issues. Although there would be a single secretary of national defense,
he would leave "full administration of their respective services to the Secretaries of War, Navy, and Air." And in a second objective attributed to the
president, the letter agreed to the preservation of the Navy's "integrity and
autonomy so as to insure the retention of those imponderables of spirit
and morale so essential to a military service." Truman would not accept
the evasive reply, advising Forrestal by phone "in no uncertain terms," as
the Navy secretary recounted it, "that, if I wouldn't go along with a single
secretary and a single department of defense, he would transfer naval
aviation to the Air Force and the Marine Corps to the Army."[48]

Two days later, the Senate Military Affairs Committee reported a revised version of S. 2044, incorporating the decisions of the two secretaries and the president. On 2 July the Senate Naval Affairs Committee began its hearings on the revised legislation. For five days the Navy outlined its opposition to the amended bill. On 11 July the hearings ended. That day, the chairman of the Senate Naval Affairs Committee inserted into the record a 5 July letter from Forrestal, then observing the atomic bomb tests at Bikini in the Pacific, which described the revised bill as "an administrative monstrosity." The Navy secretary was convinced that it was "utterly impossible" to incorporate the directives of the president's plan into the framework of the legislation as it stood and believed that there must be an "entirely fresh approach to the problem."[49] Under such circumstances, it was apparent to Truman that it would not be useful to force further unification efforts on a Congress that was approaching its final adjournment. On 19 July 1946 the president recommended to the Senate that the unification issue be postponed until the 80th Congress convened early in 1947.

CHAPTER ELEVEN

Creation of the National Security State, July 1946–March 1950

I have been back from Europe exactly a year. It has been a most difficult period for me, with far more frustrations than progress.

DWIGHT D. EISENHOWER

Now General Eisenhower, it is a pleasure to have you here. I note in the paper whenever they get in hot water down at [the] Pentagon they send for you. When we want you, you always come and are always welcome.

CARL VINSON

T HE STANDOFF ON THE unification issue created only a momentary lull. In July 1946 the Senate Joint committee investigating the Pearl Harbor attack published its final report, in which an entire section was devoted to unity of command. All the evidence adduced thus far, the report began, revealed "the complete inadequacy of command by *mutual cooperation* where decisive action is of the essence."[1] The congressional report led inevitably to the broader issue of unification by concluding that the dual structure of the chain of command was a major cause of the debacle. From Pearl Harbor the Army chain had run from the commanding general of the Hawaiian Department, to Marshall, to Stimson, to Roosevelt. In a similar manner, the Navy chain had begun with the commander in chief, US Fleet and Pacific Fleet, up to the chief of naval operations, to the Navy secretary, and finally to the president. Below the level of the president, in short, there had been no exercise of authority, no unity of command over the two commanders at Pearl Harbor. Back in Washington, operating under a system of separate departments, the report concluded, there was "the basic deficiency of conflicting interests which precipitate serious and unnecessary obstacles to the solution of pressing military problems."[2] Truman had already made this critical linkage as vice president. "Granting neglect and derelictions," he had written in 1944, "what stands clearer than that the root cause of the Pearl Harbor tragedy was the lack of a single secretary set-up, and the fact that two secretaries in Washington issued their separate commands to two field commanders each reared in the tradition that cooperation carries the risk of endangering independence."[3]

The Pearl Harbor report caused Eisenhower in August to initiate a joint effort with Nimitz to ensure implementation of the committee's recommendation "that immediate action be taken to insure that unity of command is imposed at all military and naval outposts."[4] On 17 September the War Department submitted Eisenhower's outline to the JCS for "sound unified command arrangements" in various theaters throughout the globe.[5] During the remainder of the fall, the Army chief of staff conducted intense negotiations with the other services in order to translate his wartime experience with unified commands into a worldwide military command-and-control structure designed for the new concept of US national security. As a consequence, the JCS on 12 December presented President Truman with a plan that stipulated as an "interim measure for the immediate postwar period" the eventual establishment of seven unified commands around the world.[6] The result, however rudimentary, was the first unified command plan, a quantum leap from Eisenhower's days in OPD, when he struggled to establish the ABDA Command. The new plan, he realized, would serve not only as a building block for further expansion of the unified command concept and system, but as an example of interservice cooperation for the unification struggle in Washington.

By late summer 1946 it was already apparent that the services alone would not be able to solve the unification issue, particularly since it was inextricably enmeshed with the problem of roles and missions definitions. On 10 September, Truman hosted a conference that included Patterson and Forrestal as well as Eisenhower, Nimitz, and Leahy. Also in attendance was Clark Clifford, the president's confidant and White House counsel. Patterson began by stating his willingness to have the legislation stipulate that a secretary of common defense would not, where avoidable, become involved in the administration of the services, normally limiting himself to broad policy issues. This was an important War Department concession, but Forrestal acted as if it had not been granted. Growing increasingly agitated, the Navy secretary called for the creation of an Office of Deputy to the President to be headed by an overall defense secretary with limited functions who "should not try to get down into the administration of each Department." He understood the need for the president to have the support of his cabinet members, Forrestal concluded harshly, but if he could not support the administration's bill with "conviction and sincerity," he would have to request that the president accept his resignation. Truman responded somewhat dryly that he anticipated no such necessity.[7]

Eisenhower ventured into the discussion with the techniques of conciliation that had served him so well throughout the war. All the participants, he pointed out, had already accepted the broad principle of a secretary of common defense. The details could be worked out later. Moreover, it was inconceivable to him that the Navy should fear that any actions in the wake of the legislation "would impair its ability to perform its mission." Forrestal replied testily that he could not agree to the Army recommendations. "I was again constrained to say that the Navy *did have* deep apprehensions as to what would happen to it under such a plan as the War Department has proposed," he noted in his diary.[8]

Despite the dismal outcome of the September meeting, the differences had narrowed considerably from the previous year. The president had decided against the single chief of staff and against curtailing the combatant functions of the Marine Corps. And the Senate subcommittee had rejected in S. 2044 control by the JCS of the military budget. Finally, all parties had agreed to the general concept of some kind of overall secretary. At the same time, however, the exact definition of the secretary's authority over the services remained the centerpiece of the disagreement. Moreover, there were still questions concerning a separate air force, the control of the Navy's land-based air, and whether the matter of service roles and missions was to be handled statutorily by Congress or by the executive branch.[9]

In any event, both Eisenhower and Patterson were increasingly ready to make concessions as the year came to an end. For the Army chief, it was vital to get the process under way. If a unification bill was not submitted to Congress soon, there would be little chance for a law before 1948—an unacceptable development in the current security environment. It would be "unconscionable," he told Clifford, for the United States to fight another conflict organized as it had been in World War II.[10] On 16 January 1947 the two secretaries dispatched a joint letter to the president outlining their agreement on all aspects of the unification bill. Like Eisenhower, Truman was willing to tolerate concessions in order to move on with the process. He released the letter to the public the same day and replied that he was "exceedingly pleased" to receive it. The agreement, the president added, "provides a thoroughly practical and workable plan of unification and I heartily approve of it."[11]

On 26 February, President Truman sent the draft unification bill to the newly convened 80th Congress. The proposed legislation incorporated most of the Patterson-Forrestal agreement and was introduced in the House as HR 2319 on 28 February and in the Senate as S. 758 on 2 March. By that time, the congressional committee structure had changed dramatically with the merger in each house of the Military Affairs and Naval Affairs committees into new Armed Services committees. On 18 March the new Senate committee began nineteen days of hearings on the bill that would last until 9 May.

The process of agreement had been excruciating, and as a consequence, both parties were committed to the passage of the tightly negotiated legislation. The two departments agreed in advance on those officials who would testify before the Senate Armed Services Committee and on ensuring that those witnesses would not propose any changes to the bill. The noncontentious tone was set by Forrestal as the first witness on Tuesday, 18 March. Secretary Patterson followed suit a few days later by giving his "unqualified support" to the bill and by concurring completely with Forrestal's testimony.[12]

On 25 March, Eisenhower opened his testimony on a similarly positive note, describing the bill as "a great start" and urging its speedy enactment. Beneath the surface of his opening statement, however, there were intimations of his frustration at the course of events concerning the problem of roles and missions. He was less than pliant when specifically queried on the status of the Marine Corps and naval aviation. In terms of aviation, he pointed out that there would always be "a shadowland" along coastlines that might require at different times in different circumstances forces from different services. "And I would say that no blueprint in advance is ever going to work it out." In response to more detailed questions, Eisenhower indicated that he looked upon both naval aviation and the Marine Corps as basic and integral components of the Navy and would not, therefore, be opposed to their protection in statutory language legislated by Congress. "But," he added, "there can be many questions as to size, composition, method of training, method of equipment, that are not basic. They are what I would call operational and organizational details."[13]

If this lack of personal commitment to the compromise agreement was not enough to disquiet the Navy, Eisenhower also chose to vent his frustration concerning the unreformed status of the JCS. To specific questions concerning the efficacy of that organization under the new bill, he returned to his concurrence the previous May in President Truman's elimination of the proposal for a supreme chief of staff of common defense. The decision continued to rankle him, and he could not resist a last thrust. "Now, distinguishing my personal conviction as opposed to what I now believe we should recommend," he stated, "I . . . believed in the single professional Chief of Staff . . . but I have come to the conclusion that it is one of these argumentative points that should be eliminated from the bill. . . . Time may bring it about." In the meantime, he emphasized in a response that further reawakened Navy fears that the new, powerful position of an overall secretary, "directly superior to the Joint Chiefs of Staff," would ensure prompt decisions even in the face of indecision on the part of that organization. Typically, Forrestal captured the essence of what bothered the Navy most about the testimony in his diary entry: "General Eisenhower . . . said, in effect, that he was sorry there wasn't a single Chief of Staff but he hoped that the development would come in the future."[14]

Eisenhower had moved in subtle and not so subtle ways well beyond his charter as a conciliatory witness testifying to support compromise legislation. It was true, of course, that he had not directly opposed the bill. But he had been needlessly aggressive in responding to questions concerning service functions that were poised on a delicate balance of compromises and carefully crafted phrases. Moreover, Eisenhower had also expressed his doubts concerning the elimination of an overall chief of staff, a concession decided upon by the president and agreed to by the Army chief of staff. All in all, it was a petulant, stubborn performance by the five-star general, not at all in keeping with his normal conciliatory philosophy and far removed from his evolutionary approach to the issue of unification.

In June the Senate committee favorably reported an amended version of the bill. On 9 July the Senate passed S. 758 by voice vote and sent it on to the House.[15] The compromise unification bill had even a more difficult passage through the House, where the Republican leadership decided not to refer it to the merged Armed Services Committee. Instead, the bill was sent to the Committee on Expenditures in the Executive Departments, chaired by Representative Clare E. Hoffman of Michigan, an isolationist considered to be neither interested in nor knowledgeable about military affairs. As it turned out, Hoffman was a combative, tough-minded critic of the compromise legislation, particularly worried about what he perceived as threats to the functions of the Marine Corps revealed in Eisenhower's 1478 JCS series memoranda of March and April 1946 and his recent unguarded testimony in the Senate on S. 758. On 2 April, Hoffman began the House hearings on the compromise bill.[16]

In his opening remarks before the committee, the Army chief of staff explained that since he had been accused during the previous year of being an enemy of the Marine Corps, he had reexamined his early statements. In terms of the 1478 JCS series, the "exchange of letters between the Navy and ourselves was merely a way to get something started." It was necessary in that context to mention the Marine Corps, but "certainly no hostility was shown against it." And in fact, Eisenhower emphasized, he considered his proposal in that exchange of a troop strength of fifty thousand to sixty thousand for the Marines to be "a reasonable figure," since it was approximately three times as large as the Corps's prewar numbers. "I am nonplussed," he concluded, "to find out why I have been considered an enemy of the Marines."[17]

Hoffman did his best to clear up Eisenhower's professed confusion on the subject. He began by reviewing obvious statements from Eisenhower's spring 1946 proposals, particularly the contention that "the emerging development of the Marine forces during the war should not be viewed as assigning to the Navy a normal function of land warfare." Was not this, Hoffman queried, the source of the apprehension concerning the Army's intention toward the Marines?[18]

The House hearings on H.R. 2319 were uncomfortable for Eisenhower, who was accustomed to more deference from congressional committees. He was at times evasive and disingenuous, particularly in his responses during the discussion of the JCS 1478 series of memoranda. The fact that Hoffman had those papers was described by Marine observers as a "shattering discovery . . . as if General Eisenhower had found himself in the middle of a minefield."[19] Nevertheless, Eisenhower remained consistent on two principal points in terms of service functions. The first was that the Marine Corps should not be built up to be used in sustained land operations, such as the protracted campaign from Normandy to the Elbe. From this perspective, he pointed out, the four-month Marine campaign on Guadalcanal did not qualify because of the limited objectives. "Fundamentally," he concluded, "the Marines are a fleet arm."[20] The second was that the service roles and missions should remain in a separate executive order and not be incorporated into the unification bill. The compromise bill was simply too fragile. "If we start writing details applying to any particular service or any particular function or any particular type of organization or administration," he concluded, "we will be writing bills for many, many months."[21]

After Eisenhower's testimony, there was the matter of a post-Army career for the chief of staff. The trustees of Columbia University had been attempting to persuade him to take over from the aging president of the university. On 23 June, "conscious of my own shortcomings . . . in the field of scholarly attainment," Eisenhower accepted the offer to head the university beginning in June 1948.[22] In the meantime, Patterson had turned down Truman's offer to be the first secretary of defense and had also resigned as secretary of war, to be replaced in that position by his deputy, Kenneth Royall. Forrestal was the improbable second choice, a man who had labored so skillfully in opposition to the president as an advocate of service autonomy and decentralization in order to render the new position ineffective.

On 26 July, the last day of the first session of the 80th Congress, a congressional delegation rushed the engrossed copy of the unification bill to Truman from the Capitol. The president was waiting to fly to Missouri. Shortly after noon, sitting in his plane, Truman signed the bill into law. At the same time, he handed the congressional leaders the nomination papers for the new position. As the plane departed, the congressional delegation rushed the nomination back to the Senate, where in the early hours of 27 July, Forrestal was confirmed as the first secretary of defense by a voice vote a few minutes before adjournment.[23]

The National Security Act (P.L. 253) was compromise legislation designed to accommodate a variety of views and thus fully satisfy none. The act consisted of three parts. Title I dealt with much of the coordinating machinery for national security outlined in the Eberstadt Report, such as the National Security Council and the Central Intelligence Agency. Title III addressed miscellaneous items concerned with such transitional issues as administration, personnel, and funding. The compromise featured most prominently in the powers provided in Title II to the secretary of defense. Instead of presiding over one single executive-branch department as Truman had originally recommended, the secretary was to head a National Military Establishment (NME) consisting of, with the addition of the Air Force, three executive departments, one for each service and each headed by a cabinet-level secretary. This was in keeping with the act's initial declaration of policy that provided for the "authoritative coordination and unified direction under civilian control" of the three services but not their merger. The secretary was "the principal assistant to the President in all matters relating to national security," charged with establishing "general policies and programs" for the NME as a whole, with "general direction, authority, and control" over the military departments.[24]

At the same time, the two military organizations retained their status as "individual executive departments"—still primarily autonomous structures with almost complete control over their internal affairs. To them was added the Department of the Air Force. In addition, those powers and duties not specifically assigned to the overall secretary would be integrated into the authority of each department secretary. Moreover, those secretaries could appeal any decisions by the secretary of defense to the president or the budget director after notifying the secretary of their intentions. There were equally far-reaching protections for the Navy and the Marine Corps, with specific guarantees in the law of their aviation components and of the use of land-based aircraft for key functions that included antisubmarine operations, naval reconnaissance, and shipping protection. The Marine Corps also emerged not only without curtailment of its World War II combatant functions but with those functions enshrined for the first time in law, particularly "for the conduct of such land operations as may be essential to the prosecution of a naval campaign." Finally, reacting to fears that a defense head might become a "super-secretary" surrounded by a Prussian-style general staff, Congress limited his statutory staff to no more than three special assistants, while making no provision for an undersecretary or any assistant secretaries.[25]

Under Title II, the National Security Act provided the Joint Chiefs a statutory basis for the first time as the "principal military advisers to the President and the Secretary of Defense." Among their key duties were to prepare strategic plans and provide strategic direction to the armed forces, formulate policies for joint military training, oversee major personnel and supply requirements, and establish unified commands on a global basis in key strategic areas. The statutory members of the JSC were to consist of the uniformed chiefs of the three services and, "if there be one," the chief of staff to the commander in chief. To support the JCS, the new act created a permanent full-time joint staff limited to one hundred officers who would operate under a military director.[26]

On 17 September, in the Navy Department building, James Forrestal was sworn in by Chief Justice Fred M. Vinson as the first secretary of defense. The next day, the Air Force officially became a separate service, and the new secretary visited the Pentagon to examine his office and attend the swearing in ceremony of John L. Sullivan as secretary of the Navy and W. Stuart Symington as secretary of the Air Force. The third member of Forrestal's team was Kenneth Royall, who automatically made the transition from secretary of war to secretary of the Army. In this new capacity, he hosted the Pentagon ceremony.

Forrestal approached the new post with a customary determination that showed none of the joy and excitement he had displayed when appointed secretary of the Navy. "This office," he wrote, "will probably be the greatest cemetery for dead cats in history."[27] This prescience notwithstanding, the new secretary seemed oblivious in his first press conference to the basic contradictions of his authority as a result of a federative rather than a unified structure. The intent of the new law, he began, was to allow the services to run their own operations: "I hope to disappear, frankly, as quietly as possible from the public eye." The reporters were amazed. Wasn't he the only cabinet officer who could speak for the combined services? Forrestal acknowledged this but emphasized that "preservation of the integrity of these services is most important." Then what would happen, the reporters pressed, if one service differed with his views or those of the president, or if the service positions were in conflict with one another? It would not be a matter of force, Forrestal replied. "This is a team of people working toward a common end. If you have to use authority, why you'd better get out of your job."[28]

Nowhere was this optimism more misplaced than with the JCS, which were increasingly called on in the fall of 1947 to provide professional military advice on issues that ranged from the Soviet threat in Europe and US base requirements in the Pacific to the civil war in China and the custody of atomic weapons within the US government. The requests from

Forrestal's office soon overwhelmed the JCS organization, due in part to the limitation imposed on the joint staff of one hundred officers. The primary cause, however, was simply that the unreformed JCS remained a committee of equal military service commanders, completely tripartite in structure and philosophy. Without a single overall chief of staff or even a presiding chairman, the Joint Chiefs were rarely able to reflect a unified position, normally responding in "split papers" as members of three different organizations, each combining service interests with subjective strategic viewpoints, on which there could be no compromise.

The result was organizational deadlock on issues concerning the nature of the next war, the type of weapons to be developed for that conflict, and the accommodation of service interests as the president began to impose tighter military budgets. Most serious, in Eisenhower's estimation, many of these issues could not be resolved under the current structure except by the president—in effect, a regression to the wartime modus operandi of Roosevelt, who even with the acceptance of open-ended budgets and duplication and waste as the price of victory, often had to personally adjudicate struggles within the Joint Chiefs. All this was not likely to change, given the JCS structure, the new law's equivocal language, and the determination of the new secretary of defense to work by consensus. "If each member comes to regard himself merely as the special advocate or pleader of the service he represents," Eisenhower cautioned in a valedictory memorandum to Forrestal in early 1948, "I fear that in the long run the body will be little more than an agency for eliminating from proposals and projects inconsequential and minor differences—a body of 'fly speckers.'"[29]

On 22 January, Eisenhower also wrote to the president to confirm the impending succession of Bradley as Army chief of staff. "You are likewise aware," he informed Truman, "that I shall always hold myself available for any military duty that the Government may require of me."[30] At noon on 7 February 1948, Eisenhower administered the oath of office to Bradley in the secretary of the Army's office. President Truman then pinned a fourth Distinguished Service Medal on the former chief of staff and presented a silver cigarette box on behalf of him and the service chiefs.

The next day, after thirty-six years of continuous military service, Dwight Eisenhower departed the Army and began to work on his account of the European war from his perspective as supreme commander. His model was Grant's memoirs, which he had always admired "because of their simplicity and lack of pretension."[31] On 2 May the Eisenhowers departed Quarters One at Fort Meyer after a simple ceremonial farewell by the Old Guard of the Third Infantry Regiment. In the late afternoon they arrived in New York City to be welcomed by a crowd of two hundred people in front of their new house at 60 Morningside Drive. At 10:00 A.M. on 7 June, Eisenhower officially became president of Columbia University when he received the keys to the university in a small ceremony held in the Trustees' Room.[32]

In the meantime, Secretary Forrestal was attempting to rewrite the executive order (9877) on service functions that had been issued at the time of the National Security Act. The Joint Chiefs could not agree on the new draft and on 8 March 1948 forwarded a split roles-and-missions paper to the secretary of defense with a request that service functions be "resolved by higher authority."[33] In his farewell memorandum, Eisenhower had suggested that Forrestal get away from Washington with the Joint Chiefs to settle the issue. The secretary acted on this advice and met with the JCS at the Key West Naval Base from 11 to 14 March. At that meeting and one on 20 March in Washington, assignments of service roles and missions were hammered out. The agreement was provided to the president, who approved it on 21 April.[34]

In terms of the JCS, the basic principle of the Key West Agreement was to operate the armed forces "under unified command whenever such unified command is in the best interests of national security." The JCS was authorized to establish these organizations, to determine what means were required for exercise of the unified command, and to assign to individual members the responsibility for providing such means. Equally important, the Joint Chiefs were authorized to continue the practice of designating one of their members as executive agent for each unified command, thus perpetuating the implication that the service that raised and supported forces also employed them. The National Security Act had intended that the JCS would serve as advisers and planners, not in a direct command status of the unified commands. But the Key West Agreement on executive agents led to a widespread perception that the JCS was in the chain of command, a perception that was reinforced by the fact that in practice the Joint Chiefs functioned as though that were the case. Finally, the overwhelming interest of the Joint Chiefs at Key West was to maintain control of their own service operations in operational commands involving more than one service. The result was the "service component command," a device adopted to protect department integrity, but a source of future tensions between the authority of the unified commanders and the service chiefs.[35]

As for military functions, the new document moved away from the broad delineation of the 1947 executive order and outlined the primary and secondary, or "collateral," responsibility of each service. The primary functions remained the same. To these were added the collateral roles and missions that each service was to perform in support of or in collaboration with the service executing the primary function. The new system ensured redundancy by preventing one service from making exclusive claims for jurisdiction over roles and missions and thus over the weapons, facilities, and technology required to implement those functions. This had immediate implications for two issues: the size and functions of the Marine Corps and the role of the Navy in strategic air warfare. To begin with, the Army dropped its insistence that Marine units be limited to less than division size, agreeing that there would be no attempt to abolish the Marine Corps or to restrict it unduly in its mission. To avoid unnecessary duplication, however, it was agreed that for planning purposes, the Marines should not exceed four divisions or have a larger than corps-sized headquarters.[36]

The issue of strategic bombing was more complex, with both the Air Force and the Navy making claims to the associated roles and missions. To this end, the Air Force was developing the B-36 super bomber and the Navy was initiating construction of flush-deck supercarriers, from which it could launch its version of a nuclear bomber. For the Navy, the Key West Agreement represented at least a partial victory on the issue. Despite the agreement's reaffirmation of the primary Air Force responsibility for strategic air warfare, the Navy was permitted as a collateral mission "to be prepared to participate in the overall air effort as directed by the Joint Chiefs of Staff." Moreover, the "collateral" aspect of the mission did not "prohibit the Navy from attacking any targets, inland or otherwise, necessary for the accomplishment of its mission." Finally, in the 26 March memorandum for record concerning the entire agreement, the Navy succeeded in inserting the stipulation that if naval considerations did not justify a supercarrier, the contribution that the carrier could make to strategic air warfare "might be enough to warrant its construction."[37]

By that time, as Clark Clifford noted, Forrestal had undergone a "dramatic metamorphosis" in terms of unification. The fundamental flaw in the original National Security Act, the defense secretary had come to believe, was the idea that military services that retained their autonomy could be made to operate as a unified entity. The realization began immediately after Forrestal moved to the Pentagon, when he had to operate under the restrictions that he had been so instrumental in creating: a minuscule staff, no deputies, and a limited mandate, almost bereft of real power and authority. As a consequence, in May 1948 a dissatisfied Forrestal arranged for his old friend Ferdinand Eberstadt, already a member of former President Herbert Hoover's Committee on Executive Branch Reorganization, to head that committee's Task Force on National Security Organization. In August, less than ten months in office and faced by a loose confederation of feuding service rivals that he had helped to create, the secretary of defense realized that he faced an impossible task. "I was wrong," he admitted to Clifford. "I cannot make this work. No one can make it work."[38]

One result of the Forrestal epiphany on unification was increased correspondence and contact during the fall with the president of Columbia University. In late September, after negotiations with the Soviets on the Berlin blockade had broken down, Eisenhower advised the secretary that based on his wartime experiences, the "common danger" of the crisis might help Forrestal in fostering more of a "sense of interdependence" among the services. He ended his letter with an apology for bothering the secretary in such a hectic period. Forrestal, however, was grateful. "You need never apologize," he replied, "for sending me any of your thoughts."[39] Another result was that Forrestal became more public in his call for changes to the National Security Act. On 30 September he so testified to the Eberstadt Task Force, citing "our general experience to date."[40] And on 5 October, Forrestal admitted to President Truman that he was ready to support revision of the 1947 bill. The president accepted what at best was a difficult admission without gloating and directed the secretary of defense to lead a team to draft proposed legislative amendments to the act.[41]

On 12 October, Eisenhower was formally installed as president of Columbia University. By that time, a pattern had begun to emerge in his dealings with the defense secretary. On 4 October he assured Forrestal that he would "always answer to any quick call." A few days later in a "Dear Ike" reply, Forrestal emphasized that whenever Eisenhower was in town, he would "set aside some time in which we can talk fundamentals."[42] At the end of the month Eisenhower was in Washington for three days of briefings on problems associated with unification. During those meetings, he began to work through the director of the joint staff, Major General Alfred M. Gruenther, a longtime friend and fellow bridge aficionado who had served in World War II as chief of staff of General Mark Clark's US Fifth Army in North Africa and Italy. Gruenther was the main connection between the Office of the Secretary of Defense and the JCS, especially trusted by Forrestal, who at one point referred to him as "my principal advisor."[43] At the conclusion of the briefings, Forrestal wrote to thank Eisenhower for a "most helpful visit" which he hoped could be "renewed from time to time."[44]

In actuality, the secretary of defense had more detailed plans. On 9 November, a week after Truman's surprise reelection, he asked the president to invite Eisenhower down to Washington for three or four weeks to preside over the JCS, emphasizing "that the talents of Ike, in terms of the identification of problems and the accommodations of differing views, would be highly useful."[45] Forrestal was primarily concerned with revision of the National Security Act and more specifically in establishing a chairman of the Joint Chiefs with power to make direct recommendations to the secretary of defense. He was well aware that Carl Vinson, soon to take over as chairman of the House Armed Services Committee, would be opposed to a position that in any way appeared to resemble a single chief of staff for the armed forces. From this perspective, Eisenhower would be invaluable as an example of a senior military adviser interacting with the JCS. "With Ike here for sixty days I think we can get the pattern set and prove its workability by pragmatic experience."[46] A few weeks later, Eisenhower accepted the offer to come to serve as Forrestal's military consultant for several months beginning in the new year.[47]

From 20 to 27 January 1949, Eisenhower visited Washington for conferences and briefings with the JCS and the individual services. On 22 January he began his temporary, nonstatutory duties as principal military adviser and consultant to the president and the secretary of defense. By the end of what he termed "a week of struggle in the Pentagon," Eisenhower was angry, frustrated, and disgusted by the conflict between the Air Force and the Navy, which he perceived as "personal as well as organizational and so noticeable that it is never absent from any discussion." He was more convinced than ever of the need for majority vote in the JCS and for direct presidential intervention to convince the Joint Chiefs that continued split decisions and failure to agree would "breed contempt and ridicule that can destroy any group."[48]

The fundamental problem still concerned service functions. The Key West conference had clarified roles and missions to a great extent and provided a structure for further discussions. With technology, weapons, and strategy in constant flux, however, the most carefully negotiated compromise could not anticipate new developments. Furthermore, a legacy of mistrust that lingered from the unification struggle had been temporarily overcome but was never far from the surface. In his first annual report in December, Forrestal correctly predicted the issue with the most potential divisiveness: "What is to be the use, and who is to be the user of air power?"[49] By January 1949 the interservice disputes over strategy, missions, and budget had begun to resolve themselves into a struggle concerning this issue, in particular the question of strategic bombing and the two weapons systems in contention for the mission, the Navy's supercarrier and the Air Force's B-36 bomber. A definitive solution appeared impossible, and Eisenhower was already beginning to regret his agreement with Forrestal. "Except for my liking, admiration and respect for his great qualities," he wrote, "I'd not go near Washington—even if I had to resign my commission."[50]

On Monday, 31 January, Eisenhower returned to Washington for five days on a commute from New York City that was already becoming a "familiar monotonous and dreary process through familiar train yards and past endless billboards."[51] The week began with two days of separate Navy briefings that confirmed his impression that the Navy now viewed its main mission not as control of the sea but as projection of American air power. Equally important, he learned that his idea of majority rule for the JCS was unacceptable to that organization. He continued, too, to be concerned about Forrestal's mental state and about the secretary's high expectations for his new adviser. "He exaggerates greatly the possibility that I will materially help in his task of 'unifying' the services," Eisenhower noted on 2 February in his diary.[52] Two days later, his diary fairly bristled with his reaction to the continued acrimony on the strategic bombing issue. "Well—something has to snap, and so far as I'm concerned it will have to be the patience of the Pres & Sec. Def.," he wrote. "They are going to have to get tough! And I mean tough!"[53]

That day Eisenhower sent a memorandum to Forrestal that strongly recommended presidential intervention in the form of a meeting with civilian secretaries and assistant secretaries as well as the JCS and the vice chiefs in order to emphasize that *"joint work will take precedence over any personal or individual service matter."*[54] Eisenhower described the meeting as "most satisfactory," certainly an understatement considering the results. The president insisted on service compliance with directives, supported the strongest possible Air Force, and cut some of the Navy's "assumed missions." Finally, in addition to creating the position of undersecretary of defense, Truman decided either to establish a chairman of the JCS by law or by appointing a general selected by Eisenhower to be presidential chief of staff. In the meantime, Eisenhower agreed to act as JCS chairman "for a brief (I hope) period pending change in law or formal arrangements for getting 'unification' on the rails."[55]

At the same time, work on amending the National Security Act was proceeding swiftly. On 10 February, Forrestal and Clifford completed an eleven-point legislative program that was remarkably similar to the president's original 19 December 1945 unification message, particularly in terms of increased authority for the secretary of defense. Forrestal also wanted the proposed JCS chairman to be the principal military adviser to the secretary and the president. At the same time, he concluded that, in order to eliminate parochial service allegiances and foster a broader focus on US national interests, the Joint Chiefs should not have operational control of their respective services. But the secretary also recognized the extent of military and congressional opposition to such moves and recommended only a presiding chairman of the JCS, with the remaining chiefs retaining command of their services.[56]

On 15 February the Hoover Committee on Executive Branch Reorganization echoed these recommendations in its findings. Significantly, however, that organization's vice chairman, Dean Acheson, led three members in dissent. What was needed, they asserted, was someone to exercise control over the JCS—to be called "the Chief of Staff and not 'chairman,' 'responsible head,' 'principal adviser,' or some other temporizing title." He would not have command functions but would preside over the JCS with power to initiate and terminate discussions, to bring all recommendations from the JCS—whether agreed or not—and give his own recommendation to the secretary. It would be a post, they concluded, "to which every young professional soldier, naval officer, and airman would aspire, instead of, as now, to be the head of a separate service." Moreover, this was not a new solution. "Elihu Root, when Secretary of War," they emphasized, "found the cavalry, infantry, and artillery immersed in dangerous service rivalries. . . . He recommended that the post of Chief of Staff be created in the Army. Through the years since it has often been filled by our most brilliant officers."[57]

Eisenhower was also concerned with what he classified as "lip service at the altar of 'unification'" on the matter, and on 4 March he pressed unsuccessfully to propose the JCS chairman as the coequal of the undersecretary of defense, also a new position, but under separate consideration by Congress. The principal virtue of this alternative, he pointed out, would be to establish the chairman "as the immediate and direct subordinate and associate of the Secretary of Defense."[58] Despite this setback, the president did incorporate Eisenhower's earlier wording in his proposal to Congress the next day for changes in the 1947 National Security Act, recommending the establishment of a chairman of the JCS "to take precedence over all other military personnel, and to be the principal military adviser to the President and the Secretary of Defense."[59]

At almost the same time, there was a change of leadership in the Pentagon. In January, Forrestal had submitted a postelection, pro forma resignation to President-elect Truman. It was generally assumed that he expected to continue as defense secretary. But the president accepted the resignation on 1 March and on 3 March announced the appointment of Louis Johnson to the position. Within a short time, the new secretary of defense assembled almost a completely new Pentagon team. Francis P. Matthews, a lawyer and a friend of Johnson's who had worked with him raising funds for Truman, became secretary of the Navy. And Secretary of the Army Kenneth Royall was replaced by his undersecretary, Gordon Gray, a lawyer and newspaper publisher from North Carolina. Only Stuart Symington remained in office, as secretary of the Air Force. As for the "part-time and informal" chairman, Johnson made it immediately clear that he wanted Eisenhower on the job. "J. is *insistent* that I make no plans to terminate my Washington duties for next 6 mos. *at least*," Eisenhower recorded in his diary. "He says he told Pres. He'd take job only if I'd stay on."[60]

However gratifying these sentiments, Eisenhower's dealings with the services did not improve. On the afternoon of 21 March he became ill with a severe stomach disorder. His physician recommended complete rest, and on 28 March, Eisenhower flew on the presidential plane to convalesce at the president's vacation home in Key West. From 7 to 12 April,

Eisenhower was joined at Key West by the Joint Chiefs to discuss force structure and budget issues. On 16 May he arrived back at Columbia after more than two months' absence. Less than a week later he learned of Forrestal's death by suicide. On 25 May, a bright, clear spring day, Eisenhower was one of nine honorary pallbearers as the first secretary of defense was buried with full military honors in Arlington National Cemetery.

In the meantime, the supercarrier–B-36 issue began to reemerge. The new secretary of defense initiated the process on 15 April by asking Eisenhower and the Joint Chiefs for their views on the military advisability of completing the USS *United States,* the construction of which had been approved by the president and Congress the previous spring. At Eisenhower's suggestion, the JCS addressed the matter without waiting for his return to Washington. Predictably, the chief of naval operations, Admiral Louis E. Denfeld, was for completion and the Air Force chief of staff, General Hoyt S. Vandenberg, was against. General Bradley had approved the construction in May 1948, but he now agreed with the Air Force that it was "militarily unsound" to add to the current carrier force. Eisenhower sided with Vandenberg and Bradley. Confronted by a split decision, Johnson decided with the majority. After receiving the president's approval of this decision, the defense secretary ordered the cessation of work on the supercarrier on 23 April.[61]

On 26 June, while John L. Sullivan was still Navy secretary, he fired off an angry letter to Johnson, protesting that the cancellation of a project already approved by executive and legislative leaders would "result in a renewed effort to abolish the Marine Corps and to transfer all naval and marine aviation elsewhere." The consequences could be "tragic," he concluded, "in so drastically and arbitrarily changing and restricting the operational plans of an armed service."[62] In the next two months, allegations spread throughout the higher naval echelons of Johnson's anti-Navy bias and of problems with the B-36 concerning technical capabilities, contract fraud, and conflict of interest. In early June the House of Representatives authorized its Armed Services Committee to investigate not only the B-36 allegations but the supercarrier cancellation decision, the Air Force strategic bombing plan, and the broader service roles and missions issue as well. The entire business for Eisenhower was an unedifying spectacle that brought no credit to any service. "I have been very proud of membership in the Armed Services and have felt that, jointly they provide to the country the greatest body of honest, selfless, intelli-

gent public servants that could be found anywhere," he wrote to Swede
Hazlett. "Consequently, it hurts me to see a public impression growing up
that these men do nothing except to quarrel and fight among themselves
for access to the taxpayers' pocketbook."[63]

The Navy–Air Force issue tended to overshadow the successful progress
during that period on President Truman's proposed National Security Act
amendments. On 24 March the Senate Armed Services Committee began
hearings on a bill that generally conformed to the president's recommended changes. All service witnesses broadly supported the proposals,
with the Army and Air Force predictably more in favor than the Navy and
the Marines. "I do not think," the Marine Corps commandant asserted
at one point, "the National Security Act has been given a fair trial."[64] On
26 May the Senate approved a slightly revised bill. Vinson's House Armed
Services Committee began hearings on 28 June and favorably reported a
House version on 14 July. A conference report was agreed to by the Senate on 28 July and by the House on 2 August. On 10 August, President
Truman signed Public Law 216, the National Security Act Amendments
of 1949.

The new legislation increased the defense secretary's power and authority. The National Military Establishment became the Department of
Defense, an executive department with cabinet status, and the three service departments became "military departments." The service secretaries
would still "separately administer" these departments, but specifically
under the unqualified, not "general," "direction, authority, and control"
of the defense secretary. At the same time, the service secretaries lost two
important privileges: their statutory membership on the National Security Council and the right to appeal decisions to the president and the
budget director. Some compensation was provided by granting the secretaries as well as the JCS the new right of making reports on their own
initiatives to Congress. The end result, however, was that the services became semiautonomous administrative subdivisions in the new executive
department, with their civilian leaders denied cabinet status and a direct
role in defense policymaking.[65]

The changes were equally significant for the JCS. The new act abolished the position of chief of staff to the commander in chief and replaced
it with a full-time JCS chairman. With the creation of this position, Congress could not resist reiterating as a declaration of policy in the bill its
opposition to a "single Chief of Staff over the Armed Forces," empha-

sizing that the chairman would not exercise military command over the JCS or any of the services. At the same time, the legislators denied the chairman a "vote" in JCS deliberations—a meaningless gesture useful only as a decoy, as Eisenhower had long before suggested, since the Joint Chiefs were advisers who neither voted nor decided. Finally, citing the traditional fear of a "military staff," Congress rejected the president's recommendation to do away with all limitations on the size of the joint staff, agreeing only to an increase from 100 to 210 officers.[66]

The total impact of these changes was important for the JCS, which of all the agencies retained its direct involvement in defense policymaking. With their removal from the National Security Council and withdrawal of their cabinet status, the service secretaries lost considerable power in 1949. This decline produced a situation similar to that in World War II when Secretaries Stimson and Knox had been bypassed by the JCS. At that time, the focus was on the president; after 1949 it was on the secretary of defense. Then, as in 1949, the Joint Chiefs were individually responsible to their service secretaries. Collectively, however, they remained the principal military advisers of the defense secretary; and since they were the only service departmental representatives provided a statutory role in the defense policy process, they became, as they had been in the war, the spokesmen for their services. In this position, the Joint Chiefs were relatively isolated from civilian interface even as they continued to direct their military departments. To this was added a provision in the new bill that explicitly prohibited any of the hard-won major combat functions for each of the services from being "transferred, reassigned, abolished, or consolidated" by the secretary of defense.[67]

In the end the 1949 amendments moved dramatically from the decentralized approach to authority incorporated in the original National Security Act. There would still be problems in the future. But national unity of command and effort had improved in an evolutionary fashion, and President Truman could be forgiven some optimism in the wake of the new bill. "We finally succeeded in getting a Unification Act that will enable us to have Unification," he wrote, "and as soon as we get the cry babies in the niches where they belong, we will have no more trouble."[68]

The passage of the act on 10 August was good news for Eisenhower, as was President Truman's announcement the next day that he had nominated Bradley as the first chairman of the Joint Chiefs of Staff. In July,

Eisenhower had turned down an invitation from Johnson to assume the post once it was passed into law. He was ready to return full-time to Columbia, "convinced that Washington would never see me again except as an occasional visitor."[69] In the meantime, the House Armed Services Committee concluded the first phase of its hearings—that concerned with the B-36 investigation. By 25 August the committee had determined that the charges of favoritism and corruption against the secretaries of defense and the Air Force were baseless.

Eisenhower was not pleased with the second phase of the committee hearings that began on 6 October and focused on the broad issues of strategy and unification. At the outset, the chief of naval operations, Admiral Denfeld, challenged not only the strategic concepts and the functions of the JCS but the efficacy of the unification process itself. "We are quite depressed over the tone," Gruenther wrote in forwarding a copy of Denfeld's testimony to Morningside Heights. "The bitter fight still goes on in Washington," Eisenhower noted in his diary, "with the Navy cursing the other services. The whole performance is humiliating."[70]

On 19 October, Eisenhower agreed to testify at the House hearings. That day, his former subordinate and now the chairman of the JCS provided testimony, which the New York Times characterized as "one of the most extraordinary tongue lashings ever given to high military officers in such a forum."[71] Bradley began by reminding the committee of the unanimous JCS ratification the previous February of the Air Force investment in the B-36. He was unsparing, in words that could have been drawn from Eisenhower's earlier postwar testimony, when it came to the most contentious roles and missions issues. "I would like to point out . . . that I have participated in the two largest amphibious assaults ever made in history," he asserted. "In neither case were any Marines present. And in neither case were any Navy carriers used."[72]

The principal problem in all this, Bradley concluded, was a lack of commitment to full unity of command in Washington. "Despite protestations to the contrary, I believe that the Navy has opposed unification from the beginning, and they have not in spirit as well as deed, accepted it completely to date." The lesson from Pearl Harbor, "a Sunday morning within the memory of all of us," was that the military must be one team— "in the game to win regardless of who carries the ball. This is no time for 'fancy dans' who won't hit the line with all they have on every play, unless they can call the signals. Each player on this team—whether he shines in the spotlight of the backfield or eats dirt in the line—must be an all-American."[73]

Eisenhower's brief testimony the next day was, by design, pallid in comparison. "In unity there is strength," he exhorted the committee, "and this country unified can whip the world." At the same time, however, disunity could cripple the national security establishment just the way domestic strikes and labor disputes (then ongoing in the coal and steel industries) were creating economic paralysis in the United States. It was a situation that was causing a "certain general staff in this world" to shout "with glee." In particular, he believed that "seething antagonism" within the Defense Department could not fail to encourage Soviet hopes to weaken America. "I am going to be no party," Eisenhower concluded, "to anything that I think gives aid and comfort to any potential enemy."[74]

The next day, the *New York Times* correctly interpreted the statement as "a friendly but plain rebuke today to all officers involved in the controversy with the armed forces, including his old wartime subordinate, General Omar N. Bradley."[75] Eisenhower attempted to limit the damage. He wrote Bradley of his support and cautioned him not to be bothered by some speculation about his future usefulness as chairman because of his use of terms that were considered "belittling." In a postscript to his letter, he advised Bradley: "Don't defend yourself—/Don't explain/Don't worry!!"[76]

After his testimony in October, Eisenhower's involvement with events in the nation's capital declined precipitously. Toward the end of the year, however, Chairman Vinson unofficially solicited his ideas for the report that the House Armed Services Committee was preparing on the recent hearings. On 3 January 1950 Eisenhower complied by providing a detailed draft to Vinson, who used much of the input without alterations in his final report.[77] This interaction was Eisenhower's last major involvement with the unification issue from Morningside Heights. His role in Washington had been a frustrating one. "Sometimes I was an umpire between disputing services," he recalled much later; "sometimes a hatchetman on what Fox Conner used to call Fool Schemes."[78] Moreover, since he generally visited Washington only a few days each month, Gruenther as director of the joint staff ran the day-to-day administrative business and continued to perform the majority of duties that had been his before Eisenhower's appointment. Thus, although the acting chairman became involved in strategic planning and budget estimates, he could never master the detail that was part of a daily routine and key to playing a consistent role in the complex issues. Under these circumstances, Eisenhower presided over only twelve JCS meetings and could simply not keep up. The position of acting chairman was, in short, a part-time, informal job, which in Stephen Ambrose's estimation "gave Eisenhower maximum exposure and minimum influence."[79]

Ambrose's judgment is too severe when applied to what was institutionally possible in 1949. The Truman administration may have wanted Eisenhower's prestige more than his advice. But the fact remains that both the president and the secretary of defense listened to and acted on many of his recommendations concerning unification issues and the formulation and passage of amendments to the National Security Act. At the same time, Eisenhower's impartial conduct as acting JCS chairman played a major role in gaining congressional acceptance for that position. Even more important, his new perspective as chairman only reinforced Eisenhower's conviction of the dangerous inadequacies of the unreformed JCS system in a period in which the concept and means of national security were rapidly changing. And as he also realized, even with statutory authority, the chairman position that emerged from the 1949 legislation had no more power over the Joint Chiefs than he had possessed in his temporary capacity. The move to increase the authority of the defense secretary was long overdue, he believed, but overall global unified command from Washington would not be complete until that process extended to the chairman in terms of the JCS. He had consistently advocated this course of action since late 1948 and in another form in his testimony on the Collins Plan in 1945. But it was time now to regroup and trust in the evolutionary process of unification, already demonstrated in the 1949 legislation.

PART FIVE

Peacetime Unity of Effort and Command, 1950–1952

CHAPTER TWELVE

The Great Debate, April 1950–March 1951

To produce Allied co-operation for World War II was far easier than developing a military defense in NATO and peace. This was an enterprise without precedent.

DWIGHT D. EISENHOWER

I am particularly confident that any man named to Supreme Commander must approach it *studiously* and *gradually*. . . . Much of what we did in World War II has no application whatsoever to any future conflict into which we might be forced. But these experiences and lessons that deal with human beings—and particularly when these human beings are placed into positions of such responsibility that they involve capacity to damage the coalition as well as to rivet it tightly together—should, if remembered and heeded, do much to smooth out future difficulty and to expedite the true business of soldiers, which is merely to win victories and then to retire to the rear of the stage.

DWIGHT D. EISENHOWER

The nation's security problem is not as simple a black-and-white matter as the "Great Debaters" would like to make it appear.

DWIGHT D. EISENHOWER

E ISENHOWER'S RETURN TO Columbia University would not last long. Events had been in train for several years in Europe and throughout the world that would inexorably draw him back to the scene of his greatest military triumph, where once again he would face many of the problems of unity of command and effort that he had experienced in World War II, this time rendered more complex in a peacetime environment of reduced European budgets combined with the residual grievances of the American unification effort. During 1948, in response to Soviet moves in Czechoslovakia and Berlin, five Western nations formed the Western European Union (WEU), an early attempt at collective security that foundered as old rivalries among the European great powers emerged. On 4 April 1949 the United States joined Canada and ten European nations to form the North Atlantic Treaty Organization (NATO). The move committed the United States to a transatlantic bargain by which it agreed, as part of a collective defense effort, to respond to any external acts of aggression against any member nation. This unprecedented decision was tied into the emerging perception of the Soviet threat, as well as the expanding postwar concept of American national security, with its fundamental assumption that the political and economic survival of Europe was closely linked to vital US national interests.

The evolving structure of NATO soon reflected that organization's unique membership and mission. The North Atlantic Council (NAC), NATO's governing body, consisted of the foreign ministers of the treaty nations, who met periodically in various locations. When the NAC was not in session, its policies were carried out by the Council Deputies operating in London in continuous session. Under the council, the Defense Committee, consisting of treaty defense ministers, met periodically and was charged with preparing combined unified command plans. Operating in a subordinate role to this committee, the military chiefs of staff of the alliance countries also met periodically as NATO's Military Committee. The policies formulated by this organization were executed on a continuing basis by the American, French, and British chiefs of staffs or their deputies, who formed the Standing Group for the Military Committee and met regularly in Washington. These types of intricate structures reassured Europeans that the United States did not intend to revert to its military isolation, leaving them to deal with either the Soviets or a resurgent Germany. Equally important, the detailed involvement by the United States in NATO's evolving organization reinforced the perception of its commitment to Europe as a particular American sphere of influence, serving notice to the Soviets not to interfere in the region.[1]

Guiding the formation of NATO was the president's new secretary of state, Dean Acheson, who had replaced General Marshall in January 1949. Acheson was a lawyer who had served in the State Department as an assistant secretary during World War II and for two years after that conflict as undersecretary before returning to private practice. He was feisty, articulate, and eloquent in speech and writing, both of which he could employ from time to time in savage criticism. He was also known, however, for his loyalty, famously illustrated by his devotion to the president—an incongruous relationship based on mutual trust and celebrated by Acheson in his memoirs, which he dedicated to Truman, "The captain with the mighty heart." Those memoirs were entitled *Present at the Creation,* actually an understatement from a man who not only was present at the creation of the postwar world but was one of its chief architects, whether it was the Bretton Woods agreements, the Truman Doctrine, or the Marshall Plan.

The new NATO structure was also one of Acheson's achievements. But by spring 1950 it was evident that neither the United States nor the European members were prepared to field the requisite standing military forces for the collective defense of Europe. In April 1950, spurred by Communist China's victory in the Chinese Civil War and the Soviet detonation of a nuclear device the previous fall, the Acheson State Department produced a draft grand strategy focused on containment of the Soviet Union on the Eurasian landmass supported by a massive conventional-force buildup. It was soon apparent, however, that the new strategy, known by its National Security Council document number, NSC-68, would not be implemented given the president's determination to maintain low defense budgets.

In a similar manner that month, NATO's Defense Committee approved a detailed four-year Medium Term Defense Plan (MTDP) anchored in Germany and the Netherlands on the integrated defensive Rhine-Ijssel line in the East. The plan required at least ninety divisions, more than one thousand combat ships, and almost nine thousand aircraft to be in place by 1954. At the time, the alliance was represented on the Continent by fourteen divisions of uneven quality and strength and one thousand aircraft, none of which was either optimally deployed for defense or under any unified authority. In contrast, the Soviets had approximately twenty-five divisions supported by about six thousand aircraft positioned in forward areas in Eastern Europe for immediate attack, plus a huge mass of land and air units in the USSR—all operating under a highly centralized and well tested command structure. On 15 June 1950 Field Marshal Bernard Montgomery, in his capacity as chairman of the Commanders in Chief Committee of the WEU, reported that "as things stand today and in the foreseeable future, there would be scenes of appalling and indescribable confusion in Western Europe if we were ever attacked by the Russians."[2]

Ten days after Montgomery's report, North Korean forces invaded South Korea. Eisenhower flew to Washington that day to discuss the situation with senior officials. He approved of the Truman response through the United Nations and the decision by the president to give General MacArthur as the commander in chief, Far East (CINCFE), authority to use all Army forces available to him. "I believe we'll have a dozen Koreas," he noted in his diary, "if we don't take a firm stand."[3] And a few days later in a Fourth of July address to forty-seven thousand Boy Scouts at their second national jamboree at Valley Forge, Pennsylvania, Eisenhower tied Truman's "inescapable" decision to assist in Korea to the most fundamental lesson of his generation in dealing with aggression. "The alternative would be another kind of Munich," he concluded, "with all the disastrous consequences that followed in the wake of that fatal error 12 years ago."[4] As for the choice of the overall commander in Korea, it was an accretion of power for MacArthur unforeseen in the unified command plan battles of 1946, but generally welcomed with confidence and support. James Reston of the *New York Times* was one of the few dissenters. In a prescient column two weeks after the North Korean attack, he pointed out that that whereas Eisenhower was widely known for his "international teamwork," the new UN commander in Korea at seventy years of age was "a sovereign power in his own right with stubborn confidence in his own judgment. Diplomacy and a vast concern for the opinions and sensitivities of others are the political qualities essential to this new assignment, and these are precisely the qualities General MacArthur has been accused of lacking in the past."[5]

One of the most important results of the outbreak of the Korean War in June 1950 was that it appeared to confirm the assumptions of the moribund US grand strategy in NSC-68 that called for a buildup of conventional forces to contain the Soviet Union. To begin with, the North Korean attack ended the myth of atomic deterrence. The United States' possession of atomic superiority, in other words, did not mean that the Soviets or their surrogates would not attempt to break out of the containment belt with conventional forces. The attack on 25 June also seemed to bear out the implicit conclusion in NSC-68 concerning the indivisibility of interests. South Korea had been defined in January 1950 by Acheson in his famous National Press Club speech as being outside US vital interests. And yet because of the nature of the North Korean attack, the United States responded, and the survival of South Korea became a vital interest. Finally, events in Korea appeared to support the most fundamental contention of NSC-68, that the United States could generate enough forces and resources to plug up the containment belt anywhere the Soviets and their surrogates might attempt to expand. In the wake of the June attack, Truman sent a much increased defense budget to Congress. That body required less than forty-eight hours to approve a new budget that tripled the amount the president had requested.[6]

The North Korean aggression shocked the Europeans. Since they, like the Americans, assumed at the very least Soviet concurrence in the attack, it undermined a predominant European view that Soviet actions since 1945 had been focused only on creating a barrier of Communist states across the traditional invasion routes into Russia. From this perspective, the Soviet Union would not resort to an overt attack on Western Europe. The immediate US response in Korea, of course, was reassuring. But the Western European governments, now increasingly apprehensive about Soviet intentions, were also aware of the inadequacy of European defenses as well as of the very real possibility that those defenses might soon be tested. The NATO Medium Term Defense Plan had fixed the Rhine-Ijssel line as the primary defensive demarcation. In early summer 1950 a series of phased withdrawals from Germany and even France seemed more realistic. On 13 July the JCS and service secretaries advised Secretary of Defense Louis Johnson that the United States should help NATO countries expand their forces, send additional military equipment to those forces, and, most important, send more American forces to Europe.[7]

The major mark of progress at this point in terms of NATO, as Acheson later admitted, was that "where we were naked we began to admit it."[8] The realization caused urgent US efforts that summer to correct the ends-means military disconnect in NATO and thereby prevent the Europeans from retreating into what the Department of State termed a "fear and resignation psychosis" that could tear away the "moral tissue" of the alliance.[9] But early attempts to elicit military increases from member nations were hampered by the lack of military structure in NATO. France, for example, linked contributions not only to the addition of American and British troops but to the creation of a unified military command with a World War II–type combined chiefs of staff organization to create overall strategy and act as a general staff. Equally problematical and directly linked to French participation was the growing American belief that military participation by the still-occupied West Germany was essential for a viable European defense. Even before the Korean conflict, the JCS had agreed that rearming that country was "of fundamental importance" and that France must "be persuaded to recognize that the USSR is a greater menace to [her] independence . . . than is Germany."[10] Truman agreed, observing at the time that with German participation, the Allies could transform NATO's military efforts from "a rear-guard action on the shores of the Atlantic Ocean" to a "defense in depth."[11] Soon the linkage of German rearmament to the issue of NATO's command arrangement became an important part of the detailed discussions between the departments of State and Defense concerning the dispatch of more American troops to Europe.

On 8 September the president received the joint recommendations from the two departments calling for the commitment of additional US troops to Europe "at the earliest feasible date."[12] These forces would include from four to six divisions, which would join a European defense force with an international staff initially under an American chief of staff and "eventually" an American supreme commander. The NATO nations would make firm commitments concerning the forces that would pass immediately to the supreme commander as well as those that would be placed under his command in war. To this structure, the secretaries recommended that German contingents be added at the division level to serve under NATO corps and higher units. Finally, the two department heads stipulated that the United States should accept supreme command responsibility only if the NATO members requested it and only if they undertook to fulfill their force commitments.[13]

On 9 September, Truman announced, without providing specific details of the extent and timing, the "substantial increase" of US forces to be stationed in Western Europe. He was acting, the president emphasized, in "the sincere expectation" of similar Allied efforts.[14] But the public commitment of American forces undercut US negotiating leverage with the Allies—a development Truman was apparently ready to accept in order to stimulate European morale.

The announcement triggered a spate of newspaper speculation that Truman would soon support either Eisenhower or Bradley to head the NATO forces. General Gruenther, now the deputy chief of staff for plans and combat operations on the Army staff, sent Eisenhower one such article. "My own prediction," he wrote his friend, "is that one of the two gentlemen will be tagged."[15] On 12 September the president removed Louis Johnson as secretary of defense and announced that he would nominate General Marshall to fill that position. Marshall's only stipulation was that his return to service from his Leesburg, Virginia, home would not exceed one year. As his deputy, he selected Robert A. Lovett, an investment banker who had served under Henry Stimson in World War II as assistant secretary of war for air and under Marshall as undersecretary during the general's 1947–1949 tenure as secretary of state. Eisenhower immediately wired congratulations to his mentor, who accepted the good wishes, noting, however, that he was entitled "to your sympathy too because there are going to be hard days ahead."[16] Marshall's prediction was immediately realized at his congressional confirmation hearings, during which, as Acheson noted, "the primitives in the Senate reached a crescendo of vituperation" as they questioned the competence and loyalty of the former Army chief of staff and secretary of state.[17]

On 26 September 1950 the North Atlantic Council communiqué emphasized the progress that had been made and the work yet to be done. There was agreement on the formation "at the earliest possible date" of an integrated force acting under the political guidance of NATO and the strategic direction of the Military Committee's Standing Group. The force would operate under a supreme commander supported by an international staff and authorized to organize and train national contingents in peacetime into an effective integrated whole in the event of war. The new position, the council emphasized, would be filled as soon as there was assurance that "national forces will be made available for the integrated force adequate to enable the latter to be reasonably capable of fulfilling its responsibilities." In order to implement the council's recommendation, the foreign ministers asked for recommendations from the Defense Committee "as a matter of urgency" concerning the organization, command, and strategic direction of the force. The committee was also to make recommendations on the method and timing concerning allocation of national units in being to the integrated command, as well as on the method by which Germany could make its most useful contribution, "bearing in mind . . . that it would not serve the best interests of Europe or of Germany to bring into being a German national army or a German general staff."[18]

These latter concerns became irrelevant on 24 October with the introduction of the so-called Pleven Plan and its quick and decisive passage in the French National Assembly—a remarkable achievement in the Fourth Republic. The plan, named for its primary sponsor, the French premier, called for simultaneous activities, one within and one outside NATO. Within the alliance, all current plans for increased forces and production would be maintained, including the French goal of committing twenty divisions by 1954. Outside the alliance, the plan called for a European defense minister who would direct a new experimental NATO force composed of integrated Allied and German contingents with an initial total strength of one hundred thousand troops and with German formations limited in size to battalion level. Once trained and operational, these units would eventually be assigned to the supreme commander in NATO.[19]

For the Americans and many of the Allies, the Pleven Plan was at best ambiguous and at worst unworkable. Bradley believed the Pleven Plan to be "entirely impractical," and Acheson considered it to be "hopeless," while Marshall admitted that he was unable to "penetrate the miasma" of the plan.[20] Eisenhower agreed, describing it as "a complicated form of partial German rearmament and hodgepodge organization" that would remain largely on paper and provide more opportunity for debate than for action.[21]

Even though speculation was increasing that Eisenhower would be given a role as NATO's supreme commander of integrated military force, he had not been invited for consultations on any of the fall events involving the future of that organization. But that began to change. On 19 October, Truman referred to the issue in a letter to Eisenhower. "First time you are in town, I wish you'd come in and see me," he added in a handwritten postscript. "If I send for you, we'll start the 'speculators' to work."[22]

Eisenhower arrived in Washington at midnight on Friday, 27 October. Early the next morning he met in the Pentagon with Army Chief of Staff General J. Lawton Collins, Secretary of the Army Frank Pace, and General Gruenther. From them he learned that NATO's Military Committee, chaired by General Bradley, had unanimously indicated its desire that the commander of NATO's forces should be an American and even more specifically had named him as their choice. Later that day, he met with the president, who immediately offered him the NATO military command. Eisenhower was enthusiastic about the possible assignment, an absolutely critical military job in what he believed to be a "world crisis." "I rather look upon this effort," he wrote Swede Hazlett, who considered the possible assignment a demotion, "as about the last remaining chance for the survival of Western Civilization."[23]

In the meantime, the NATO ministers were making a great deal of progress. The United States agreed to provide an American supreme commander and troops to an integrated NATO force, provided the principle of German participation in that organization was accepted and steps begun to implement it. To this end, the French agreed to the incorporation of German troops on a basis of full equality into NATO's unified command as regimental combat teams, self-contained units of approximately six thousand troops, on condition that the Allies approve the long-term goal of a European defense force. This departure from the original French demand that a European political superstructure precede initiatives to rearm Germany was a major concession.[24] These proceedings were followed on 12 December by a Military Committee meeting in London at which its members recommended to the Defense Committee their additional report on the detailed establishment of an integrated NATO force and a supreme headquarters, and on the reorganization of the overall military structure, including terms of reference for the supreme commander, Atlantic Powers in Europe.[25] On 13 December the Council Deputies and the Military Committee met to approve the political and military reports.

Eisenhower monitored these events through newspaper accounts, updates from the joint staff, and, on 9 December, a two-hour meeting with the JCS. He was apparently surprised at some of the information, as well as at the accelerated pace of events, all of which may have added to his growing misgivings. The Military Committee's report on NATO's military structure recommended "a separate overall Naval Command directly responsible to the Standing Group," the latter defined as "the authority responsible for coordinating the requirements of all Fronts."[26] This "staff" desire to separate the Mediterranean from the main theater, Eisenhower emphasized to Marshall, was typical of the degree "to which some of the papers are filled up with detailed conditions, circumstances and arrangements for command, all of which gives rise to the suspicion that people are more engaged in . . . insisting upon limitations upon unified command than in supporting with their full strength the efforts of the selected commander."[27]

In response to the complaints about command arrangements in the Mediterranean, Marshall and Lovett assured Eisenhower that the Joint Chiefs would recommend that every American soldier and sailor be placed under him "in case of need." Most important, as Lovett reported to Acheson, Eisenhower's point of view on American forces in Europe was now "elastic," and he had abandoned the idea of not accepting the command appointment until the establishment of a sizable NATO force. He was more realistically and pragmatically inclined on the matter, not the least because of Lovett's appealing reminder that as supreme commander he would occupy the position around which the European nations would rally and coalesce. As a result, Eisenhower ended the meeting by concentrating on quality rather than quantity, emphasizing the need for well-trained and well-equipped units immediately capable of swift expansion.[28]

On 18 December at the Brussels meeting of the North Atlantic Council and NATO's Defense Committee, the French minister of defense proposed Eisenhower, an officer who "stood out above all others," one who "was in the minds of everybody," as supreme commander. The council responded enthusiastically with a unanimous recommendation of the American general in recognition of his "incomparable prestige, proven ability, and the highest order of leadership." The next day, Acheson announced that as the council had requested, Truman had appointed the five-star general as the first supreme Allied commander, Europe (SACEUR), and would soon increase the number of US troops under him.[29]

Eisenhower would have "direct control over the higher training of all national forces allocated to SHAPE [Supreme Headquarters Allied Powers, Europe] in peacetime." And he would have direct access to each country's chief of staff. This type of access was also extended to each head of government if it were necessary to facilitate the SACEUR's mission. Most critical, the report also authorized Eisenhower as supreme commander to make recommendations to national chiefs of staff "on the peacetime deployment of National forces placed or to be placed under his control, and on logistic and administrative matters affecting the efficiency or readiness of these forces." Finally, in wartime, the terms of reference provided the SACEUR with "full powers" in matters of operations and training.[30]

In his 19 December announcement of Eisenhower's appointment as supreme commander of an integrated NATO force, Truman also reaffirmed his intention to assign additional US troops to Europe as part of that force. The president cited article 3 of the North Atlantic Treaty, which called for "continuous and effective . . . mutual aid," a type of preventive support to the "collective capacity to resist such an attack."[31] In response the next day, Herbert Hoover delivered a twenty-minute radio and television address that inaugurated what came to be called the Great Debate concerning this unprecedented decision. Citing the need to preserve the Western Hemisphere as a "Gibraltar of Western Civilization," the former president reminded his audience that it was possible for the forces of the Communist-controlled Eurasian landmass to turn Western Europe into the "graveyard of millions of American boys," while tying the US into a "war without victory." To send another American soldier or dollar before the Western European nations had established and equipped sufficient divisions would only create another situation like Korea.[32]

Senator Robert A. Taft of Ohio joined in the attack on 5 January 1951 by maintaining that the North Atlantic Treaty did not legally obligate the US to dispatch forces to Europe and that in any case the president needed congressional approval for such action. This was followed on 8 January by Senate Resolution 8, introduced by Senator Kenneth S. Wherry of Nebraska, which stipulated that no American ground forces could be deployed to Europe for NATO purposes before Congress formulated "a policy with respect there to."[33] Truman would not let this opening legislative salvo of the Great Debate go unanswered, contending that as commander in chief, he could "send troops anywhere in the world" without involving Congress. "I don't ask their permission" he remarked at an 11 January press conference, "I just consult them."[34]

In the meantime, Eisenhower was preparing for what he had described to Truman as a "survey trip," a whirlwind three-week visit to eleven NATO capitals.[35] He began his tour in Paris, where he described the synergism in unified and combined command, emphasizing that there was "power in our . . . resourcefulness on sea, land and air. Aroused and united, there is nothing which the nations of the Atlantic Community cannot achieve."[36] Later that day in a radio broadcast beamed throughout the NATO countries, however, he was careful to point out that he represented no panacea and that ultimate success lay with European efforts. "I return to Europe as a military commander," he began, "but with no miraculous plans, no display of military force."[37] Nevertheless, as Eisenhower well realized, what he did bring was the power and prestige of his name and reputation. This was evident at an initial NATO planning conference in which the participants focused solely on the weakness of the alliance military forces. "I never heard more crying in my life," one observer recalled.

> And I could see General Eisenhower becoming less and less impressed with this very negative approach, and finally he just banged that podium, got red faced, and said in a voice that could have been heard two or three floors below that he knew what the weaknesses were. "I know there are shortages, but I myself make up for part of that shortage—what I can do and what I can put into this—and the rest of it has to be made up by you people. Now get at it!" And he banged the podium again and he walked out. Just turned around, didn't say another word, just walked out. And believe me there was a great change in the attitude. Right away there was an air of determination—we *will* do it.[38]

Eisenhower continued this type of exhortation with all the European leaders. Nowhere was the effect more dramatic than in Paris, where he emphasized to Premier René Pleven that the French did not have "enough confidence in their own potentialities" and that France should begin to live up to its reputation as a great nation. Pleven, he urged, should "beat the drums to reaffirm the glory of France." The premier was profoundly affected. "I thank you," he responded; "you have aroused new confidence in me already." Afterward, when Gruenther told Eisenhower that he had been "superbly eloquent," the supreme commander snorted: "Why is it that when I deliver such a good talk, it has to be an audience of one?"[39]

At the same time, Eisenhower did not mince words. In each capital he stressed the necessity of being able to convince the US Congress and public upon his return that the NATO partners were doing their share. In short, there was a need to report that Europe was not waiting to see what the United States would do but was moving forward rapidly to build up its forces. From this perspective, he emphasized repeatedly that Europe was "behind time" and that each nation must "rise above local political considerations" and find ways to increase its efforts. It was simply "a matter of heart."[40]

Eisenhower's last meeting of the tour was in Ottawa on 26 January. The next day he flew to New York City and from there to West Point, where he spent four days at the Hotel Thayer writing a speech that he was to deliver to Congress. It was a difficult task. "Few speeches have ever given me so much trouble," he recalled years later.[41] On the one hand, Eisenhower had to convince the members of Congress of the magnitude and imminence of the Soviet threat. On the other, his task was to persuade those politicians that the United States could meet that threat without excessive cost. At the same time, it was necessary for Congress to understand that while the nations of Western Europe were too weak to defend themselves, they possessed the spirit and determination to reach this goal if provided American aid. Finally, in terms of at least part of that assistance, Eisenhower had to convince Congress that as SACEUR he required immediately more US troops in Europe, but that the numbers would not be large nor the duration long. In the end, it was a matter of symbols and morale. "NATO needs an eloquent and inspired Moses," he observed to Lovett, "as much as it needs planes, tanks, guns and ships."[42]

On 31 January, Eisenhower arrived in Washington. At Blair House the president escorted the general to a meeting with the cabinet that also included the vice president and the House speaker. He had asked "Ike," Truman said, to give them his impressions of the European trip. The new SACEUR emphasized that the American contribution was necessary to implement his strategic concept of defense based on the synergism of land, sea, and air forces in a combined unified command. Europe was shaped like "a long bottleneck," he explained. The wide part of the bottle was Russia; the neck was Western Europe, stretching down to Spain. On either side of the bottleneck were bodies of water controlled by NATO with land on the far side of the water to be used for airbases. To the north was the North Sea, with Scandinavia behind it. To the south was the Mediterranean, with North Africa and the Near East on the other side. As a consequence, it would be possible to apply great air and sea power on the flanks and rely on land power in the center. "Then," Eisenhower concluded, "if the Russians tried to move ahead in the center, I'd hit them awfully hard from both flanks. I think if we build up the kind of force I want, the center will hold and they'll have to pull back."[43]

The following morning, 1 February, Eisenhower addressed an informal, limited joint session of Congress in Coolidge Auditorium at the Library of Congress. That afternoon he entertained questions in a two-hour combined executive session of the Senate Armed Services and Foreign Relations committees, and the next day he conducted a similar session with the equivalent House committees. He used questions on his future command structure to register his concern about what he already perceived as assaults on the unity of his new command: "I do not see how strategically . . . you can separate the Mediterranean and the North Sea from Europe." At the same time, his estimate of up to thirty years' sustentation of NATO's state of preparedness stunned the legislators, not yet adjusted to the protracted outlook of the Cold War. In any event, he emphasized, it was important not to underestimate NATO's strength or Soviet problems. "No man ever thought clearly when he was scared to death. The staff officer you have to throw out is the man who comes in and says, 'My god, you're licked. Let's run.'"[44]

Eisenhower had performed well in muting the contradictions inherent in many of the themes he presented to Congress. In his prepared remarks, he effectively linked the concept of US national security to NATO's military viability, stressing the need for US forces, equipment, and leadership as well as patience. In the subsequent hours of congressional questioning "almost to the point of cross-examination," he maintained the theme that alliance unity was a feasible goal, that it was possible to deter Soviet expansion, and that there should be no limitations placed on the number of US divisions for Europe.[45] At the same time, his testimony served to quiet some congressional opposition by demonstrating that fears of a requirement for a much larger force were unwarranted. Even Senator Taft was impressed. "General Eisenhower has made progress in persuading the European pact members that their own safety depends on arming themselves adequately," he wrote. "Our aim should be to make Europe sufficiently strong so that American troops can be withdrawn from the continent of Europe."[46] But Eisenhower's success before Congress was also due to the aura that he radiated of optimism, confidence, and integrity. At one point in a response to a senator's query as to the best future course for the country with respect to NATO, Eisenhower responded, "We have just got to prove ourselves worthy of our own history." "God bless you!" the senator replied.[47]

The joint hearings of the Senate Armed Services and Foreign Relations committees on the Wherry Resolution touched on many of the themes addressed in the congressional interaction with Eisenhower. On 15 February the secretary of defense opened the proceedings by revealing the administration's plans to dispatch four divisions to Europe to augment the two already on occupation duty in Germany. The total of six divisions, Marshall stated, was essential for Eisenhower, who "had been given one of the hardest jobs that has ever been given an American citizen." That number was sufficient for the present, but he could not predict "off hand" what might be required in the future.[48]

Marshall's revelation was designed to reinforce Eisenhower's assurance that US forces would constitute only a minor part of the proposed integrated force. And in fact, the figure did deflate much of the opposition. But it also stimulated some to question the feasibility of the project, to counter that the limited forces in the West could not hold out against the Soviet Union, particularly with the American addition of, in former President Hoover's description, "such pitiable forces."[49] Instead of additional ground forces, Senators Taft and Wherry argued in this regard, the United States should focus on strategic bombing and control of the seas. One solution to the feasibility problem, of course, was to increase American commitments—a possibility that went to the heart of the opposition's concerns as expressed in the Wherry Resolution. "I'm trying to find out," one exasperated senator declared, "whether this is only the camel getting its head under the tent, and whether 4 divisions will require 6 more and then the 10 will require 12 more, and where we are going, what we have to look forward to."[50]

For the rest of the month, political and military witnesses for the administration attempted to answer the congressional concerns. The additional four divisions, they countered, should be evaluated in terms of the deterrent effect of the existing forces. Moreover, as Acheson pointed out in an argument that must have delighted Eisenhower, the feasibility of the entire force must be considered in terms of the effect of joint synergism on the ability to deter. "It is not the case that ground forces would or could be sufficient by themselves," he explained, "or that air or sea power by themselves could or would be sufficient, but that the three elements of our deterrent forces, taken together, are the best means of preventing an attack from taking place."[51]

As the hearings proceeded, it became increasingly evident that constitutional issues remained at the heart of the Great Debate. Many of the Republicans, led by Taft, asserted that the president had exceeded his powers when he announced his decision to deploy additional US divisions without obtaining prior congressional approval. Administration officials outlined precedents to bolster their arguments that it was well within the power of the president as commander in chief to deploy American troops as he believed necessary. The secretary of state was particularly effective in continuing Eisenhower's contention that the North Atlantic Treaty was not limited to the collective defense of article 5 in terms of what should be done by member nations subsequent to an attack. Congress, he maintained, had recognized the need to build defenses in Europe before an attack when it passed the Mutual Defense Assistance Act in 1949. That recognition was also expressed the same year in the NATO Treaty, approved by the Senate, with its emphasis in article 3 on continuous and effective mutual aid by the organization's members. That provision clearly indicated, Acheson concluded, "the intent of all 12 nations to work out an integrated defense now, not to wait and develop such a defense only if an attack occurs."[52]

In the end, the Republicans abandoned the idea of legislation and resorted instead to resolutions without the force of law. On the second anniversary of the signing of the North Atlantic Treaty, two such resolutions passed. The president hardly saw this end of the Great Debate as a watershed event in executive-legislative relations. At a news conference on 5 April he did not address the subject of congressional approval. At the same time, he was deliberately ambiguous in dealing with a question concerning the dispatch of more troops to Europe without congressional authorization. He had always consulted the Senate on any major policy, the president responded, "and that situation will develop in the usual manner."[53]

Left largely unaddressed as the Great Debate ended was the German issue, despite the fact that the assignment of US ground forces to Europe was, in large part, to strengthen an integrated NATO structure that could accommodate eventual participation of German forces without risking an imbalance in European power. This implied a commitment to permanence that the administration could not admit to Congress. As a consequence, the Great Debate was incomplete, leaving the Congress unaware of the centrality of the German question in determining the scope and structure of the US military commitment to NATO. By that time, the SACEUR was already operating from Europe. Eisenhower found the greeting on his return to France as supreme commander to be "especially charming." The toasts to him were frequent and grandiose. He replied in his halting French, the sound of which, he recalled, approximated "that of a Kansas threshing machine with gear trouble."[54]

CHAPTER THIRTEEN

The European Command Test, February 1951–May 1952

I am always ready to refute the viewpoint of the pessimist who is ever present to remind us that alliances such as ours are historically irresolute and unstable.

DWIGHT D. EISENHOWER

I sometimes wonder at myself when I find I am still outside a mental ward.

DWIGHT D. EISENHOWER

EISENHOWER'S INITIAL TASK was to create a headquarters and a command organization for his disparate NATO forces. To this end, General Gruenther traveled from the North Atlantic Council meeting at Brussels to Paris on 18 December 1950 with five US officers. The SACEUR's creation of the command structure was tied into his "bottleneck" strategy for the defense of Europe that he had outlined to President Truman and his cabinet on 31 January. On 20 March, NATO's Standing Group approved SACEUR's establishment of Northern, Central, and Southern subordinate commands to be located, respectively, in Oslo, Fontainebleau, and Naples. That day, Eisenhower announced the appointment of Field Marshal Montgomery as his deputy supreme commander. Some had reservations about the choice, but Eisenhower told Averell Harriman that he found Montgomery to be "a fine team-mate."[1] At the same time, Eisenhower also appointed a British air marshal as his deputy for air and a French admiral as his sea deputy. These deputies, he informed Marshall, had no command functions and would be involved instead in "tasks of an administrative, advisory, consultative, and preparatory nature, involving contacts both with my own staff and with the governments of NATO."[2]

The correspondence with Harriman, the president's special assistant for foreign affairs, was a new communications link for Eisenhower. Harriman was the son of a railroad tycoon and an old friend of both Acheson and Lovett. He had been a special envoy from President Roosevelt to Britain and the Soviet Union during World War II and was closely acquainted with both Churchill and Stalin. Eisenhower had met the tall, stoop-shouldered diplomat in London during the war and had maintained warm relations with him ever since. Now, as SACEUR, he began to use Harriman as a sounding board and a source of advice and, because of his special relationship to Truman, as a conduit for communicating with the president.

On 2 April 1951, two days before the second anniversary of the signing of the North Atlantic Treaty, the supreme commander formally activated Supreme Headquarters Allied Powers, Europe (SHAPE), as well as Central and Northern commands. Eisenhower took personal responsibility for Allied Forces, Central Europe, and named two French officers as commanders of its land and naval forces and an American to head its air forces. A British admiral was his choice to command Allied Forces, Northern Europe, as well as that command's naval forces. A US general was in charge of air, and Danish and Norwegian generals commanded their respective national land components.[3]

With the activation of SHAPE, Eisenhower assumed operational control of all forces assigned to his command in peacetime, with the concomitant responsibility to ensure they were properly organized, equipped, and trained. There were also "earmarked" forces that the member nations had agreed to place under a NATO commander at some future time in peace, or automatically in the event of mobilization or war. Eisenhower was authorized to deal directly with national authorities on how the assigned forces should be deployed in peacetime and on the priority in which earmarked forces should be mobilized and come into his organization. And although each nation had logistic support responsibility for its own forces, it was SACEUR's responsibility to ensure that those national arrangements were coordinated.

The activation of the Central and Northern sectors emphasized Eisenhower's precarious theater strategic position. His command consisted of less than fifteen combat-ready divisions and fewer than one thousand operational aircraft, many of them obsolescent and situated on exposed airfields that were not strategically located or interrelated. In addition, his logistical support lines had been located primarily for occupation duties and were incorrectly placed to face the Soviet threat. At one point, as the

SACEUR began his first series of briefings at SHAPE on the situation, he asked one of his staff officers what the Russians would require to march to the English Channel. "Shoes, sir," was the reply.[4]

Eisenhower's principal problem was of substance, of getting hold of something concrete in the new organization. In a series of messages, he bombarded political and military leaders in Washington with complaints about SHAPE's "hazy, almost chimerical character" and its status as "far more of a mere conception than . . . a real organization." Another "thousand obstacles" in administrative details ranged from living conditions for the staff to nonexistent national and international budgets. To Bradley, Eisenhower complained of a "woeful lack of visible progress," and in his diary he lashed out at what he termed "this dismaying and unattractive assignment." Above all, his early task of organization was "cursed," as he described it to Collins, with all of the old conceptions of national and service prestige. "At the end of World War II," he wrote Harriman in this regard, "I thought that nations and services had learned well the rudiments of the principles applicable to unified military effort among Allies and would be prepared, in the future, to act accordingly. I was wrong!"[5]

In the meantime, the SACEUR found himself in the opening months of his command increasingly involved in nonmilitary matters; he perceived himself as "a modern Ishmael" in the "nebulous organization which we call NATO."[6] Because NATO was still in its conceptual stages, he complained to the secretary of defense, it lacked the offices and facilities for use in nonmilitary ministerial functions. Marshall, of course, had heard similar complaints from his protégé concerning nonmilitary responsibilities during the North African campaign. Perhaps conscious of this, Eisenhower emphasized the uniqueness of the peacetime structure, which was infinitely more complicated than that of World War II because of the increased number of nations, and the fact that "the economic and political functions enter into *everything* we do." And yet in this complex environment, the Council Deputies had not yet even agreed upon a cost-sharing method of apportioning the construction and operating costs of the different NATO headquarters. "Budgets and a dozen other administrative problems," Eisenhower concluded, "just sort of hang in the air for want of a definite and decisive authority to act on them."[7]

In May the North Atlantic Council acknowledged that military and economic issues could not be considered separately from the political sphere by incorporating the committees dealing with defense and economics. The council henceforth would not be a group of foreign ministers but instead the sole ministerial body in NATO, still run on a daily basis by the Council Deputies, which now became the permanent working organization representing all ministries of their governments concerned with NATO affairs. There was less success in centralizing the NATO agencies, in particular the proposal to shift to Paris the Military Committee's Standing Group from Washington and the Council Deputies from London. Such transfers, the Joint Chiefs advised Marshall, would "subject SACEUR to direct political pressure which might be detrimental to him militarily." Moreover, they pointed out, the proximity of the Council Deputies to SHAPE would diminish the authority of the Standing Group, in which US influence was currently "more predominant."[8] Eisenhower, who knew something about the political pressures inherent in co-location from his experiences in London prior to OVERLORD, was in complete agreement. There were also other factors, he added, ranging from shortages of accommodations to increased security risks. Most important, the current distribution of key NATO agencies among Washington, London, and Paris helped to sustain the interest of national leaders in the alliance.[9]

For Eisenhower, the basic problem was that the nascent organizational machinery of NATO adversely affected the unity of his command. Under the current arrangements, his chain of command starting with the Standing Group and extending upward to the North Atlantic Council was "well nigh useless" because of the time required for deliberations on critical issues, which included clearing decisions on a daily basis with NATO agencies and national staffs affected by the decisions. In addition, there were serious problems with the Council Deputies, which had been particularly helpless in dealing with his budget. At SHAPE, he noted in his diary, he had no one "to take over ministerial functions in finance, construction, policy etc etc," and no compensatory capability from the Council Deputies. "The weak unarticulated mechanism that tries to serve as the NATO overhead is futile," he concluded.[10]

Eisenhower continued to raise the subject of NATO reorganization in his visits to alliance capitals. The requirements of the SACEUR, he emphasized, had to pass through the time-consuming machinery of the committee system. If the governments could be represented by top-level officials with much greater authority in NATO bodies, more rapid progress would be possible. In order for alliance machinery to function efficiently, this authority must be delegated to the Council Deputies to exercise between the annual meetings of the North Atlantic council. The council, in any event, needed to meet more frequently, at least on a quarterly basis, in order to demonstrate unity of purpose and to bring public opinion along on major issues.[11]

All these problems associated with producing "efficiency in the *Allied* machinery," Eisenhower believed, could be addressed by first creating overall unity of command in the form of one NATO official charged with running the alliance on a regular basis. This "top Allied man" ideally would be an American who could also make final recommendations to Washington on the Military Defense Assistance Program. The supreme commander would be his principal military adviser. This unity of command would also extend to Washington, where one man "of Cabinet stature," responsible only to the White House, should be appointed to direct all NATO-related activities for the United States in terms of foreign aid and security matters. That official would "ride herd" on the entire interagency operation as a means "to get rapid action and solution to many questions which are now batted about among the different agencies in Washington for protracted periods of time."[12]

Despite these problems, the overall situation improved by summer. Montgomery was doing well as the deputy SACEUR, bringing his stature and professional expertise to focus successfully on building an integrated NATO force. And Gruenther had quickly become indispensable both personally and professionally as the Allied chief of staff and, equally important, as Eisenhower's American deputy to deal with US activities. By this time, the Council Deputies had not only approved the SHAPE budget but agreed on a final plan for apportioning the cost for the headquarters among the NATO nations.

A brief vacation was a momentary respite from Eisenhower's brutal schedule to build support for NATO in Europe. This involved numerous trips to alliance capitals, where he was always careful to talk not only to government officials but also to opposition political leaders, trade union leaders, intellectuals, and anyone who could mould public opinion. The initial obstacle, as he well understood, was more psychological than military. "Our problem," he advised General Collins, "is . . . one of selling and inspiring."[13] The key was to lift confidence by providing the reassurance that the United States was firmly aligned with Western Europe. The supreme commander accomplished this task in numerous visits by way of his personal prestige combined with his natural charm and magnetism and backed by the obvious political influence he could wield. This type of influence was on display early in this tenure as SACEUR, when Eisenhower traveled to Paris to attend a dinner given by the president of France for Margaret Truman, the U.S. president's daughter. After dinner at the Elysée, the party attended a performance at the Comédie Française, a moment captured by a visiting journalist and author: "The blasé audience paid only the minimum of polite attention to Miss Truman and the President of the Republic; then a few seconds later, Eisenhower entered the presidential box. There had been no announcement that he would be there but he was instantly recognized, and the entire house rose spontaneously and cheered. No greater tribute could be paid in France to *anybody*."[14]

At the same time, Eisenhower constantly reiterated to NATO leaders that Europe in the long run would have to provide "the heart and soul" of its own defense. It was not possible or desirable that the Continent should be "defended by legions brought in from abroad somewhat in the fashion that Rome's territories vainly sought many hundred years ago." On the seventh anniversary of D-Day, Eisenhower delivered a Europe-wide radio broadcast from Normandy to remind the Europeans of their stake in providing for a viable integrated force in NATO. "Never again," he emphasized, "must there be a campaign of liberation fought on these shores."[15]

Eisenhower devoted as much time to building support for NATO among the "veritable stream" of American visitors to SHAPE. Over and over again, Eisenhower urged a broader sense of national security on his visitors—that the true defense of the United States was on the Elbe River, that in fact the American way of life depended upon resources that came only from Europe and European colonies and upon other intercourse with the Continent ranging from trade to scientific exchanges. "I have never worked harder in my life," he noted at the time, "—even the hours that I get away from this office are normally involved in meeting with people who want to discuss NATO. . . . Since it is exceedingly important that people understand this thing if we are to have any chance of successful accomplishment, I feel it necessary to give such persons what ever time is required."[16]

On every front Eisenhower could see some improvement. But he warned against thinking that the task was "comfortably in hand." Real success would require time, effort, and understanding. On 16 July, *Life* magazine provided a review of SHAPE during its initial seven months, outlining some of Eisenhower's problems while describing "elements of hope" that stemmed from the supreme commander's determination for Europe to become unified and self-sufficient. Because of Eisenhower's "energy, resolution, lucidity and almost boyish enthusiasm," the article concluded, "the heart of Europe is beating more strongly than at any time since World War II."[17]

In the spring an opposition deputy in the French National Assembly castigated the supreme commander's decision to retain overall unified command of the central region. Eisenhower was not granting French General Alphonse Juin, the commander of Allied Army Forces, Central Europe, as much power as had been granted the northern region commander. Juin, in fact, did want operational control of the air forces in the central region. For Eisenhower, as it had been in his assumption of overall ground command after OVERLORD, the issue concerned the provision of joint resources, this time complicated by peacetime national and political variables. As a result, he mollified Juin by pointing out that the French general's plan would give both the British and American air forces the excuse to hold back allocations of air units to the central command. As overall commander in chief of the region, he promised he would ensure that the primary mission of the central air forces would be to support the land battle, "to include gaining air superiority," and that those air forces would not be withdrawn without his personal order.[18]

More serious command problems with the British affected Eisenhower's concept of defending Europe in terms of the security of both his Atlantic lines of communication and his southern flank. In December the NATO Defense Committee had decided that the appointment of a supreme Allied commander, Atlantic (SACLANT), should quickly follow that of SACEUR. On 19 February 1951 the Council Deputies nominated an American admiral to fill the position. Churchill, from the opposition bench, attacked the Attlee government's acceptance of the nomination, demanding whether there were no British admirals capable of filling the post. Attlee's promise to reconsider the issue touched off a bitter public debate in Britain. On 9 March the United States decided to delay NATO action on the SACLANT appointment while both sides worked on a compromise.

The search for a solution to the Atlantic command opened up another

Anglo-American command issue concerning the Mediterranean that would prove even more intractable. The British desired a military position in NATO equal to Eisenhower's, if not SACLANT, then supreme Allied commander in the Mediterranean. Such a command, however, posed serious problems for Eisenhower's plan of organization for his southern flank, which included the US fleet under Admiral Robert Carney as US commander in chief, Naval Forces, Eastern Atlantic and Mediterranean (CINCNELM), with jurisdiction from just east of the Azores to a point east of India and from the North Pole to the equator. On the one hand, the supreme commander was very much aware that his national authorities had not fully considered the "super-sensitiveness" of the British to "anything and everything Naval." The United States should therefore "be generous in the matter of titles" in the Mediterranean, even calling "the British commander 'Supreme' even though our contribution was greater." It was "absolutely necessary," he added, that the Royal Navy take over an important position in the command structure of the Mediterranean, as had Field Marshals Alexander and Wilson as successive supreme Allied commanders in that area from 1944 to 1945. On the other hand, Eisenhower also insisted that any British command in the Mediterranean "would not include control over the American Naval Forces given to me for protection of my right flank nor would it interfere in any way with my scheme of command for the protection of Western Europe."[19]

The result was a compromise. At a 8 June meeting in London between the chairman of the JCS and the British Chiefs, the British agreed to Eisenhower's arrangement for the Southern European Command on the understanding that the issue of future overall command in the Mediterranean was yet to be settled. On 14 June the Standing Group approved the command arrangements. Four days later, SHAPE announced the appointment of Admiral Carney as commander in chief, Allied Forces, Southern Europe (CINCSOUTH), and as commander of the Allied naval forces, Southern Europe, which he would operate with a separate staff. In the latter position, Carney would have control of the US Sixth Fleet, and until the evolution of a command system for the entire Mediterranean, he would coordinate his activities with those of Allies in adjacent areas. An Italian general was to command the Allied land forces of southern Europe, an American general the Allied air forces. With this solution to what he termed his "annoying little 'Southern problem,'" and with the establishment of his third subordinate major NATO command,

Eisenhower's framework for his "bottleneck" strategy was virtually complete.[20]

The SACLANT problem was solved in the new year with the January arrival of Winston Churchill in Washington for a conference with President Truman. Churchill, who had again become prime minister in October, still considered the Atlantic Command plans to be "utterly unnecessary" and a "deep humiliation for the British Navy."[21] At the second meeting, the president began by asking for Churchill's comments. The prime minister replied with what Acheson considered to be "one of Mr. Churchill's greatest speeches," requesting that Britain be allowed to play her historic role "upon that western sea whose floor is white with the bones of Englishmen." After more negotiations and a subsequent break, Acheson proposed a communiqué that would permit the British leader, "while not withdrawing his objections," to agree to the American proposal for a combined unified command. Churchill studied the communiqué for what seemed to Acheson an "interminable" minute before looking across to the president. "I accept every word of it," he responded. Truman was in agreement and declined a suggestion that the communiqué be reviewed for style before public release. He and the prime minister had examined it, he said, and one of them, at least, "used fair English."[22]

There were other unity-of-command issues for Eisenhower that stemmed from problems with his own national authorities concerning the role of US commands within the NATO military structure. During his tenure as acting chairman of the JCS, Eisenhower had come to accept a forward defense strategy for Europe that called for the Allies to defend on a line as far to the east as possible, using ground troops and tactical air and naval support, complemented by the strategic bombing of Soviet fuel plants. And in fact while occupying that position, he had directed the development of OFFTACKLE, a war plan based on the concept of forward defense in Europe and the Middle East. Among his reasons for this conversion were the pressure from European Allies, the realization of how difficult reentry into Europe would be, and the belief, based on his experiences in the unification "wars," that the forward strategy could resolve interservice rivalries by providing roles for all services.[23]

In August the SACEUR sent SHAPE force requirements to the Standing Group for a forward strategy with a "strong defense zone between the Iron Curtain and the Rhine," a strong German contribution, and sufficient Atlantic naval forces to provide direct support of NATO ground troops.²⁴ Like Eisenhower, the JCS recognized that the forces available to the United States and its allies were not sufficient to prevent the Soviet Union from overrunning Western Europe. This had been a fundamental assumption of OFFTACKLE and still obtained in the new US war plan, IRONBARK, issued in 1951. There was a fundamental difference, however, between how the Joint Chiefs and the supreme commander chose to plan for that assumption. IRONBARK called for defensive actions against stronger Soviet Forces as the Allied forces in Germany withdrew to the line of the Rhine. Any further withdrawal was to be directed by Eisenhower. Nevertheless, the US commander was also to prepare plans to extricate American forces "by withdrawal through western or southern French ports to the United Kingdom or to northwest Africa."²⁵

This stipulation struck at the heart of Eisenhower's concept of combined unity of command because of the reluctance by him and most of the European NATO and SHAPE leaders to plan for withdrawals from Germany in the event of war. The adverse political impact of such planning, the supreme commander believed, would simply outweigh any possible military advantages as he attempted to perform his primary task of building European confidence and morale. The result was a strongly worded message to the Joint Chiefs citing "serious differences of understanding" with them over IRONBARK. Eisenhower began by recognizing the JCS responsibility to have worldwide emergency war plans. "However, with respect to my area of responsibility," he pointed out, "the fact that the US has taken the lead in establishing a unified allied command structure, and has, with other nations, agreed to place its forces under that command, makes it mandatory that US emergency plans recognize clearly my authority as the Supreme Allied Commander Europe." Under such circumstances, he concluded, "unilateral national action with respect to forces under my command would be a complete breaking of faith. I consider, therefore, that it must be made absolutely clear that the directive of the President, placing all US forces in Europe under my operational command for the accomplishment of my mission, has no qualifications or limitations other than the responsibility to ensure the evacuation of US civilians in the event of an emergency."²⁶

The Joint Chiefs were adamant, however, and their response only emphasized the differing concepts of operation held by NATO and US planners. In the end, the supreme commander was forced to compromise with his own national authorities by operating under both the NATO and the

US concepts of emergency action. The SHAPE plan continued to reflect the forward strategy and emphasized engagement of the Soviet forces east of the Rhine. The more pessimistic US plan, which Eisenhower continued to coordinate on a not releasable to foreign nationals (NOFORN) basis, still contemplated a retreat from central Europe.[27]

The struggle to narrow the gap in alliance force goals also brought the supreme commander into a higher, grand strategic realm concerned with a unified framework for NATO and for Western Europe. The gap had been exacerbated by Eisenhower's focus on a sufficient combat-ready force that could act effectively early in his forward defense strategy and thereby also serve as a major deterrent. But the fact remained, as the SACEUR fully realized, that no matter how successful he was in persuading the NATO nations to increase their spending in defense, he would not even approach the achievement of his force goals without a German contribution. At the end of the day, he observed of the linkage, "we are either going to solve the German problem or the Soviets will solve it for us."[28]

On 24 July the six-nation European Defense Force (EDF) conference in Paris endorsed the concept of German rearmament administered as part of the European Defense Community (EDC) by a European minister of defense. In Washington, President Truman approved on 2 August a new American policy that favored German rearmament within the EDF structure. Under these arrangements, the EDF would not constitute a separate field army but would be based on the concept of supplying European contingents to NATO from the EDC to be used by the SACEUR "in accordance with military necessity."[29]

The experiences with the German issue only reinforced Eisenhower's belief that NATO's organization needed to be more unified in order to consider all elements of power in the evaluation of alliance military force goal contributions. SHAPE was only a military headquarters, he wrote to the chairman of the North Atlantic Council in early September, and its successful functioning was dependent on the "vitality and vigor" of the NATO machinery in taking political and economic as well as military issues into consideration.[30] A week later, Eisenhower returned to this theme in his written report to the seventh session of the council, which was meeting in Ottawa from 15 to 20 September. He began by supporting the Military Committee's request that member governments "fill the gap" between their level of forces and equipment and what the NATO military authorities considered essential for the defense of the North Atlantic area. At the same time, however, he emphasized that NATO must reorganize itself in order to supervise all implications of military contributions by alliance members.[31]

Nevertheless, because of the May reforms, for the first time member governments were represented at Ottawa by foreign, defense, and economic or financial ministers. Most significant, in response to Eisenhower's urgings, the ministers established a Temporary Council Committee (TCC) charged with reconciling the requirements of "fulfilling a militarily acceptable NATO plan for the defense of Western Europe and the realistic political-economic capabilities of the member nations."[32] In attempting to strike the balance of whether the military authorities were asking too much or whether governments were offering too little, the North Atlantic Council empowered the TCC to solicit information and assistance from all member governments and from the military and civilian agencies of NATO. To this end, the TCC established a three-man Executive Bureau, soon known as the "Three Wise Men," headed by the committee chairman, Averell Harriman, and the French and British vice chairmen.[33] The TCC began with an initial meeting at SHAPE to review the applicable military issues and to address the related problems, as Eisenhower observed, "that the existing civil machinery has failed to solve."[34]

On 24 November the eighth session of the North Atlantic Council convened in Rome to receive the progress reports on the initiatives from the Ottawa meeting and to prepare for final decisions at the next session, to be held at Lisbon in February 1952. The council instructed the deputies to consider a recently completed draft treaty and to make recommendations at Lisbon on the desired relationship between NATO and the EDC. The Council Deputies were also to examine an interim report by the TCC and be prepared at the next meeting to discuss changes that might be necessary in the organization of NATO's civilian agencies. At the same time, the defense ministers approved a new Military Committee midterm plan (MC 26/1), which provided Eisenhower for 1954 with forty-six divisions at the start of hostilities and ninety-eight ready and reserve divisions within thirty days. Although the JCS still considered these requirements to be austere, the council ministers asked the TCC to consider the feasibility of the plan in terms of nonmilitary capabilities and report back at Lisbon. Eisenhower agreed with this approach in his opening remarks to the council, praising the ability of Harriman's temporary committee "to get away from pious statements and get results." The key was to find ways to increase the NATO force while recognizing that "economic life [was] equally [as] valuable as creation [of] military strength."[35]

By that time, Eisenhower was dealing with increased attention and pressure focused on his intentions concerning the next presidential election. On 7 January, the day after his name had been placed in the New Hampshire primary without his permission, he issued a carefully crafted public statement. While acknowledging his Republican Party voting record, he said that he would not seek the nomination nor would he participate in any preconvention activities; he would, however, accept "a clear-cut call to political duty."[36]

On 20 February the ninth session of the North Atlantic Council began at Lisbon. The ministers began by welcoming Greece and Turkey into the alliance. Based on a report by the TCC, they agreed to provide for "the earliest possible build-up of balanced collective forces to meet the requirements of external security within the capabilities of member countries." To this end, NATO forces by the end of 1952 were to consist of approximately fifty divisions, four thousand aircraft, and "strong naval forces."[37] In the future, force goals would be projected three years ahead and examined annually in a process that would balance the requirements of NATO's military leaders against the financial, political, and economic capacities of alliance nations.

To Eisenhower's delight, the council also approved the draft treaty from the Paris conference to establish the European Army and recommended reciprocal security agreements under article 5 between NATO and the EDC member nations, thus providing formal linkage of West Germany to the North Atlantic Alliance.[38] Eisenhower was also particularly pleased with the ministerial efforts to reorganize NATO's civilian sector into a more unified and efficient structure. The council members fulfilled his wish for a "top Allied man" by creating the position of secretary general to be responsive to them and preside over an international staff in a permanent, unified secretariat. All civilian agencies, including those in London, were to be centralized in Paris, and some, such as the Council Deputies, were to be dissolved and their functions transferred to the North Atlantic Council as the only formal civilian body. The ministers also answered one of Eisenhower's major concerns by placing the council in continuous session under the secretary general through appointment of permanent ambassadors who would head their country delegations except for those occasions, at least three times a year, when the council was required to meet in ministerial session. Finally, the ministers at Lisbon expanded the SACEUR's power relative to the Standing Group by adjusting his terms of reference to provide him even greater responsibilities for planning the provision of equipment and logistic support. As the conference drew to a close on 25 February, Acheson wired an exultant final report to the president. "We have something pretty close to a grand slam," he concluded.[39]

The success of the Lisbon conference, along with his March victories in the New Hampshire and Minnesota primaries, brought more pressure on Eisenhower to declare his political plans. One result was that on 2 April he requested relief from his duties as SACEUR effective 1 June. At the same time, Eisenhower issued the first annual SACEUR report, which stressed that "the tide has begun to flow our way and the situation of the free world is brighter than it was a year ago."[40] He emphasized the more than fifty divisions promised to NATO by the end of the year, the new focus on creating priority reserve divisions, and the prospects of German contributions through the EDC. Moreover, as he prepared to depart, his command had thirty-five active and ready divisions and almost three thousand aircraft—more than double SHAPE's strength when he had activated the headquarters a year before. And thanks to command-post exercises in the fall, those units had greatly improved their cohesion and combat readiness. At the same time, SHAPE and the subordinate headquarters were beginning to function effectively together and were well advanced in the construction and improvement of airfields and communication facilities, as well as in the provision of support troops.[41]

The supreme commander, in fact, had no illusions about the situation and warned at the beginning of the report that despite progress, "there is no real security yet achieved in Europe; there is only a beginning."[42] From this perspective, he understood that the complete Lisbon force goals were probably unattainable. Moreover, it was impossible to ignore the 103 divisions deployed by the Soviet Army in Eastern Europe and the western USSR, which caused some humorists to note the similarity of NATO at three years of age to the Venus de Milo—all SHAPE and no arms. But Eisenhower also realized that the Lisbon goals bolstered the public perception of the intentions and capabilities of the alliance, while providing impetus to efforts at increasing the quantity and quality of forces for SHAPE. A major part of that impetus would come from the annual defense review procedures that he had helped to institute in NATO. Thanks to Eisenhower's efforts, the reviews were to be conducted on an international basis with the information provided by the NATO governments on the details of their national military, industrial, and fiscal programs to be more extensive and more complete than allies had ever exchanged either in war or peace.

Eisenhower could also look back on other specific accomplishments during his sixteen months as SACEUR. He used the sweeping authority granted to him by the Allies to deal with political and military leaders in order to create an effective integrated force that successfully militarized NATO. During that period, there were parochial national problems with the unity of the combined command that he created, not only from old allies but from his own government as well. Many of these problems stemmed from his abiding belief in the synergism of joint land, sea, and air action. He jealously guarded those joint assets that were under his combined command or supported that command, particularly if, as in Admiral Carney's case, they contributed to his "bottleneck" strategy. At the same time, his dealings with Washington on such matters only reinforced his strong conviction that the overall American unification process was in great need of improvement, particularly in terms of a more streamlined political-military chain of command and the mitigation of service rivalries. Eisenhower dealt with most of these issues successfully by adjusting the hard-earned lessons acquired during his previous wartime command in Europe to the peacetime limitations of the Cold War. The result was that the first SACEUR was the successful purveyor of the concept that combined and joint command under NATO could work, and that integrated forces and headquarters could serve as an effective deterrent to the Soviets.

Eisenhower also used his power and prestige to exert pressure for reform of the nascent NATO machinery. Just as he had translated under his vision of overall unified command the concepts of theater unity of command and effort to the need for unification at the national level after 1945, so too during 1951 did he move from his efforts at unified military integration of national forces to those involving a unified NATO structure capable of addressing holistically political and economic as well as military considerations. This pattern of overall unity was part of Eisenhower's larger vision of a United States of Europe with an integrated multinational European Army capable of absorbing the German contribution so necessary to the achievement of NATO'S future force goals. And because of his efforts, three days before he turned over his command to General Ridgway, the Europeans signed a treaty creating the EDC. In the future, the treaty would not be ratified by the French. But it would make possible alternatives that during Eisenhower's tenure as president would ensure West German rearmament and key contributions by that nation to NATO forces.[43]

As SACEUR, Eisenhower also came to symbolize the American commitment to Europe. He often talked of his NATO position as being only one-twelfth American. But as he realized, the NATO members also perceived him as the leading US spokesman and, to a degree, a roving ambassador. European statesmen often sought him out to gauge the US response to various policies while also attempting to obtain his support for national positions. In this capacity, by backing the American presence with appropriate force and military assistance commitments, the first SACEUR reassured the Europeans that they could count on US support against any possible Soviet incursion.

Eisenhower was able to fulfill this function successfully because he worked on his ties to Washington even more assiduously than he had in World War II. That conflict had been a far simpler time, when his American chain of command had consisted of General Marshall as his principal contact. For the supreme commander in peacetime, the task was more complex. In the new environment, he became particularly effective in maintaining good relations with the president either by communicating directly with him or through his special assistant, Averell Harriman. It was an important achievement, especially at a time when Eisenhower's proconsul counterpart in Asia, General MacArthur, was locked in a bitter struggle with civilian authority. At the same time, he was equally successful with Congress, nurturing favorable ties in countless briefings to visiting congressmen that paid dividends in the form of legislative support for NATO.[44]

In the end, when Eisenhower departed Europe, he left considerable achievements. Soviet power had not spread in Europe, the United States had increased its presence there, and NATO had a well-integrated defense force as well as a mechanism to coordinate the military, economic, and political strands of power in the overall defensive effort. Through his prestige, power, and personal magnetism, Eisenhower had created the kind of unity in his command that had occurred in the past only after war had forced nations to join in a common cause. In fact, from his perspective, the establishment of a successful unified command in peacetime was the best way of assuring that nations would not be forced to join such a command for war. It was this peacetime unity of command and unity of effort, backed by the US presence and Eisenhower's direct leadership and diplomacy, that was so instrumental in raising the morale and self-confidence of the Western Europeans. This had always been the supreme commander's primary goal. If many of his accomplishments were more of the spirit than in the achievement of the number of troops in the field and in reserve that he desired, the fact remains that they were the bedrock of the structure for the most enduring peacetime alliance and combined unified command in history.

PART SIX

Peacetime Unification and Unity of Effort and Command, 1952–1958

CHAPTER FOURTEEN

Executive Reform and the New Look: Strategic Strains on the Concept of Unified Command, 1953

> As a former soldier who has experienced modern war at first-hand and now as President and Commander in Chief of the Armed Forces of the United States, I believe that our Defense Establishment is in need of immediate improvements.
>
> DWIGHT D. EISENHOWER

> I don't believe that any of us are smart enough—and I put in 40 years in that business, as you know—I don't believe any of us are smart enough to lay out a blueprint for a perfect organization. I believe you have to try something and correct it a little, and try something else and correct it a little.
>
> DWIGHT D. EISENHOWER

DWIGHT EISENHOWER ENTERED office as president of the United States with a blend of military-political experience unmatched by any of his predecessors, including George Washington and Ulysses S. Grant. In nonstop assignments since he entered the War Department in late 1941, the new chief executive had developed extraordinary insight into the grand strategic problems of integrating all facets of military power with the political, economic, and psychological elements of national power. Consequently, he began his administration with a clear conception of what he later called "logical guidelines for designing and employing a security establishment."[1] The conception was tied to the expanded post-1945 vision of US national security, from which had emerged a grand strategic consensus for US global involvement to contain the Soviet Union on the Eurasian landmass, a vision to which Eisenhower fully subscribed.

The consensus on containment survived arguments over whether the resultant policy should be particularistic or universalistic or whether the primary threat was the ideological menace of communism or the geopolitical form of the Soviet great power. There was, however, a price to pay for the consensus. The ability of each administration to remain in office after 1945 became dependent on reducing the tension between the foreign and domestic components of US national security, a tension increasingly exacerbated, as Eisenhower assumed office, by the requirements of containment. One result was that the application of national ways and means of implementing grand strategy during the Cold War fell into two distinct patterns: cost minimization and risk minimization. Strategic actions designed to minimize cost tended to escalate risks, while those aimed at minimizing risks tended to drive up costs. The alternation between the two patterns had profound social, political, economic, and military implications.[2]

The cost minimization approach to containment allowed the United States to choose not only the time and place of responding but the appropriate elements of national power as well. The basic requirement of the strategy was to distinguish between vital and peripheral US interests. At the heart of this approach was the belief that any attempt to generate enough means to meet all possible threats in implementing the grand strategy could bankrupt the country or at the very least have seriously adverse societal impacts.[3]

The Truman administration officially promulgated the strategy of containment in the March 1947 Truman Doctrine. But despite the apparent open-ended, global commitment implicit in that strategy, the administration quickly adopted the cost-minimizing pattern of implementation. The basic problem with that approach, however, as Korea would prove, was that the strategic premise of making rational distinctions between vital and peripheral interests did not take into consideration psychological insecurities, in which losses of peripheral areas to Soviet domination might be perceived as damaging to more vital ones. For such scenarios, minimizing costs appeared to add the possible loss of deterrent credibility to the concomitant increase in risk. These insecurities, as John Lewis Gaddis has pointed out, "could as easily develop from the distant sound of falling dominoes as from the rattling of sabers next door."[4]

The second pattern of strategic ways and means—risk minimization— also emerged in the Truman years, outlined in NSC-68. That document officially enshrined the strategic objective of containing the expansion of the Soviet Union for an indefinite period until the Kremlin "[modified] its behavior to conform to generally accepted international standards."[5]

NSC-68 outlined a risk-minimizing strategy based on the fundamental assumption that the United States could generate enough means to defend its interests wherever they existed. Accordingly, there was no need to differentiate those interests that were vital from those that were not. But as risks were lowered, the costs inevitably increased. Additionally, the decision to respond wherever aggression occurred placed the United States in a reactive mode, leaving it to potential adversaries to determine how and under what circumstances American resources would be expended. When the Korean War dragged on, public frustration mounted. With the prospect of indefinitely high expenditures of men and matériel for a type of conflict alien to American tradition, this public frustration began to erode the authority of the Truman administration to pursue its approach to grand strategy.

As a result, Eisenhower began his administration with a new national security policy called the New Look, a cost-minimizing reaction to the risk-minimizing strategy of the last years of the Truman administration. The new president perceived that any attempt to generate enough means to protect undifferentiated interests against all possible threats would require a degree of fiscal austerity that would alter American society— that any attempt at absolute risk-free security might destroy what the United States was trying to achieve. For Eisenhower, ever conscious of the tension between foreign and domestic policy, national security and economic stability went hand in hand. He believed that if the American public perceived the cost of internationalism as indefinite national sacrifice, the result would be isolationism. No one more eloquently than this former soldier tied together the domestic and foreign implications of the national security state as it emerged in the long twilight war:

> Every gun that is made, every warship launched, every rocket fired signifies, in the final sense, a theft from those who hunger and are not fed, those who are cold and are not clothed. . . . The cost of one modern heavy bomber is this: a modern brick school in more than 30 cities. It is two electric power plants, each serving a town of 60,000 population. It is two fine, fully equipped hospitals. It is some 50 miles of concrete pavement. We pay for a single fighter plane with a half million bushels of wheat. We pay for a single destroyer with new homes that could have housed more than 8,000 people.[6]

The focus on the balance of security and economic solvency caused Eisenhower to expect the Joint Chiefs to subordinate their positions as heads of their respective services to their corporate duties as members of the JCS, dealing with "the great decisions which increase or decrease the chance of war" without descending into "minute details of tactical and operational procedures."[7] The Joint Chiefs, however, found it difficult to adapt completely to such a role. Agreement on ways and means of deterrence and war fighting was a difficult proposition for officers who, less than a decade after the passage of the National Security Act, had been shaped by years of parochial service approaches to military strategy. The problem was only exacerbated in a time of drastic budget reductions when the Joint Chiefs were forced to allocate scarcity. The results were disagreements within that organization that in 1952 were perceived by the public as a tendency for the individual members of the JCS to place service interests above those of the nation. All this buttressed a general consensus by that time that the five-year-old defense establishment was badly in need of change. The Republican presidential candidate agreed, charging in a September 1952 campaign speech that the military unification process still consisted of "too much form and too little substance" and that the Department of Defense wasted "time, money, and talent with equal generosity." At the same time, Eisenhower called for the creation "at the earliest possible date next year" of a commission made up of "the most capable civilians in our land" to study the operations and functions of the department.[8]

The consensus for change was generally bipartisan, particularly as far as the departing Democratic secretary of defense, Robert A. Lovett, was concerned. When Lovett took over the Defense Department at Marshall's request in September 1951, he had expected to work within the existing system. But because of the unprecedented growth of the military establishment during the Korean War, he was forced to operate in a structure that he increasingly perceived as defective. Lovett expressed his dissatisfaction in a letter to Truman on 18 November 1952 in response to the president's earlier request for suggestions concerning Pentagon organization where unification might be "profitably continued."[9] At the outset, Lovett framed the issue in blunt terms, emphasizing that the United States "should not deliberately maintain a Department of Defense organization which in several parts would require drastic reorganization to fight a war." In order to remedy the situation, he outlined issues still outstanding from the amended National Security Act of 1949 and proposed a series of changes long advocated by Eisenhower. There were still "contradictions and straddles" in the legislation, he believed, that rendered ambiguous his authority and power over the military departments and the JCS, as well as his primacy as adviser to the president on defense matters. Questions in this regard were being raised by "legal beavers" and should be "clarified definitively."[10]

In the meantime, preparations were under way for the new administration. Eisenhower was diligently searching for Lovett's replacement. "We have tried two investment bankers, a lawyer, and a soldier—and we are not yet unified," he wrote Gruenther on 26 November. "I believe it takes a man who is used to knocking heads together and who is not easily fooled."[11] That man was Charles Wilson, an engineer born in 1890, the same year as Eisenhower, who had worked his way up in the automotive world to become the president of General Motors in 1941. For Eisenhower, Wilson appeared to be just the type of tough-minded businessman that was required to advance unification in the Pentagon and thus ensure that the military establishment worked together to combine maximum efficiency with minimum cost. That establishment was currently headed by members of the JCS whose appointments from the Truman administration would expire the following summer. All were old acquaintances of the president-elect, and he counted three of them, Generals Bradley, Collins, and Vandenberg, as personal friends.

These men and the rest of the newly formed cabinet were present on 20 January 1953 as Eisenhower was sworn in on the Capitol steps as the thirty-fourth president of the United States. After the ceremony, he reviewed a gigantic ten-mile inaugural parade that included eighty-five-ton atomic cannons and ten floats depicting scenes from his life. At one point, a mounted cowboy acting with permission of the Secret Service threw a lasso around the president's shoulders. As he watched the West Point cadets march by the reviewing stand opposite the White House, the new president recalled his participation as a cadet in a similar parade forty years earlier for Woodrow Wilson. He was equally reflective the next day, his first in the new job. "Plenty of worries and difficult problems," he noted in his diary. "But such has been my portion . . . since July '41—even before that!"[12] By that time, Lovett's 18 November letter had entered the public domain with a front-page article in the *New York Times* entitled "Lovett Criticizes Defense Machine as Weak in Crisis." A few days later, the Pentagon released the original letter, adding to the growing public impression of organizational problems in the Department of Defense.[13]

Both Eisenhower and Wilson were receptive to Lovett's ideas and en-sured that he was a member of the new committee named by the presi-dent on 19 February 1953 to recommend organizational improvements in the Department of Defense. The committee was headed by Nelson Rockefeller, the energetic scion of the famous and wealthy family, who was already chairing the President's Advisory Committee on Government Organization. In addition to Lovett, the panel's members included Eisen-hower's brother, Milton, and JCS Chairman General Omar Bradley. Wil-son also assigned a five-man staff and later, as consultants, three retired service chiefs, Admiral Chester Nimitz and Generals George Marshall and Tooey Spaatz. In his written instructions to Rockefeller on 26 Feb-ruary, the new secretary of defense emphasized Eisenhower's interest in the proceedings and the desire to explore a "gray area" in regard to the relationship of the secretary of defense and the JCS and "their relative direct and indirect relationship with the President."[14]

The committee moved expeditiously. Two dozen witnesses appeared, made up of former service secretaries and assistant secretaries of defense as well as the current members of the JCS—civilian and military person-nel who, in Rockefeller's estimation, "had the most intimate contact with the operation of the Defense Department since passage of the National Security Act of 1947."[15] On 11 April, Rockefeller sent the final report to the secretary of defense, noting in his cover memorandum that the commit-tee's findings could achieve "maximum security at minimum cost." This conclusion was bound to please Wilson, who found the recommenda-tions "sound and constructive" and dispatched them to the president on 13 April.[16]

Upon receipt of the Rockefeller report at the White House, Eisen-hower's special legislative assistant supervised its conversion by his team of specialists into the brief sections of the reorganization plan. Some committee recommendations could be implemented without "excessive difficulty" by executive action and were not included in the plan. But others required congressional action and were thus incorporated into the reorganization proposals. The question then centered on how to get the plan approved. To avoid the legislative process altogether, the White House decided to forward the plan in keeping with the Reorganization Act of 1949 as recently reconfirmed by the February 1953 Senate bill that granted the president authority to create new executive agencies or alter those already established. This approach, however, still required submission of the reorganization plan to Congress, where it would go into effect after sixty days unless either the House or Senate passed a resolution of disapproval by absolute majority. There was no danger of amendments with this approach since the law stipulated only the use of a simple up-or-down vote in the proceedings. At the same time, it was expected that the use of the plan option might make the "Armed Services crowd angry" since those members had a "proprietary interest" in dealing with the issue as legislation in their committees.[17]

On 30 April, Eisenhower transmitted a message to Congress containing Reorganization Plan No. 6—the sixth plan in 1953 concerned with improving organization in agencies ranging from the Executive Office of the President to the Export Import Bank. As a former soldier and now as commander in chief, he had come to believe six years after the enactment of the National Security Act that the Defense Department was "in need of immediate improvement." To that end, the president emphasized three major objectives in his message. First was the need for the military establishment to be based on fundamental constitutional principles and traditions, particularly those dealing with "clear and unchallenged civilian responsibility." To guard these principles, Eisenhower elaborated, it was necessary to reorganize the "basic channels of responsibility and authority" prescribed in the National Security Act through the civilian secretaries of the military departments and to make clear that the Joint Chiefs were "not a command body" but rather principal advisers to the president and the secretary of defense.[18]

As a result, the president advised Congress, he had instructed the defense secretary to issue by executive action a revision of that provision of the Key West agreement by which the Joint Chiefs could designate one of their members as executive agent for each unified command. Like the Rockefeller Committee, he believed that the provision had led to "considerable confusion and misunderstanding" concerning both the relationship of the JCS to the secretary of defense and that of the military chief of each service to the civilian secretary of his military department. He had therefore directed the secretary of defense to designate a military department as the executive agent for each unified command. Under this new arrangement, Eisenhower emphasized, "the channel of responsibility and authority to a commander of a unified command will unmistakably be from the President to the Secretary of Defense to the designated civilian Secretary of a military department."[19]

Eisenhower's second broad objective in the message focused on "effectiveness with economy" in order to maintain "an adequate national defense for the indefinite future." To accomplish this, the reorganization plan called for the abolition of defense boards recommended by the Rockefeller Committee. Reorganization Plan No. 6 authorized the addition of six assistant secretaries of defense to the three existing positions, all to be assigned the functions vested in the abolished agencies. The reshuffle of these functions would increase the central authority of the secretary and thereby the cost effectiveness of the Department of Defense.

Eisenhower's last objective stressed the need to improve the existing machinery for strategic planning. Since the national security legislation provided that the JCS would have primary responsibility for such planning, the president explained that he was taking administrative action as well as incorporating changes in his reorganization plan concerning that organization. The Joint Chiefs were "clearly overworked" and thus must be encouraged to delegate lesser duties to subordinates in their service staffs. In his memoirs, Eisenhower was more direct. "My objective," he recalled, "was to take at least one step in divorcing the thinking and the outlook of the members of the Joint Staff from those of their parent services." [20]

Reorganization Plan No. 6 was designed to place greater responsibility upon the chairman of the Joint Chiefs for organizing and directing the subordinate JCS structure. The JCS chairman would be directly responsible for managing the joint staff and its director. The selection of the director would be subject to the secretary of defense's approval, while the chairman would approve the selection of service officers for the joint staff. In the interest of broadened involvement in the strategic planning process, the chairman was also directed to provide for participation by civilian scientists and engineers within the JCS substructure. Taken together, the president emphasized, the combination of administrative changes and measures in the new document would "lead to the development of plans based on the broadest conception of the overall national interest rather than the particular desires of the individual services." [21]

Criticism in the press of the new initiative came from many longtime opponents of unification. Hanson Baldwin of the *New York Times* was opposed to any plan based on the "dangerous and absurd suggestions advanced by the Rockefeller Committee." Baldwin, an Annapolis graduate and longtime advocate of the Navy's approach to unification, emphasized that the plan was replete with hidden "jokers," such as the addition of new assistant secretaries to work for the secretary of defense, transforming his office into "something of a Hydra-headed monster." Moreover, the "seemingly innocuous" proposals concerning the JCS chairman gave that position power, prestige, and functions it was never intended to have. "It tends to 'box-in' the Joint Chiefs of Staff," Baldwin observed, "between a chairman, superior to them in rank and prestige, and a staff ostensibly serving them, but actually selected by their superior chairman."[22] David Lawrence agreed in a series of articles in the *Washington Evening Star*, which concluded that unless the plan was rejected in Congress by either house within sixty days, "America is to be given the Hitler system as a Chief of General Staff to do as he pleases with the armed services, thus reversing the entire tradition of American military history."[23]

As the spring progressed, Reorganization Plan No. 6 moved smoothly through the Senate. But in the House, the suspicion still lingered even within his party that the president was trying to centralize power by "Prussianizing" the high command. At the same time, Representative Clare Hoffman, Eisenhower's nemesis from the spring 1947 House Government Operations Committee hearings on unification, had sprung into action. Hoffman was still head of that committee and very much opposed to enlarging the powers of the JCS chairman. As a consequence, on 27 May he introduced a resolution allowing all provisions of Reorganization Plan No. 6 to be implemented except the two that authorized the chairman to manage the joint staff and its director and to approve the selection and tenure of that staff. It was time to discuss this issue, Hoffman announced as he opened the four-day committee hearings on 17 June, since the "people and the Congress heretofore have opposed a Prussian type military chief of staff in this country." The president's denial of any specter in his reorganization plan of a "man on horseback" was not convincing. "I believe he is well on the road," the committee chairman concluded, "and riding fast."[24]

On 22 June the Committee on Government Operations by a vote of 14 to 12 favorably reported on the Hoffman resolution for enacting Reorganization Plan No. 6 except for the two provisions affecting the JCS chairman. On 24 June, after the House Rules Committee denied a rule for the consideration of the resolution, the Government Operations Committee by a vote of 16 to 14 approved another resolution rejecting the entire reorganization plan. The administration immediately swung into action with intense lobbying efforts throughout Congress. On 26 and 27 June the entire House of Representatives debated the new resolution before defeating it 235 to 108. On 30 June 1953, since neither the Senate nor the House had taken unfavorable action within sixty days after the president's transmittal message, Reorganization Plan No. 6 became effective.[25]

With the new plan, Eisenhower was able to advance centralization in the Department of Defense about as far as he could and certainly farther than any other president could have at the time. Ultimately, however, he was successful because his reorganization goals were modest and were presented convincingly as such. He began by using the bipartisan Rockefeller Committee to emphasize incremental change in the Pentagon. And during the congressional hearings, his officials consistently stressed the administrative nature of the reorganization effort. This was also the theme during the presidential press conference on the day he transmitted the reorganization document to Congress. The plan was "not radical," he emphasized; and to a follow-up question on the uniqueness of his efforts with the defense establishment, he interrupted: "Not radical, not radical."[26]

On 1 October 1953 Secretary Wilson implemented Eisenhower's directions by issuing a revision of the Key West agreement, which substituted the military departments for the JCS as executive agents for unified commands with a line from him to the designated civilian secretaries of those departments. The revision, however, still included an "important proviso" from the Rockefeller Committee deliberations that had emerged intact in the president's 30 April message to Congress. The secretary of a military department was still required to authorize the military chief of that department to act for it in its executive agency capacity in terms of strategic direction and the conduct of combat operations in emergency and wartime situations. Wilson was careful to point out in the revision that in such circumstances the military chief would be acting in the name and under the direction of the secretary of defense and that promulgated orders would directly state that fact. But there was no disguising the de facto continuation of command status for the JCS under this provision—a status captured during the House hearings when one congressman, addressing the executive agency caveat, plaintively wondered "why we create something here that might possible [sic] be needed only in peacetime; and then when we get into a [sic] emergency, we revert back to what our experience has been in the last war and we are presently using."[27]

The compromise on executive agency was an unsuccessful attempt to square the circle of avoiding service interest orientation by the three service chiefs while recognizing that planning without responsibility was futile. But with that responsibility came factional perspectives; and this remained the unassailable fallacy in the expectation for the 1953 reorganization effort that if the Joint Chiefs could be relieved of some time-consuming service administrative burdens, they could rise above their service interests. This idea that rationality could be purchased with time assumed that there was a single right answer for the chiefs to discover if given sufficient amount of that commodity. But as Eisenhower would find out in his first term, group rationality concerning complex problems was not always possible even by patient deliberation. Equally fallacious was the idea that a service chief operating between staff and line was free to ignore the conditions of his office. In actual fact, he remained in effective control of his service only so long as he retained its confidence, which could be quickly lost if he was perceived to have abandoned his role as service spokesman in the JCS.[28]

The institutional basis of the JCS compromise also rested on the small increments in the reorganization plan to the powers of the chairman and the functions and structure of the joint staff. But even this progress was misleading since the chairman was still limited by the linkage of his staff to service interests, despite his own independence from such ties. This was buttressed by the principle of equal service representation which only strengthened the assumption that the members of the joint staff had some representative responsibilities. Moreover, members of that staff were still shaped by a lifetime of serving their particular service and often disagreed on the best courses of action to serve national interests—as the JCS had done even during the exigencies of World War II.

In the end, the effectiveness of Reorganization Plan No. 6 would depend on how well the president consolidated his first-term defense team to support the major changes he envisaged in the realm of national security policy and strategy, military force levels, and the defense budget. The head of that team was Secretary of Defense Wilson, who was Eisenhower's choice to manage the massive logistical functions of the Defense Department, ranging from procurement and storage to transportation and distribution. But Wilson was not to involve himself as Lovett had done in foreign policy or strategy. He was, in fact, as the president bluntly informed him, to "run" the Department of Defense in the sense of implementing national security policy, not of making it. Otherwise, Eisenhower, who clearly understood Wilson's limitations as well as his strengths, would be his own defense minister.[29]

To support the new secretary, Eisenhower decided that a new JCS was in order. He was influenced by Senator Robert Taft and other Republican leaders who perceived the current Joint Chiefs as partisans of Truman administration policies. Taft, in particular, who believed that General Bradley in his capacity as JCS chairman had overstepped his position in supporting the administration focus on Europe at the expense of Asia and on land power at the expense of air and sea power, had pledged during his campaign for the Republican nomination to replace Bradley if elected. Eisenhower's decision for the change was eased by the fact that the terms of the JCS members would expire in the summer of 1953. In May the president nominated General Nathan F. Twining, the vice chief of staff of the Air Force, to succeed General Vandenberg; Admiral Arthur W. Radford, the current commander in chief, Pacific, to succeed General Bradley as chairman; General Matthew B. Ridgway, the current supreme Allied commander, Europe (SACEUR), to replace General Collins as the Army chief of staff; and Admiral Robert B. Carney, commander in chief, Allied forces, Southern Europe, to be the new chief of naval operations.[30]

The president made it abundantly clear that the changes did not stem from any dissatisfaction with "my old friends," the outgoing chiefs, whom he had found through "years of experience" to be "loyal and dedicated men." The appointment of the chiefs, he emphasized to reporters, gave the secretary of defense the new team that he desired and did not mean abrupt strategic changes. Nevertheless, his administration would take a new strategic approach that would be made "without any real chains fastening to the past."[31] Eisenhower had good reason to be satisfied with his appointees. The new service chiefs were old friends or close associates. And all four of the Joint Chiefs had globalist views, with extensive experience in Asia as well as in Europe. Most important for the president, each of the new members had been a commander in chief of a unified command and could therefore be expected to think from a broader, joint and unified perspective on national interests with minimal service biases.[32]

At first blush, Admiral Radford was a curious choice for JCS chairman. A forceful, articulate, and assured 1916 graduate of the Naval Academy, he had been a spokesman for naval air power after World War II and a bitter opponent of the unification compromise in 1947. During the B-36 and unification hearings in 1949, Radford had opposed any strategy that relied primarily on retaliatory strategic nuclear bombing and provided a prepared statement to this effect that was so explosive that the secretary of the Navy requested that it be discussed in executive session. At that session, the admiral pointed out that he did not believe that a strategic nuclear capability would be "an effective deterrent to a war, or that it will win a war." In fact, he concluded, "there is no short cut, no cheap, no easy way to win a war. We must realize that the threat of instant atomic retaliation will not prevent it, and may even invite it."[33]

Eisenhower first met Radford on the trip to Korea in December 1952 as the president-elect. During the flight, the plane stopped at Iwo Jima, and Radford, as unified commander in the Pacific, joined the presidential party. The admiral remained with the party on the return voyage aboard the cruiser USS *Helena*. During that time, there were many opportunities for him to brief the president, and he found both Eisenhower and Wilson receptive to his outlook on the strategic and the global situation. US forward-deployed forces, Radford emphasized, were overcommitted around the world, particularly in Asia. As an alternative, the primary reliance should be on local defense using indigenous forces, which would allow many US forces to be concentrated as a "mobile strategic reserve" in or near North America. Most important, the admiral assured the president-elect that he had been "wrong in 1947" in his "disapproval of a unified command" and that he had come to share Eisenhower's belief that "the need for close co-ordination of land, sea and air forces in a nuclear war called for a removal of the old barriers between the services."[34]

In his new role, Radford would increase the independence and power of the position of JCS chairman beyond that suggested by its statutory basis. Reorganization Plan No. 6, of course, provided him somewhat more formal authority in terms of managing the joint staff. But one of the admiral's greatest advantages was that he supported the president's fundamental concept of national security, arguing that the economic stability of the United States was "of military importance" and that military professionals must "take economic factors into consideration."[35] At the same time, he had considerable influence over an essentially functionalist secretary of defense with little strategic understanding who normally deferred to the chairman in JCS disputes. "Usually, and I know of no case to the contrary," one general recalled of Wilson, "he took the advice of the Chairman of the Joint Chiefs of Staff regardless of the views of the separate service chiefs."[36]

Radford's most important advantage was that he was able to transcend the administrative and liaison roles of the chairman and serve instead as a type of executive subordinate to the president and the secretary of defense. Using this approach, he soon became as much an envoy for Eisenhower and Wilson to the JCS as he was for the Chiefs in dealing with their civilian superiors. His aggressive advancement of the president's strategic views within the JCS predictably angered the military leaders, one of whom later described the chairman as "an able and ruthless partisan, who did his utmost to impose his views upon the Chiefs."[37] Eisenhower naturally came to see Radford in a different light, as "a tower of strength in struggling for better teamwork among the services." Equally important for the president, his chairman "was nearly unique among professional military men in his understanding of the relationships between national military and economic strength."[38] This type of confidence ensured a positive symbiotic relationship between the two men in terms of strategic formulation that was unique in the evolution of the national security state. "Admiral Radford," Samuel Huntington observed in this regard, "probably played a more important role in shaping strategy than any other military man in military office between 1946 and 1960."[39]

As the chairman's relationship with the president evolved, it directly affected the functioning of the JCS and the state of civil-military relations at the highest level. As principal military advisors, the Joint Chiefs normally presented their views to the defense secretary or the president by memorandum that reflected either consensus on an issue or divergent ("split") opinions. Radford was authorized to present his own opinion on any issues on which the Chiefs were split, a function, he realized, that gave him considerably more responsibility and authority than appeared in law. "I have often pointed out to the Chiefs," he testified before Congress at one point, "that the more they disagree, the more power they hand to the Chairman."[40] On occasion, Eisenhower would assert that there were no expectations for the Joint Chiefs to "abandon their basic convictions or conclusions about security needs," and that he did not have all the final strategic answers. In this regard, he made clear to the Chiefs that his door was "open to them at any time," and that those who wished could always come "along with Admiral Radford" to see him—an important qualifying condition.[41]

The National Security Council (NSC) also played an important role in Eisenhower's relations with the JCS. The Joint Chiefs had a representative on the NSC Planning Board, which offered them an opportunity to influence papers that were going to the council for discussion. And the secretary of defense normally provided the papers to the JCS for comment in preparing the Defense Department position before an issue was addressed by the NSC. In addition, the president was also prepared to use the council as an outlet for the Chiefs to debate his policies. But thereafter, he expected his decisions to be supported and the military leaders to refrain from any public airing of differences. In this manner, he used the NSC to create more support for decisions already made in smaller, informal meetings, and at the same time to explain more fully to his key subordinates why he was making the decisions. Eisenhower prided himself on delegating a great deal of authority to the heads of his departments and agencies, his "operating lieutenants," and then "growled a good deal" if they escalated problems to him that he thought should be solved at their level.[42] But this really did not apply to the Pentagon, where, ironically, he was attempting in his reorganization plan to increase the power and authority of his principal civilian leader. For the fact remained throughout his time in office that Eisenhower dominated the policy-fiscal dialogue between the JCS and the principal civilian officials by acting, in effect, as his own defense secretary in dealing with the chairman on strategic matters and with the secretary of defense on budgetary issues.[43]

In order to deal with the Pentagon as well as other government agencies, the new president organized the White House staff along military lines. All papers for him were cleared through a secretariat headed by Colonel Andrew Goodpaster, the staff secretary who had overall responsibility for supervising White House paperwork and administrative operations. Equally important, Goodpaster was authorized to be a liaison officer with the Defense Department and often acted as an unofficial national security adviser to the president, providing briefings and ensuring that decisions were implemented. Goodpaster occupied a main-floor West Wing office and saw and briefed the president an average of one or two times a day. He was liked and trusted by all senior officials, whether in the cabinet departments or in the White House. McGeorge Bundy, in a January 1961 appraisal for the new president, described the Army engineer officer and his role as "tending the door and handling urgent messages silently—a wise and good man."[44] In addition, at Eisenhower's direction, Goodpaster attended meetings held by the president with various officials, particularly the Joint Chiefs and the secretary of defense. In this capacity, he always prepared memoranda of these conferences, the precision, accuracy, and objectivity of which, as Stephen Ambrose has observed, made them "the single most reliable source for what happened in the Eisenhower presidency."[45]

The evolving staff procedures of the new administration were initially focused on the 1954 fiscal year defense budget of more than $46 billion bequeathed by the Truman presidency. The debate between Eisenhower's civilian and military advisers on this budget continued throughout March and April and only reinforced his determination to reform the Pentagon and to replace the Joint Chiefs. Pitted against the JCS was Secretary of the Treasury George Humphrey, a businessman from Cleveland, who believed in balancing the federal budget and emphatically stated, "From now on out this Government must pay its way."[46]

At the end of April, the president approved NSC 149/2, a new national security policy that documented the administration's abandonment of the policy from the Truman years of US preparation for global war by the mid-1950s. Based on the guidelines for the new military program in NSC 149/2, Eisenhower approved a revised defense budget for fiscal year 1954 that was drafted by the Office of the Secretary of Defense and the military departments without the assistance of the JCS. On 7 May 1953 the revised budget of $36 billion was presented to Congress, which cut the appropriations request even further due in large part to the president's successful public campaign. It was necessary in terms of US national security, he advised the nation in a radio address, to take a "middle way," between "a needlessly high rate of Federal spending" and a "penny-wise, pound-foolish policy that could, through lack of needed strength, cripple the cause of freedom everywhere."[47]

On 16 August the new Joint Chiefs formally assumed office. It was a time of rapid changes in the international situation, marked by the signing of the Korean armistice at Panmunjom on 27 July and by the Soviet explosion of a hydrogen bomb on 12 August, less than a year after America's first thermonuclear detonation. On 13 October, at a meeting of the NSC to address the budget for fiscal year 1955, the JCS provided uncoordinated and virtually unchanged service-recommended force levels as a basis for that budget. Since the thermonuclear tests by the Soviets, Eisenhower was increasingly worried about an apparently endless rise in defense spending and what he perceived as the associated necessity for tighter economic controls and higher taxes. The Joint Chiefs were to reconfigure their force levels "on a genuine austerity basis" without cuts in combat strength; the defense secretary was to recompute his defense budget for fiscal year 1955 in accordance with the JCS actions.[48]

An equally important message from the president in the 13 October proceedings was his displeasure with the performance by the new Chiefs, all of whom were in attendance at the meeting. The Joint Chiefs, he stated, should not look for "a perfect defense." Instead, the utmost that they could hope to achieve was, in George Washington's words, "a respectable posture of defense."[49] Eisenhower's differences with the Joint Chiefs spilled over into a tense meeting of the NSC on 29 October, convened to finalize the new national security policy as NSC 162/2. Admiral Carney was the only member of the JCS present at the meeting. It was thus left to the chief of naval operations to make the military case on the interrelated issues of force redeployment from overseas and nuclear weapons. Eisenhower did not dispute the redeployment premise that overextended forward-deployed US forces should be disengaged and repositioned; the "real issue was not the pros and cons of redeployment" but the timing and scale involved in carrying out the concept.[50]

Carney was equally unsuccessful with nuclear policy. Throughout the fall, it had been obvious that the new approach to containment would focus primarily on deterrence through offensive retaliatory capability, chiefly provided by strategic nuclear weapons as well as through continental defense. Since that capability primarily involved strategic air power, it meant subordinate status for other parts of the military establishment, such as conventional ground forces. The NSC Planning Board called for the development and maintenance of a "strong military posture with emphasis on the capability of inflicting massive retaliatory damage by offensive striking power." The JCS position was that the "strong military posture" should merely "include" this capability with no reference to "emphasis," thus widening the choice of forces as elements of offensive strength.[51]

Eisenhower ended the impasse with a firm restatement of his preference: "In effect, we should state what we propose to do, namely, to keep the minimum respectable posture of defense while emphasizing this particular offensive capability." After all, deterring a war was even more important than winning one; and there was nothing in terms of deterrence that could compare with this retaliatory striking power. The president was adamant that he would "tolerate no notice of a JCS dissent in the record of action." The Joint Chiefs provided him military advice; he made the decisions.[52]

Beyond nuclear policy, the New Look addressed all the elements of national power—political, economic, and psychological as well as military. Containment of the pervasive threat of communism would succeed in the long haul because a strong and resolute United States would be able to exert a steady but flexible counterpressure to any Kremlin aggression. In the meantime, one outcome of the 13 October NSC meeting was a renewed attempt to create a military strategy that would justify smaller forces for fiscal year 1955 and "for the long pull ahead." In this strategy, the Joint Chiefs agreed to total strength of 2,815,000 by fiscal year 1957, a reduction from the current figure by 600,000 and a severe reallocation of the remaining personnel among the services. Wilson approved an end strength for fiscal year 1955 of little more than 3,000,000 personnel, with force levels that called for a 23 percent cut in the Army, 13 percent for the Navy, and 7.5 percent for the Marines, with slight increases for the Air Force. Based on these changes, the defense secretary was able to propose a fiscal year 1955 budget of approximately $31 billion and brief it to the National Security Council on 16 December.[53]

The new national military strategy called for a 28 percent reduction in force levels and large reductions in the defense budget by fiscal year 1957. And the most salient point in the new defense budget for fiscal year 1955 was the total estimated expenditure of about $37.5 billion, which compared favorably with the current annual spending rate of $44 billion. The president concluded as he and the NSC approved both documents that the program would be "kept under continuous scrutiny in relation to world developments," and any service could request a review of its program if changes were deemed necessary.[54]

Thus a year and a half after becoming president, Eisenhower had his strategic policy in the form of the New Look. Congress, in fact, never really examined the basic premises and concepts of that policy, and the administration's image of unanimity concerning it was marred only slightly during the congressional phase by Ridgway's defection, which always appeared more implicit than actual. The result was congressional passage of a Defense budget for fiscal year 1955 of almost $29 billion in final appropriations, approximately $1 billion less than even the president had requested. When Eisenhower signed the bill into law on 30 April 1954, it was a victory for his administration and the concept of the New Look.

For the Joint Chiefs, however, the result was a reflection of just how much the formulation of the New Look was a top-down process driven by the president and how relatively little it was affected by advice from the JCS. The Army chief touched upon this in his memoirs when he insisted that "the size and strength of the Army—in fact the pattern of the whole military establishment under the new administration—had already been decided upon, in outline at least, long before."[55] In any event, when the Joint Chiefs did not cooperate, Eisenhower certainly exerted pressure on them to expand their role beyond the military sphere in order to gain unanimity on a program consistent with the fiscal policy of the administration. At the same time, the president's emphasis on economy and the acceptance of the assumption that desired reductions could be made only by a shift in strategy calling for greater focus on nuclear striking power tended to pull civilian authorities into the strategic arena, just as his insistence on unanimity by the Joint Chiefs on a fiscally limited New Look program forced the JCS to move into the realm of economic national security.

In achieving his overall national security policy and his first defense budget, Eisenhower had grounds to be optimistic concerning the efficacy of Reorganization Plan No. 6 and the prospects of a unified perspective in Washington. But as the remainder of his first term would prove, this optimism was premature. Ridgway had already demonstrated the potential problems in attempting to persuade the Joint Chiefs to subordinate their professional service viewpoints in order to enhance the political acceptability of the New Look's military requirements. The attempt to "politicize" the JCS in this fashion resulted in confusion over the meaning of military professionalism that would have adverse consequences among the senior military leadership during the Vietnam War.[56] Furthermore, the strategic equation was already beginning to change. NSC 162/2 had referred to the future development of "mutual atomic plenty" on the part of both superpowers.[57] But the early emergence of Soviet strategic capabilities and weaponry would create a "balance of terror" that would undermine the New Look's two key assumptions: that America's military dominance would not begin to diminish drastically until the late 1950s and that the threat of US nuclear retaliation could deter both large and small aggression across the spectrum of conflict.

CHAPTER FIFTEEN

The Strains Deepen:
The President and the JCS, 1954–1956

While the Army is adapting itself readily to the employment of new weapons and new techniques, nothing currently available or foreseeable in war reduces the essentiality of mobile, powerful ground forces, the only forces which can seize the enemy's land and the people living thereon, and exercise control of both thereafter.

GENERAL MATTHEW RIDGWAY

The Chief of Staff of the Army, the Navy, the Marines, the Air Force, each one . . . puts in a bill of goods that if you just took it and added them up and put them on top of each other, they would reach the top of the Washington Monument. . . . But then someone who has a higher decision to make has to get this thing leveled out. Now we're having a New Look every day.

DWIGHT D. EISENHOWER

THE NEW LOOK NATIONAL STRATEGY rested on the basic assumption that the global situation would not deteriorate appreciably. Beginning in 1954, however, and extending through Eisenhower's first term, external developments began to turn discussion toward ends and ways rather than means in order to determine what national security goals were possible in the context of the new international environment. The French defeat in Indochina, the growing Soviet nuclear capability, and the crises in Suez and Hungary contributed to the president's deteriorating relationship during his first term with the JCS over issues that ranged from global strategy and the defense budget to service roles and missions.[1]

Planning for the defense budget for fiscal year 1956 began early in 1954 against the background of a deep recession that by March had reduced the gross national product in constant dollars by 4 percent from a year earlier and had caused unemployment to surge to a peak of four million. That same month, the cost estimates for fiscal year 1956 submitted by the services to the JCS totaled more than the estimates in the December 1953 New Look military strategy. At the same time, international events cast further doubts on the planned force reductions. The increasingly uncertain French position in Indochina caused the suspension of the administration's plans to withdraw US forces from the Far East. And in Europe, ratification by the French Assembly of the six-country European Defense Community treaty became more problematical, diminishing the prospect of the speedy addition to NATO of a West German component consisting of twelve fifteen thousand–man divisions plus naval and air units. Under these circumstances, Secretary of Defense Wilson began to agree with his military advisers that a second New Look might be necessary. "The next few months are obviously critical ones in world affairs," he explained, "and what happens in Europe and Asia during this period may force a soul-searching review of our specific policies, plans, objectives and expenditures."[2]

That type of review began in earnest with the fall of Dien Bien Phu on 7 May and the subsequent withdrawal of French forces into the Mekong Delta. On 21 May, in a somber military appraisal of the prospects for the free world, the Joint Chiefs warned of the increasingly dim likelihood of early and effective contributions by the Japanese and West Germans to the defense of their respective regions, which could lead to problems in maintaining sufficient ground forces for a strong mobile central reserve in the United States. Any delay in the organization of the central reserve, they emphasized, would probably necessitate a new look at personnel and force ceilings for fiscal years 1956 and 1957. The Joint Chiefs concluded by warning that time was running out for the United States to use its nuclear superiority. "With respect to general war," they reported, "the attainment of atomic plenty by both the United States and the USSR could create a condition of mutual deterrence in which both sides would be strongly inhibited from initiating general war." Under such circumstances, the Soviets might pursue global domination through a succession of either covert or overt local aggressions.[3]

The defense economy program of the New Look seemed to have come to an end. In early September, Chinese Communist forces began to shell the Nationalist Chinese offshore Quemoy islands. On 17 September the secretary of defense tentatively approved new JCS force levels, which in the cost estimates by the services in October were approximately $8 billion above the congressional appropriations for the fiscal year 1955 budget. On 7 December, Wilson announced that the administration would not make any plans for further cuts in defense spending unless the international situation improved. "We are close to the bottom," the defense secretary stated.[4]

The next day, these trends began to unravel. On the morning of 8 December the Joint Chiefs met with Wilson to discuss a program worked out by their planners to increase service strengths and force levels by the end of fiscal year 1957. The scheme involved maintaining the current strengths of the Air Force and the Marine Corps, while increasing the sizes of the Navy and the Army. The Army proposal, in particular, was stunning, calling for the creation of four more divisions, an increase of 179,000 troops above the strength ceiling approved in July. Perhaps the entire program reminded Eisenhower of how the New Look defense economy structure was slipping. In any event, he quickly responded that it was "unacceptable," and at the same time not only reaffirmed the manpower-reduction goals he had announced in December 1953 but directed that they be achieved a year earlier, by the end of fiscal year 1956, with some cutbacks to be achieved before the end of the current fiscal year.[5]

Eisenhower outlined his decision to the NSC on 9 December, emphasizing the continued centrality of strategic retaliatory forces, but with a greater focus on guided missile development, the mobilization base, continental defense, and ready reserve forces. The funding of these new priorities would be provided in part by money saved by personnel reductions. The president was anxious to have his military advisers on board. For even though the Army was the only service significantly affected by his new personnel cuts, the Joint Chiefs and the service secretaries were united in their opposition to a revision currently under way of the basic national security policy, in which they believed that the president and the secretary of state were seriously underestimating the increasing military strength of the Soviet Union.

That battle had been joined in a contentious and inconclusive NSC meeting on 24 November. At a subsequent meeting on 3 December, General Ridgway led off the agenda with his dissident views on force structures, force deployments in peacetime, and war strategy. His particular emphasis was on the Army's role in a general war and the need to avoid the use of nuclear weapons. In this regard, the general stressed, the Soviets would not resort to nuclear use unless the United States did, and the nation that used nuclear weapons first would incur the hatred of mankind. The logical consequence of this, he concluded, was that the United States must develop capabilities to deal with aggression across the entire spectrum of conflict.[6]

This rejection of the most fundamental of the New Look shibboleths ensured that the president's request for questions at the end of the general's presentation was met with deep silence. The president thanked Ridgway, who then left the room. In the postmortem, both Eisenhower and Treasury Secretary Humphrey dismissed the idea that the Soviets would not resort to nuclear attack in general war unless precipitated by the United States, and they reaffirmed that the country would destroy its fundamental economy and institutions if it attempted to field "all kinds of forces designed to fight all kinds of wars at all times."[7]

The general dissatisfaction of his military advisers was never far from the surface as the president made his budget decision public in the next few weeks. As a consequence, Eisenhower met with the Joint Chiefs and the defense secretary at the White House on 22 December to insist on their wholehearted support of his manpower and budget decisions. Now that he had made the decisions in his capacity as commander in chief, the president concluded, he was entitled to the full support of his subordinates, and he expected to receive it.[8]

A week later, the NSC Planning Board circulated a new draft national security policy paper, which the JCS still considered unacceptable; some days later, Eisenhower approved the amended policy as NSC 5501. The new policy affirmed the State Department's prediction of an indefinite extension of hostile coexistence due to military stalemate and mutual deterrence. At the same time, it reasserted such familiar themes as the need to develop and maintain "effective nuclear-air retaliatory power" and to preserve US national security without "seriously weakening the US economy." But unlike NSC 162/2, NSC 5501 also asserted that by itself, massive retaliation was insufficient for full security. Given the standoff of nuclear parity, the United States must develop forces in addition to those assigned in NATO in order to apply power "selectively and flexibly." These "properly balanced, sufficiently versatile, suitably deployed, highly mobile" forces would be capable of preventing limited conflict from escalating to total nuclear war.[9]

The inclusion of strategic nuclear retaliatory capability as merely one part of a varied force structure required to deal with the communist threat marked a key concession to Ridgway and a quantum leap from the second-class status accorded to general-purpose forces in NSC 162/2. From a policy standpoint on this major issue, the NSC had in fact responded both to the prospect of eventual nuclear parity and mutual deterrence and, in the short term, to the triumph of the Indochinese Communists in a conflict marked by the absence of overt military intervention on the part of other communist nations. If that policy had been implemented as written, the Defense Department would have focused on a more flexible structure, emphasizing those force requirements in the JCS military strategy document that were more conducive to limited war, such as sea and air transport capability, a quickly expandable mobilization base, and sufficient ground forces for a mobile strategic reserve. But Eisenhower's December intervention in terms of force levels and budgets for fiscal year 1956 ensured that those sections in NSC 5501 calling for conventional force increase would not be implemented.[10]

The JCS position on policy appeared to be vindicated on 10 January when the Chinese Communists began once again to attack the Chinese Nationalist offshore islands. The ensuing Formosa Strait crisis threatened to develop into a full-scale war and, until it subsided in early spring, formed a background for the congressional hearings on the fiscal year 1956 budget that Eisenhower submitted to Congress on 17 January. Given Ridgway's opposition to the accelerated manpower cuts ordered in December, his testimony before the House Armed Services Committee on 31 January promised to be controversial. But the Army chief of staff's prepared statements contributed nothing significant to the issue of personnel cuts. And it was only under direct questioning that he affirmed his belief that Army reductions during the current Far East crisis adversely affected US national security. Even then, the effect was mitigated by Ridgway's now familiar refrain that it wasn't up to him as an officer in uniform "to oppose a decision by the constituted authorities of our government."[11]

Eisenhower was hardly mollified. When questioned at a press conference in early February 1955 about the Army chief's testimony, he emphasized that his decision concerning Army cuts was reached after long study and conformed to his own "best judgment." Ridgway had been queried as to his personal convictions; "naturally, he had to express them." But, Eisenhower reminded the reporters, the general's responsibility for national defense was "a special one, or in a sense, parochial," in contrast to Eisenhower's overall responsibility as commander in chief. As for continued meetings with the JCS on defense issues, the president replied that he was never out of touch with the Joint Chiefs, conferring with them through the chairman several times a week. "I know their opinions," he added somewhat ominously, "and I know who agrees with me and who doesn't."[12]

To concerns about future JCS testimony voiced by Republican congressional leaders at a White House meeting, the president revealed a deeper resentment in his relations with his military advisers. He began quietly with the familiar acknowledgment that the service chiefs like Ridgway had to give their personal opinions when asked by members of Congress. But then the anger began to emerge. "Each service . . . has traditionally had at its head," he added dismissively, "people who think that their service is the only service that can ultimately save the United States in time of war. They all want additional manpower and they always will." Soon the subject turned to Ridgway's assertion that more divisions were required for deployment abroad in the event of a general war. Eisenhower became more emotional, pounding the table for emphasis. "What do you people think would happen if this city were hit today by an H-bomb?" he demanded. "Do you think you would vote or ask me to send the troops at Fort Meade overseas—or would you be knocking at my door to bring them in to try to pick up the pieces here in Washington? . . ."

> Suppose that attack were to occur tomorrow on fifteen of our cities. God damn it? It would be perfect rot to talk about shipping troops abroad when fifteen of our cities were in ruins. . . . Do you think the police and fire departments of these cities could restore order? Nuts! That order is going to have to be restored by disciplined armed forces. . . . That's the trouble with Ridgway. He's talking theory—I'm trying to talk sound sense. He did the same thing at SHAPE. I was there before Ridgway went over and he tried to ruin it with the same sort of talk.[13]

By that time, Eisenhower had decided not to appoint Ridgway to a second two-year term as Army chief of staff after expiration of his tenure at the end of June. On 18 February, General Maxwell Taylor was ordered back from his duties in Korea and Japan as commander of Army forces in the Far East to meet with the secretary of defense and the president. Like Ridgway, Taylor had been a division commander under Eisenhower in World War II, and as West Point superintendent after that conflict he had corresponded frequently with his former commander, by then the Army chief of staff. The president conducted a searching cross-examination, emphasizing that there were two requirements for the Army position.

First, Taylor must "wholeheartedly accept" that his primary responsibility was concerned with joint duties. Second, he must "hold views as to doctrine, basic principles, and relationships" that were in accord with those of the president. "Loyalty in spirit as well as in letter is essential," Eisenhower concluded.[14]

Although "surprised to be put through such a loyalty test," Taylor "had no trouble in responding without reservations."[15] He, of course, knew of his service's problems with the New Look. The Army's basic field manual on operations published the previous fall was highly critical of strategic airpower, pointing out that it was needlessly destructive and politically limited in small wars, in contrast to the Army's ability to fight decisively across the spectrum of conflict. For this reason, the manual concluded, Army officers were normally the natural choice to lead joint, unified commands.[16] At the same time, however, Taylor was aware that the most recent national security policy recognized that with the possibility of mutual deterrence, the United States would need versatile, ready forces to cope with limited aggression. All this, he concluded, "represented a most encouraging trend away from reliance on Massive Retaliation and provided what appeared to be authoritative guidance in support of a more flexible strategy."[17]

With Taylor on board to replace Ridgway, Eisenhower turned to Admiral Carney. In spring 1954 the chief of naval operations had testified to Congress that he accepted the fiscal year 1955 budget without reservation. In early 1955 his testimony clearly indicated that there were qualifications to his acceptance of the defense budget for fiscal year 1956. He would naturally carry out the reductions directed by the administration, but if conditions continued to increase overseas deployment strains, he might have "to ask for some adjustment."[18] This budding conflict was compounded on 28 March when the president was informed that Carney was the source of leaks to reporters concerning pessimistic views on the possibility of imminent fighting by US forces in the Formosa Strait. Eisenhower "exploded," talking "rapidly and forcefully" as he walked around the room. "By God, this has got to stop," he emphasized. "These fellows like Carney and Ridgway don't yet realize that their services have been integrated and that they have, in addition to myself, a boss in Admiral Radford."[19]

The final catalyst occurred on 10 May when the secretary of the Navy informed the president that he did not intend to ask for Carney's re-appointment. Eisenhower agreed, particularly because, as he noted in his diary, the admiral had rejected a fundamental tenet of Reorganization Plan No. 6 in his belief that "he has an authority entirely independent of his Secretary."[20] To replace Carney, Eisenhower agreed to consider the Navy secretary's recommendation of Admiral Arleigh A. Burke, a 1923 graduate of the Naval Academy and famed as a World War II combat commander in the Pacific, where his dashing emphasis on speed in operations had earned him the nickname of "31 knot Burke."

Burke, who had been a relatively low-level commander of the Atlantic destroyer force since January, was subjected on 17 May to a cross-examination and a lecture on teamwork and loyalty by the president similar to that experienced by Taylor. It was acceptable for an officer to fight for his opinions "within the family," Eisenhower began. But once the decision had been made at a higher level, the officer must obey it much "as he would a decision in an ordinary battle." In an earlier time, this had been the hallmark of the military. More recently, he added, "we began to break out, write articles ourselves, argue about whether a decision [was] good or not and to hell with what the President or anybody else thought." This had led to the idea of using Congress to override the president— a practice that must cease. "I am very much annoyed at the habit that seems to be springing up of a man seeking, or inadvertently finding, opportunities to talk on the outside," Eisenhower concluded to Burke. "That habit might belong to a bunch of politicians, not to the military."[21]

The decision to replace Ridgway and Carney did not solve Eisenhower's fundamental differences with his military advisers concerning strategic policy, the defense budget, and roles and missions. On 18 March 1955 the JCS sent Wilson a status report demonstrating that major decisions taken in 1953 and 1954 to reshape the US military force structure had not solved many of the deficiencies that existed two years earlier. Army and Navy forces were still overextended, the mobilization base was still inadequate, and no strategic reserve had yet been established. All in all, the Joint Chiefs pointed out, the administration's budgetary decisions had emphasized only two of the original eight requirements they had outlined as necessary for their military strategy: retaliatory air power and continental defense.[22] In large part due to Eisenhower's efforts with the service chiefs, this discontent was muted in JCS testimony on the defense budget in February and April before the House, which on 12 May passed the budget virtually unchanged.

In the meantime, the international situation was calming down. In late April at the Bandung Conference, the People's Republic of China announced that it was prepared to negotiate the Formosa issue. In May a sovereign rearmed West Germany joined the West European Union and NATO. That month, after almost a decade of Western effort, the Big Four concluded an Austrian State Treaty, which ended the Allied military occupation of that country and guaranteed its neutrality. By late spring, plans were under way for a Four-Power Geneva summit in July. Reacting to these trends, Congress proved even more fiscally conservative than Eisenhower, passing a fiscal year 1956 military budget on 30 June of only $31.9 billion, one billion dollars below the administration's original proposal.[23]

In August, after Congress had adjourned, the president and Mamie left for an extended vacation in Denver. In the early morning of 24 September at his mother-in-law's house, Eisenhower suffered a heart attack, a coronary thrombosis, and he was admitted to Fitzsimons Army Hospital near Denver. The president's convalescence was rapid, helped no doubt, as he noted, by the fact that he could not have selected a better time to have a heart attack: the economy was booming, Congress was not in session, and the international environment was unthreatened by any major crisis.[24] He was also encouraged by a wire from Swede Hazlett, who had suffered a second heart attack in 1953. "Welcome to the Cardiac Club!" his old friend wrote. "I'm sure you won't find our by-laws too restrictive, and that you can still do *most* of the things you enjoy doing."[25] On 11 November, Eisenhower returned to Washington, where he was greeted at the airport by five thousand people, including members of the cabinet, Congress, and the diplomatic corps. Thereafter, he began two months of convalescence primarily at his Gettysburg farm.

By that time, the Defense Department was in intense negotiations with the Bureau of Budget concerning the services' budget estimates for fiscal year 1957. Eisenhower was kept informed of the proceedings by Wilson and Radford in their visits during the fall to Gettysburg. In the end the president settled for a little more than $35.5 billion, $2 billion more than he had originally envisaged but substantially less than the original requests by the services.

Shortly thereafter, General Ridgway published the first two of six weekly installments in the *Saturday Evening Post* of his memoirs, which concluded that the tendency of "making military decisions on the basis of political considerations constitutes a danger to the country."[26] At a subsequent press conference, when directly queried on the Ridgway allegations, Eisenhower replied that he had never "made a military decision out of deference to internal politics"—certainly an overstatement, considering the nature of the New Look. Since 1940, he added, he had been receiving advice from every kind of military assistant. That advice, he continued, was "often expressing their own deeply felt, but, let us say, narrow fears. If I had listened to all the advice I got during those years, there never would have been a plan for crossing the Channel. Indeed, I think we wouldn't have crossed the Atlantic Ocean."[27]

By then Eisenhower was also heavily involved in reelection politics. His first conscious thought after rallying from his heart attack had to do with the end of any second-term ambitions: "Well, at least this settles one problem for me for good and all."[28] Nevertheless, encouraged by his physicians and his improving health and despite advice from his son, his brother Milton, and Swede Hazlett, the president announced his decision to run again at a 29 February news conference and in a subsequent radio and television address to the nation.[29]

At the same time, Eisenhower was caught up in the system that had evolved in his administration of beginning each year with the formulation of both a national security policy document and a new draft defense budget. Ideally, military plans were designed to provide linkage between policy and budget. On 12 March the Joint Chiefs produced a memorandum to the secretary of defense, stark in its pessimism concerning the "deteriorating" situation in the West that could place the United States in a short number of years in a position of "great jeopardy."[30] The next day, reacting to this "very dark picture," Eisenhower ordered the Joint Chiefs to rewrite their paper in order to avoid "a misleading impression" in terms of the military situation, the US alliance systems, and the global role of military power.[31] Two days later, the president did not even acknowledge the JCS memorandum when he approved the amended national security policy as NSC 5602/1. The result, as it had been with NSC 5501, was a lack of clear guidance needed by the JCS to translate policy into specific plans and budgets. Both calculated and uncalculated ambiguity made it possible, as General Taylor pointed out, "to find language in the 'Basic National Security Policy' to support almost any military program."[32]

On 17 April the Joint Chiefs submitted a new version of their 12 March report. Although the tone of the paper was less depressing than its predecessor's, it still retained its gloomy outlook. As a consequence, the services opened the new budget deliberations in mid-May with initial estimates for fiscal year 1958 that added up to more than $48 billion. This figure was far in excess of the highest JCS figure and in striking contrast with the $34.9 billion request for fiscal year 1957 currently being considered by Congress. It virtually assured severe disagreements with the president during the remainder of 1956.[33]

By that time, interservice disputes had taken a fundamental turn, with the Army under General Taylor increasingly challenging the basic premise of the New Look. Although the Army chief of staff did not discount massive retaliation as a response to a general Soviet air attack on the United States, he believed it was also vital to have a flexible response strategy for the most likely contingency of Soviet incremental expansion through aggression by indigenous forces or surrogates or by the encouragement of insurrection and subversion. At a meeting in early March, Taylor had not been successful in selling the JCS on the strategy, noting that "my colleagues read this Army study politely and then quietly put it to one side."[34]

Taylor's lack of success led to direct action by a group of "young Colonels" at the Pentagon, assembled as a special secretariat for the chief of staff of the Army in what was known as the Coordinating Group. The officers were charged to decide what the Army's requirements and thus budget would be and to evaluate proposals by the other services. Like Taylor, they believed that massive retaliation was unsuited to a new world of brush-fire wars and would cause the withering away of the Army. As a consequence, some of the more outspoken officers, in what came to be known as the "revolt of the colonels," leaked a number of the group's classified studies to the press on the Army's case for flexible response over massive retaliation. The studies, published in two *New York Times* articles on 19 and 20 May, caused a sensation, particularly because of their assaults on the other services. Despite the president's acceptance of the need to fight lesser conflicts, one of the studies complained, the United States continued "to pour excessive manpower and money into an Air Force which has been substantially neutralized" and "to divert large quantities of . . . military capacity into a Navy that is seriously threatened by a nation with practically no naval experience or tradition."[35]

An infuriated Wilson immediately broke up the Coordinating Group, ordering the colonels not to return to their offices. "There's a bunch of eager beavers down in the Army Staff," he told reporters, "and if they stick their heads out again I'll chop them."[36] On 21 May the defense secretary held a press conference, attended by JCS members and service secretaries, in which he denounced "partisan service representatives."[37] The service leaders joined Wilson in rejecting self-aggrandizing service publicity efforts. Taylor, who apparently had known of the activities by the "colonels," declared that there was "no mutiny or revolt in the Army." The next day, he circulated a memorandum indicating his "strong disapproval" of public statements that might incite interservice rivalry, pointing out that there were "ample means within the Department of Defense for rectifying of differences."[38] In all his actions in the wake of the "revolt," the Army chief of staff masterfully disassociated himself from the leaks without disavowing the contents of the Army studies.

To queries at a press conference on 23 May concerning interservice rivalry, Eisenhower began by cautioning the reporters to keep the service differences in perspective. But when the president was pressed on the subject, his equanimity began to fade. "I will tell you this: the day that discipline disappears from our forces, we will have no forces, and we would be foolish to put a nickel into them. . . . The President, constitutionally, is the Commander in Chief and what he decides to do in these things, in the form and the way that you arm and organize and command your forces, must be carried out."[39]

After all this, Taylor unbelievably made one more attempt at modifying the New Look when he accompanied Radford to the White House on 24 May to meet at his own request with the president. The Army chief of staff began with the familiar arguments for flexible response in a future state of mutual deterrence. The president was hardly inclined to make any concession. It was "fatuous," he pointed out, to think that both superpowers "would be locked into a life and death struggle without using such weapons." And as to local wars, "the tactical use of atomic weapons against military targets would be no more likely to trigger off a big war than the use of twenty-ton 'blockbusters.'" He would not, he emphasized, deploy and tie down US forces in small wars around the Soviet periphery.[40]

Eisenhower concluded his talk with Taylor by reemphasizing the need for "corporate judgment" by the Joint Chiefs. If they were unable to develop that type of judgment on the great problems facing the country, he finished, "the system as we now have it will have failed and major changes must be made."[41] In actuality, the president was already inclined to think, as he informed Wilson at the time, that the current JCS system had failed. The solution, therefore, was for the defense secretary to find an organization that would allow him to receive disinterested, competent advice, then decide on a program, and firmly hold to that decision by "setting his teeth."[42]

Eisenhower's dissatisfaction with the functioning of the Department of Defense increased, if anything, throughout the remainder of 1956. The Senate budget hearings for fiscal year 1957 became more turbulent in June as the Democrats, sensing an advantage in an election year, sided with the military, particularly the Air Force, in its more pessimistic outlook on future Soviet capabilities. On 11 June, General Curtis E. LeMay, the commander in chief of the Strategic Air Command (SAC), testified on the inadequacy of the overall 1957 Air Force budget in the light of what he believed was a necessary SAC expansion plan. He supported the current budget, he stated, "because that is the way my boss wants it done. My original requirement was for a much higher figure."[43] Eisenhower fought to contain the renewed pressure for more defense money, and on 29 June from a bed at Walter Reed Hospital, he signed the fiscal year 1957 bill, which increased his proposed budget by more than $800 million.

The president was at the hospital due to a severe attack of stomach pains marked by tenderness and swelling in his abdomen. He had suffered from such ailments before, but for the first time they were correctly diagnosed as ileitis, an inflammation in the lowest section of the small intestine. The first days after the operation, he acknowledged, were "miserably uncomfortable," but the operation was a complete success and provided, he noted, "the sternest test that my heart could have."[44] On 30 June the president was discharged from the hospital for convalescence at his Gettysburg farm.

Within a few weeks, Eisenhower was once again in his familiar cycle of budgetary disputes with the Joint Chiefs. His final encounter on 24 May with General Taylor had settled for the remainder of his time in office the doctrinal dispute in favor of the New Look over increased flexible conventional capability. But that still left the matter of the proposals by the service chiefs for annual defense budgets for fiscal years 1958–1960 of more than $48 billion, $12 billion more than the president had indicated he would support. Eisenhower was adamant about control of service costs and forbade any attempt by the service chiefs to go to Congress with an expenditure program beyond the limitations to be set by his administration. "Put every single person on the spot to justify every single nickel," he instructed Wilson in late July. "You have got to be willing to be the most unpopular man in the government. . . . You people never seem to learn whom you are supposed to be protecting. Not the generals, but the American people."[45]

Eisenhower's work on the budget and his relationship with his military advisers were complicated by the Suez and Hungarian crises in late October, "the start of the most crowded and demanding three weeks of my entire Presidency."[46] The United States was unlikely to become involved militarily in the anti-Soviet revolt in Hungary, but the alliance of Britain and France with Israel in operations along the Suez Canal threatened to draw the two superpowers into armed confrontation. As a consequence, the JCS began to examine the administration's expectations for personnel cuts in fiscal year 1958. Equally important, the Suez crisis validated the concerns of the flexible-response advocates by creating a situation that could not be resolved by threats of strategic nuclear bombing. This caused Admiral Burke to join General Taylor in pointing out that budget trends of the New Look had overfocused on preparation for all-out war. "In the present situation," the chief of naval operations charged, "the usefulness of naval power and the consequences of its neglect are well demonstrated."[47] On 15 November the Joint Chiefs followed up with a memorandum to the secretary of defense that registered their opposition to any sharp reductions in force levels and personnel strengths, adding that increases might even be required if there were any marked deterioration of the global situation.[48]

In the meantime, Eisenhower won reelection in early November with 58 percent of the popular vote, approximately 35.5 million ballots, and an electoral vote of 457 to 73. The Republican candidate carried all but seven states, including Louisiana for the first time since 1876. "Louisiana," the president remarked. "That's as probable as leading in Ethiopia."[49] At the same time, however, the Republicans failed to carry either the House or the Senate, the first such rebuff to a president-elect since 1848. Nevertheless, it was a great personal victory for Eisenhower. General Montgomery sent back congratulations from Europe, where he was still serving as deputy SACEUR. And from Eisenhower's longtime mentor, there was a touching handwritten note. His reelection, General Marshall wrote, demonstrated an "unprecedented vote of approval, affection and encouragement in a turbulent world."[50]

The reelection did not produce any noticeable advantage for Wilson as he attempted to bridge the fiscal year 1958 budgetary gap between the Joint Chiefs and the known predilections of the president. Eisenhower maintained the pressure on his military advisers. On 21 December, in a NSC meeting convened specifically to discuss the fiscal year 1958 budget, the president gave each service chief the opportunity to explain how he would use the funds allocated to him and what problems would exist in his service programs absent any funding increase. In the end, each military leader, in effect, agreed to what he perceived in the budget as the minimum requirement for his programs. Subsequently, under the president's insistent grilling, the service secretaries agreed that given the need to balance service requirements with those of the economy, they had created the best possible programs for the money.[51]

As the 21 December NSC meeting came to an end, Treasury Secretary Humphrey understandably complimented the "marvelous coordination and teamwork" in what he considered the "finest budget performance" since the administration had come to power.[52] It was obvious that the president had bludgeoned the reluctant service secretaries and chiefs with his budget proposal. Given the history of earlier New Look budget struggles, both Wilson and Radford were concerned about the continued support for the fiscal year 1958 administration figures by these officials during the congressional hearings. On 29 December they discussed the situation with Goodpaster and other White House officials. Goodpaster's impression was that Eisenhower believed that the JCS in their recent meetings with the president had accepted that the budgetary program involved an acceptable risk. Radford was not so sure. Although the service chiefs had sat "like bumps on a log" in the meetings, they now gave the appearance of being ready to distance themselves from the budget as soon as there was an opportunity. In particular, Air Force leaders viewed their portion as an "imposed ceiling" and that in making their case to Congress, their attitude was "not . . . to let the President get in their way."[53]

As a consequence, Goodpaster drafted a memorandum of clarification to be signed by the service secretaries and the Joint Chiefs for use in the president's remarks to congressional leaders on 1 January 1957. Those officials, the statement began, had given their views on the fiscal year 1958 military program; and while each had designated specific areas in which increases would be desirable, each had also indicated that "viewed as a whole" the program was "well balanced and satisfactory." Each of the civilian and military leaders, therefore, had assured the president of his "wholehearted support" for the program "as involving an acceptable degree of risk and providing a reasonable and wise degree of security."[54]

The last day of 1956 was a momentous one for Colonel Goodpaster. It began with Eisenhower's "Dear Andy" note informing him that the Senate would confirm his nomination to the temporary grade of brigadier general the next day. "Daily—hourly—I realize my good fortune in having you in your particular assignment," the president wrote.[55] The day was also marked by Goodpaster's meeting with the Joint Chiefs and service secretaries at the Pentagon to obtain their confirmation of his memorandum—an example of the great tact and unofficial power of the president's staff secretary, as well as an indication of how precarious relations had become between Eisenhower and his key advisers on military affairs. Wilson was also present, and he began by pointing out that there would be no problems if Eisenhower were willing to indicate that he set the "ceiling" for the budget. Goodpaster was not about to accept such loaded phraseology and indicated that as he understood the process, the president had not established a ceiling "but had decided upon a figure between the present program and the one proposed, after considering and discussing the main elements of the program." The president would, of course, acknowledge that the budget determination was his, Goodpaster added, but he wished to know and to state that his advisers joined him in it.[56]

This curious interplay, which succeeded in obtaining the Pentagon's support for the fiscal year 1958 budget, was a natural result of the evolution of civil-military relations in the first Eisenhower term. During that time, there was increasing criticism of the administration's defense policies focused on the charge that the president was subordinating security to economy and as a consequence could not control the military establishment. This perception was bolstered by acrimonious public interservice disputes over roles and mission that included an unpleasant reminder in the "revolt of the colonels" of the more momentous "revolt of the admirals" in the 1949 heyday of fierce unification fights. Then too, congressional testimony by the Joint Chiefs and their subordinates at times explicitly and more often implicitly criticized aspects of the national security strategy.

From the president's perspective, these problems stemmed not from his strategy but from the continued inability of the Joint Chiefs to function as a corporate body, a defect Lovett and his reformers in 1953 had

attempted to remedy by strengthening the authority of the defense secretary and the JCS chairman. For Eisenhower by 1956, that reorganization plan had clearly not been adequate to create the type of unity of
command and effort in Washington that he had come to expect with the
unified commands at the theater level. His background in multinational
and joint organizations had long since largely emancipated him from service parochialism, which he normally viewed as irrelevant or counterpro-
ductive. As a consequence, throughout his first term, Eisenhower was
surprised, disappointed, and then incensed by what he perceived as the
self-serving lack of broader vision on the part of the service chiefs. Each
of them, he came to believe, still thought that the sums allocated to the
others were sufficient for national security, but that the amounts for his
own service were inadequate. "The result was that budgetary decisions
had to be made, rather than approved at the civilian echelon," he concluded, looking back on this period. "Thus the internal differences in our
highest military mechanism tended to neutralize the advisory influence
they should have enjoyed as a body."[57]

In his unwillingness or inability to understand the opposing views of
his military advisers, Eisenhower ignored military cultures built up over
many years. The traditional goal for each of the most senior flag officers
in this environment was to head up his own service. From that viewpoint,
it was normal to attempt to expand the service or take on new missions
or compete with the other services. It was not, however, a perspective
that Eisenhower was likely to tolerate in his second term any more than
in his first, particularly since defense costs such as those stemming from
duplication in weapons development were growing exponentially. There
was no evidence that unless specifically directed by him, the Joint Chiefs
would focus their efforts on reducing their demands for resources in accordance with the middle way of solvency and security that featured so
prominently in each of his national security policy documents beginning
with NSC 162/2. It was increasingly clear to the president that absent
some new, more far-reaching attempt at Defense Department reorganization, the Joint Chiefs would remain mired in their service cultures,
an impediment to the further progress of unification begun in 1947 and
to his goal of a more unified command structure at the highest national
level.

CHAPTER SIXTEEN

Impetus from Space:
New Life for the Unified Command
Concept, January 1957–January 1958

Oh Little Sputnik, flying high
With made-in-Moscow beep,
You tell the world it's a Commie sky,
And Uncle Sam's asleep.

You say on fairway and on rough,
The Kremlin knows it all,
We hope our golfer knows enough
To get us on the ball.

MICHIGAN GOVERNOR G. MENNEN WILLIAMS

The older I grow, the more I come to respect balance—not only in budgets but in people.

DWIGHT DAVID EISENHOWER

ON 21 JANUARY 1957 Dwight Eisenhower started his second term as president. The first year of the second term began with increased assaults on his fundamental New Look policy. And by the middle of the year he would also have to adjust to important changes in his national security team. In the fall, he would contend with the Little Rock crisis and, most important, with the international and domestic reaction occasioned by the Soviet launch of *Sputnik,* the first satellite orbited in space. The *Sputnik* crisis posed a severe challenge to the administration. But it also offered an opportunity for the president to return to the triad of unity of command, unity of effort, and unification, which in the form of an overall unified command structure at the national level had preoccupied him for more than a decade. By that time, based on his experiences with his military and civilian defense advisers in his first

term, the president believed, as he told his cabinet, that his initial defense reform effort in 1953 had produced a "useless thing."[1] *Sputnik* would
allow him to pour his enormous reservoir of knowledge and experience
concerning the concept of unified command into one last effort at reorganization of the Department of Defense.

In late May, Eisenhower was successful in maintaining the nuclear
focus of his national security policy with the replacement of NSC 5602/1
by NSC 5707/8. The approval of the new policy document by the president and the NSC marked a firm rejection of the view that in an era of
approaching nuclear parity, there was a need for a more flexible response
capability to prepare for local or limited war. Nevertheless, the effect of
nuclear stalemate on national security policy was often debated in public
as that threat appeared increasingly, even imminently, possible. By the
summer of 1957, Hanson Baldwin warned in the *New York Times* that with
the trend toward such parity, conflicts appropriate to massive retaliation
would become less possible, leaving those that could be settled only by
"men on foot with guns in their hands and artillery behind them."[2] He
was joined by such defense intellectuals as William Kaufman, Robert
Osgood, and Henry Kissinger, who directly challenged the New Look
contention that the forces created for the most dangerous contingency
of nuclear war at one end of the spectrum of conflict could be used automatically to fight limited wars at the other end. In particular, Kissinger's
best selling critique, *Nuclear Weapons and Foreign Policy,* had enormous
public impact with its emphasis on creating a broad menu of US military
capabilities that would include more mobile, self-contained forces than
those required for nuclear deterrence.

The president followed the limited-war discussions closely and, as
John Eisenhower recalled, had the details of the arguments "absolutely
at his fingertips."[3] In any case, Eisenhower was bent on sticking with the
nuclear centrality of NSC 5707/8. And as the pressures mounted in late
1957 for developing a larger defense budget for fiscal year 1959, he would
return with ever increasing fervor to the most extreme interpretation of
the New Look.

In the meantime, the president prepared for major changes in his
national security team. In July, George Humphrey was replaced at the
Treasury. In August, Admiral Radford retired and was replaced as JCS
chairman by General Twining. Twining's position as Air Force chief of
staff was filled by his deputy, General Thomas R. White, who had the

distinction of having graduated from West Point in 1920 at the age of eighteen. Wilson's departure soon followed that of Radford. On 7 August, Eisenhower submitted the name of Neil H. McElroy as Wilson's replacement to the Senate, which confirmed the nominee two weeks later. The longtime president of Procter and Gamble was fifty-two years old, and his six-foot-four-inch height added to a commanding leadership style. The new secretary was almost obsessive about thorough preparation and soon impressed the president and Pentagon subordinates as a quick study, particularly in his ability to master rapidly the arcane details of the missile and satellite programs. Despite this favorable picture of a no-nonsense, knowledgeable decision maker, McElroy was also inclined to avoid confrontation deliberately when testifying before Congress and to move slowly on major issues, always reluctant to repudiate Wilson's policies.[4]

McElroy insisted as a condition of his acceptance that his tenure would be limited to two years. His approach to the new position was much like that of his predecessor's, with an emphasis on administration rather than strategy formulation. Because of his lack of technical background, he came to depend considerably on the advice of his deputy, Donald A. Quarles. Quarles was a trained scientist who had served as an executive at Western Electric, assistant secretary of defense for research and development, and secretary of the Air Force. From a military standpoint, McElroy looked to the JCS for similar guidance. But as he informed the Joint Chiefs, he was puzzled and disturbed by the sharpness and frequency of their disagreements on major issues. "You have spent your lives in the military, you are the top men in the field," he asserted. "I am an industrialist from the soap works. Yet I ask you what should be done on a military matter, and you say you can't agree. So I have to make the decision."[5]

Before McElroy assumed office, a crisis emerged with the 4 October announcement by the Soviets that on the previous day they had launched *Sputnik,* the first man-made satellite. There was an enormous amount of public consternation throughout the United States at the news, initially focused on the blow to American pride and prestige inflicted by the 184-pound satellite. The "Father of the H-Bomb," physicist Edward Teller, compared the shock of the event to that of the Pearl Harbor attack and when queried as to what future American space explorers would be likely to discover if they reached the moon, he responded: "Russians."[6]

Soon, concerns turned to the lead taken by the Soviet Union in an area of scientific research that had obvious long-range military implications—all exacerbated by the news on 7 October that the Soviets had successfully tested a new hydrogen bomb warhead that could presumably be used on an intercontinental ballistic missile.

Newspaper editorials were generally critical of the administration for what they perceived as a lack of vigorous emphasis on satellite and missile programs; the drive to balance the budget, the pundits wrote, had come at the expense of national security. The opposition also predictably joined the attack. "It is not very reassuring to be told that next year we will put a 'better' satellite into the air," Democratic Senate Majority Leader Lyndon Johnson announced. "Perhaps it will even have chrome trim—and automatic windshield wipers."[7] As for the "chilling beeps" of the radio signals emitted by the satellite as it circled the globe at eighteen thousand miles an hour, they were nothing more, one former Republican official commented, than "an intercontinental outer-space raspberry to a decade of American pretensions that the American way of life was a gilt-edge guarantee of our material superiority."[8]

Eisenhower would not be hurried, rejecting proposals for emerging satellite programs. In a news conference on 9 October the president continued to exude confidence and resolve. He acknowledged that with *Sputnik,* the Soviets had "gained a great psychological advantage throughout the world" but cautioned that there was no reason "to grow hysterical about it."[9] Later that same day, the president bade formal farewell to Secretary Wilson, awarding him the Medal of Freedom. Immediately thereafter, he administered the oath of office to his new secretary of defense. After the ceremony, Eisenhower met with McElroy, Quarles, the service secretaries, and the JCS to emphasize that there was to be a "no comment" policy concerning *Sputnik.*[10] But in the confines of the White House throughout the rest of the month, the president revealed a seething frustration at the mounting post-*Sputnik* criticism, particularly that leveled by the Democrats. "The idea of them charging me with not being interested in defense!" he exploded. "Damn it, I've spent my whole life being concerned with defense of our country." Nor was there much comfort in his own party, where "Republican right-wingers" were "no damn better."[11]

These types of results led Eisenhower to refocus and renew his efforts to make extensive changes in defense organization. From his perspective, as troubling as the *Sputnik* crisis was, it also offered an opportunity to take a major step on the evolutionary path toward his grail of operational and national unity of command and effort by presenting Pentagon reorganization as a way to hold down the expanding costs of preparedness brought on by the pressures for new technology in the wake of that crisis. The current climate of what he considered public and congressional overreaction to *Sputnik*, the president pointed out to his economic advisers, had opened the way for "a giant step toward unification" as a "necessary counteraction," from which a huge cost savings would result.[12]

Interservice rivalry was already emerging as a particular culprit in the press and in congressional hearings, stigmatized, for example, as the cause for the development of three separate intermediate range ballistic missile (IRBM) programs: the Army Jupiter, the Navy Polaris, and the Air Force Thor. The message to the public was that service duplication led to waste and inefficiency, exacerbating the Soviet advantage in the field. Eisenhower was ready to place this connection solely in the context of his struggles with the service chiefs and the need for reform in the Defense Department. But the president was treading a fine line. On the one hand, there was his desire to proceed slowly and prudently in response to *Sputnik*, the basis for his efforts to persuade Congress and the public that the Soviet launch of that satellite did not pose a threat to US national security. At the same time, however, if he wished to inaugurate meaningful defense reorganization, he would have to appeal to the sense of peril to that security as a result of the perceived Soviet lead in science and technology, an approach that also had the potential for use by the services and Congress to escalate the developing fiscal year 1959 budget.

In any event, there was no hesitation on the part of the president. In the immediate aftermath of *Sputnik*, he instructed Nelson Rockefeller, the chairman of the President's Advisory Commission on Governmental Organization, to begin to formulate new ideas on Pentagon reorganization. Rockefeller, a veteran of the 1953 reform efforts, instituted discussions at once between members of his committee and the Bureau of the Budget, the organization with statutory responsibility for reorganization of the executive branch.

On 14 October, Percy Brundage, the Bureau of Budget director, produced a staff memorandum on Defense Department reorganization as a result of collaboration between his office and Rockefeller's group. The document, described as a concept, not a blueprint, addressed many of

Eisenhower's concerns, particularly the "confusion" in command structure; a JCS "incapable of performing unified planning"; and armed services marked by waste, extravagance, and "triplification"—the latter
defined as the process by which each of the three services organized separate, self-sufficient forces of its own, duplicating, not complementing the
military functions of the other services. In all this, the report emphasized,
only the president could initiate steps leading to an organizational solution.[13]

Much of that solution, the 14 October memorandum elaborated,
had to do directly or indirectly with the unified command system, which
caused confusion at two levels. Within the operational commands, the
authority of the unified commander over his "supposedly subordinate"
component commanders was not clear. The commander in chief (CINC)
might well command the units from his service in his command; but the
units from the other services were under the unified commander only for
operational control, "a dangerous concept since it implies something less
than full command." This tendency was exacerbated because the service
components in the unified command were separately administered and
largely separately supplied. In a similar manner, the report continued, the
CINCs were unable to create a unified, integrated headquarters since the
staffs that they were authorized to organize were "at best . . . composed
of officers from each service, all of whom have primary responsibilities to
their separate services."[14]

At the higher level, the Budget Bureau memorandum pointed out
that there was equal confusion due to the overlapping command channels to the unified commands. Command organization was most effective
when there was a minimum of organizational levels between the president as national commander in chief and his major operational commanders. "Each intervening level," the report stipulated, "courts delay,
indecision, reinterpretation of reports and commands, and confusion of
authority." The secretary of defense "rightfully" belonged in the chain of
command below the president. The interposition of any other intervening
layer would only "weaken and confuse" the relationship that the president should maintain with his operational commands. "Certainly there
should be no committee such as the Joint Chiefs of Staff at any point in
the command structure." In this organization, then, the defense secretary should be authorized to establish operational commands, with the
approval of the president, as well as to assign combat functions and roles

and missions directly to those commands, not to separate services. "The commanders should accordingly report directly to the Secretary of Defense and receive their orders from him," the memorandum concluded, "thus eliminating any need for 'executive agencies.'" In this manner, the peacetime defense structure would be so designed that, without major reorganization, it could facilitate the execution of military operations necessary for war or any emergency involving operations short of war.[15]

A few days later, Rockefeller added some thoughts of his own in a nineteen-page draft "Notes on the Reorganization of the Department of Defense." Traditional roles and missions boundaries among the services had been "almost obliterated" by new weapons and equipment. "Today, no service can achieve its primary mission without either trespassing on the role of the other services or calling on them for assistance," he pointed out. "And cooperation among the services is difficult unless there is an agreement on doctrine, the practical manifestation of which would be that all services hold the same view as to what constitutes an essential target." The tendency for each service, therefore, was to hoard weapons in order "to develop a capability for winning a war by itself." Moreover, since the secretary of defense possessed neither the staff nor the organization to shape service disagreements over doctrine, he remained at best an arbiter of doctrinal disputes, a referee in interservice rivalry. "And it is the nature of a referee's role," Rockefeller emphasized, "that problems come to him only *after* positions have hardened."[16]

Eisenhower's focus on defense reorganization became more intense on 3 November, four days before the fortieth anniversary of the Bolshevik Revolution, when the Soviet Union announced the orbiting of a second Sputnik, this one weighing more than half a ton, as compared with the six-pound American *Vanguard* that was still in its development phase. Estimates of the rocket thrust to launch the new satellite were at least 500,000 pounds, more than enough to send an ICBM approximately five thousand miles across the globe. All this was dramatic refutation of those who hoped that *Sputnik I* represented all that the Soviets were capable of achieving. In addition, the new satellite also carried a dog, named Laika, which not only offended many animal rights proponents but suggested that the Soviets had plans for future manned space flights.[17]

The next day, the president had three meetings that directly or indirectly helped crystallize his thoughts on Pentagon reform. Over breakfast, he worked with Rockefeller and Brundage on reorganization proposals that they agreed were essential to any final program. Eisenhower was particularly enthusiastic about the proposal to move the operation of unified commands from the supervision of whatever service was designated executive agent to the overall supervision of the Defense Department and the JCS. This shifting of operational responsibilities from the services to the Joint Chiefs, he responded, would lead to "a marked decrease in inter-service rivalry." In the end, the meeting allowed Eisenhower to provide guidance on general recommendations for improving unified commands; creating a new chain of command to the operational commanders, bypassing the military departments; substituting an integrated military planning organization for the Joint Staff; and placing the control of all research and development projects in the Office of the Secretary of Defense.[18]

Eisenhower's second meeting on 4 November was to receive a briefing on the so-called Gaither report. The previous April, the president had appointed a "security resources panel" to evaluate a proposal to build blast and fallout shelters to protect the US population in a nuclear attack. The panel was named for its chairman, H. Rowan Gaither, a San Francisco lawyer, who was head of both the Rand Corporation and the Ford Foundation. The final committee report was drafted by Paul Nitze, who during the Truman administration had outlined the Soviet threat in stark terms for NSC-68, a document that called for quantum increases in defense spending—without, however, a specific price tag. Now in the Gaither report, this confirmed Cold Warrior outlined again in urgent and unequivocal language the need for another huge leap in defense expenditures, this time with figures, as part of a sweeping overhaul of national security policy.[19]

Only a small group from the committee, which included old friends such as John J. McCloy and Robert Lovett, provided an oral report of its findings on 4 November to the president. Eisenhower's response was more cautionary than enthusiastic. He rejected the alarmist tone of the report concerning the Soviet threat, suggesting instead that US strategic forces were stronger than the committee had indicated.[20] But that was as far as he would go. The problem was that the president knew something that the committee did not. Since 1956 he had been receiving intelligence concerning the Soviet ICBM program provided by American U-2 planes flying high above the USSR. The information from that program clearly indicated that the Soviets were still conducting early tests of their missiles and were not currently prepared to deploy them. Disclosure of the program would have silenced many of the president's critics, but he was unwilling to jeopardize such an important project, only hinting at his frustrations to Swede Hazlett: "In . . . our relative position with Russia in arms development, you can understand there are many things that I don't dare to allude to publicly, yet some of them would do much to allay the fears of our own people."[21] At one point, Dulles urged him to reveal the U-2 evidence that the United States did not lag behind the Soviet Union in the missile race, but the president continued to resist. "Ike took the heat, grinned, and kept his mouth shut," Barry Goldwater later observed.[22]

Eisenhower was also appalled on 4 November at the Gaither report's call for a total increase of forty billion dollars in defense expenditures over a period of five to eight years—a figure that the report contended "would not pose significant problems" for the nation and was "well within our economic capabilities."[23] The president did not agree. The type of crisis response necessary for such a buildup simply could not be sustained for the long haul. "The crux is, therefore, how to keep up interest and support without hysteria," he instructed the group.[24]

There were also some aspects of the Gaither report that Eisenhower found useful, particularly the section entitled "Improvement of Management of Defense Resources," which addressed many of his Pentagon reform concerns. The principal theme of the section, much like that of the Brundage memorandum, was that new weapon systems cut across service lines and created new problems for the management of defense resources. Some "urgently needed" steps could be taken without Congress, but that body would be needed for an amendment of "present legislation, which freezes the organization of the Defense Department along lines which . . . are clearly inappropriate today and may become intolerable in the near future." The defense secretary, the Gaither report emphasized, should be "directly and solely" in charge of a command post–type group, "organized as a staff, not as an interagency committee," to assist him in both command and control and in long-term planning.[25]

This subject was addressed briefly in the 4 November meeting with the group from the Gaither committee, eliciting the only enthusiastic response from the president. Typically, it was John J. McCloy, Eisenhower's old ally in the early unification struggles, who raised the need for organizational improvement of the Pentagon, pointing out that interservice bickering and rivalry were adversely affecting the management of defense resources and thus degrading US national security. Moreover, he added, those disputes were spreading to institutions, such as industry and universities, which tended to be tied to particular services. The president responded that the underlying question for the problem was "Why can't we be one in national defense?"—a question he planned to pose to the top military and civilian Pentagon leaders that evening at a White House dinner. Then drawing on his breakfast discussions, Eisenhower noted that he was beginning to think that the services should become establishments solely for training, logistics and administration and that the Joint Staff should become completely unified and integrated. One of the advantages of having a new secretary of defense, he added, was that he could take such organizational steps without fixing blame or engaging in recriminations.[26]

Following a stag dinner that evening for the Joint Chiefs and the secretaries of the military departments, the president met with them in the White House Red Room for what he termed a "kind of seminar." He began by pointing out that in his previous conferences that day, the underlying theme had been that the American people were "deeply concerned" over rivalry in the military establishment. "The question was repeatedly raised," Eisenhower emphasized, "are we sufficiently unified? Are we getting the best personal judgment of our officers, rather than a parroting of service party lines?" The Joint Chiefs immediately objected. The struggle over missiles, General White protested, was good "competition," not "harmful rivalry." General Taylor added that a clear distinction should be made between missile development and missile use in this regard, an assertion that led to an argument with General Twining over the range of Army missiles—the very type of bickering that the president had described.[27]

Eisenhower brought the Joint Chiefs back to the subject by insisting they must be above narrow service considerations. He did not, he explained, "regard organization as an answer in itself, except as it leads individuals to take a broader outlook." Turning once again to his SHAEF and SHAPE experiences and to his discussions earlier that day, the president indicated that he wanted to draw up a major reorganization proposal, in which the JCS would remove operational functions from the military departments, leaving the service staffs concerned with mobilization, administration, and logistics. The joint staff would then be organized on an integrated basis, reporting to the JCS as a corporate body. At the same time, each chief would turn over the executive direction of his service to his deputy in order to concentrate on his joint responsibility as a "soldier-statesman."[28]

Once again, the Joint Chiefs fought the linkage of interservice disputes with the need for reorganization. Admiral Burke argued that individual chiefs had different experiences going back many years, as did the service members of the joint staff. JCS disagreements occurred not because of service connections, he contended, but because of the individual experiences of the members. It was always easy to generate a group eager to please the top men, Burke concluded; but with complex issues not always susceptible to final solutions, it was essential to have the deep judgment that could be brought to the problems under the current procedures. The president could not let the traditional naval argument against unification go unanswered. Why, he asked the chief of naval operations with some force, would it not be better to have "composite, well-thought positions reflecting the experience of many people of differing backgrounds and of differing services," instead of his own service?

The Army was similarly defensive when Eisenhower elaborated on his proposal for unified commands that should report directly to the JCS, which would study their problems, take account of all resources to be provided by the services, and use the joint staff to assist in using those resources operationally. General Taylor instantly attempted to head off the implications of the proposal for his ever narrowing flexibility to determine the programs and end strength for his service. Such an approach, he responded, would require an overhaul of the existing commands since the problem was a budgetary one of relating the needs of the CINCs with what could be provided from available service funds. What he had in mind, the president countered disarmingly, was that the Joint Chiefs could tell the CINCs what was generally available from the services and then work out the best use of those resources.[29]

What was abundantly clear to Eisenhower from this last of his meetings on 4 November was that he could expect JCS opposition in the future to any major Pentagon reform efforts. As a consequence, he ended the discussion with a not so subtle reminder that he wanted to keep in close touch with the Joint Chiefs and service secretaries, particularly as the reorganization efforts moved forward and bipartisan meetings were scheduled with congressional leaders. It was essential that the group remain together, the president emphasized. They must stand "firmly behind" a plan that might not meet everybody's wishes. Eisenhower concluded, once they had agreed to it, "they should say this is what *we* believe."[30]

On 7 November the Gaither committee rendered its report to the full NSC in one of the largest gatherings of that body in history, with sixty-nine in attendance. Generally, Eisenhower was content to let Dulles strongly reject the proposals for reasons ranging from excessive cost, which would drain funds from more vital programs such as foreign aid, to the possibility, in the case of a civil-defense program, that allies would be alarmed and the Soviets encouraged to initiate even more massive arms build-ups.[31] Later that day the president made a radio and television address to explain the steps he was taking for improvement of the situation, including the creation of the Office of Special Assistant to the President for Science and Technology, and the acceptance of the position by Dr. James R. Killian, president of the Massachusetts Institute of Technology.[32]

On 15 November, Rockefeller and Brundage submitted a joint memorandum to the president, enclosing a report of major reorganization proposals. It was "extremely important," the two officials emphasized, that the president be in a position early in the next session of Congress to put forward the administration's Pentagon reorganization recommendations. "We hope that Secretary McElroy will be able to give a high priority to the development of a comprehensive reorganization proposal." To facilitate the development of such a plan, McElroy "might be well advised to bring together as soon as possible a special committee on organization, similar to the one which Secretary Wilson established in 1953."[33]

On Monday morning, 25 November, Eisenhower informed Goodpaster that he had read the joint memorandum and the draft report "with great interest." He liked the plan and even suggested that the administration should be ready with legislation "this year" for a "few key actions" to begin that improvement. He was also pleased with the idea of an advisory study group focused on organizational change in the Pentagon. Many of the things that were undesirable from a unity-of-command-and-effort perspective in the activities of the military services, he concluded, could be eliminated only by organizational change.[34]

That day, shortly after lunch, Eisenhower complained of dizziness; while dictating to his personal secretary, Ann Whitman, he began to jumble his words. She quickly summoned the White House physician, who diagnosed a stroke and ordered the president to bed. By 27 November his speech had returned, and after attending Thanksgiving service the next day, he departed for a long Gettysburg weekend. That following Monday, 2 December, a week after the stroke, the president was back at work in the White House, "chipper and entirely sure of himself," in Whitman's estimation.[35] Still, there were residual effects, such as a tendency, Eisenhower wrote Swede Hazlett, to occasionally use the wrong word— "for example, I may say 'desk' when I mean 'chair.'"[36] And in a meeting with congressional leaders from both parties on 3 December, Eisenhower opened the proceedings by stating that although he apparently had no physical defects as the result of his "most recent illness," he still had difficulty "articulating" and therefore would leave the discussions to others.[37]

There was, of course, a great deal of concern about the president's third major illness in twenty-six months. Anxious to dampen rumors and buoyed by his dramatic recovery, Eisenhower decided two days after his stroke to attend a NATO summit previously scheduled for 15 December. The trip was an enormous success. The president reassured the public about his health and vigor with a grueling schedule that included up to ten hours a day in negotiations and long motorcades through Paris in an open car. Equally important, he achieved his primary mission of reassurance with the acceptance by the European allies of forward-deployed IRBMs as proof of US commitment and determination not to be deterred by Soviet intercontinental ballistic missile (ICBM) developments. "IRBM PLUS NATO EQUALS ICBM," one French newspaper headline read.[38]

The NATO summit seemed to lift Eisenhower from his apparent puzzled and depressed initial reaction to *Sputnik*. The work of Rockefeller and Brundage on defense reorganization had in the meantime been reinforced by James Killian and his newly created President's Science Committee, a group of seventeen scientists and public figures that was to act as a conduit between the president and the scientific community. In terms of the missile program, the committee reported to Eisenhower, the impact of interservice rivalry had been "wasteful" and "damaging." It was time to establish a new policy of central direction in the Pentagon, what Killian termed "modernization of organization," in order "to give focus and purposefulness to military technology."[39] This was also a theme in the ongoing hearings by Senate Majority Leader Lyndon Johnson's Defense Preparedness Subcommittee, which had begun on 25 November to investigate why the Soviets had been first into space. From the testimony before that committee emerged a picture of interservice disputes that caused bureaucratic confusion and duplication of effort. To this was added the picture of a president skimping on national security with a budget ceiling that had resulted in limitations on the US missile program. Under heavy questioning, both McElroy and Quarles confirmed that Congress had appropriated $1.5 billion more in the preceding four years for defense than had been requested by the White House.[40]

By the end of December, Eisenhower was satisfied that he had a solid base for defense reorganization efforts in the New Year. But he was increasingly concerned with the effect that testimony by civilian and military Pentagon leaders might have on those efforts in his dealing with a Congress that was traditionally opposed to Pentagon reform, particularly if it strengthened the executive branch. The best chance for such reform, the president reasoned, would stem not from any personal bipartisan appeal on his part but from a plan devised in the Pentagon that included compromises with the Joint Chiefs and service secretaries. The basis for this approach, he believed, was the advisory group recommended by Brundage and Rockefeller, which would work under the secretary of defense to produce a report from which a defense reorganization bill could emerge "that would command my approval and overwhelming support in the Congress."[41] As a consequence, he instructed Rockefeller and Brundage to keep their draft plan secret until he could arrange for the Pentagon to take the lead.[42]

The key to the Pentagon role was the secretary of defense, whose reluctance to tackle defense reform immediately was already apparent. The new secretary believed that Wilson should have addressed defense reorganization before leaving office. Moreover, McElroy always prided himself on his mastery of issues; Pentagon reform was simply too complex for him to address so soon after assuming office and after having been through what he termed "an interesting education" in the *Sputnik* period. As a result, he later recalled, "I tried to persuade the President that it would really be better for me to take another year on this, and I'd know more about what I could recommend to him."[43] Eisenhower was not in a receptive mood. In late December the president called McElroy into his office and directed him to get on with the defense reorganization efforts. "You have a free hand," he said.[44]

By that time the glow of the NATO summit had faded and pressures on the president from a variety of issues were mounting. After the initial *Sputnik* launch, he had committed the United States to place a satellite in orbit by December. But the December liftoff of the Navy's three-stage *Vanguard* rocket with a grapefruit-sized satellite on top reached only a few feet before exploding—a televised national humiliation, not helped by a report that, in Eisenhower's words, a "goddamn three-star general" had rejoiced at the news of the Navy's failure.[45] On 20 December a *Washington Post* article leaked portions of the Gaither report, asserting that the classified document portrayed the United States "in the gravest danger in history"—a "nation moving in a frightening course to the status of second-class power" by the "missile-bristling Soviet Union."[46] Public concern at these revelations was exacerbated on 6 January 1958 with the release of a report on the military aspects of national security, produced under the auspices of the Rockefeller Brothers Fund, which predicted that unless current trends were reversed, "the world balance of power will shift in favor of the Soviet bloc."[47] Senator Johnson immediately used the public outcry concerning the Gaither and Rockefeller reports in his hearings. US national security was being jeopardized, he suggested, by both interservice rivalry and the president's stubborn refusal to spend funds for protection from new threats revealed by the launch of *Sputnik*.[48]

The results of the Rockefeller report were not all negative for the administration. It had been drafted by a panel directed by Henry Kissinger as part of a series of six studies under the overall direction of Nelson Rockefeller. Not surprisingly, then, the conclusions of the report concerning defense organization reflected many of the ideas and proposals that Rockefeller and Brundage had worked through with the president in November.[49] The reaction to this section of the report proved invaluable for an administration without a ready reorganization plan to gauge the opposition that could be expected from future Pentagon reform proposals.

The most immediate and visible opponents were the chairmen of the Senate and House Armed Services committees, who were veterans of the naval affairs committees that had merged in 1946 into the current organizations they headed. Both men favored the traditional Navy approach of decentralization in defense organization. Senator Richard Russell of Georgia was, as he stated, "not a single department man." And his House counterpart from the same state, Carl Vinson, rejected all the Rockefeller report's organizational proposals, denouncing the idea of a single chief of staff in the form of the JCS chairman as "a road to national suicide" and praising interservice competition as a healthy development in contrast to the growth of the Defense Department into a "fifth service."[50]

In the meantime, the president used the entire first week of the New Year to prepare for his 9 January 1958 state of the union speech. His primary writer was Bryce Harlow, a member of the White House congressional liaison. Eisenhower was pleased with the way the Oklahoma native approached major issues, observing at one point in a handwritten note to him: "Good job! You think like I do."[51] In the coming months, Harlow would become indispensable to the administration's defense reform efforts, serving the president, as one White House colleague noted, "with more energy, devotion, tirelessness, street-wise counsel, and selflessness than almost anyone else."[52]

Harlow would need all his skills on the state of the union message. For the Pentagon reform advisory group had not yet even been formed, and the president wished to avoid detailed recommendations that lacked what he believed was the necessary imprimatur of that group. In the forty-five-minute address, Eisenhower left no doubt that his top priority initiative was defense reorganization. He notified Congress that he had this "never-ending problem" under special study and would soon finalize his conclusions. At that time, he would take such executive action as necessary and, in a separate message, present appropriate recommendations to Congress. In the meantime, the president emphasized, without anticipating the detailed form that reorganization should take, he could outline its major objectives: "real unity" in military activities, clear military subordination to civilian authority, and the end of interservice rivalries by means of "clear organization and decisive central control." He was not attempting at this time to pass judgment on the charge of harmful service rivalries, he assured Congress. "But one thing is sure. Whatever they are, American wants them stopped."[53] At the end of his address, Eisenhower received a standing ovation and returned to the White House "in fine spirits."[54]

But the euphoria would not last. Without specifics, his speech fell short of his goal to focus national attention on defense reorganization. On 15 January, at his first press conference since his stroke, reporters pressed him to expand on the reorganization principles in the state of the union message and explain how unification in the Pentagon "in reality" could move "from the discussion to the actual stage." The president responded vaguely with a reminder that he had given "many active hours" to reviewing the military record on the subject of unified command as he had known it for forty-five years, and in particular since 1947. As a consequence, he believed, his views on the subject were "completely objective," without personal bias. But he would remain the national commander in chief for only three more years, and his personal convictions, no matter how strong, could not be the final answer. "There must be a consensus reached with the Congress," he emphasized, "with the people that have the job of operating the services, to get the very finest kind of organization we can."[55]

For the reporters, accustomed to Eisenhower's assertion of executive power on major issues and well aware of his strong feelings on defense reorganization, the president's approach appeared disingenuous. "You are not saying, sir, or are you," one reporter asked, "that you will not fight for unification of the services?" Eisenhower replied testily that he was trying to put an effective plan before Congress. This would involve many discussions and conferences involving a great deal of argument. And he would do his best to express his views in a process that required the involvement of both Congress and the civilian and military leaders of the services. "I am certainly hopeful," Eisenhower concluded, "that it goes in the direction of what I believe."[56]

CHAPTER SEVENTEEN

Reform Proposals and Congressional Gauntlet, January–June 1958

Military organization was a subject I had long lived with. . . . I had definite ideas of the corrective measures that needed to be taken.

DWIGHT D. EISENHOWER

All we're trying to do is to set up an establishment that will function in peacetime, as it necessarily must in wartime, under the Secretary of Defense.

DWIGHT D. EISENHOWER

Now on some of these matters—such as the inner mysteries of a hydrogen atom—I certainly have no direct personal knowledge. But I do know something about the insides of a certain large five-sided building.

DWIGHT D. EISENHOWER

EISENHOWER'S PUBLIC COMMITMENT to defense reorganization in the state of the union address put further pressure on the secretary of defense. On 17 January, McElroy announced the members who had agreed to sit on the Pentagon reform advisory group, much to the relief of the president, who stressed the amount of "political heat" the administration was receiving on the issue.[1] There were no surprises in the group. Eisenhower had discussed each member with Rockefeller, McElroy, and Brundage since the fall and was pleased with what he considered "a distinguished body of broadly experienced individuals," who, he believed, would add more credibility to the reform package he would eventually send to Congress.[2] The members consisted of former JCS Chairmen General Bradley and Admiral Radford, the current chairman, General Twining, and Nelson Rockefeller. Robert Lovett declined because of ill health, but his former deputy secretary of defense, William Foster, now head of the Arms Control and Disarmament Agency, agreed to serve. In addition, General Gruenther would consult occasionally. To head the group,

McElroy selected Charles A. Coolidge, a well-known Boston lawyer and a former assistant secretary of defense, who had drafted the 18 November 1952 report by Lovett to President Truman that had become so influential in the reform proposals of Reorganization Plan No. 6.

On the morning of 25 January the president, accompanied by Bryce Harlow and General Goodpaster, traveled to the Pentagon to meet with the Coolidge group. Eisenhower attended the meeting primarily to demonstrate his interest. But in the discussions, he was disturbed that some of the participants appeared "too eager to prove that things were perfect as they were," and that many of the others "wanted to avoid any radical change, feeling that the best chance of getting some improvement rested on cautious attempts to change a number of small things." As a consequence, when McElroy asked for his views and comments, the president took control of the meeting, which had already lasted more than two hours. He was not trying to dictate a particular solution, he began, although, he added forcefully, he had "very decided ideas" as to what "the right solution" would be. But he wanted to ensure that the group did not become complacent. It was impossible to "laugh off" the present criticism of the Defense Department's performance, he warned; "it won't do simply to justify everything now being done."[3]

Eisenhower's overall impression, he informed the participants, was that they had been talking about details rather than basic concepts. Large rather than incremental changes would be required. To illustrate this point, he returned to two of his favorite reform issues, which he believed had been addressed only superficially during the meeting. To begin with, the JCS system as it existed was much too complicated. A large part of the solution, he urged, was the elimination of joint committees and the organization of the joint staff as an integrated entity, with the head of each section as part of "a real G-2/G-3 staff" reporting to the JCS operating corporately as a single chief of staff. As for the idea of an executive agent for strategic direction, the entire process was "crazy." The service secretaries, he stressed, should be interested not in strategic planning but instead in the administrative support required by the operational field commanders. In this regard, the group was losing focus on the principal point that under the secretary of defense, the JCS must be supreme if interservice rivalries and duplication of effort were to be reduced. From this concept, Eisenhower concluded, would flow the necessary organizational lines, "simple clear and free of delaying service obstructions. The

Joint Chiefs system as it now exists is too complicated to work in warfare when minutes will be as precious as months have been in the past."[4]

Eisenhower's meeting at the Pentagon, as Coolidge noted, "started the ball rolling" for his group's efforts. The panel began to hold meetings twice a week, with McElroy and Quarles, now acutely aware of the president's overriding interest, usually in attendance. As witnesses testified at these meetings, Coolidge would capture their ideas and circulate them in memoranda to the members of the panel. He also remained in close contact with Bryce Harlow and General Goodpaster at the White House. Both men, "who knew what the President thought completely," were at Coolidge's disposal "all the time," allowing him to clear up any points made by Eisenhower in the initial and subsequent meetings on defense reorganization. This was particularly important for the panel director, who had not seen the president since his stroke and was "deeply worried" by what he perceived as Eisenhower's difficulty on 25 January in expressing himself.[5]

By 19 February the Coolidge group had finished with testimony and assembled the input into ten major subjects to be addressed in terms of defense reorganization. Two days later, the group, accompanied by the secretary of defense, flew to Ramey Air Force Base in Puerto Rico for a weekend of "hammering" out a plan.[6] On 27 February, McElroy and Coolidge briefed the president on the results of the panel's work in Puerto Rico. Coolidge used three organizational charts that soon drew Eisenhower into detailed discussions.[7] Over the next several months, Eisenhower reworked the successive drafts of the reorganization message to Congress. On Sunday, 30 March, he dictated to Ann Whitman over the phone from his Gettysburg farm a memorandum to Goodpaster on the changes.[8] All in all, he told UN Ambassador Henry Cabot Lodge, he had been "going to town" on the message to Congress. "I am determined to make it, in all respects, 'mine.'"[9]

On 1 April the president hosted Republican congressional leaders to brief them on the latest reform plan. The presentations went smoothly until Coolidge introduced the idea of a change in the appropriations process: the fiscal year 1960 defense budget would not be divided among the three services. Instead, as Eisenhower had worked out with the panel, Congress would appropriate some funds to eight broad defense categories as well as to the services. The secretary of defense would then allocate the funds from the categories to the military departments as he deemed proper. The recommendation represented a compromise on the part of the president, who wanted all defense appropriations to go directly to the secretary. Nevertheless, it elicited strong reaction from the legislators, who concluded the meeting by insisting that the appropriations proposal would prevent the president from realizing his desire for widespread defense reform. He needed to realize, one senator pointed out, the "great concern" of Congress with maintaining the power of the purse, a power that it would "not surrender lightly."[10]

The reorganization message that Eisenhower sent to Congress on 3 April was uniquely his own in expression and organization despite the mammoth incremental vetting process that had been under way for months at the White House and Pentagon. Into the seven thousand–word document he poured ideas concerning his concept of unified command at the national and operational levels and linked them specifically to his unique and extensive experiences in both peace and war. From that perspective, it was only natural for him to begin with his fundamental governing principle that "separate ground, sea and air warfare is gone forever. If ever again we should be involved in war, we will fight it in all elements, with all services as one single concentrated effort. Peacetime preparatory and organizational activity must conform to this fact."[11]

The president then turned to six broad objectives and specific recommendations for action focused on "the vital necessity for complete unity." The first objective was to organize US fighting forces into operational commands that were "truly unified." The entire defense organization must exist to make those unified commands the "cutting edge" of the US military machine. As a consequence, it was his intention that, except for units personally approved by him, all operational forces would be organized into unified commands, established at his direction as part of the Defense Department, but separate from the military departments with missions and force levels that conformed to national objectives. He was not seeking to merge or abolish the traditional services, Eisenhower added; but for unified commands to succeed, any legal restrictions on the CINCs of those organizations should be repealed. "Because I have seen the evils of diluted command," he concluded, "I emphasize that each unified commander must have unquestioned authority over all units of his command. Forces must be assigned to the command and be removed only by central direction—by the Secretary of Defense or the Commander in Chief—and not [by] any orders of individual military departments."

The second objective, closely aligned to the first, was to "clear" command channels so that orders would proceed directly from the president and secretary of defense to the CINCs of the operational commands. Eisenhower began by describing the existing chain of command he had established in 1953 that ran to the unified commands through whatever service secretary was designated as the executive agent. It was clear, the president acknowledged, that the service secretaries and chiefs should not direct unified operations and that this chain of command had become "cumbersome and unreliable in time of peace and not usable in time of war." Every additional headquarters in the chain courted confusion of authority and diffusion of responsibility; and when military responsibility was unclear, civilian control was uncertain. He had therefore directed the secretary of defense to discontinue the use of military departments as executive agents for unified commands and was now requesting that Congress repeal any statutory authority that vested responsibilities for military operations in any official other than the defense secretary.

Given this assault on the military departments, Eisenhower sought to reassure the services with a third objective: that they must continue as agencies to administer their primary training and logistics functions for the service component forces under the CINCs of the unified commands—a mission they would be better able to discharge after being relieved of direct responsibility for military operations. The changes in the organization and support of the operational forces would also require a fourth objective concerned with the Joint Chiefs. The JCS concept, the president explained, was "essentially sound" and should continue as currently provided in law. But given the shift that he had directed in operational channels, the JCS must be further unified and strengthened in order to provide the operational and planning assistance previously furnished for the most part by the staffs of the military departments. To accomplish this, he had directed the secretary to add an integrated operations division and to discontinue the interservice committees positioned between the JCS and the joint staff. The committee system, he emphasized, existed because each military department felt obligated to judge independently each product of the joint staff. "Had I allowed my interservice and interallied staff to be similarly organized in the theaters I commanded during World War II," Eisenhower emphasized, "the delays and resulting indecisiveness would have been unacceptable to my superiors."

To aid in strengthening the JCS, the president also requested that

Congress raise or remove the statutory limit on the joint staff and authorize the JCS chairman to assign duties to that staff and, with the secretary's approval, to appoint its director. At the same time, in the interest of correcting any misunderstanding of JCS procedures, Eisenhower also requested repeal of the current provision of the National Security Act stipulating that the chairman should have no vote. It was wrong to "so single out" that position, he explained, since the JCS did not act by voting. In addition, the president proposed legislative change enabling each chief of a military service to delegate major positions of his service responsibilities to his vice chief. The dual-hat problem for the Joint Chiefs had not yielded to past efforts, but it was time to find a solution, particularly because of the new strategic planning and operational burdens being imposed on the JCS and the Joint Staff. Once Congress had changed the law, Eisenhower promised, the defense secretary would "require the chiefs to use their power of delegation to enable them to make the Joint Chiefs of Staff duties their principal duties."

The president's fifth objective was to reorganize the research-and-development function of the Defense Department in order to make the best use of scientific and technological resources. Just as he had in his 1953 reorganization message, Eisenhower returned to the rapidly changing environment, in which war had been revolutionized by new technology and techniques. As a consequence, he considered it "essential" that the defense secretary's control over organization and funds for his department's research and development be made "complete and unchallengeable." To this end, he proposed to establish the position of director of defense research and engineering, ranking immediately after the service secretaries and above the assistant secretaries of defense. This official, who should be nationally known as a leader in science and technology, would eliminate unpromising duplicative programs, release promising ones for development or production, and initiate projects to ensure that such gaps as might exist were filled. Above all, he would plan research and development to meet national military objectives, instead of the "more limited requirements of each of the military services."

Eisenhower's final objective was couched in the broadest of terms concerning the need to remove "all doubt" as to the defense secretary's "full authority." That official, he began, was accountable to the president and Congress for the unified direction of the nation's largest single activity. And yet his authority had been "circumscribed and hedged about" in a manner that not only increased his burdens but worked against the effective unified direction of national security activities. As a consequence, the president pointed to three key areas that required attention. As a start, he recommended that Congress in the future make appropriations for the Defense Department in such a fashion as to provide the secretary "adequate authority and flexibility" in money matters "both among and within the military departments." In keeping with a last-minute decision to soften this aspect of his message, the president made no reference to lump-sum appropriations. Nor did he provide specific recommendations other than to point out that the need for centralized control of funding was particularly acute in terms of the secretary's missions of strategic planning and operational control and that the current methods for providing funds worked against the unity of the Pentagon as an executive department of the US government.

The second area had to do with the current "inconsistent and confusing" language of the National Security Act, which gave the secretary "direction, authority and control" over his entire department, yet also provided that the military departments were to be "separately administered." Such contradictory concepts, the president pointed out, "unavoidably abrade the unity of the Defense Department." It was time to be done with "prescribing controversy by law." He therefore recommended eliminating from the current law the provision for separate administration and other "needless and injurious restraints" on the secretary's authority. In terms of those restraints, Eisenhower also specifically called attention to the need of the defense secretary for greater control in the Pentagon over the distribution of functions. It was time, he proposed, for removing any doubts concerning the secretary's authority to transfer, reassign, abolish, or consolidate the functions of the Defense Department.

A final area was focused on personnel recommendations to enhance the centralization of authority. To facilitate administration of the reorganized department, Eisenhower proposed that in addition to the new research and engineering position, there was a need for seven assistant secretaries of defense and a general counsel of equivalent rank. The president conceived these positions as being empowered to give instructions for implementing policies approved by the secretary of defense and subject "at all times," he was careful to point out, to the rights of service secretaries to raise contested issues with the secretary. One of the positions would be responsible for legislative liaison, part of a new centralized focus on this field as well as on public relations. He had directed a review of service activities in both areas with the intention of increasing the secretary's supervision over them without impeding the flow of information to Congress and the public. "We do not want defense dollars spent on publicity and influence campaigns," Eisenhower emphasized, "in which each service claims superiority over the others and strives for increased appropriations or other Congressional favors."

In relatively minor personnel policies, the president also announced that he was instituting procedures to provide the secretary of defense the authority to transfer officers, with their consent, between services in order to ensure a distribution of proper technical skills among the military departments. At the same time, in order to promote jointness at the highest military level, he would approve flag officers for advancement to the two highest ranks in the future only on recommendation of the defense secretary after he had consulted with the Joint Chiefs. To achieve such promotions, the officers must have demonstrated "the capacity for dealing objectively—without service partisanship—with matters of the broadest significance to our national security." Eisenhower ended his message by advising the House and the Senate that the secretary of defense would soon transmit draft legislation to carry out those items in his message that required legislative action. "I urge the Congress to consider them promptly," he concluded, "and to cooperate fully in making these essential improvements in our Defense Establishment."

The effort concerning the proposed legislation was under the supervision of Robert Dechert, the Defense Department general counsel, working with the Bureau of the Budget Director and various members of the White House staff. On 16 April the president sent the draft bill on defense reorganization to Congress, along with a detailed analysis of its contents. In his letter of transmittal to the president of the Senate and speaker of the House, Eisenhower pointed out that he had already begun to take some initiatives through executive administrative actions and that those actions combined with the proposed legislation would allow him to carry out the reorganization recommendations in his 9 January state of the union address and his 3 April message to Congress. He was acting, he assertively reminded Congress, under his constitutional obligation to recommend such measures as he judged "necessary and expedient." At the same time, however, he confirmed his retreat on funding by calling attention to the fact that the draft bill contained "no provisions relating to the appropriation of funds to the Department of Defense."[12]

The issue of congressional testimony had not been addressed in the president's 3 April message. Consequently, it became the object of more attention and controversy with the release of the draft administration bill, which repealed that part of the current law that allowed service secretaries or JCS members to present recommendations to Congress on their own initiative after notification of the defense secretary. The remaining provisions of the proposed legislation reflected in more detail those aspects of the president's earlier recommendations that required statutory changes. The administration also sought to soften the request to eliminate the phrase "separately maintained" for the military departments by emphasizing its commitment to maintain separate services. It was also hoped that this commitment would provide assurance that the secretary could not use his authorization in the proposed legislation to transfer or abolish functions as a device either to merge or to eliminate military departments. This was important since the new proposal required the repeal of the existing law's specific prohibition against any action by the defense secretary concerning combatant functions. Instead, the new bill lumped together both combatant and noncombatant functions, the latter never prohibited in the past, and permitted the secretary to abolish or transfer both types with thirty days' advance notification to the congressional Armed Services committees.[13]

Carl Vinson responded immediately by scheduling hearings to begin on 22 April and by attacking all aspects of Eisenhower's proposals in an emotional, hourlong speech on the House floor. In terms of the president's theme of changing needs in the missile age, Vinson argued that "space ships, satellites and guided missiles cannot abrogate the Constitution of the United States." And as for the JCS, the bill would destroy "this sound, effective and war-proven system" by increasing the power of the JCS chairman.[14]

Vinson also promised a thorough examination of the reorganization bill and those testifying before his committee. For some of the administration witnesses, he warned on 20 April, "it may be a painful experience . . . similar to the Spanish bullfighter's 'moment of truth' when he stands sword in hand, before the horns of the charging bull."[15] The first of these was Secretary McElroy, who led off the testimony before the

House Armed Services Committee on 2 April. The secretary read a pre-pared statement that referred to the "lifetime of personal experience in peace and war, of the President, whose judgment in such matters as these has deeply marked every element of the proposal now before your com-mittee." The focus of the legislation, he continued, was on the concept of unified command as the "heart and soul" of the president's reorgani-zation program. From the "continuing refinement" of that concept since the beginning of World War II had emerged the need for unified strategic planning, an improved joint staff, and sufficiently clear authority in the Office of the Secretary of Defense to make certain that the unified com-mands had the support necessary to carry out their missions.[16]

In the questioning that followed the statement, there was a general concern that the unified-command concept could be used as a precursor to the merger of the services, particularly if the defense secretary could transfer or abolish the combat functions of the military departments. McElroy repeatedly explained that while the administration bill provided for the unified direction of the three departments, it specifically prohib-ited their mergers, as it did the designation of a single chief of staff over the services or an armed forces general staff. But would it not be possible, one committee member pressed, for a future secretary, if so inclined, to use the new command structure to transfer all service personnel into uni-fied commands—in effect eliminating the separate services and unifying the armed forces by executive order. That "could happen," McElroy ad-mitted, even conceding before the committee adjourned until the next day that it would also be possible to organize support forces into unified commands.[17]

The defense secretary's testimony was cited the next day in a presi-dential news conference. Sarah McClendon, a reporter for a small Texas paper, held that the House committee had "wrung an admission" from McElroy that it might be possible in the future to have a "dictatorial" president and secretary of defense, who under the new legislation might transfer all troop units from the military departments to unified com-mands and leave none under the service secretaries and chiefs. "Now," she asked, "would that not enable our man someday to have a personal-ized military force if he were of such a turn?" An obviously angry presi-dent responded immediately. "Well, I've got one question to ask you: have you read the law?" Her affirmative answer did not satisfy him. "No you haven't, I don't think," he began as he attempted to explain that the military services were not being weakened. "Now look, Mrs. McClendon," Eisenhower concluded, "it might be just as, well, sensible for you to say that the Congress is suddenly going nuts and completely abolishing the Defense Department. . . . I think it is just not possible if we are sensible people."[18]

That same day, McElroy returned to Congress for three more days of questioning. The secretary of defense held his own on most issues. But when it came to the provisions concerning the JCS chairman and the joint staff, he encountered difficulties despite his detailed explanation of the reasons why the changes proposed in the bill were "really minimal." From his first day as a witness, McElroy had been pummeled with queries concerning the proposed repeal of the right of service secretaries and chiefs to appeal on their own initiative to Congress after notifying the defense secretary. Under continued questioning on the issue, the defense secretary retreated. "Well, I would simply like to say," he responded, "that our feet are not in concrete on this, and if the committee decides that this is an important privilege to retain, I personally would not oppose it." Instantly, Vinson was alert to the concession. "Did you catch the distinguished Secretary's last statement?" he asked the other members. If they hadn't, McElroy clarified his position under questioning two more times before he finished his testimony at the end of the week. The administration believed that the legislation would be "cleaned up," he stated, with the removal of the provision in question. But if that was not regarded by the Congress as something in the public interest, he would not oppose its retention, "and I don't think any of the rest of us will."[19]

A second issue concerning the power of the secretary of defense involved even greater concessions. McElroy was unable to convince the committee that the provision for "separately administered" military departments diminished the secretary's direct authority and control over those departments. Committee members were particularly skeptical in light of the proposed bill's authorization for the newly created assistant defense secretaries to issue instructions in the secretary's name to the military departments. As Vinson pointed out, those new positions, as well as the proposed Office of Research and Engineering, would considerably increase the size of the Office of the Secretary of Defense. McElroy admitted as much, even volunteering to "come clean" on the subject by pointing out that increased centralization of public affairs and legislative liaison would entail some movement of personnel from the services to the secretary's office. More important, the defense secretary acknowledged that the new bill provided him more authority than he ever intended to use. His attorneys had advised him, he stated, that "unnecessarily broad" language was required to ensure the type of authority he desired. "Now then," he continued, "if we can find . . . in those particular areas ways in which we can say these things without being unduly restrictive, then I would think it would be all right."[20]

Once again, the chairman sensed an opening. Could the secretary then, Vinson asked, accomplish what he wanted without such a broad repeal of the present statutes? McElroy acknowledged that this was possible, an answer that was still too vague for Democratic Representative F. Edward Hébert. "In other words," the Louisiana congressman stated, "you are not wedded to the language of the bill that was brought up here in the President's message." That was correct, the secretary responded. "Our approach is flexible," he added.[21]

Word of McElroy's "flexibility" reached Eisenhower from a report in a local newspaper at Augusta, Georgia, where he was vacationing. The president had stated earlier that he did not regard the bill's exact language as necessarily sacrosanct. But he knew at once that the new testimony had opened the way for Vinson to change some of the key provisions of the bill. The president immediately called the defense secretary, who assured him that no changes in the meaning of the bill had been implied by any testimony of his and agreed with Eisenhower that there could be "no compromise" on the legislation.[22] Eisenhower then dictated a statement to his press secretary, stating that while McElroy had been correct in not insisting on "rigid adherence to words and phraseology," his testimony had not implied an alteration in the meaning of any feature of the proposed bill. Both he and the secretary, the president emphasized, agreed that there could be "no compromise on or retreat from the essentials" of the legislation.[23]

Eisenhower was about to embark on a three-pronged campaign under the direction of Bryce Harlow in order to increase pressure on Capitol Hill in favor of the reorganization bill. The first approach was to include in almost every one of his public speeches some reference to his reform efforts. The second effort of Harlow's campaign focused on gaining support from both sides of the aisle. "Here Bryce's abilities absolutely shone in turning around, almost completely, the top Congressional leaders," Goodpaster recalled of his White House staff colleague. "Other than the

President himself, no one but Bryce could have done it. Bryce was the key figure."[24] Democratic Party support was predictably more problematical. Eisenhower was thus grateful when President Truman spoke out for the reorganization efforts. And he telephoned his "warm thanks" to Clarence Cannon, chairman of the House Appropriations Committee, for making what the president considered a "statesmanlike" speech, in which the Missouri Democrat had couched the reorganization issue in apocalyptic terms. "This is not an academic discussion," Cannon stated. "A thousand years of civilization weigh in the balance."[25]

Eisenhower's third method of lobbying for the reorganization bill was to write directly to hundreds of influential business executives to "explain the issues at stake" and to ask them to make "their own conclusions known to the members of Congress."[26] The "regular letter," as Ann Whitman termed it, was enormously successful, resulting in what the president characterized as a "flood of messages" favoring the bill to congressional offices.[27] One recipient reported that he had sent twenty thousand letters of his own to ask friends and employees for their help. Some congressional members quickly accused the president, as he noted, "of the heinous offense of 'going over the head of Congress,'" welcome criticism to Eisenhower, who considered it as evidence that the effects of his efforts were "being felt in the proper places." Some of the more outspoken critics of the bill, he recalled, "suddenly began to see many virtues in it."[28]

In the meantime, Vinson's Armed Services Committee continued its hearings with testimony by the Joint Chiefs, which was generally supportive of the bill. Admiral Burke's statement, however, was also tinged with a hint of doubt. "The important thing about making changes is to be sure that they are really improvements," he cautioned. "Change is not in itself progress." Under questioning, the chief of naval operations acknowledged that he had expressed "apprehensions" about some elements of the draft legislation, a good many of which had been eliminated. "That is somewhat of an indictment," the always attentive Vinson commented.[29]

As the committee probed further, Burke revealed that he was against eliminating the right in the current law for JCS members and service secretaries to appeal to Congress. Nor was he in favor of unrestricted expansion of the joint staff, which would then, he believed, interfere in the operations of the unified commands and "crank out more papers than the Joint Chiefs of Staff can read and study." At the same time he professed indifference to the replacement of the executive agent system with the

JCS, noting that there was "nothing wrong with either." And when pressed on the issue of using force assignments to unified commands in order to eliminate or reduce the services, Burke, like McElroy, admitted the possibility that under the proposed legislation some future secretary of defense could use the "rather wide language" to do "drastic things which nobody intends at the moment." The committee quickly expanded the subject to the proposed repeal of the prohibition on any actions by the defense secretary with service combatant functions. The admiral admitted that he was apprehensive about the future ability to "stretch" interpretations of the functions provisions in the bill to eliminate naval aviation or the Marine Corps, and that the mandated thirty-day notification of Congress provided "no safeguard at all." At the conclusion of the testimony, a grateful Hébert advised Burke, "Until you appeared here this afternoon, I was getting a little discouraged about this committee getting the real facts in the case except by pulling teeth."[30]

At the same time, in response to Vinson's request during the opening week of testimony, McElroy submitted written answers for the record based on discussions with Coolidge and Twining and cleared by Harlow and others at the White House. These concise, well-organized responses presented in logical order the reasons why the administration bill would not create a single chief of staff or a supreme, monolithic general staff and would pose no threat of service merger through changes concerning combat functions. To this was added the testimony of General Counsel Dechert, a former Army officer who had fought alongside the Marines at Belleau Wood in World War I and who refused to accept the simplistic answers offered by some committee members for complex questions. In precise, often esoteric detail, Dechert skillfully defended the phrasing of the legislation he had written, at one time admonishing Vinson that "these pieces of language which you, sir, have indicated are not intended to deprive the Secretary of Defense of full power, have nevertheless been used by numerous people to indicate that the Secretary of Defense does not have that full power."[31]

There was equally unyielding and effective support by Admiral Radford and General Bradley. Radford began by emphasizing his "full accord" with Eisenhower's objectives, Bradley by declaring his full agreement with the recommendations of "our President." Both former JCS chairmen then attempted to defuse many of the congressional concerns with the administration bill. Bradley assured the committee members that service merger was not a possibility. "You wouldn't let it happen," he emphasized, "regardless of the wording." Radford focused on the need for control of service functions by the defense secretary to provide him flexibility in a time of great change that he had "never envisaged in 1949." Both men agreed that the defense secretary's power was confusedly contradicted by the provision for the services to be "separately administered by their respective Secretaries." Many of the congressmen were not fully convinced. "Can you suggest to the committee," an exasperated Vinson demanded of Bradley, "any English word that carries more authority than 'direction, authority and control'?"[32]

Throughout the House hearings, Vinson had the committee staff translate daily developments into "proper legislative language." On 12 May, the last day of the hearings, he was thus able to send to the White House his committee's own draft bill, which included the majority of the provisions sought by Eisenhower. There were, however, several important differences. The new bill eliminated the phrase "separately administered" in accordance with the administration's recommendations but required that the military departments be "separately organized" and that the control by the secretary of defense be "exercised through the respective Secretaries of such departments." In keeping with Eisenhower's proposals, most functions could be transferred by the secretary after a thirty-day notification period to Congress. But in the committee draft, this did not apply to "major combatant functions." Instead, a sixty-day waiting period was stipulated for this type of function, during which Congress could block the transfer by concurrent resolution. At the same time, any member of the JCS was authorized to define what functions belonged in the category of "major combatant" and thus would be subject to the sixty-day congressional vetting process, a potential veto for each of the Joint Chiefs. The committee draft also retained the provision from the National Security Act, eliminated in the administration's bill, which allowed the service secretaries and Joint Chiefs to appeal to Congress. Finally, the joint staff was limited to four hundred officers, who could operate according to conventional staff procedures but were specifically prohibited from organizing as an armed forces general staff or from exercising any type of executive authority.[33]

That day, Harlow briefed the committee draft "section by section" to the president and the secretary of defense, both of whom agreed that the bill was "much too restrictive to be acceptable."[34] Between Tuesday, 13

May, and Thursday, 15 May, Harlow worked through three drafts, shut-
tling back and forth between McElroy on the one hand and key committee leaders and their staff on the other. On Thursday evening Harlow, who
had once worked on Vinson's staff, called the chairman at home concerning the latest committee draft. Vinson was in no mood for further negotiation. He requested a letter from the president endorsing the amended
bill. Otherwise, the committee would be unable to report the legislation
out to the House.[35]

Later that evening, Harlow informed the president, providing him a
copy of the committee bill and a positive draft response to Vinson. Eisenhower was in a quandary. On the one hand, as both McElroy and Harlow
had reminded him, the amended legislation incorporated most of the
provisions he had sought. On the other hand, three issues still remained
unsatisfactorily resolved for the president. His solution was to compromise. On 16 May he dispatched a letter to Vinson that he intended "to be
mild in tone, polite in tenor, but unmistakable so far as my dissatisfaction
with important details are concerned."[36] He began by toning down some
of the more positive aspects of Harlow's draft. Nevertheless, he devoted
most of the letter to congratulating Vinson on the "constructive efforts"
and the "progress" made by the committee on reorganization, acknowledging that "by and large the bill seems to deal positively with every major
problem I presented to Congress." At the same time, he added a cryptic
paragraph at the end of the letter, which informed the chairman that he
was sending over his views on "two quite important" issues and that he
hoped the language could be "suitably adjusted" on the House floor.[37]
Harlow delivered the letter to Vinson in person and explained that the
president had jettisoned the issue of appeal to Congress and was focusing
his objections on the requirement for the defense secretary's control to
be exercised through department secretaries and on the limitations governing his transfer of functions.

Eisenhower's gingerly approach to the two issues was hardly designed
to impress Vinson. On 16 May the chairman read the president's response
to the entire committee, described the interaction by his subcommittee
with the administration since the end of the hearings, and promptly set
about persuading the committee members to reject the two proposals
mentioned in the letter. At the end of the meeting, some members still
had doubts and questions. But Vinson was an immoveable force. "I want

this bill accepted, just like we have written it," he stated, "and let the country know we agreed on a bill." As a consequence, the committee was to decide immediately with "no hemming and hawing about it." And when the members voted unanimously for the committee bill, the satisfied chairman announced that a formal roll call would be held the following Wednesday after the legislation was introduced formally. That day, Vinson released a press statement that described the committee bill as "a meeting of the minds" that was "in harmony with the objectives of the President and is based upon the testimony of the Secretary of Defense and the Joint Chiefs of Staff."[38]

The president did not see things that way. It was obvious, as Harlow reported, that "Vinson has now reached the point where he believes he should not change the bill any further."[39] What was equally clear to Eisenhower was that he had been outmaneuvered and left with unattractive choices. Given the generally conciliatory tone of his letter, which Vinson had released publicly, a fight on the bill might seem vindictive, if not wildly inconsistent. On 19 May, the day Vinson introduced the amended bill as H.R. 12541, an angry Eisenhower met with GOP congressional leaders to review his limited options. Some of the legislators advised against attempting to have the bill amended on the House floor, something that would risk public defeat, given the Democratic majority. Instead, they proposed, once the Senate had addressed the bill, it might be possible to persuade the subsequent conference committee of both houses to eliminate the offending provisions. Others reminded the president that Vinson had a reputation for toughness in conference committees. House Minority Leader Joseph Martin agreed, recommending a fight on the House floor, which he believed could result in victory with Eisenhower's strong support. The president's final agreement to a House fight was hardly a model of confidence. "I've licked old Uncle Carl for 20 years," he concluded. "But I know how tough and dictatorial he can be."[40]

On 21 May the House Armed Services Committee unanimously approved HR 12541, and the next day the committee favorably reported it to the House. On 26 May, in a meeting with McElroy, Eisenhower reconfirmed his intention to oppose the two provisions of the committee bill that he had cited in his letter to Vinson. To this, he added once again his objection to the provision that authorized the right of appeal to Congress by service secretaries and JCS members. The next day the president met with Republican congressional leaders and vowed to fight the three provisions, which represented nothing more than "one man's arrogance and pride and egotism."[41]

On 28 May, after meeting with McElroy, the president argued in an unusually hard-hitting and pithy statement released to the press that the reported committee bill, which continued "to imply Congressional approval of wasteful duplications, administrative delays and interservice rivalry," "directly conflicted" with his reorganization legislation. The House committee had acted commendably on most of the needed changes, he acknowledged, but "pretty good is not good enough"; "America, having started on this reorganization, wants the job right." The first of the three "objectionable" committee changes added the new provision for the secretary to exercise his authority "through" the secretaries of the military departments. This was nothing more, Eisenhower explained, than a *"legalized bottleneck,"* which constricted the defense secretary's authority by putting "a premium on intransigence by lower Pentagon levels" and was couched in language ensuring that "frictions, delays, [and] duplications in the Defense Department would be given the color of legality."

The second committee change involved the sixty-day window during which Congress could veto any action by the secretary of defense concerning major combatant functions, as well as the authorization for any JCS member to determine what constituted such a function. Eisenhower described this amendment as the *"everyone's out of step but me"* provision, which would vest "astonishing authority" in one officer without regard to his civilian leadership while repudiating the concept of flexibility of combatant functions. In short, the committee change would constitute "an endorsement of duplication and standpattism in defense and of the concept of military superiority over civilian authority." Finally, the president characterized the provision restoring the right of appeal to Congress as *"legalized insubordination."* It not only invited interservice rivalries and insubordination to the president and the defense secretary, he emphasized, but it enforced the idea of disunity, blocked defense modernization, and suggested that Congress *"hoped"* for such disobedience and disputes among the services.[42]

Much of the press was startled, as Hanson Baldwin described it in the *New York Times,* by Eisenhower's "brusque," "rather astonishing" response. If successful, Baldwin concluded, the president's "unfair and extreme language" would shift the focus from the Soviet lead in Sputniks and long-range missiles to "service whipping boys and to a White House battle with an apparently recalcitrant and backward Congress."[43] Baldwin's *Times* colleague Arthur Krock accused Eisenhower of endorsing the House bill on 16 May and reversing the position on 28 May. The president responded the same day in a personal and confidential "Dear Arthur" letter to the columnist. His approval of the committee's work had been "sincere," he pointed out, subject to certain "important" exceptions. But he had failed to realize that his "general statement" of approval could be used as a vehicle for disregarding those exceptions. "I am not again going to make the mistake," Eisenhower concluded, "of assuming that a polite indication of disagreement—which in my former life was taken seriously indeed—can be interpreted as a weakness in will."[44]

As if to signal this determination, an unrepentant president only fueled the increasing partisan debate by seeking to solidify Republican ranks. Incensed at the approval of the House bill by all GOP committee members, he decided to send every Republican member of the House a copy of the defense modernization bill, as he described it, with a "plea" for solidarity on the three issues. The Democrats reacted to what they perceived as complete abandonment of a bipartisan approach on the part of the administration. Some members of Vinson's committee were upset that the president had rejected what they considered was a compromise worked out with his emissaries. House Speaker Sam Rayburn of Texas considered the Republican efforts at "corralling votes" on the three issues to be a blatant attempt to "crush" the Armed Services Committee. As for the chairman of that committee, it was the first time in his forty years in Congress that he could remember a national security issue having become "a subject of partisan politics."[45]

On 12 June attempts to amend the Vinson bill on the House floor to meet the president's objectives failed primarily on party lines by a vote of 192 to 211. At the same time, the House accepted an amendment that authorized the secretary of defense to use a single agency in order to carry out supply or service activity common to more than one military department. This single-manager amendment specifically exempted such activity from being a "major combatant function." Coolidge correctly perceived that this major concession, combined with the bill's authorization for the secretary to assign new weapons as he chose, provided the secretary considerably more power in terms of functions than when the president's bill was drafted.[46] A few days later, Eisenhower noted in a letter to a member of Congress that he believed that had party discipline not been "tightly drawn" by the Democrats, the "needed" amendments would have prevailed by a substantial margin. "That the House would divide along political lines in considering our national defense requirements is very disappointing," he concluded; "certainly at no point in the development of this legislation did I desire or expect strictly party considerations."[47]

And yet the vote along party lines was due in large part to the president. He regretted sending the 16 May congratulatory message to Vinson, who he believed had betrayed him by rejecting the two proposals referred to in the letter and later specifically explained to the chairman by Harlow. As a consequence, Eisenhower had resorted to increasingly shrill counter-moves, making it inevitable that his three proposals would be treated in a partisan manner. The result was an unnecessary and humiliating defeat for the president. With Vinson's bill, Eisenhower had achieved almost all his reorganization objectives. Moreover, there was a good chance that Vinson's action on the remaining three issues was in part a face-saving tactic that might have yielded to quiet compromise in conference after the Senate hearings and vote. That outcome was much less likely as the partisan tone on reorganization spread to that body.

CHAPTER EIGHTEEN

Executive-Legislative Reform: The 1958 Defense Reorganization Act, June–December 1958

Now, looking back over all the years since 1911 when I entered military service, I find it hardly surprising that a defense revision agitates partisans and traditionalists. . . . We can expect the same kind of resistance to the new modernization proposals.

DWIGHT D. EISENHOWER

B Y THE TIME THE SENATE hearings on the House bill began on 17 June, Bryce Harlow and Defense Counsel Robert Dechert were already working with the Senate committee on possible compromises. In his capacity as Senate Armed Services Committee chairman, Senator Richard Russell of Georgia was open to attempts at bipartisan efforts despite the partisan outcome that had been so disastrous for the administration in the House.

The proceedings ended on 9 July. On 17 July the Senate Armed Services Committee reported out substitute legislation that was passed unanimously by the Senate the next day. Vinson promptly accepted the compromise worked out by Russell with the administration. It required only twenty-seven minutes for the House-Senate conference committee to report out the final bill. That day, Eisenhower issued a short statement thanking both chairmen for the "praiseworthy job" by their committees. "Except in relative minor respects," he concluded, "the bill adequately meets every recommendation that I submitted to the Congress on this subject."[1] On 6 August 1958 the president signed the bill into law, issuing a restrained statement, which merely noted that the legislation represented "a major advance" in defense organization and that he expected the "faithful execution" of its provisions.[2]

The struggle resulting in the new reorganization legislation had been surprising from a number of perspectives. Eisenhower, as the historian Clinton Rossiter noted at the time in *The American Presidency,* was likely to go down in history as one of the "earth-smoothers," not one of the "earth-shakers."[3] But when it came to his reorganization efforts in 1958, Eisenhower's natural inclination for conciliation with Congress faded before his absolute conviction based on his years of experience that he knew more about how the armed forces should be organized from the national to the theater level than any other person currently in active public life.

In the new legislation, Eisenhower achieved the majority of his objectives within his first goal of improving strategic planning and advice, because many of his proposals were relatively modest. Certainly, his approach to strengthening the authority of the JCS chairman was governed by congressional fears of a man on horseback. In 1953 he had attempted to provide the chairman authority to organize and direct the strategic planning staff system without weakening the ability of the Joint Chiefs to provide military advice as a group. In his 1958 proposals the president attempted to make the joint staff directly responsive to the independent authority of the JCS chairman by authorizing him to assign duties to the joint staff and to select its director. Congress, however, continued to limit the chairman's authority over the joint staff. The final act authorized the JCS chairman to select the director of the joint staff, but only "in consultation with" the Joint Chiefs, and directed the joint staff to perform its duties as prescribed not only by the chairman but by the JCS as well. Finally, the 1953 authorization for the chairman to manage the joint staff and its director was mitigated with the addition in the new act of the phrase "on behalf of the Joint Chiefs of Staff."[4]

At the same time, by abolishing the executive-agent system, the president emphasized the primacy of the Joint Chiefs as strategic planners and advisers unencumbered by command responsibilities. Congress also designated specific authority, at Eisenhower's request, for the service chiefs to "delegate" or "prescribe" many of their service duties to their vice chiefs.[5] It was his hope that through these changes the emphasis on the corporate duties of the Joint Chiefs would become overriding. Nevertheless, as Goodpaster recalled, Eisenhower "acknowledged some doubt" since he understood that his organizational changes in 1958 would not eliminate the natural wellspring of service parochialism in the dual-hat system.[6]

Eisenhower's last major effort in terms of improving strategic planning and advice focused on transforming the military staff working for the JCS into an independent one with a unified national perspective. To this end, Congress responded to the president's request to eliminate the statutory ceiling of officers in the joint staff by raising that ceiling from 210 to 400, even as Eisenhower eliminated by executive order the joint staff committee system in an attempt to reduce service influence. All this notwithstanding, the evolutionary progress in terms of the structure and procedures of the joint staff was still enough to raise the traditional civil-military fears of Congress, which stipulated in the new law that the joint staff "shall not operate or be organized as an overall Armed Forces General Staff and shall have no executive authority."[7]

As he had with strategic planning and advising, the president met his second goal concerning resource allocation to forces, programs, and weapons partly by scaling back the objectives. The primary compromise had to do with his desire for congressional approval of lump-sum budget authority for the secretary of defense. Recognizing the adamancy of congressional objections from both sides of the aisle, Eisenhower jettisoned this proposal during the period between his 3 April message to Congress and the 16 April submission of his reorganization bill. With this matter settled, Congress proceeded to fulfill the president's request of statutory authorization for the new position of defense research and engineering director. This official, who would rank in precedence just behind the service secretaries, would act as the principal scientific and technical adviser to the secretary; supervise all research and engineering activities in the Defense Department; and direct and control assignment and reassignment of those activities that the secretary "deems to require centralized management." In this manner, the director could stop the rush by the services for new roles and missions that had characterized the Pentagon since World War II. To emphasize their agreement with the need for this type of centralization, both Armed Services committees specifically authorized the defense secretary "to assign or reassign, to one or more departments or services, the development and operational use of new weapons or weapons systems."[8] In effect, this provision allowed the secretary to decide how the services would be armed—a power formerly the exclusive prerogative of the professional military.

Eisenhower's third major goal and his dominant theme for defense reorganization concerned the need for unity of command and unity of effort from the highest national level down through the theater level, commensurate with the increased centralization of authority in the Pentagon brought about by progress in the unification process. Congress recognized the president's interest and expertise in this area by agreeing to most of his requested changes despite some inconsistent and even illogical responses at some points by administration witnesses. The new law authorized the president through the secretary of defense and with the advice and assistance of the JCS to establish unified or specified commands, now also termed "combatant" commands, to assign them missions, and to determine their force structure.

Congress also honored Eisenhower's desire to create a clear line of command to the CINCs from him through the secretary of defense, with the JCS acting as the secretary's operational staff. The combatant theater commanders, the new law stipulated, were responsible in turn to both the president and the secretary for implementing assigned missions. To this end, Congress delegated the CINCs full "operational command" over land, sea, and air forces, the assignment of which could be transferred only with presidential approval. In this regard, the Reorganization Act specifically removed any references to command by the services, authorizing the service chiefs to exercise supervision over the members and organizations of their respective services "in a manner consistent with the full operational command vested in unified or specified combatant commanders." That this type of arrangement provided the CINCs new authority was demonstrated in the JCS definition approved by the president, which stipulated that the functions of operational command over assigned forces involved "the composition of subordinate forces, the assignment of tasks, the designation of objectives, the over-all control of assigned resources, and the full authoritative direction necessary to accomplish the mission."[9]

The new chain of operational command to the combatant forces also excluded the military departments and their service staffs from direction and control of military operations. The service secretaries and chiefs were, in effect, reduced to roles as "providers and maintainers" of the forces assigned to the unified commands. The beneficiary of this division of labor was the secretary of defense, who continued the trend since 1949 of increasing the power and authority of his position under the evolving unification process at the national level at the expense of the military departments. Given congressional fears concerning civilian supremacy, Eisenhower understood that his proposals for more centralization in his overall concept of unified command must focus on the position of defense secretary rather than on his longtime desire for dramatic increases in the authority of the JCS chairman. Even then, Congress balked at three administration proposals that affected the secretary's authority.

The first issue addressed the elimination of any statutory constraints on the formal authority of the defense secretary or any other legislative provisions that protected the authority of the individual services. Carl Vinson had helped craft the language in the 1949 amendments to the National Security Act that provided the secretary the "direction, authority, and control" over the "separately administered" military departments. His committee acceded to the president's request for elimination of the "separately administered" phase, providing "separately organized" as a substitute acceptable to the administration. At the same time, however, the committee added that the secretary's direction, authority, and control over the military departments would be exercised "through the respective Secretaries of such departments," a provision that reflected congressional fears of encroachment by assistant secretaries of defense. The 1953 plan had stipulated that those assistant secretaries should not be in a direct line of administrative authority between the defense secretary and the three military departments. But in his 3 April message to Congress five years later, Eisenhower referred to the power of the assistant secretaries "to give instructions appropriate to carry out the polices approved by the Secretary of Defense."[10]

The administration chose to interpret the new phrase inserted by Congress as an attempt to keep individual service secretaries in the operational chain of command despite specific commitments throughout the draft congressional reorganization bill to the new streamlined chain of command. In the end the president was successful in eliminating the phrase, but only at the cost of an addition to the Reorganization Act directing that no assistant secretary of defense would have authority to issue orders to a military department unless the defense secretary had delegated specifically such authority to him in writing. For Eisenhower in retrospect, the issue was "one of the less important ones," useful primarily as a "red herring" to draw fire, "allowing the whole major undertaking to proceed virtually unscathed."[11]

Eisenhower had less apparent success with the issue of transferring, merging, reassigning, or abolishing major combatant functions. The 1949 amendments contained the first explicit statutory limitation of executive alteration of combatant functions, an ironic development since the purpose of those amendments had been to clarify and strengthen the defense secretary's power. The president's call for repeal of this restriction nine years later foundered on the reluctance of Congress to diminish its constitutional authority in the assignments of roles and missions. He was successful in eliminating the House addition that empowered any member of the JCS to define a "major" combatant function, the "everyone's out of step but me" provision that allowed one or more of the Joint Chiefs to throw any proposed change up to Congress. But after prolonged negotiations, the final reorganization bill stipulated that in making a "substantial transfer" of a major combatant function, the defense secretary had to report such action to the House and Senate Armed Services committees, which then had thirty days to report out any resolution against the action. If either committee did so, the bill gave both houses of Congress an additional forty days to approve the resolution. If either the House or Senate so approved, the function transfer could not occur.[12]

Despite these restrictions on his original proposal, Eisenhower came to view them as making "a small hole in the doughnut." After all, as Harlow pointed out, Congress had provided authorization in the new legislation for the secretary of defense to deal with functions on an unrestricted basis during emergencies or imminent threats; to assign or reassign to the services responsibility for development and operational use of new weapons; and to direct single-management supply or service activities common to more than one military department without such operations being considered as actions involving major combatant functions. In a similar manner, Eisenhower glossed over his clear defeat concerning the retention in the final bill of the provision that he termed "legalized insubordination," which authorized the service secretaries and chiefs to go directly to Congress with any recommendations relating to the Department of Defense that they "may deem proper."[13] Still, he consoled himself by dwelling on a reaction to similar circumstances by the only West Pointer to precede him as president. "I cannot make the Comptroller General change his mind," he recalled Ulysses S. Grant once stating, "but I can get a new Comptroller General."[14]

There was still unfinished executive action required on the reorganization effort. In August the Defense Department under the supervision of Deputy Secretary Quarles began to revise two basic department directives in order to make them conform to the new reorganization act and the president's 3 April message to Congress. DOD Directive 5100.1 was concerned with the functions of the armed forces and the JCS, and DOD Directive 5158.1 dealt with JCS operations and the relationship of the Joint Chiefs with other departmental agencies. In addition, the JCS made necessary changes in the unified command plan designed to strengthen the command authority of the unified commanders, to fix their force structure, and to eliminate the designation of military departments as executive agents. The phasing in of the new system would begin with the European Command (USEUCOM) on 15 September, Twining informed the president, and would be completed by the coming of the New Year. At the same time, the JCS chairman elaborated, the joint staff system would come into effect, establishing parallel functional lines for the JCS with the headquarters staffs of the unified and specified commands as well as the service component forces under the CINCs. Eisenhower, Goodpaster reported, "heartily welcomed" the arrangement that he had long sought.[15]

By the early fall there seemed to be evidence that Eisenhower's reorganization efforts were having a calming effect on the nation. The United States had also launched four satellites, compared with three by the Soviets, a reassuring trend in the space effort somewhat mitigated by the fact that *Sputnik III* was eighty times the weight of *Explorer III*. But politically, the president's position was being undermined by his insistence on fiscal restraint in a period when the Democrats were demanding increased spending to combat the recession at home while matching the Soviet challenge abroad. The result was a sweeping Democratic victory in the 4 November midterm congressional elections, which resulted in Democratic gains of thirteen seats in the Senate and forty-seven in the House, as well as the addition of five governors, leaving control of thirty-four state capitals in the hands of the other party.

This humiliating defeat adversely affected Eisenhower's efforts to put a ceiling of forty billion dollars on the fiscal year 1960 defense budget. Earlier, he had warned Twining that the military must assist him, particularly concerning duplication of weapons with similar missions. The Pentagon did not comply, proposing once again a huge total in individual service requests, which even when pared down by McElroy still exceeded the president's goal by three billion dollars. The Berlin crisis in November only increased the demands for more funds by the services and the Democratic congressional majority. On 8 December, Eisenhower accepted a final figure of just under forty-one billion dollars for defense expenditures. The Joint Chiefs asserted that this was the minimum necessary for national security. The president, as he admitted to McElroy, believed that he had been "dragooned" and that he that he had no other choice.[16]

In the meantime, meetings continued throughout the fall on the two Pentagon directives for implementation of Defense Department reform. By late October an increasingly assertive JCS had raised several issues concerning relations with the secretary of defense and the Office of the Secretary of Defense (OSD). To begin with, the Joint Chiefs pointed out that their organization should not be considered one of the staff elements of OSD cited in the current "relationship" 5158.1 directive, as well as in the president's 3 April message to Congress. They were responsible, after all, not only to the defense secretary but by statute to the president and the National Security Council. Moreover, unlike OSD civilian officials, their duties were prescribed by law and required special training and expertise. At the same time, the Joint Chiefs concurred with the reorganization act's requirement that authority to issue orders to military departments must be delegated by the secretary in writing. But they also proposed that this authority be given only to assistant secretaries of defense and not extended to assistants of the secretary in the revision of the "functions" 5100.1 directive. Finally, the JCS proposed that 5100.1 should also be amended to include not only the new chain of operational command but a statement that the Joint Chiefs were in that chain.[17]

The White House staff was less than enthusiastic about the new draft 5100.1, which did not reflect "the full spirit of change the President seeks to install."[18] During the next month, Harlow worked out compromises with the Pentagon on the various issues. In particular, negotiators from both sides of the Potomac agreed to allow the Joint Chiefs to maintain the amendment that placed them "in the chain of operational command," but only with specific emphasis on their functions as advisers and military staff to the secretary and as coordinators and channels of communications to the unified and specified commanders. This concept of the Joint Chiefs as transmitters, not originators, of command orders was further embellished with the added assertion in 5100.1 that the CINCs of the operational commands were responsible only to the president and secretary of defense for the accomplishment of their military missions. The chain of command, the addition stipulated, ran "from" the president "to" the defense secretary "and through" the JCS to the CINCs. "Orders to such commanders will be issued by the President or the Secretary of Defense or by the Joint Chiefs of Staff by authority and direction of the Secretary of Defense."[19]

On 22 December, the president met with McElroy and Quarles to address 5100.1. Harlow was in attendance, as were the Joint Chiefs. Quarles acted as the spokesman for the department, assuring Eisenhower that the provisions of the directive incorporated agreed working relationships within the Defense Department and provisions of the new unified command plan. The major exception was the proposed revision by the Joint Chiefs that placed the JCS outside OSD. General Twining expressed the JCS rationale for the revision, citing the unique responsibilities of the Joint Chiefs and the fear that their incorporation into OSD would place them under assistant secretaries of defense.[20]

Eisenhower was somewhat sympathetic. He recognized that assistant secretaries might be inclined to "oversupervise" with direct JCS inclusion in OSD. Those secretaries, he added, were created in order to make the job of the Joint Chiefs easier, not to be their superiors. If he were secretary of defense, he would not object to anything designed to maintain the dignity of the JCS. Having said this, the president also warned against getting involved in organizational details, what he described as "straining at a gnat." Regardless of the wording of the law, he emphasized, the fact remained that the Joint Chiefs were the secretary's military staff, his "direct subordinates," who should be organized as he desired. In this primary service to the secretary, Eisenhower concluded, the Joint Chiefs were far more important as a corporate body than as a collection of individual service chiefs.[21]

At that juncture, presumably on cue, General Taylor showed the president a proposed chart that depicted the JCS and OSD as separate organizational boxes under the secretary of defense, with each connected to the secretary by a solid line. Another solid line also connected the JCS to the president. Eisenhower acknowledged that the military chiefs had always been technically considered advisers to the president, but he also stressed his concern that the Joint Chiefs be recognized primarily as a military staff for the defense secretary. As a consequence, his solution was to leave a solid "direct line of responsibility" from the Joint Chiefs to the secretary and a dotted "close coordination" line from them to the president. The dotted line to his office, he acknowledged, indicated the additional responsibility of the Joint Chiefs, whom he would always be willing to see on an individual basis. That same dotted line, he directed, should also connect the JCS and OSD boxes to indicate the close working relationship between the two organizations that must exist in serving the secretary of Defense.[22]

A good deal of the remaining discussion centered on the attempt in the directive to affix budgetary responsibility. Quarles outlined a proposed procedure, by which the CINC of a unified command would make his military requirements known to the JCS while the services would transmit logistic requirements through the Joint Chiefs to the defense secretary. Harlow objected that this would establish two separate "provisioning" channels, since the service component commands under the CINCs dealt directly with their respective services for support. Admiral Burke and General Taylor attempted to reassure the president that the CINCs were aware of what their component commands were doing in terms of their channels to their service chiefs. But Harlow insisted on specific wording that required the component commanders to ensure that their logistic requirements transmitted to their services be consistent with "the agreed defense military requirements" transmitted by the CINCs of the unified commands to the JCS. The president brought the organizational discussion to a close by repeating his desire that there be a "realization" of the fact that the Joint Chiefs were responsible to the secretary of defense and that that they constituted a corporate group and not a "collection" of service chiefs. To these objectives for his last two years in office, he added his wish for the "amalgamation" of the joint staff into "a truly single staff."[23]

The next day, the Pentagon issued a new draft directive based on the president's decisions. Coordination between Quarles and Harlow continued in writing and by telephone until after Christmas. On 31 December 1958, after final White House approval, McElroy issued revised Department of Defense directives 5100.1 on functions and 5158.1 on relationships. Both directives served to complete the panoply of requirements outlined in the president's state of the union address, his message to Congress, and the Defense Reorganization Act of 1958.[24]

The results justified the effort. It was true, of course, that the Department of Defense was still far removed from Truman's vision of "one team, with all the reins in one hand." But as Douglas Stuart points out, "it was much closer to this ideal than anyone had reason to expect following the passage of the 1947 National Security Act."[25] The new legislation represented, in fact, a major move from the coordinate philosophy that had triumphed in that act to Eisenhower's desired concept of centralized civilian authority. That authority extended on the one hand in a direct operational line to the CINCs and, on the other, in an administrative and support line to the subordinate component forces of those commanders through the military departments. In theory, those two lines would be brought together for the secretary within the JCS advisory system. The effort would be led by the chairman, gradually moving toward the overall chief-of-staff status outlined so long ago in Eisenhower's interpretation of the Collins Plan. Under this system, the Joint Chiefs would focus on strategic planning and advice, acquiring a broader perspective as a corporative group in their interaction with the CINCs on national security that would be used to enrich their dealings with the services on force capabilities and programs. Finally, as the president summed it up, the Defense Reorganization Act provided authority to the CINCs that "was even more sweeping than that I exercised over all the American Forces assigned to OVERLORD in World War II."[26]

At the same time, Eisenhower was aware from his years of experience that effective organizational approaches to his concept of unified command at the national and theater levels normally must be evolutionary in nature and that this applied to the results of his latest efforts. At the 6 August signing of the Defense Reorganization Act, he reminded his associates "that the law was just another step toward what the majority of experienced military men knew was necessary."[27] In other words, the 1958 legislation combined with his executive implementing actions constituted progress in what he understood was an imperfect process replete with problems, some of which were not yet understood. It was an understanding that he had expressed in his 1949 testimony concerning the first changes to the National Security Act. "We are expecting perfection too quickly," he stated at the time. "It is just exactly, gentlemen, as when we were waging a great war in Europe. . . . We get a set-back, deliberately risked to get ahead with this war. . . . These set-backs are an inescapable part of all group activity."[28]

Epilogue
The Unified Command Legacy:
Goldwater-Nichols and Beyond

Unless we get better coordination, better cooperation between the services, we will ultimately have to go further than we go in this bill. . . . I have no illusions that things are going to change very fast . . . but I will say that if the bill is modified, as the President and the Secretary of Defense have recommended, as least it will be a step in the right direction. If it doesn't work, then, within a couple of years the administration, whoever it is, will have to be back up here and ask for more authority.

ADMIRAL ARTHUR W. RADFORD, 1958

President Eisenhower's proposals remain the last serious attempt in this century to correct these serious flaws in our unified command system; 1958 was a long time ago, but the problems Ike identified have not been corrected. And it is clear that the Department of Defense won't make the necessary changes. It is going to be up to the US Congress. This is our challenge; this is our responsibility under the Constitution . . . [since] the problems that General, and later President, Eisenhower identified persist.

SENATOR BARRY GOLDWATER, 1985

Your operational performance has been so piss poor, you guys would have trouble defending the [Pentagon] River Entrance from an attack by a troop of Boy Scouts.

SENATOR BARRY GOLDWATER, 1985

ON WEDNESDAY, 5 MAY 1982, General Andrew J. Goodpaster appeared before the Investigations Subcommittee of the House Armed Services Committee to testify concerning reorganization proposals for the Joint Chiefs of Staff. In the almost quarter of a century since the Defense Reorganization Act of 1958, Goodpaster had served as assistant to the JCS chairman, director of the joint staff, deputy commander in Vietnam, and supreme Allied commander, Europe. After retiring as a four-star general, he had been recalled to active duty temporarily as the superintendent at West Point, with the rank of lieutenant general, to help his alma mater through a difficult time. Now, in the spring of 1982, Goodpaster was responding to a resurgence of interest in extending further the reform efforts on which he had worked in 1957 and 1958. It had been Eisenhower's hope, the general began, "though he acknowledged some doubt," that through the changes that were put into effect in 1958, there would be "overriding" emphasis on the corporate duties of the Joint Chiefs. "I think that the system," he added, "has not measured up to his hopes in that regard."[1]

Certainly, Eisenhower would have been astounded in 1982 at the statutory void on defense reorganization since 1958. After all, he had participated in major changes in the Department of Defense in just the eleven years between the National Security Act and his administration's reorganization efforts. Moreover, in the decades after those efforts, there were three presidentially initiated critical studies of the Defense Department. In 1960 President Kennedy created the Committee on the Defense Establishment under the chair of Stuart Symington, whose report was largely ignored by Secretary of Defense Robert McNamara, involved in his own managerial reforms. A decade later, President Nixon responded to the report of his Blue Ribbon Defense Panel in a similar manner due to the ongoing Vietnam conflict and potential congressional resistance. Finally, President Carter failed to act on the 1978 recommendations of his panel concerning the national military command structure, also known as the Steadman Report for its principal author.[2]

The three administrations also may have been deterred from action on the reports by Eisenhower's struggle with Congress despite his military status and prestige. Moreover, the panels also undermined their effectiveness by proposing politically unfeasible measures that included the elimination of the JCS and the military departments. In any event, the studies were perceptive in examining the imbalance between the roles of the services and those of the joint structure, particularly the continuing impact of the JCS dual-hat system and service parochialism on that structure. For incomplete centralization, all three reports agreed, allowed a degree of service dominance that adversely affected the ability of the secretary of defense to integrate senior military advice in terms of three key functions concerning national security strategy.[3]

The first function was strategic planning and advice. In his 3 April 1958 message to Congress, Eisenhower had warned that "service responsibilities and activities must always be the branches, not the central trunk of the national security tree." But his reform efforts that year left the dual-hat concept virtually untouched, despite the legislative encouragement for the service chiefs to use their vice chiefs more fully in terms of activities concerning the military departments. As a consequence, the JCS continued to lack the structure to provide the national, cross-service perspective necessary for strategic planning and advice. Bureaucratic politics and service interests continued to overshadow broad strategic thinking. As early as 1960 the Symington Report concluded in this regard that "no different results can be expected as long as the members of the Joint Chiefs of Staff retain their two-hatted character, with their positions preconditioned by the Service environment to which they must return after each session of the Joint Chiefs of Staff."[4]

The reports also noted that the continuation of joint staffing procedures usually ensured that JCS advice was both untimely and so diluted as to be virtually unusable by civilian officials. The 1970 Blue Ribbon Defense Panel described JCS procedures as "ponderous and slow," and at one point Paul Nitze observed of the Joint Chiefs that "it would sometimes take them three days to blow their nose."[5] Part of the problem was the joint staff, which remained an undesirable career option, as did other joint assignments. As a consequence, positions in that organization generally attracted officers awaiting retirement, as well as, in one flag officer's judgment, the "sick, lame and lazy."[6] Most important, despite the demise of the JCS committee system because of Eisenhower's efforts, the JCS continued an overly complex coordination procedure, sometimes referred to as the "flimsy-buff-green-red stripe" system, for the colors and sequence demarking how the joint staff coordinated draft issue and policy papers with each of the services. If there was no agreement between the services and the joint staff at one level, the paper was simply elevated to a higher one. Throughout the process, the services retained great leverage because of the requirement that remained for JCS consensus, which in turn provided an incentive for resistance by a military department until its position was satisfied. The system, the 1978 Steadman Report concluded, ensured that joint planning and advice would remain generally devoid of a corporate outlook and thus ineffective.[7]

The dual-hat conflict of interest also continued to prevent the use of the JCS organization as an effective forum for the second essential function of rational, cross-service resource and force structure planning and allocation. Service parochialism, in effect, prevented any type of JCS

agreement on resource allocation issues except for that of increasing
forces without taking resource constraints into consideration. "A Chief
cannot . . . be expected to argue for additional carriers, divisions, and air
wings when constructing a Service budget," the Steadman Report observed in this regard, "and then agree in a joint forum that they should be
deleted in favor of programs of other Services."[8] This dilemma continued
to be exacerbated after 1958 by the lack of realistic strategic planning,
which left each service to pursue its own vision of the next war and the
forces that it would need for that conflict. In the absence of genuine strategic guidance, the services expressed their ends or objectives in terms
of their force structures, whether it was a six hundred–ship Navy, an
eighteen-division Army, or a forty-wing Air Force. In this manner, service
goals tended to supplement strategic ones, reversing the logic of creating
force structures as a function of strategy.[9]

Incomplete centralization and service dominance also undermined
Eisenhower's division of labor between the operational and administrative lines of authority, thus adversely affecting his concept of unified command at the theater and national levels and the key function of conducting effective joint military operations. In December 1958 Eisenhower had
agreed to the Defense Department directive that described the newly
streamlined chain of command from the president and defense secretary
to the combatant commands as passing "through" the JCS. The president's intention was for the JCS to act as a "channel of command," a
mechanism by which his orders and those of the secretary were transmitted to the CINCs. In practice, however, the service chiefs, in their
dual role as members of the JCS acting as the military link between the
secretary and the combatant commanders, continued to have dominant
influence in operational planning and direction. Much of this was due
to their overwhelming influence on the joint staff and because of their
involvement in the selection of the CINCs. This continued dominance
was heightened because of the relatively limited interaction between the
Office of the Secretary of Defense and that of the JCS, despite the close
cooperative communication between the two offices envisaged by Eisenhower in 1958 when he allowed the JCS to be an entity separate from the
secretary's office. By 1970 the Blue Ribbon Defense Panel determined
that the operational chain had become unresponsive because of the presence of the Joint Chiefs, which despite their ostensible function as staff
transmitters, not originators, of commands, provided "a forum of inter-

Service conflicts to be injected into the decision-making process for military operations."[10]

Much of the 1970 report was based on the American experience in Vietnam, which was marked by distortion of Eisenhower's concept of unified command at every level and by the consequent lack of integration among the services as each sought to carve out a large mission for itself. At the theater level, the conflict occurred within the area of PACOM, the Pacific geographical unified command headed by a Navy admiral (CINCPAC). As Army forces increased in the country, CINCPAC created a military assistance command, Vietnam (MACV), in effect a sub-unified command under an Army general. At a later date, the Marines established another sub-unified command in South Vietnam's northern provinces. At the same time, the forces operating over Vietnam from the carrier task forces in the South China Sea and the B-52 bases in Guam remained under CINCPAC. Even in defeat, as the US armed forces sought to evacuate Saigon in spring 1975, responsibility was split between separate land and sea commands, each of which established a different time for execution, causing delays and confusion. That type of service parochialism and lack of integration was mirrored at the national level and was one reason, General Colin Powell concluded in his memoirs, why "the Joint Chiefs had never spoken out with a clear voice to prevent the deepening morass in Vietnam."[11]

The influence of the service chiefs in the operational chain of command to the combatant commanders was mirrored in the administrative chain. For under the post-1958 system, each single-service component commander was responsible to his CINC concerning operational matters and to his service chief for everything else, which as Samuel Huntington has pointed out, "in peacetime is almost everything of importance."[12] This meant control by the services over recruitment, training, personnel, logistics, and maintenance for their forces. It also meant service dominance in the component commands at the expense of the CINCs. "I had three bosses: American unified commander, NATO regional commander, and Air Force chief," a former head of the Air Force component command in Europe recalled of his assignment in the early 1970s. "The chief had the greatest influence on me because he assigned my people, gave them jobs, and had the money."[13]

Continued service dominance in the dual chains of command established by the Eisenhower reforms also weakened the CINCs in other ways. In their capacity as members of the JCS, the service chiefs in November 1959 issued their basic joint publication, *Unified Action Armed Forces* (*UNAAF*), which despite changes in the ensuing years, continued to favor service dominance at the theater level. Whether it was authorization for the military departments to develop operational doctrine or a narrow interpretation of the command chain that hindered a CINC from selecting and commanding units he believed necessary for a given contingency or mission, the basic joint publication for unified action retained a distinct orientation on maintaining single-service integrity. These types of pressure were reflected in the lack of attention paid by the CINCs to all those things necessary for the conduct of joint operations ranging from joint training and planning to the development of meaningful ways to gauge joint readiness in the combatant forces. At the same time, the military education system combined with service career development patterns did little to encourage expertise in joint military operations.[14]

Equally serious was the lack of direct control by the CINCs of the resources allotted to their commands. In theory, both the services and the Office of the Secretary of Defense would solicit the needs of the unified commands in this regard. In practice, although the Eisenhower administration had arranged for the CINCs to use their component commanders to pass on their resource priorities, the services were not required to act on them in submitting their budget requirements. And as both the secretary's office and the combatant commanders would discover in the coming years, there were limits on the ability of a civilian staff to gain control over budgets and programs that were still primarily under service administration. For no matter how powerful and direct the scrutiny of the defense secretary, it would still be up to the service chiefs to draft basic documents and defend and justify them through each stage in the process of congressional appropriations. The combatant commanders, in short, were still not permanent institutional players in the budget and resource allocation process. Nor did the JCS chairman have a meaningful role in that process.[15]

In the end, the CINCs were caught after 1958 between powerful structures above and below them that encouraged single-service perspectives. The services still dominated the determination of what forces, weapons, and capabilities were to be available to implement US national military strategy. Moreover, they generally continued to use their own institutional priorities to develop their organizational structures. One consequence was that the forces assigned to the combatant commanders continued to reflect service interests, priorities, and decisions. An equally serious result was that the CINCs still lacked influence over the capabilities and readiness of the forces they commanded, some of which might ultimately be configured to fight a different type of war than envisaged by the heads of the unified commands in the near-term contingency plans they drafted.

These problems were duly reported in the defense studies during the decades leading up to General Goodpaster's testimony in 1982. "Despite the establishment of the unified command concept in the Defense Reorganization Act of 1958, as requested by President Eisenhower," the 1970 Blue Ribbon Defense Panel observed, "the relationship and relative authority between the Unified Commanders and the component commander, and between the component commander and his Military Department, remain substantially unchanged."[16] The 1978 Steadman Report was even more explicit, noting that the combatant commanders "have limited power to influence the capability of the forces assigned to them. . . . The CINCs' forces are trained and equipped by their parent Services, who control the flow of men, money, and materiel to the CINCs components. The Services (and the components) thus have the major influence on both the structure and the readiness of the forces for which the CINC is responsible."[17]

Various solutions had been considered before Goodpaster's testimony in 1982 as a way of rectifying the service dominance of the joint structure in spite of the Eisenhower reforms. At one end of the centralization spectrum was the traditional armed forces general staff model, headed by a single uniformed chief of staff with command authority over both the operational commands and the military services and supported by a multiservice general staff entirely independent of the services. Eisenhower had initially supported the Army variant of the model in the 1945 Collins Plan and had revealed his continued support in his testimony before Congress in the spring of 1947, even after Truman had jettisoned the concept because of congressional opposition. A few years later, outgoing Secretary of Defense Robert Lovett briefly considered a version of the general staff system in his 18 November 1952 letter to President Truman before abandoning it because of "unnecessary apprehension" on the part of Congress.[18] In the 1958 congressional reorganization hearings and debates, there were still supporters of the centralized general staff model, like Senator Barry Goldwater. "I believe the ultimate organization of the armed services," the Arizona Republican stated on the Senate floor in July, "must be one military, one uniform, a General Staff, and a Chief of Staff, surrounded by proper civilian protection and surrounded by Congress and the President, so as to eliminate any chances that there might occur what some people seem to think could possibly occur under such a system."[19]

Goldwater was referring, of course, to the specter of the model as a danger to civilian control of the military, a risk perceived by many in Congress as an inevitable and unacceptable trade-off for ending the JCS dual-hat system by eliminating the Joint Chiefs. As a consequence, Congress placed a statement in the National Security Act amendments of 1958 identical to that of 1949 emphasizing that the intent of the legislation was not to establish a single chief of staff over the armed forces or an armed forces general staff. When the joint staff was expanded in 1958, the provision was added that it "shall not operate or be organized as an overall Armed Forces General Staff and shall have no executive authority."[20] This type of apprehension did not noticeably lessen in the subsequent decades, and by the early 1980s the general staff model had failed to attract many supporters.

The second solution was simply to improve on the Eisenhower attempts to balance service influence in the joint system by enlarging the power of the JCS chairman, the joint staff, and the CINCs. That enhancement, as the 1978 Steadman Report pointed out, had not been sufficient for a proper balance, given the strength of the dual-hat system. Four years later, Air Force General David C. Jones, at the end of his tenure as JCS chairman, built on the report's recommendations. He began by throwing down the gauntlet in his 3 February 1982 testimony on another subject before Congress, repeated his comments in a widely publicized magazine article that month, and elaborated on them with greater specificity in testimony before the same session of the House Armed Services Investigations Subcommittee that Goodpaster attended.

Jones was an up-from-the-ranks general who had enlisted in the Army Air Forces in 1942. By 1971 he was commanding US Air Forces in Europe (USAFE), a service component of the US European Command (EUCOM), an assignment that impressed him with the power of the services at the expense of the unified commands. In 1974 Jones became the Air Force chief of staff, and in 1978 the chairman of the JCS. In April

1980 he observed firsthand the failure of the Iranian hostage rescue mission, marked by serious defects concerning unity of command and effort, as forces from several services were pulled together on an ad hoc basis under ambiguous command-and-control arrangements. Now, in 1982, as he prepared to retire in June, Jones recalled that at the signing of the 1958 reorganization act, Eisenhower had reminded those present that the legislation was just another step toward what ultimately would be necessary. "I believe he would be disappointed," Jones concluded, "that further steps have not been taken."[21]

Like Eisenhower, Jones sought to promote an independent joint military perspective within the existing system. To this end, he supported a more independent JCS chairman, who with increased authority could work with the Joint Chiefs and the CINCs to provide the civilian leaders with military advice and planning that was integrated across service boundaries. The chairman would replace the JCS, Jones proposed, as the principal military adviser to the president, the secretary of defense, and the National Security Council. Supported by a new four-star deputy, he would offer this advice based on his own judgment after considering the counsel of the other JCS members.[22]

At the same time, Jones called for the JCS chairman to be given greater authority over the joint staff, with that organization reporting directly to him instead of all the Joint Chiefs. The chairman should also play a larger role, Jones said, in the selection and promotion of joint staff members, who would be provided more incentives to serve in joint assignments and to develop a wider cross-service national perspective. "In our system," Jones emphasized in this regard, "Clausewitz would probably make full colonel, retire in 20 years, and go to work for a think tank."[23] In a similar manner, he proposed using the rejuvenated JCS chairman to strengthen the CINCs by authorizing him to supervise the combatant commands and represent their interests in terms of plans and decisions concerning allocation of resources. The JCS would remain the operational military staff for the secretary of defense, but the chain of command, Jones recommended, would run from the president to the secretary through the chairman, rather than the JCS, to the CINCs.

Following the lead of General Jones, the Army chief of staff, General Edward C. Meyer, recommended a third reorganization solution in early 1982. A highly decorated infantry commander in the Korean and Vietnam conflicts, Meyer was a quintessential man of action who also possessed great intellectual curiosity and a well-developed strategic expertise. In keeping with the pattern of Army chiefs since Marshall and Eisenhower, he was concerned generally about overall unity of command and in particular more centralized unified direction of the armed forces. Like Jones, Meyer recommended a more powerful JCS chairman. But unlike the Air Force general, the Army chief of staff was also bent on eliminating the JCS's dual-hat status by separating the functions of joint military advice, planning, and operational direction from the supervision of the services. The vehicle for this "major surgery" was a national military advisory council, reminiscent of General Bradley's preference for a group of "superchiefs" in the Coolidge group deliberations in 1958 or General Taylor's consideration in 1960 of what he termed the "Supreme Military Council."[24]

The council would consist of four-star officers from each service who would have no service responsibilities or functions and would not return to their services upon completion of their council tours. Presided over by the chairman and supported by a strengthened joint staff, the new organization would develop military strategy and translate civilian policy guidance into programming instructions for the military departments. At the same time, the chairman would transmit orders from the president and the secretary of defense to the combatant commanders. In this manner, Meyer emphasized, the joint military structure could produce more rational, comprehensive strategic planning and direction. In any event, he warned on 21 April as he led off testimony before the House Armed Services Investigations Subcommittee, "tinkering will not suffice"; it would be necessary to take on "some of the issues which in the past have been put in the box which says, 'Too tough to handle.'"[25]

On 5 May, in his testimony before the subcommittee, General Goodpaster was asked how he thought Eisenhower would respond to the Jones-Meyer proposals. The general was hesitant initially "to speak for" his former boss, but then relented. "I suppose I have had as much discussion with him on issues of this kind," he reflected, "as any other human being." In essence, he conjectured, Eisenhower would agree with Jones's proposals to strengthen the role of the chairman, limit service involvement in the joint process, and broaden the training, experiences, and rewards for joint duty. He sympathized with Meyer's desire "to eliminate dual hatting," but considered his additional proposal concerning a national military advisory council as too revolutionary, as opposed to the strong-chairman model, "which is a distinct evolutionary step." In any event, he warned the subcommittee, it would not be easy to overcome the "inevitable institutional opposition" to the systemic reform inherent in the new proposals. Success would depend on mobilizing support from many sources. "I do know," Goodpaster concluded, "that it took the unique experience of an Eisenhower administration and the unique confidence in his military judgment to accomplish the reform measures of 1958, and even those did not go as far as he desired."[26]

After the testimony in spring 1982, both houses conducted almost continuous reorganization hearings for the next two years. With the departure from the Joint Chiefs of Jones in June 1982 and Meyer in July 1983, the JCS and Secretary of Defense Caspar W. Weinberger generally opposed reorganization that strengthened the JCS chairman, the dominant model that began to emerge from congressional hearings. In January 1983 Congressman Bill Nichols of Alabama, a World War II veteran who had lost a leg in the battle of the Huertgen Forest, assumed the chair of the House Armed Services Investigations Subcommittee. In September, forty-five-year-old Senator Sam Nunn of Georgia, whose great-uncle was Carl Vinson, became the ranking minority member of the Senate Armed Services Committee. On 23 October 1983 a truck filled with explosives rammed into the Beirut Airport barracks of the US Marine contingent assigned to the multinational peacekeeping force in Lebanon. Two days later, the invasion by US armed forces of the tiny Caribbean island of Grenada revealed further command-and-control problems. On 2 November former Secretary of Defense James R. Schlesinger reacted to these events in his testimony before the Senate Armed Services Committee by denouncing the degree of service independence and the problems of the JCS structure, "in which log-rolling, back-scratching, marriage arrangements" could flourish. "In all our military institutions, the time-honored principle of 'unity of command' is inculcated," he concluded. "Yet at the national level it is firmly resisted and flagrantly violated. Unity of command is endorsed, if and only if, it applies at the service level."[27]

Senator Goldwater was equally concerned when he assumed his duties at the beginning of 1985 as the chairman of the Senate Armed Services Committee. The crusty seventy-six-year-old Arizona Republican had been interested in the reorganization of the armed services his entire career, even writing a lengthy paper on the subject as a member of the Air Force Reserve, from which he retired in 1967 as a major general.

Goldwater was open to new ideas and had long since moved from his concentration on the extreme centralization of the general staff model for the overall military structure. Most important, he was ferociously bipartisan in his approach and soon formed a highly effective working relationship with Senator Nunn, the ranking minority member of his committee.

The two senators were aided by an NSC staff proposal in January 1985 to form a senior policy group on Defense Department reform that would give President Reagan credibility on the subject and take some of the initiative from Congress. The predictable Pentagon resistance to the proposal was mitigated in the next few months by press reports of such military acquisition mismanagement as Navy expenditures of $659 each for ashtrays in new surveillance aircraft. On 7 June the president agreed to the NSC proposal, and on 11 June he selected David Packard to head a sixteen-member commission. Packard was a cofounder in 1939 of the Hewlett-Packard Company and a former deputy secretary of defense. Within a day of his appointment, he met separately with Goldwater and Nunn. And throughout the summer and fall, members of the Packard Commission, as the President's Blue Ribbon Commission on Defense Management was called, held discussions with members of the Task Force on Defense organization established by the two senators.

Over an eight-day period in early October, Goldwater and Nunn made a series of speeches from the well of the Senate in an attempt to focus attention on their reform efforts. They began by addressing the role of Congress in national security, then presented a historical examination of US military organizational problems. The final speeches were focused on deficiencies in the JCS, the combatant commands, and the military budget process. Not surprisingly, there were several pointed references to the last major effort at defense reform. "In 1958," Goldwater emphasized, "President Eisenhower proposed changes to the 1947 act to strengthen the unity of the Armed Forces and the ability to conduct joint operations. . . . But unfortunately, the influence of the individual services remained too strong. Although Congress approved Eisenhower's proposals, the concept of unified command that Ike articulated has not been adequately implemented by the Department of Defense at any time over the last 27 years. *They should have listened to Ike.*"[28]

The speeches assured maximum media attention, particularly because they were followed a week later by the briefing of a new comprehensive report to the Senate Armed Services Committee commissioned by the two senators. The document was dubbed the Locher Report for the study director, James R. Locher III, who presented it to the committee on 16 October to inaugurate a new series of hearings. The 645-page report fed a growing consensus for defense reorganization in Congress with detailed analyses of problems and specific recommendations for overhauling the organization and decision-making process of the Pentagon. The primary desired outcome was a strengthened JCS chairman, but the study also took more extreme stances, such as substituting a joint military advisory council for the JCS in order to provide, as Locher recalled, "maximum negotiating room."[29] That such room would be necessary was evident during the briefing of the report to the Pentagon leadership, when the deputy secretary of defense deplored the document as a symbol of the exaggeration that had marred the entire campaign. "How much evidence do you want?" the normally slow-to-anger Nunn responded. "For forty years, the Pentagon's problems have been repeatedly cited by one presidential commission after another. And each operational failure has served to reinforce these studies."[30]

The Pentagon reaction, however, represented only one, albeit important, response to the congressional reform initiatives. At the White House, at least one member of the NSC staff was working to build presidential support for the Packard Commission's efforts. Mike Donley had moved from his staff position on the Senate Armed Services Committee to one on the National Security Council the previous July. By November 1985, as the work of the commission neared its close, he had come to believe that the recommendations of that panel might produce changes that would rival the importance of the Eisenhower initiatives. As a consequence, he made a trip to the Eisenhower Library at Abilene, Kansas, in order to "get a handle on how Eisenhower bureaucratically handled reorganization." Donley expected that the history of Eisenhower's role in 1958 would "resonate" with the president "as a good example for how to address reorganization." Moreover, he concluded, that history would "reinforce with Reagan that he had every right and reason to be interested in what was going on" and thus "make sure that he was personally involved."[31]

The information from Donley's trip also sparked interest among the members of the Packard Commission, some of whom personally interviewed General Goodpaster in mid-January 1986 concerning Eisenhower's role in the defense reorganization efforts of his administration.

Goodpaster had remained actively involved with the issue since his testimony before the House subcommittee in spring 1982. Most notably, he had served in the interim as a vice chairman of a reorganization project by Georgetown University's Center for Strategic and International Studies, the results of which he had personally briefed to Goldwater in December 1984, two months before public release of the study. "Failure to complete the reforms proposed by President Eisenhower in 1958," the project report stated at the outset, "is among the root causes of current problems within the defense establishment."[32] And in December 1985 before Goldwater's committee, Goodpaster continued to provide testimony that basically favored the JCS chairman model. As a result of Donley's research and the interview with Goodpaster, the commission members acquired a detailed picture of Eisenhower's initiatives. "We had a fairly good feeling of what he wanted to do and what he did not get done," Packard recalled. "That had an influence on what we tried to do."[33]

In February 1986, just as the Packard Commission was preparing to release its interim report, National Security Adviser Admiral John M. Poindexter provided President Reagan a memorandum containing the results of Donley's research. "Ike faced a Congress that was opposed to change," the document began; "today, it is Congress that is pushing for more extensive and detailed changes in defense management and organization." Given this reversal and playing to the widely known antipathy of Secretary Weinberger and the JCS to the congressional initiatives and in particular to the Locher Report recommendations, Poindexter characterized the commission's efforts as almost the lesser of two evils for the president: "So where the Eisenhower initiatives were intended to push Congress into doing something they would otherwise resist, we hope to use the Packard Commission initiatives as a substitute for the more objectionable legislation being forcefully advanced by Congress." At the same time, the memorandum also emphasized to the president the commission's positive continuity with Eisenhower's earlier efforts, which in turn represented continuous effort back to 1947 toward enhancing unified command at the theater and national levels:

> There are many parallels between the recommendations of the Packard Commission and the Eisenhower initiatives of 1958. The commission's conclusions are consistent with the historical trend of enhancing the authority of the secretary of defense and JCS as a means of improving the integration of the military departments in support of strategic plans,

while still maintaining the integrity of the individual services and their responsibility for program execution. . . . While Packard's recommendations are significant, and to some may appear as a departure from current practice, they in fact represent realignment back to the original intent of the National Security Act, which President Eisenhower tried so hard to implement.[34]

Events moved swiftly on reorganization thereafter. In April 1986 President Reagan endorsed the preliminary recommendations of the Packard Commission, many of which were incorporated in the Senate version of the reorganization bill that passed on 7 May, in a surge of bipartisan support for reform, by a vote of 95 to 0. The House approved its version on 5 August by 406 to 4. On 12 September, Congress published its joint conference report. Four days later, the Senate approved the legislation, followed the next day by the House. On 1 October 1986 the president signed the Goldwater-Nichols Act in a low-key ceremony that reflected the divisive nature of the issue within the executive branch. In a short, bland, three-paragraph press statement, he cited a peculiar mix in his pantheon of heroes, praising the act as a responsible course of action that affirmed "the basic wisdom of those who came before us—the Forrestals, Bradleys, Radfords, and Eisenhowers—advancing their legacies in light of our own experience."[35]

Goldwater-Nichols continued the 1958 reform model, rejecting, as Eisenhower had done, more centralized structures that would have more completely fulfilled his concept of unified command, but impracticably at the expense of JCS existence. Instead, the legislation of 1986 concentrated on Eisenhower's organizing principle of striking a balance between maintaining and employing the forces and on making it work. To that end, the most fundamental provisions of Goldwater-Nichols were designed to achieve the counterpoise to the services anticipated in Eisenhower's 1958 concept, but not fully realized until twenty-eight years later.[36]

The first step in achieving the balance was to improve the capability for the joint structure to provide military advice and conduct strategic planning. To accomplish this, Goldwater-Nichols transferred the duties and functions of the corporate JCS to the chairman, who was now to become the head of that organization and in that capacity to act as the principal military adviser to the president, the secretary of defense, and the National Security Council. The new legislation also made the joint staff directly subordinate to the chairman, while creating the position of vice chairman to assist him in his new and expanded duties, which included participation in NSC meetings, subject to the president's direction, and supervision of certain defense agencies and field activities when assigned by the defense secretary. In terms of strategic planning, the new duties included preparing a national military strategy to support the president's annual national security strategy, itself a new requirement of Goldwater-Nichols. The chairman also became responsible for the preparation and review of near-term contingency plans to ensure conformance with the secretary's policy guidance and the translation of that policy with specific planning tasks for the CINCs, who were then to develop theater operations plans to be submitted to the chairman for approval. Finally, the act also required the chairman to prepare global strategic plans to integrate the regional and functional plans created by the separate combatant commanders.[37]

The second step in creating equilibrium between the joint structure and the services was to establish more centralized rationality in resource allocation and force development. The problem was that the principal focus of the CINCs was on readiness—the ability to field in the near term well-equipped, well-supplied, and well-trained fighting forces. The services, on the other hand, were primarily procurement agencies and thus tended to emphasize the longer-term requirements of investment and modernization. Service dominance in this area was basically unchanged by the Eisenhower reforms and continued over the intervening years, to be reinforced by such actors as defense contractors and congressmen in promoting major weapons systems. To combat this, Goldwater-Nichols designated important duties for the chairman focused on resource and force requirements identified by the combatant commanders. To begin with, Congress authorized the chairman to solicit these requirements and provide analysis of them at the national level, including the extent to which programs proposed by the services satisfied sufficiently and effectively what the CINCs required. Aiding this rational approach were associated provisions in the legislation that made the chairman responsible for developing doctrine concerning joint employment of the armed forces; for appraising the functions assigned to the services; and for reviewing the missions, responsibilities, and force structures of the unified and specified commands.

The increase in the authority and responsibility of the JCS chairman was also tied to the expanded power of the combatant commanders, the final step in creating more balance in the joint-service relationship. That expansion was designed to reduce the influence of service parochialism and improve the focus of Pentagon planning on the needs of the CINCs. At the theater level, Goldwater-Nichols specifically addressed the tendency of the services since 1958 to use the *Unified Action Armed Forces*, the publication with final authority for joint operations, to give significant authority to the service component commanders, thereby restricting the authority of the CINCs. The new bill clarified unity of command and effort in even greater detail, authorizing each CINC within his theater to organize commands and forces; prescribe the chain of command; select or suspend subordinate commanders and staff; and direct those subordinate commands in all aspects of military operations, joint training, and administrative and logistic support necessary to achieve their assigned missions. At the same time, Congress provided for the JCS chairman, at the secretary's discretion, to be responsible for oversight of the CINCs and designated him as "spokesman" for those commanders, particularly on requirements for the effective operational direction of their forces.

Goldwater-Nichols also provided further reinforcement of authority for the combatant commanders by clarifying the operational chain of command from the president to the secretary of defense to the CINCs. As had been the case in the 1958 legislation and the implementing Defense Department directive, the new bill deliberately excluded the service chiefs and secretaries from operational command responsibilities. The difference was that the 1986 act substituted the chairman for the JCS as the transmitter of communications for employing the combatant commands, thus reinforcing the division of labor between operations and administration by eliminating a committee dominated by service interests as the operational middleman between the secretary and the CINCs. Moreover, Goldwater-Nichols specifically directed the service secretaries to assign all forces from the military departments to the unified and specified commands with the exception of units required to perform service functions. If the implications of these moves were still not clear to the military departments, Congress held the secretaries specifically responsible for meeting the future operational requirements of those commanders as synthesized by the JCS chairman.

Finally, in a move that would particularly have pleased Eisenhower, Goldwater-Nichols promoted a more effective management of officers in terms of training and orientation toward joint matters. The intent of the new management provisions was to improve the quality not only of the joint staff but of the combatant command staffs as well. To accomplish this, Congress outlined requirements for joint specialty officers, specifying minimums in education, promotions, and tour length in joint duty positions, all in an effort to transform the military culture.

In the years since the passage of the Goldwater-Nichols Act, the debate has continued concerning joint and service influences on US military activities. Some critics believe that the increased power of the JCS chairman and the more effective joint staff undermine civilian control of the military. At the very least, critics contend, the chairman represents a growing politicization of the military. At the most, he is becoming a decision maker, not merely an adviser, whose support is actively cultivated by each incoming administration.[38] Others warn that jointness may weaken beneficial interservice competition and constrain innovation. Balanced military judgment and combat effectiveness, they contend, are also dependent upon service individuality, culture, and training. "Remember that effective jointness means blending the distinct colors of the services into a rainbow of synergistic military effectiveness," former Marine Corps Commandant Carl E. Mundy points out in this regard. "It does not suggest pouring them into a single jar and mixing them until they lose their individual properties and come out as a colorless paste."[39]

Generally, however, the 1986 legislation has been considered a success in accelerating the process of unification by fundamentally changing the manner of raising, training, commanding, and employing the US armed forces. In the wake of Operation Desert Storm, the regional CINC for that conflict testified that "Goldwater-Nichols established very, very clear lines of command authority and responsibilities over subordinate commanders, and this meant a much more effective fighting force."[40] And on the tenth anniversary of the act, General Powell noted the dramatic improvement of the joint staff to the point that it had become "the premier military staff in the world."[41] For that same commemoration, Senator Nunn summed up what was generally perceived as the most important result of the act. "The Pentagon's ability to prepare for and conduct joint operations," he wrote, "has improved more in ten years—since passage of the Goldwater-Nichols Act—than in the entire period since the need for jointness was recognized by the creation of the Joint Army-Navy board in 1903." At the same time, the Georgia senator warned that in the increasingly complex post–Cold War environment, new reforms to establish unity of effort across the entire government would be necessary, particularly in terms of the interagency system. "The old days of the Pentagon doing the entire mission are gone for good," he concluded.[42]

Nunn's broader focus presaged a series of reports similar to those after every major defense reform effort since 1947. The 1997 National Defense Panel examined the inadequacies of the interagency process in dealing with complex contingencies. In early 2001 the Phase III Report of the US Commission on National Security in the 21st Century had as its theme the need for altering the overall national security structure in order to provide more flexibility throughout the government to anticipate unexpected security challenges. One such challenge, the terrorist attacks of 11 September later that year, increased the awareness of problems associated with coordination within the executive branch, spurring a series of new reports that called for agencies outside the Pentagon to increase their operational and planning capabilities in the interagency system. Those capabilities, they concluded, resided almost entirely in the Department of Defense.[43]

This interest in overall security-related government reform is likely to increase in the future. Anxieties concerning homeland security will certainly not abate soon; nor will stresses on the active and reserve components of the all-volunteer force and increases in security-oriented outlays just as the "boomer" generation heads into retirement. But, as Eisenhower could attest, the task of reorganizing the Pentagon pales before that of reforming the government interagency process. The legislative defense reforms from 1947 through 1986 all represented movements toward fulfillment of his concept of unified command. Each act was marked in varying degrees by attempts to reconcile the structural decentralization of the constitutional system with the requirements for national defense in a time when the concept of US national security was changing.

Now, in the era after the 2001 terrorist attacks, if those efforts are to be extended to the entire executive branch, each of the three elements of Eisenhower's concept would be either weak or nonexistent. Most of the agencies in that branch lack operational cultures and capabilities necessary to conduct effective interagency operations in the sense allowed by the process of unification for the military services, which in turn facilitates unity of effort. Equally important, even as current security challenges demand solutions that more effectively integrate the nonmilitary elements of power, the constraints of the American political system virtually assure that this will have to be done absent complete unity of command. For while the secretary of defense has statutory "authority, direction and control" over his department, subject to the direction of the chief executive, Congress has failed to give the president the same authority over the other executive branch agencies, unless he chooses to invoke his temporary emergency powers.[44]

Still, there is no reason to think that Dwight Eisenhower would avoid the new challenge. In his military and civilian career, he observed and personally led the gradual evolution of his unified command concept, first in the ad hoc juncture of the War and Navy departments under the JCS during World War II, and then later in the Department of Defense. From these experiences at the theater and national levels, he would understand that reforms driven by the executive branch often lack staying power and that the role of Congress in the process is essential. In that regard, he also would appreciate how the shock of 11 September 2001, much like that of *Sputnik*, could be used to galvanize efforts by both the legislative and executive branches. Moreover, given his predilection for the evolutionary approach to Defense Department reform, Eisenhower would undoubtedly caution against sweeping changes to existing institutions and capabilities in the broader, more complex work of dealing with all executive branch agencies involved in national security. Finally, he would include himself with typical honesty and with typically suitable credit to others as an example of how the role of critical individuals at various points in the reform process could shape the ultimate outcome of reform efforts. In the end, it is easy to imagine Dwight Eisenhower addressing the new problem with his boundless enthusiasm and infectious grin, providing the same signal to reformers of the new era that he had to his subordinates at his rain-soaked headquarters in the early-morning hours of 5 June 1944. "Okay," he would say, "let's go."[45]

Notes

Introduction

The epigraph to this chapter is drawn from Dana Priest, *The Mission: Waging War and Keeping Peace with America's Military* (New York: Norton, 2004), 24.

1. Ibid., 112.

2. Ibid., 116–117. See also Christopher J. Fettweis, "Militarizing Diplomacy: Warrior-Diplomats and the Foreign Policy Process," in *America's Viceroys: The Military and US Foreign Policy,* ed. Derek S. Reveron (New York: Palgrave Macmillan, 2004), 44–70.

3. In 2002 the Bush administration discontinued use of the acronym CINC for military officers, substituting the title Combatant Commander for the heads of the unified and specified commands. The title Commander in Chief, Secretary of Defense Rumsfeld directed, would "be used [only] to connote or indicate the President of the United States of America." At the same time, the secretary called for a phasing-in period to save money: "Utilization of current material (signs, stationery, etc) for military officers that indicates the title 'Commander in Chief' is permitted until supplies are exhausted, or until the next regular maintenance period during which signage may be changed without any undue additional cost to the taxpayers." Unclassified 24 October 2002 Secretary of Defense Memorandum, Subject: The Title "Commander in Chief."

4. Joint Chiefs of Staff, *Joint Publication 1. Doctrine for the Armed Forces of the United States* (Washington, DC: GPO, 1970), GL-11.

5. Center for Strategic and International Studies (CSIS), *Beyond Goldwater-Nichols: US Government and Defense Reform for a New Strategic Era* (Washington, DC: CSIS, 2005), 139.

6. William Faulkner, *Requiem for a Nun* (New York: Random House, 1951), 92.

Chapter 1. Reform and Education

The epigraphs to this chapter are drawn from John P. Marquand, *Melville Goodwin, USA* (Boston: Little Brown, 1951), 252; "Assembly Visits General Eisenhower," *Assembly* 27 (Spring 1968), 4; and Dwight D. Eisenhower, *At Ease: Stories I Tell to Friends* (Garden City, NY: Doubleday, 1967), 81.

1. Eisenhower, *At Ease*, 4. See also Stephen E. Ambrose, *Eisenhower*, vol. 1, *Soldier, General of the Army, President-Elect, 1890–1952* (New York: Simon and Schuster, 1983), 43; Joseph Ellis and Robert Moore, *School for Soldiers: West Point and the Profession of Arms* (New York: Oxford University Press, 1974), 12.

2. Stephen E. Ambrose, *Duty, Honor, Country: A History of West Point* (Baltimore: Johns Hopkins University Press, 1999), 250. "A feudal fief in the midst of an early American paradise, West Point is an anachronism within an anachronism." Ellis and Moore, *School for Soldiers*, 4–5.

3. H. H. Arnold, *Global Mission* (New York: Harper, 1949), 6–9. After reading the Ambrose study on West Point, Eisenhower noted in the foreword to that book that he "was amazed at how little some things change." Ambrose, *Duty, Honor, Country*, ix.

4. Henry L. Stimson and McGeorge Bundy, *On Active Service in Peace and War* (New York: Harper, 1947), 32.

5. Thomas J. Fleming, *West Point: The Men and Times of the United States Military Academy* (New York: William Morrow, 1969) 268.

6. Stimson and Bundy, *On Active Service*, 39.

7. Ibid.

8. Ibid., 450–451.

9. War Department, "Report for 1902," 1 December 1902, in *Five Years of the War Department Following the War with Spain as Shown in the Annual Reports of the Secretary of War, 1899–1903* (hereafter *Five Years*) (Washington, DC: GPO, 1904), 293. See also Philip C. Jessup, *Elihu Root*, vol. 1, *1845–1909* (New York: Dodd, Mead, 1937), 240–264; Otto L. Nelson Jr., *National Security and the General Staff* (Washington, DC: Infantry Journal Press, 1946), 39–47.

10. "Report for 1902," 1 December 1902, *Five Years*, 297. Stimson always considered that the chief of staff reform should not be jeopardized, even unintentionally, by any change in the title and function of the position. As a consequence, as secretary of war in 1942, he vetoed the Army Staff's proposal to vest the chief of staff with the title of commander. Stimson and Bundy, *On Active Service*, 450.

11. On the controversy between General William R. Shafter and Admiral William T. Sampson, see General Shafter's testimony in *Report of the Commission Approved by the President to Investigate the Conduct of the War Department in the War with Spain*, 8 vols. (hereafter *Dodge Commission*) (Washington, DC: GPO, 1900), 7: 3195–3196; Lawrence J. Legere Jr., "Unification of the Armed Forces," Ph.D. diss., Harvard University, 1951, 50–56.

12. "Report for 1903," 7 December 1903, *Five Years*, 334. See also Legere, "Unification of the Armed Forces," 47; Vernon E. Davis, *The History of the Joint Chiefs of Staff*

in World War II: Organizational Development, vol. 1, *Origin of the Joint and Combined Chiefs of Staff* (Washington, DC: Historical Division, JCS, 1972), 1, 6.

13. "Report for 1903," 7 December 1903, *Five Years*, 335.

14. Legere, "Unification of the Armed Forces," 59–60; Louis Morton, "The Long Road to Unity of Command," *Military Review* 39 (January 1960), 6.

15. Morton, "Long Road to Unity of Command," 7–8.

16. Ibid., 8.

17. Ibid., 9.

18. Even after the US entry into World War I in spring 1917, there were no changes in the academic routine and instruction except that because of early graduation, cadets did not take the course in the art of war. Ambrose, *Duty, Honor, Country*, 251–252. See also Ellis and Moore, *School for Soldiers*, 38; Russell Weigley, *History of the United States Army* (New York: Macmillan, 1987), 325.

19. Ambrose, *Eisenhower*, 1: 51.

20. Eisenhower, *At Ease*, 16.

21. Ambrose, *Eisenhower*, 1: 65. See also ibid., 1: 56, 68.

22. Davis, *History of the Joint Chiefs*, 1: 82–84; Edward M. Coffman, *The War to End All Wars: The American Military Experience in World War I* (Lexington: University Press of Kentucky, 1998), 143–153.

23. Coffman, *War to End All Wars*, 154. Both French Prime Minister Georges Clemenceau and his British counterpart David Lloyd George were present, as well US General John J. Pershing and Chief of Staff Tasker H. Bliss.

24. Legere, "Unification of the Armed Forces," 69–70. See also Davis, *History of the Joint Chiefs*, 1: 12.

25. Demetrios Caraley, *The Politics of Military Unification: A Study of Conflict and the Policy Process* (New York: Columbia University Press, 1966), 7–8; US Congress, Senate, Committee on Naval Affairs, *Report to Honorable James Forrestal, Secretary of the Navy, on Unification of the War and Navy Departments and Postwar Organization for National Security* (hereafter Eberstadt Report) (Washington, DC: GPO, 1945), 79th Congress, 1st session, 186–187.

26. Legere, "Unification of the Armed Forces," 75; Morton, "Long Road to Unity of Command," 11; Davis, *History of the Joint Chiefs*, 1: 29.

27. Ambrose, *Eisenhower*, 1: 67; Russell F. Weigley, *History of the United States Army* (New York: Macmillan, 1967), 396, 403. In 1938 Pershing paid Conner his highest tribute: "I could have spared any other in the AEF better than you." Coffman, *War to End All Wars*, 267.

28. Carlo D'Este, *Eisenhower: A Soldier's Life* (New York: Holt, 2002), 149.

29. Eisenhower, *At Ease*, 187.

30. Kenneth S. Davis, *Soldier of Democracy: A Biography of Dwight Eisenhower* (New York: Doubleday, 1952), 197. In fact, Conner's highest praise for his protégé was: "Eisenhower, you handled that just the way Marshall would have done." Ibid.

31. Dwight D. Eisenhower, *Crusade in Europe* (Garden City, NY: Doubleday, 1948), 18.

32. Eisenhower, *At Ease,* 200.

33. Daniel D. Holt and James W. Leyerzapf, eds., *Eisenhower: The Prewar Diaries and Selective Papers, 1905–1941* (Baltimore: Johns Hopkins University Press, 1998), 45. The quotation is from an August 1926 Eisenhower paper, "On the Command and General Staff School," 43–58, later published, unsigned, in revised version as "The Leavenworth Course," *Infantry Journal,* no. 3 (1927), 589–600.

34. Mark C. Bender, *Watershed at Leavenworth: Dwight D. Eisenhower and the Command and General Staff School* (Fort Leavenworth, KS: Combat Studies Institute, 1990), 43.

35. Philip C. Cockerell, *Brown Shoes and Mortar Boards: US Army Officer Professional Education at the Command and General Staff School, Fort Leavenworth, Kansas, 1919–1940* (Ann Arbor: UMI Dissertation Services, 1993), 95.

36. Ibid., 111; Bender, *Watershed at Leavenworth,* 43; Ambrose, *Eisenhower,* 1: 80–81. The class standings were tight. Eisenhower finished less than two points ahead of Gerow, who ranked eleventh in the class.

37. *The Joint Board, Joint Action of the Army and the Navy* (hereafter *JAAN*) (Washington, DC: GPO, 1927) 4–5.

38. Report of Committee no. 9, "Subject: Joint Landing Operations," 3 March 1928, file no. 347-9, Command Course no. 25, p. 5, US Army War College Curricular Archives, US Army Military History Institute. The report provides a detailed analysis of the 1927 *JAAN.*

39. Report of Subcommittee no., 1, "Subject: A Resume of the Actual Conditions, Allied and Central Powers, Just Prior to the Operations of 1918," 9, 11, part of Report of Committee no. 16, "Subject: Strategy of the World War, Western Front, 1918, with Special Reference to the Employment of the American Expeditionary Force," 22 March 1928, file no. 347-16, Command Course no. 32, US Army War College Curricular Archives, US Army Military History Institute. Among his extensive bibliography for the report, Eisenhower listed Fox Conner's "Notes of Operations of the AEF," US Army War College Curricular Archives, US Army Military History Institute, 3.

Chapter 2. Reform and Experience

The epigraphs to this chapter are drawn from Dwight D. Eisenhower, *At Ease: Stories I Tell to Friends* (Garden City, NY: Doubleday, 1967), 197; and US Congress, Senate, Committee on Military Affairs, *Hearings on S. 84 and S. 1482, Department of Armed Forces, Department of Military Security,* 79th Congress, 1st session (Washington, DC: GPO, 1945), 204.

1. Piers Brendon, *Ike: His Life and Times* (Harper and Row, 1986), 56.

2. Ibid. See also David M. Kennedy, *Freedom from Fear: The American People in Depression and War, 1929–1945* (New York: Oxford University Press, 1999), 1.

3. Brendon, *Ike,* 64; Ernest R. May, "Cold War and Defense," *The Cold War and Defense,* ed. Keith Neilson and Ronald G. Hay (New York: Praeger, 1990), 9. See also Kennedy, *Freedom from Fear,* 131; David Brinkley, *Washington Goes to War* (New York: Knopf, 1988), xiii–xiv, 24.

4. Eisenhower, *At Ease*, 212.

5. Stephen E. Ambrose, *Eisenhower*, vol. 1, *Soldier, General of the Army, President Elect, 1890–1952* (New York: Simon and Schuster, 1983), 91. See also Kerry E. Irish, "Apt Pupil: Dwight Eisenhower and the 1930 Industrial Mobilization Plan," *Journal of Military History* 70 (2006), 50–51.

6. Daniel D. Holt and James W. Leyerzapf, eds., *Eisenhower: The Prewar Diaries and Selected Papers, 1905–1941* (Baltimore: Johns Hopkins University Press, 1998), 187; emphasis in original. See also Lawrence J. Legere Jr., "Unification of the Armed Forces," Ph.D. diss., Harvard University, 1951, 29; Vernon E. Davis, *The History of the Joint Chiefs of Staff in World War II: Organizational Development*, vol. 1, *Origin of the Joint and Combined Chiefs of Staff* (Washington, DC: Historical Division, JCS, 1972), 29.

7. Holt and Leyerzapf, *Eisenhower*, 153–154.

8. Eisenhower, *At Ease*, 212.

9. Holt and Leyerzapf, *Eisenhower*, 247.

10. Ibid., 250.

11. Ibid., 217.

12. Ibid., 248–249.

13. Ibid., 253–254; emphasis in original.

14. *Hearings on S. 84 and S. 1482*, 284. "I have no doubt," one witness testified after World War II, "the members of that Board honestly believed that 'coordinated action' through some kind of committee meetings like the Joint Army-Navy Board was just as good as a unified command—that is they believed it until the first Sunday in December 1941." Ibid.

15. US Joint Army and Navy Board, *The Joint Action of the Army and the Navy* (hereafter *JAAN*) (Washington, DC: GPO, 1935). See also Legere, "Unification of the Armed Forces," 146–147; Davis, *History of the Joint Chiefs*, 1: 21–22, 28; Louis Morton, "The Long Road to Unity of Command," *Military Review* 39, no. 10 (1960), 11.

16. *JAAN*, chapter 2, change 2, dated 30 November 1938. The 1935 *JAAN* had stipulated that unity of command could occur only at presidential direction. See also Davis, *History of the Joint Chiefs*, 1: xi, 37; Legere, "Unification of the Armed Forces," 149; Morton, "Long Road to Unity of Command," 11–12; C. Kenneth Allard, *Command, Control and the Common Defense* (New Haven: Yale University Press, 1990), 96, who points out that mutual cooperation in the late 1930s was "little more than a nonaggression pact concluded between the Army and the Navy of the United States."

17. Eisenhower, *At Ease*, 214. John Eisenhower has pointed out that his father's diaries during this period were usually upbeat, referring to long hours but never complaining. But in fact Eisenhower's work schedule almost broke his health. "I always resented the years I spent as a slave in the War Department," he commented in later years. John S. D. Eisenhower, Introduction to Holt and Leyerzapf, *Eisenhower*, xxvii.

18. Merle Miller, *Ike the Soldier: As They Knew Him* (New York: Putnam, 1987), 261; Ambrose, *Eisenhower*, 1: 94.

19. Eisenhower, *At Ease*, 213.

20. Ibid., 214; Miller, *Ike the Soldier*, 261; Peter Lyon, *Eisenhower: Portrait of a Hero* (Boston: Little, Brown, 1974), 69; Ambrose, *Eisenhower*, 1: 94.

21. D. Clayton James, *The Years of MacArthur*, vol. 1, *1880–1941*. (Boston: Houghton Mifflin, 1970), 564.

22. Eisenhower, *At Ease*, 219.

23. Memorandum for Manuel Quezon, President of the Philippines, 8 August 1940, written at the request of the secretary to the president for personal observations before Eisenhower's departure, quoted in Holt and Leyerzapf, *Eisenhower*, 488, 486, 475.

24. Davis, *History of the Joint Chiefs*, 1: 34; *Hearings Before the Joint Committee on the Investigation of the Pearl Harbor Attack* (Washington, DC: GPO, 1946), part 29, p. 2066.

25. Forrest C. Pogue, *George C. Marshall: Ordeal and Hope, 1939-1942* (New York: Viking, 1965), 290.

26. Davis, *History of the Joint Chiefs*, 1: 119; Mark Skinner Watson, *Chief of Staff: Prewar Plans and Preparation* (Washington, DC: GPO, 1950), 376.

27. Davis, *History of the Joint Chiefs*, 1: 38-39; Legere, "Unification of the Armed Forces," 197-199.

28. Dwight D. Eisenhower, *Crusade in Europe* (Garden City, NY: Doubleday, 1948), 6.

29. Ambrose, *Eisenhower*, 1: 126.

30. Eisenhower, *Crusade in Europe*, 11.

31. Ibid., 11-12. See also Eisenhower, *At Ease*, 242-245.

32. Eisenhower, *Crusade in Europe*, 12. "I still shudder," Eisenhower recalled in his memoirs concerning the vote on continuing the draft, "to think how close we came to returning trained men home, closing down the reception centers for new draftees, reassembling a fragmentized force into its Regular Army core—all within weeks of our entry into the most colossal war of all time." Eisenhower, *At Ease*, 244.

33. Eisenhower, *Crusade in Europe*, 14.

Chapter 3. Beginnings of Combined and Joint Command

The epigraphs to this chapter are drawn from Dwight D. Eisenhower, *Crusade in Europe* (New York: Doubleday, 1948), 16; and Carlo D'Este, *Eisenhower: A Soldier's Life* (New York: Holt, 2002), 287.

1. Eisenhower, *Crusade in Europe*, 19.

2. Frederick Morgan, *Overture to Overlord* (Garden City, NY: Doubleday, 1950), 8.

3. Eric Larrabee, *Commander in Chief: Franklin Delano Roosevelt, His Lieutenants, and Their War* (New York: Simon and Schuster, 1987), 419.

4. Ibid., 20; Henry L. Stimson and McGeorge Bundy, *On Active Service in Peace and War* (New York: Harper and Brothers, 1947), 382-391.

5. Forrest C. Pogue, *George C. Marshall: Ordeal and Hope, 1939-1942* (New York: Viking, 1965), 337.

6. Ibid., 338.

7. Ibid.; Dwight D. Eisenhower, *At Ease: Stories I Tell to Friends* (Garden City, NY: Doubleday, 1967), 248. Marshall wanted things done "the way he wanted them — or else," Eisenhower recalled fifteen years later. 10 January 1957 entry, Ann C. Whitman File, Diary Series, box 8, Eisenhower Library.

8. Eisenhower, *At Ease*, 248.

9. Geoffrey Perret, *Eisenhower* (New York: Random House, 1988), 148. See also Eisenhower, *Crusade in Europe*, 24.

10. Dwight D. Eisenhower, *The Eisenhower Diaries*, ed. Robert H. Ferrell (New York: Norton, 1989), 46. See also Stephen E. Ambrose, *Eisenhower*, vol. 1, *Soldier, General of the Army, President-Elect, 1890–1952* (New York: Simon and Schuster, 1983), 137.

11. Alfred D. Chandler Jr., ed., *The Papers of Dwight David Eisenhower* (hereafter *EP*), vols. 1–5, *The War Years* (Baltimore: Johns Hopkins University Press, 1970), 1: no. 341, p. 343.

12. Winston S. Churchill, *The Second World War*, vol. 2, *Their Finest Hour* (Boston: Houghton Mifflin, 1949), 16.

13. Pogue, *George C. Marshall*, 271.

14. Larrabee, *Commander in Chief*, 155. See also Pogue, *George C. Marshall*, 270–273; Vernon E. Davis, *The History of the Joint Chiefs in World War II: Organizational Development*, vol. 1, *Origin of the Joint and Combined Chiefs of Staff* (Washington, DC: Historical Division, JCS, 1972), 180–181.

15. D'Este, *Eisenhower*, 297.

16. Davis, *History of the Joint Chiefs*, 1: 181; Pogue, *George C. Marshall*, 84, 283.

17. D'Este, *Eisenhower*, 288.

18. Pogue, *George C. Marshall*, 275; Maurice Matloff and Edwin M. Snell, *Strategic Planning for Coalition Warfare, 1941–1942* (Washington, DC: Office of the Chief of Military History, 1953), 123; Grace P. Hayes, *The History of the Joint Chiefs of Staff in World War II: The War Against Japan*, vol. 1, *Pearl Harbor Through TRIDENT* (Washington, DC: JCS, 1953), chapter 2.

19. *EP* 1: no. 22, p. 24; emphasis in original. See also Stephen E. Ambrose, *The Supreme Commander: The War Years of General Dwight D. Eisenhower* (Garden City, NY: Doubleday, 1970), 25–26.

20. Robert E. Sherwood, *Roosevelt and Hopkins: An Intimate History*, rev. ed. (New York: Harper, 1950), 455. The proposal was evidently as much a surprise to Eisenhower, who attended the meeting for WPD, as for the Navy. "I express these as my personal views," Marshall began, "and not those as a result of consultation with the Navy or with my own War Plans Division." Ibid. See also Pogue, *George C. Marshall*, 276; Davis, *History of the Joint Chiefs*, 1: 153; Matloff and Snell, *Strategic Planning for Coalition Warfare*, 124; Eisenhower's memorandum for file of the Christmas meeting, *EP* 1: no. 23, pp. 25–27.

21. Pogue, *George C. Marshall*, 276.

22. Ibid., 264.

23. Ambrose, *Eisenhower*, 146.

24. *EP* 1: no. 79, p. 70.

25. Arthur Bryant, *The Turn of the Tide* (Garden City, NY: Doubleday, 1957), 234.

26. *EP* 1: no. 23, p. 26, and no. 24, pp. 28–29.

27. Matloff and Snell, *Strategic Planning for Coalition Warfare*, 125; *EP* 1: no. 24, p. 30n1.

28. Pogue, *George C. Marshall*, 279.

29. Sherwood, *Roosevelt and Hopkins*, 457.

30. Pogue, *George C. Marshall*, 280.

31. Winston S. Churchill, *The Second World War*, vol. 3, *The Grand Alliance* (Boston: Houghton Mifflin, 1950), 274.

32. Ibid., 675–677.

33. *EP* 1: no. 49, p. 48. See also ibid., no. 34, p. 37n1; Sherwood, *Roosevelt and Hopkins*, 458; Louis Morton, *Strategy and Command: The First Two Years* (Washington, DC: Office of the Chief of Military History, 1962), 606–610.

34. *EP* 1: no. 32, p. 35. See also Morton, *Strategy and Command*, 161–162.

35. Churchill, *Second World War*, 3: 675.

36. Sherwood, *Roosevelt and Hopkins*, 469.

37. Ibid.

38. Davis, *History of the Joint Chiefs*, 1: 210.

39. Ibid., 1: 166.

40. Lawrence J. Legere Jr., "Unification of the Armed Forces," Ph.D. diss., Harvard University, 1951, 216.

41. Davis, *History of the Joint Chiefs*, 1: 165, 169; Pogue, *George C. Marshall*, 282–285; Matloff and Snell, *Strategic Planning for Coalition Warfare*, 125–126; Legere, "Unification of the Armed Forces," 217.

42. Bryant, *Turn of the Tide*, 254.

43. Churchill, *Second World War*, 3: 686.

44. Charles Wilson Moran, *Churchill: The Struggle for Survival, 1940–1945* (Boston: Houghton Mifflin, 1966), 23.

Chapter 4. Unified European Theater Command

The epigraphs to this chapter are drawn from Carlo D'Este, *Eisenhower: A Soldier's Life* (New York: Holt, 2002), 302; and Dwight D. Eisenhower, *The Eisenhower Diaries*, ed. Robert H. Ferrell (New York: Norton, 1981), 44.

1. Lawrence J. Legere Jr., "Unification of the Armed Forces," Ph.D. diss., Harvard University, 1951, 259–260. See also Vernon E. Davis, *The History of the Joint Chiefs in World War II: Organizational Development*, vol. 1, *Origin of the Joint and Combined Chiefs of Staff* (Washington, D.C.: Historical Division, JCS, 1972), 180.

2. Legere, "Unification of the Armed Forces," 201; Forrest C. Pogue, *George C. Marshall: Ordeal and Hope, 1939–1942* (New York: Viking, 1965), 70. Marshall's preference was that the Combined Chiefs of Staff meet in the Federal Reserve Building, the setting for all the military meetings during the Arcadia Conference. The legal status

of the building, however, prevented the president from assigning it as the location for the Combined Chiefs meetings. On 30 January 1942 Roosevelt designated the Public Health Building as the venue. Davis, *History of the Joint Chiefs*, 1: 188.

3. Eric Larrabee, *Commander in Chief: Franklin Delano Roosevelt, His Lieutenants, and Their War* (New York: Simon and Schuster, 1987), 21; Davis, *History of the Joint Chiefs*, 1: 453.

4. Dwight D. Eisenhower, *Crusade in Europe* (Garden City, NY: Doubleday, 1948) 31. See also Geoffrey Perret, *Eisenhower* (New York: Random House, 2002), 154–155; Ray S. Cline, *Washington Command Post: The Operations Division* (Washington, DC: Office of the Chief of Military History, 1951), 94. For the reform motivation and the reorganization process, see Otto L. Nelson Jr., *National Security and the General Staff* (Washington, DC: Infantry Journal Press, 1946), chapters 7 and 8.

5. Eisenhower, *Diaries*, 48. In a 15 June 1932 entry in his diary on his previous War Department tour, Eisenhower reflected on his twenty-one years of service to the day and called Gerow "my best friend. . . . I have no language sufficiently forceful to describe his efficiency and general worth." Daniel D. Holt and James W. Leyerzapf, eds., *Eisenhower: the Prewar Diaries and Selected Papers, 1905–1941* (Baltimore: Johns Hopkins University Press, 1998), 228.

6. Eisenhower, *Diaries*, 47.

7. Eisenhower, *Crusade in Europe*, 31. See also Cline, *Washington Command Post*, 94.

8. Cline, *Washington Command Post*, 116; John C. Ries, *The Management of Defense: Organization and Control of the U.S. Armed Services* (Baltimore: Johns Hopkins University Press, 1964), 26.

9. Perret, *Eisenhower*, 155, emphasis in the original. See also Cline, *Washington Command Post*, 107–111, 118.

10. Davis, *History of the Joint Chiefs*, 1: 236. The wording came about as a result of a 26 February letter from Roosevelt to Stimson, requesting that the draft executive order be rephrased in order "to make it very clear that the Commander-in-Chief exercises his command function . . . directly through the Chief of Staff." Ibid., 1: 237. This left Stimson no formal responsibilities in strategic matters. This circumstance, he noted, might have disturbed him seriously but for the relationship of mutual confidence with Roosevelt and Marshall that ensured that he was an active participant in all grand strategic discussions during the war. Henry L. Stimson and McGeorge Bundy, *On Active Service in Peace and War* (New York: Harper, 1947), 415, 453.

11. Cline, *Washington Command Post*, 110.

12. Merle Miller, *Ike the Soldier: As They Knew Him* (New York: Putnam, 1987), 346. See also Perret, *Eisenhower*, 155–156.

13. Miller, *Ike the Soldier*, 344. The visitor was Colonel Lucian K. Truscott Jr., on his way to London to work with the British.

14. Ibid., 342.

15. Eisenhower, *Diaries*, 47.

16. Larrabee, *Commander in Chief*, 421.

17. Alfred D. Chandler Jr., ed., *The Papers of Dwight David Eisenhower* (hereafter

EP), vols. 1–5, *The War Years* (Baltimore: Johns Hopkins University Press, 1970), 1: no. 201, pp. 194–195; Winston S. Churchill, *The Second World War*, vol. 4, *The Hinge of Fate* (Boston: Houghton Mifflin, 1950), 169–170.

18. Eisenhower, *Diaries*, 49.

19. Davis, *History of the Joint Chiefs*, 1: 200–202; *EP*, 1: no. 142, p. 126n2, and no. 178, p. 176n1.

20. *EP*, 1: no. 178, pp. 174–175. See also Maurice Matloff and Edwin M. Snell, *Strategic Planning for Coalition Warfare, 1941–1942* (Washington, DC: Office of the Chief of Military History, 1953), 165–167. That day, Eisenhower noted in his diary: "ABDA area is gone. Java is occupied almost completely." Eisenhower, *Diaries*, 50.

21. Davis, *History of the Joint Chiefs*, 1: 202; *EP*, 1: no. 178, p. 176n2. See also Cline, *Washington Command Post*, 166–169; Demetrios Caraley, *The Politics of Military Unification: A Study of Conflict and the Policy Process* (New York: Columbia University Press, 1966), 18.

22. Pogue, *George C. Marshall*, 255.

23. Louis Morton, *Strategy and Command: The First Two Years* (Washington, DC: Center of Military History, 1985), 246. See also Cline, *Washington Command Post*, 166–199; and for Eisenhower's memorandum, *EP*, 1: no. 180, pp. 176–177.

24. All quotations from diary entries, Eisenhower, *Diaries*, 50–51.

25. Morton, *Strategy and Command*, 615, 618.

26. Eisenhower, *Diaries*, 48, 49. See also *EP*, 1: no. 3, p. 8n2.

27. Ibid., 49.

28. *EP*, 1: no. 204, p. 197n2.

29. Ibid., 205–207. For an earlier example of Eisenhower's thinking on these priorities, see ibid., no. 185, p. 180.

30. Eisenhower, *Diaries*, 53.

31. *EP*, 1: no. 292, pp. 292–293; emphasis in original.

32. Ibid., no. 293, p. 295.

33. Eisenhower, *Diaries*, 53–54. In 1948, fresh from the unification struggles, Eisenhower reflected on the earlier landing craft problems. "What a difference it would have made if we had co-ordinated policy and a single head at that time"; Eisenhower, *Crusade in Europe*, 39.

34. Eisenhower, *At Ease*, 252; US Congress, House Committee on Expenditures in the Executive Department, *Hearings on HR 2319, National Security Act 1947*, 80th Congress, first session (Washington, DC: GPO, 1947), 302.

35. Eisenhower, *Diaries*, 58.

36. Eisenhower, *Crusade in Europe*, 356.

37. *EP*, 1: no. 318, p. 319.

38. Arthur Bryant, *The Turn of the Tide* (Garden City, NY: Doubleday, 1957), 31n.

39. Stephen E. Ambrose, *The Supreme Commander: The War Years of General Dwight D. Eisenhower* (Garden City, NY: Doubleday, 1970), 46.

40. *EP*, 1: no. 318, p. 320. For the British charts, see ibid., 323–324.

41. Ibid., 321.

42. Ibid., no. 329, pp. 334–335.

43. Eisenhower, *Crusade in Europe*, 50; Eisenhower, *Diaries*, 62.

44. Eisenhower, *Diaries*, 62.

45. Eisenhower, *Crusade in Europe*, 51.

46. Pogue, *George C. Marshall*, 337.

47. Perret, *Eisenhower*, 160; Eisenhower, *Diaries*, 64.

Chapter 5. Unity in Theory

The epigraphs to this chapter are drawn from Harry C. Butcher, *My Three Years with Eisenhower* (New York: Simon and Schuster, 1946), 138; and Louis Galambos and Daun Van Ee, eds., *The Papers of Dwight David Eisenhower* (hereafter *EP*), vols. 14–17, *The Presidency: The Middle Way* (Baltimore: Johns Hopkins University Press, 1996), 15: no. 599, p. 750.

1. Alfred D. Chandler Jr., ed., *EP*, vols. 1–5, *The War Years* (Baltimore: Johns Hopkins University Press, 1970), 1: no. 352, p. 359n1.

2. D. K. R. Crosswell, *The Chief of Staff: The Military Career of General Walter Bedell Smith* (New York: Greenwood, 1991), 126. See also Dwight D. Eisenhower, *Letters to Mamie*, ed. John S. D. Eisenhower (Garden City, NY: Doubleday, 1978), 9.

3. *EP*, 1: no. 360, p. 369.

4. Carlo D'Este, *Eisenhower: A Soldier's Life* (New York: Holt, 2002), 326.

5. Dwight D. Eisenhower, *At Ease: Stories I Tell to Friends* (Garden City, NY: Doubleday, 1967), 252. For a slightly different version, see Harry C. Butcher, *My Three Years with Eisenhower* (New York: Simon and Schuster, 1946), 37. See also Maurice Matloff and Edwin M. Snell, *Strategic Planning for Coalition Warfare, 1941–1942* (Washington, DC: Office of the Chief of Military History, 1953), 278, 281–283; D'Este, *Eisenhower*, 334–336.

6. *EP*, 1: no. 442, p. 485.

7. Lionel Hastings Ismay, *The Memoirs of General Lord Ismay* (New York: Viking, 1960), 262. Ismay was no stranger to such canine comparisons. His nickname was Pug, derived from a face that featured an extremely short nose dominated by large, slightly protuberant, liquid brown eyes; Forrest C. Pogue, *George C. Marshall: Ordeal and Hope, 1939–1942* (New York: Viking, 1966), 310.

8. Crosswell, *Chief of Staff*, 139; Piers Brendon, *Ike: His Life and Times* (New York: Harper and Row, 1986), 85.

9. Pogue, *George C. Marshall*, 298–301; John C. Ries, *The Management of Defense: Organization and Control of the US Armed Services* (Baltimore: Johns Hopkins University Press, 1964), 62; Ray S. Cline, *Washington Command Post: The Operations Division* (Washington, DC: Office of the Chief of Military History, 1951), 105; Vernon E. Davis, *The History of the Joint Chiefs in World War II: Organizational Development*, vol. 1, *Origin of the Joint and Combined Chiefs of Staff* (Washington, DC: Historical Division, JCS, 1972), 256–257.

10. Arthur Bryant, *The Turn of the Tide* (Garden City, NY: Doubleday, 1957), 242n. See also Davis, *History of the Joint Chiefs*, 1: 260–261; William D. Leahy, *I Was There:*

The Personal Story of the Chief of Staff to Presidents Roosevelt and Truman (New York: McGraw-Hill, 1950, 1950), 95–107; Henry R. Adams, *Witness to Power: The Life of Fleet Admiral William D. Leahy* (Annapolis: Naval Institute Press, 1984).

11. Chandler, Introduction to *EP*, 1: xx; Forrest C. Pogue, *The Supreme Command* (Washington, DC: Office of the Chief of Military History, 1954), 40.

12. *EP*, 2: no. 607, p. 691. See also Eisenhower's cable to Smith in London from Gibraltar after the invasion of North Africa had begun, in which he explained his hesitancy about sending too many personal messages to Churchill. He was, Eisenhower elaborated, "jealously guarding" the sanctity of his line of communication to the Combined Chiefs: "I never want to take the slightest chance that they will feel I am short-cutting or under-cutting or trying to go through the back door"; ibid., no. 609, p. 694.

13. Dwight D. Eisenhower, *Crusade in Europe* (Garden City, NY: Doubleday), 62.

14. *EP*, 2: no. 935, p. 1080.

15. Forrest C. Pogue, *George C. Marshall: Organizer of Victory, 1943–1945* (New York: Viking, 1973), 77; Crosswell, *Chief of Staff*, 148; Pogue, *Supreme Command*, 35.

16. Butcher, *My Three Years with Eisenhower*, 71.

17. Ismay, *Memoirs*, 258, 262.

18. Eisenhower, *Crusade in Europe*, 76.

19. *EP*, 2: no. 927, p. 1071.

20. Eric Larrabee, *Commander in Chief: Franklin Roosevelt, His Lieutenants, and Their War* (New York: Simon and Schuster, 1987), 436.

21. Butcher, *My Three Years with Eisenhower*, 49.

22. Eisenhower, *Crusade in Europe*, 76.

23. Stephen E. Ambrose, *The Supreme Commander: The War Years of General Dwight D. Eisenhower* (Garden City, NY: Doubleday, 1970), 80.

24. Crosswell, *Chief of Staff*, 123, 141.

25. *EP*, 2: no. 585, p. 668.

26. Eisenhower, *Crusade in Europe*, 89.

27. Ibid., 80.

28. D'Este, *Eisenhower*, 339–340, 343; Crosswell, *Chief of Staff*, 126.

29. Ambrose, *Supreme Commander*, 83. See also *EP*, 1: no. 559, p. 628, no. 411, pp. 444–447, and no. 438, pp. 481–483.

30. Butcher, *My Three Years with Eisenhower*, 45; emphasis on original.

31. Wesley Frank Craven and James Lea Cate, eds., *U.S. Army Air Forces in World War II*, vol. 2, *Europe: Torch to Point Blank, August 1942–December 1943* (Chicago: University of Chicago Press, 1949), 56–60; George F. Howe, *U.S. Army in World War II, Northwest Africa: Seizing the Initiative in the West* (Washington, DC: Center of Military History, 1985), 37; Crosswell, *Chief of Staff*, 124.

32. Andrew Browne Cunningham, *A Sailor's Odyssey* (New York: Dutton, 1951), 471; Eisenhower, *Crusade in Europe*, 89.

33. *EP*, 1: no. 534, p. 592. See also Howe, *Northwest Africa*, 36; Cunningham, *Sailor's Odyssey*, 471.

34. Butcher, *My Three Years with Eisenhower*, 126.

35. *EP*, 1: no. 488, p. 547.

36. Eisenhower, *Crusade in Europe*, 369.

37. *EP*, 1: no. 541, pp. 603–604.

38. Howe, *Northwest Africa*, 36.

39. *EP*, 1: no. 563, p. 632.

40. Ibid., no. 559, pp. 627–628. See also Eisenhower's 21 October note on the new directive to Brigadier Hollis of the British War Cabinet: "I consider its terms completely satisfactory. In fact, it so definitely expresses the views I had with respect to appropriate instructions to a national commander, under the conditions prevailing in this case that I am forwarding a copy to the United States War Department in the hope that it will serve as a model in future cases of this kind"; ibid., no. 563, p. 633n2.

Chapter 6. Testing the Theory

The epigraphs to this chapter are drawn from Stephen E. Ambrose, *The Supreme Commander: The War Years of General Dwight D. Eisenhower* (Garden City, NY: Doubleday, 1970), 137; and Dwight D. Eisenhower, *Crusade in Europe* (Garden City, NY: Doubleday, 1948), 158.

1. George F. Howe, *US Army in World War II, Northwest Africa: Seizing the Initiative in the West* (Washington, DC: Center of Military History, 1985), 38.

2. Dwight D. Eisenhower, *The Eisenhower Diaries*, ed. Robert H. Ferrell (New York: 1981), 81–82; Harry C. Butcher, *My Three Years with Eisenhower* (New York: Simon and Schuster, 1946), 178; Alfred D. Chandler Jr., ed., *The Papers of Dwight D. Eisenhower: The War Years* (hereafter *EP*), vols. 1–5 (Baltimore: Johns Hopkins University Press, 1970), 2: no. 593, p. 679.

3. Eisenhower, *Crusade in Europe*, 116. See also *EP*, 2: no. 718, p. 838.

4. Eisenhower, *Crusade in Europe*, 119. See also Rick Atkinson, *An Army at Dawn: The War in North Africa, 1942–1943* (New York: Holt, 2002), 170.

5. *EP*, 2: no. 594, p. 680.

6. Butcher, *My Three Years with Eisenhower*, 183. See also Stephen E. Ambrose, *Eisenhower*, vol. 1, *Soldier, General of the Army, President-Elect, 1890–1952* (New York: Simon and Schuster, 1983), 209; *EP*, 2: no. 622, pp. 707–711; Howe, *Northwest Africa*, 263, 269–271.

7. Butcher, *My Three Years with Eisenhower*, 216.

8. *EP*, 2: no. 653, p. 750. See also Butcher, *My Three Years with Eisenhower*, 183; Atkinson, *Army at Dawn*, 194.

9. Butcher, *My Three Years with Eisenhower*, 234–235.

10. *EP*, 2: no. 649, p. 675.

11. By fall 1943, the AFHQ staff numbered 4,070, one of the largest command-oriented bureaucracies in the history of war, until the larger Supreme Headquarters Allied Expeditionary Force (SHAEF) was created in 1944; Carlo D'Este, *Eisenhower: A Soldier's Life* (New York: Holt, 2002), 381; D. K. R. Crosswell, *The Chief of Staff:*

The Military Career of Walter Bedell Smith (New York: Greenwood, 1991), 40. In the coming years, AFHQ would expand to 1,000 officers and 15,000 enlisted troops in more than two hundred locations in Algiers; Atkinson, *Army at Dawn,* 195.

12. *EP,* 2: no. 654, p. 752n1.

13. Ibid., no. 659, p. 750. See also D'Este, *Eisenhower,* 323; Wesley Frank Craven and James Lea Cate, eds., *US Army Air Forces in World War II,* vol. 2, *Europe: Torch to Point Blank, August 1942–December 1943* (Chicago: University of Chicago Press, 1949), 63–66.

14. Forrest C. Pogue, *The Supreme Command* (Washington, DC: Office of the Chief of Military History, 1954), 61.

15. Arthur Tedder, *With Prejudice* (Boston: Little, Brown, 1966), 369–370.

16. *EP,* 2: no. 684, p. 790. "I assumed that he did not realize," Tedder later recalled, "that I already controlled air operations in theaters under separate ground commanders including those from Malta"; Tedder, *With Prejudice,* 375.

17. *EP,* 2: no. 684, p. 790.

18. Ibid., no. 747, p. 880. See also ibid., no. 743, p. 874; Tedder, *With Prejudice,* 385.

19. *EP,* 2: no. 685, p. 791.

20. Ibid., no. 698, p. 811. See also ibid., no. 672, p. 777n3, and no. 738, pp. 867–868.

21. Ibid., no. 703, p. 820n1; Butcher, *My Three Years with Eisenhower,* 217.

22. Dwight D. Eisenhower, *Letters to Mamie,* ed. John S. D. Eisenhower (Garden City, NY: Doubleday, 1978), 73; Ambrose, *Eisenhower,* 213. See also *EP,* 2: no. 685, p. 793n5.

23. *EP,* 2: no. 705, p. 824.

24. Eisenhower, *Crusade in Europe,* 129.

25. *EP,* 2: no. 687, p. 795.

26. Ibid., no. 673, p. 781.

27. Quoted ibid., no. 753, p. 886n2; emphasis in original. See also Harold Macmillan, *The Blast of War, 1939–1945* (Garden City, NY: Doubleday, 1964), 144–161, who entitles the chapter covering this period "Everybody Gets into Eisenhower's Act."

28. *EP,* 2: no. 701, p. 818n1.

29. Harry L. Coles and Albert K. Weinberg, *US Army in World War II,* vol. 8, *Civil Affairs: Soldiers Become Governors* (Washington, DC: Office of the Chief of Military History, 1964), 47. See also Forrest C. Pogue, *George C. Marshall: Organizer of Victory, 1943–1945* (New York: Viking, 1973), 181; *EP,* 2: no. 719, p. 841n1. These were also concerns of the British. "Eisenhower far too busy with political matters," Brooke noted. "Not paying enough attention to the Germans"; Arthur Bryant, *The Turn of the Tide* (Garden City, NY: Doubleday, 1957), 436.

30. Eisenhower, *Crusade in Europe,* 124; *EP,* 2: no. 738, p. 868; Butcher, *My Three Years with Eisenhower,* 227.

31. Butcher, *My Three Years with Eisenhower,* 230. See also Howe, *Northwest Africa,* 351; *EP,* 2: no. 727, pp. 851–853. In his war memoirs, Eisenhower admitted that

in acquiescing to the French refusal to serve under Anderson, he made a monumental error; Eisenhower, *Crusade in Europe*, 146.

32. Robert E. Sherwood, *Roosevelt and Hopkins: An Intimate History* (New York: Harper, 1950), 676, 689.

33. *EP*, 2: no. 796, p. 928.

34. Albert C. Wedemeyer, *Wedemeyer Reports* (New York: Holt, 1958), 191–192. See also Atkinson, *Army at Dawn*, 288.

35. Howe, *Northwest Africa*, 354–355; *EP*, 2: no. 810, p. 943n1.

36. Pogue, *George C. Marshall*, 180.

37. Bryant, *Turn of the Tide*, 454–455. See also Tedder, *With Prejudice*, 394, who recalled "it was felt that Eisenhower could not effectively combine the roles of Supreme Commander and Military Commander."

38. Eisenhower, *Crusade in Europe*, 139.

39. Butcher, *My Three Years with Eisenhower*, 258.

40. *EP*, 2: no. 811, p. 946n2.

41. Ibid., 944.

42. Ibid.; emphasis Eisenhower's.

43. Ibid., no. 775, p. 908. Eisenhower was more explicit on the command arrangements in a 14 September 1943 memorandum to Mountbatten; ibid., 3: no. 1256, p. 1421.

44. Ibid., 2: no. 811, p. 944, and p. 946n2. See also Ambrose, *Supreme Commander*, 162; Crosswell, *Chief of Staff*, 256–257.

45. *EP*, 2: no. 811, p. 944.

46. Ibid., no. 756, p. 917n1, and no. 787, p. 919n6. On Eisenhower's promotion see ibid., no. 825, p. 963n2; D'Este, *Eisenhower*, 389; Atkinson, *Army at Dawn*, 329.

47. D'Este, *Eisenhower*, 376.

48. *EP*, 2: no. 886, p. 1033.

49. Atkinson, *Army at Dawn*, 323. See also Ambrose, *Eisenhower*, 228.

50. Atkinson, *Army at Dawn*, 324.

51. John Colville, *The Churchillians* (London: Weidenfeld and Nicholson, 1981), 152. See also Ambrose, *Supreme Commander*, 220.

52. Geoffrey Perret, *Eisenhower* (New York: Random House, 1999), 205.

53. W. G. F. Jackson, *The Battle for North Africa, 1940–43* (New York: Mason/Charter, 1975), 354.

54. Piers Brendon, *Ike: His Life and Times* (New York: Harper and Row, 1986), 106.

55. *EP*, 2: no. 832, p. 972.

56. Ibid., no. 860, p. 1006.

57. Ibid., no. 906, p. 1056.

58. Ibid., no. 945, p. 1090n.

59. Ibid., no. 945, p. 1089. See also Ambrose, *Eisenhower*, 234; Howe, *Northwest Africa*, 604–608.

60. Eisenhower, *Letters to Mamie*, 113.

61. Winston S. Churchill, *The Second World War*, vol. 4, *The Hinge of Fate* (Boston: Houghton Mifflin, 1950), 780.

62. *EP*, 2: no. 1014, p. 1149. See also Atkinson, *Army at Dawn*, 531–532.

63. Eisenhower had promised Marshall in February to reduce the size of AFHQ; *EP*, 2: no. 811, p. 945. By the end of May, the expanding requirements of the unified command structure caused him to renege on the promise. "I battle on the matter constantly," he wrote Marshall, "and yet the proof brought to me of overworking staff officers is conclusive"; ibid., no. 1020, p. 1155. See also Crosswell, *Chief of Staff*, 167, 173.

64. *EP*, 2: no. 935, p. 1081. See also Crosswell, *Chief of Staff*, 172; Howe, *Northwest Africa*, 675.

Chapter 7. Unity in Practice

The epigraphs to this chapter are drawn from Alfred D. Chandler Jr., ed., *The Papers of Dwight D. Eisenhower* (hereafter *EP*), vols. 1–5, *The War Years* (Baltimore: Johns Hopkins University Press, 1970), 2: no. 992, p. 1129, and no. 1164, p. 1315.

1. Peter Lyon, *Eisenhower: Portrait of the Hero* (Boston: Little, Brown, 1974), 208; Piers Brendon, *Ike: His Life and Times* (New York: Harper and Row, 1986), 110; *EP*, 2: no. 960, p. 1105.

2. *EP*, 2: no. 960, p. 1105n2; Andrew Browne Cunningham, *A Sailor's Odyssey* (New York: Dutton, 1951), 536–537.

3. D. K. R. Crosswell, *The Chief of Staff: The Military Career of Walter Bedell Smith* (New York: Greenwood, 1991), 164; *EP*, 2: no. 969, p. 113n1.

4. *EP*, 2: no. 949, p. 1097n2.

5. Stephen E. Ambrose, *Eisenhower*, vol. 1, *Soldier, General of the Army, President-Elect, 1890–1952* (New York: Simon and Schuster, 1983), 243.

6. Arthur Bryant, *The Turn of the Tide* (Garden City, NY: Doubleday, 1957), 522.

7. Stephen E. Ambrose, *The Supreme Commander: The War Years of General Dwight D. Eisenhower* (Garden City, NY: Doubleday, 1970), 217, emphasis in original.

8. Dwight D. Eisenhower, *Crusade in Europe* (Garden City, NY: Doubleday, 1948), 181. See also Eisenhower's 18 August letter to his son; *EP*, 2: no. 1194, p. 1344. But see Harry C. Butcher, *My Three Years with Eisenhower* (New York: Simon and Schuster, 1946), 329, in which Eisenhower asserted at the time that he would have preferred to move directly on Italy or to have assaulted both sides of the Messina Straits, cutting off the island and thus facilitating the Axis surrender with minimal loss.

9. Carlo D'Este, *Eisenhower: A Soldier's Life* (New York: Holt, 2002), 438. See, for instance, Ambrose, *Supreme Commander*, 226–227: "Nearly all military historians condemn the campaign in Sicily. . . . Eisenhower himself played practically no role in the development of the campaign."

10. Maurice Matloff, *Strategic Planning for Coalition Warfare, 1943-44* (Washington, DC: Office of the Chief of Military History, 1953), chapter 10, 211-243; D'Este, *Eisenhower*, 447.

11. *EP*, 2: no. 1121, p. 1264. See also ibid., no. 1141, pp. 1292-1293; Matloff, *Strategic Planning for Coalition Warfare*, 245-246.

12. Arthur Tedder, *With Prejudice* (Boston: Little, Brown, 1966), 459; *EP*, 2: no. 1189, p. 1339 and n2.

13. Tedder, *With Prejudice*, 462; *EP*, 2: no. 1198, pp. 1347-1348.

14. Winston S. Churchill, *The Second World War*, vol. 5, *Closing the Ring* (Boston: Houghton Mifflin, 1951), 55; *EP*, 2: no. 1138, p. 1288n1.

15. *EP*, 2: no. 1147, p. 1298. Marshall forwarded the message to the president. Eisenhower sent a similar message to Churchill; ibid., no. 1148, p. 1300.

16. Harold Macmillan, *The Blast of War, 1939-1945* (Garden City, NY: Doubleday, 1964), 302, 309. See also Butcher, *My Three Years with Eisenhower*, 372.

17. *EP*, 2: no. 1213, p. 1363.

18. Ibid., no. 1187, p. 1338n2, and no. 1213, p. 1363n1; ibid., 3: no. 1244, p. 1403n1, no. 1245, p. 1404n1, and no. 1243, p. 1402n4.

19. Ibid., 3: no. 1249, pp. 1411-1412. See also ibid., 2: no. 1240, p. 1396n2. On Eisenhower's faith that joint air and naval operations would redeem the ground situation, see his 26 September note to General Handy, ibid., 3: no. 1291, p. 1464, and his 30 September cable to Field Marshal Dill, ibid., no. 1301, pp. 1472.

20. Tedder, *With Prejudice*, 467; *EP*, 3: no. 1252, p. 1416. See also *EP*, 3: no. 1257, p. 1425n3; Wesley Frank Craven and James Lea Cate, eds., *US Army Air Forces in World War II*, vol. 2, *Europe: Torch to Point Blank, August 1942-December 1943* (Chicago: University of Chicago Press, 1949), 485-549.

21. *EP*, 3: no. 1260, p. 1260, and no. 1262, p. 1429.

22. Ibid., no. 1256, pp. 1423-1424n1.

23. Ibid., 1420.

24. Ibid., 1423; emphasis in original.

25. Ibid., no. 1375, p. 1550. See also Matloff, *Strategic Planning for Coalition Warfare*, 269-270.

26. Matloff, *Strategic Planning for Coalition Warfare*, 271-272.

27. Forrest C. Pogue, *The Supreme Command* (Washington, DC: Office of the Chief of Military History, 1954), 759.

28. Ibid., 760; Matloff, *Strategic Planning for Coalition Warfare*, 275.

29. Matloff, *Strategic Planning for Coalition Warfare*, 335, 339-341. See also Ray S. Cline, *Washington Command Post: The Operations Division* (Washington, DC: Office of the Chief of Military History, 1951), 226-228.

30. Robert E. Sherwood, *Roosevelt and Hopkins: An Intimate History* (New York: Harper, 1950), 803.

31. Arthur Bryant, *Triumph in the West* (Westport, Conn.: Greenwood, 1974), 74. See also Ambrose, *Eisenhower*, 272-273, who considers the choice of Eisenhower as supreme commander, Allied Expeditionary Force, "quite possibly the best appoint-

ment Roosevelt ever made." For the difficulty of the decision, see Sherwood, *Roosevelt and Hopkins*, 802–803.

32. Ambrose, *Eisenhower*, 272.

33. Ambrose, *Supreme Commander*, 294. See also Cunningham, *Sailor's Odyssey*, 575; Butcher, *My Three Years with Eisenhower*, 432–433.

34. Eric Larrabee, *Commander in Chief: Franklin Delano Roosevelt, His Lieutenants, and Their War* (New York: Simon and Schuster, 1987), 438.

Chapter 8. The Lessons of Unity Applied

The epigraphs to this chapter are drawn from Alfred D. Chandler Jr., ed., *The Papers of Dwight D. Eisenhower* (hereafter *EP*), vols. 1–5, *The War Years* (Baltimore: Johns Hopkins University Press, 1970), 3: no. 1469, p. 1647, and Carlo D'Este, *Decision in Normandy* (New York: HarperPerennial, 1994), 84.

1. *EP*, 3: no. 1450, p. 1632n8.

2. Forrest C. Pogue, *The Supreme Command* (Washington, DC: Office of the Chief of Military History, 1954), 43.

3. "I set no definite time for this," Eisenhower explained, noting that it was "dependent, of course, upon the progress of the initial land battles beyond the beachhead area where, as I have pointed out, simplicity of command in a narrow space was desirable"; Dwight D. Eisenhower, *Report on Operations in Northwest Europe, 6 June 1944–6 May 1945* (Washington, DC: GSO, 1946), 7.

4. D. K. R. Crosswell, *The Chief of Staff: The Military Career of Walter Bedell Smith* (New York: Greenwood, 1991), 217.

5. *EP*, 3: no. 1423, p. 1605.

6. Ibid., no. 1428, pp. 1614–1615n2; Carlo D'Este, *Eisenhower: A Soldier's Life* (New York: Holt, 2002), 472, 485; Pogue, *Supreme Command*, 46, 48.

7. *EP*, 3: no. 1428, p. 1612, and no. 1470, p. 1649.

8. Ibid., no. 1517, p. 1693.

9. Pogue, *Supreme Command*, 52–53; Eisenhower, *Report on Operations in Northwest Europe*, 3.

10. Pogue, *Supreme Command*, 53.

11. Arthur Tedder, *With Prejudice* (Boston: Little, Brown, 1966), 508; *EP*, 3: no. 1575, p. 1756n1, and no. 1539, p. 1715. See also Wesley F. Craven and James L. Cate, eds., *The Army Air Forces in World War II*, vol. 3, *Europe: Argument to VE Day* (Chicago: University of Chicago Press, 1958), 72–83; John Ehrman, *Grand Strategy*, vol. 5, *August 1943–September 1944* (London: H. M. Stationery Office, 1972), 286–304; Eisenhower, *Report on Operations in Northwest Europe*, 9.

12. Tedder, *With Prejudice*, 508–512; Harry C. Butcher, *My Three Years with Eisenhower* (New York: Simon and Schuster, 1946), 498. See also Pogue, *Supreme Command*, 124; *EP*, 3: no. 1575, p. 1756n1.

13. *EP*, 3: no. 1584, p. 1766n3.

14. Ibid., no. 1579, p. 1759n1; Pogue, *Supreme Command*, 124.

15. Eisenhower, *Report on Operations in Northwest Europe*, 16.

16. Tedder, *With Prejudice*, 522. See also Solly Zuckerman, *From Apes to Warlords* (New York: Harper and Row, 1978), 257.

17. *EP*, 3: no. 1662, pp. 1842–1844.

18. Ibid., no. 1658, p. 1839.

19. Winston S. Churchill, *The Second World War*, vol. 5, *Closing the Ring* (Boston: Houghton Mifflin, 1953), 529–530. See also Pogue, *Supreme Command*, 132; Tedder, *With Prejudice*, 529–532; and *EP*, 3: no. 1662, pp. 1844–1845n5. For the War Cabinet debate, see Ehrman, *Grand Strategy*, 5: 298–304.

20. John S. D. Eisenhower, *Strictly Personal* (Garden City, NY: Doubleday, 1974), 72. See also D'Este, *Eisenhower*, 512; Pogue, *Supreme Command*, 132.

21. Dwight D. Eisenhower, *Crusade in Europe* (Garden City, NY: Doubleday, 1948), 244, Eisenhower, *Report on Operations in Northwest Europe*, 16, 18.

22. Eisenhower, *Report on Operations in Northwest Europe*, 50; *EP*, 4: no. 1922, p. 2104.

23. Stephen E. Ambrose, *The Supreme Commander: The War Years of Dwight D. Eisenhower* (Garden City, NY: Doubleday, 1970), 367. For a counterview, see Craven and Cate, *Argument to VE Day*, chapter 6. As Pogue, *Supreme Command*, 132, points out, those official historians of the Army Air Force in World War II did not have access to German sources. For an account using sources from both sides, see Gordon A. Harrison, *US Army in World War II: European Theater of Operations*, vol. 3, part 2, *Cross Channel Attack* (Washington, DC: Office of the Chief of Military History, 1951), 198–230.

24. *EP*, 3: no. 1475, p. 1655, and no. 1476, pp. 1655–1656.

25. Churchill, *Second World War*, 5: 488. Eisenhower had not been in favor of SHINGLE but did not oppose it since he would be at his new command when the operation was carried out. Eisenhower, *Crusade in Europe*, 212–213.

26. *EP*, 3: no. 1497, pp. 1673, 1675.

27. Ibid., no. 1497, p. 1676n8.

28. Ibid., no. 1531, p. 1707.

29. Ibid., 1708n3.

30. Ibid., no. 1538, p. 1714; Maurice Matloff, *Strategic Planning for Coalition Warfare, 1943–1944* (Washington, DC: Office of the Chief of Military History, 1959), 418.

31. *EP*, 3: no. 1556, p. 1735, 1735–1736n2.

32. Matloff, *Strategic Planning for Coalition Warfare*, 420. See also *EP*, 3: no. 1561, p. 1743, and no. 1562, p. 1744n1.

33. Matloff, *Strategic Planning for Coalition Warfare*, 420–421; *EP*, 3: no. 1562, pp. 1745–1746n3, 1746n4.

34. *EP*, 3: no. 1595, p. 1776. See also ibid., no. 1593, p. 1775.

35. Winston S. Churchill, *The Second World War*, vol. 6, *Triumph and Tragedy* (Boston: Houghton Mifflin, 1953), 723. See also ibid., 716–722; Pogue, *Supreme Command*, 218–233; Ehrman, *Grand Strategy*, 5: 352–358.

36. Butcher, *My Three Years with Eisenhower*, 639.

37. *EP*, 4: no. 1892, 2067.

38. Churchill, *Second World War*, 6: 59.

39. Ibid., 6: 96.

40. *EP*, 4: no. 1910, p. 2094.

41. Ibid., no. 1911, p. 2095.

Chapter 9. The Lessons of Unity Vindicated

The epigraphs to this chapter are drawn from Alfred D. Chandler Jr., ed., *The Papers of Dwight D. Eisenhower* (hereafter *EP*), vols. 1–5, *The War Years* (Baltimore: Johns Hopkins University Press, 1970), 4: no. 2070, p. 2254; Louis Galambos, ed., *EP*, vols. 10–11, *Columbia University* (Baltimore: Johns Hopkins University Press, 1984), 10: no. 321, p. 420; and Winston S. Churchill, *The Second World War*, vol. 6, *Triumph and Tragedy* (Boston: Houghton Mifflin, 1953), 338.

1. Frederick Morgan, *Overture to Overlord* (Garden City, NY: Doubleday, 1950), 142.

2. Churchill, *Second World War*, 6: 31. See also Eric Larrabee, *Commander in Chief: Franklin Delano Roosevelt, His Lieutenants, and Their War* (New York: Simon and Schuster, 1987), 441; Dwight D. Eisenhower, *Report on Operations in Northwest Europe, 6 June 1944–6 May 1945* (Washington, DC: GSO, 1946), 8, 52.

3. John Ehrman, *Grand Strategy*, vol. 5, *August 1943–September 1944* (London: HMSO, 1956–1976), 380; Chandler, Introduction to *EP*, 1: xxvii; Stephen E. Ambrose, *The Supreme Commander: The War Years of General Dwight D. Eisenhower* (Garden City, NY: Doubleday, 1970), 532.

4. *EP*, 4: no. 1900, p. 2075.

5. Roland G. Ruppenthal, "Logistics and the Broad-Front Strategy," in *Command Decisions*, ed. Kent Roberts Greenfield (Washington, DC: Center of Military History), 1960), 419–428. See also Ambrose, *Supreme Commander*, 494–495.

6. Bernard Law Montgomery, *The Memoirs of Field Marshal the Viscount Montgomery of Alamein* (London: Collins, 1958), 243.

7. *EP*, 4: no. 1812, p. 1988; Eisenhower, *Report on Operations in Northwest Europe*, 61.

8. *EP*, 4: no. 1957, pp. 2148–2149. See also Forrest C. Pogue, *The Supreme Command* (Washington, DC: Office of the Chief of Military History, 1954), 254–255; Charles B. MacDonald, "The Decision to Launch Market-Garden," in *Command Decisions*, 429–442.

9. Pogue, *Supreme Command*, 294; *EP*, 4: no. 1979, pp. 2175–2176n; Omar N. Bradley, *A Soldier's Story* (New York: Holt, 1951), 422–423.

10. *EP*, 4: no. 1945, p. 2135n5.

11. Montgomery, *Memoirs*, 257; emphasis in original.

12. Crosswell, *Chief of Staff*, 262; Montgomery, *Memoirs*, 283.

13. Arthur Bryant, *Triumph in the West* (Westport, Conn.: Greenwood, 1974), 291–292.

14. Martin Blumenson, *The Patton Papers: 1885–1940* (Boston: Houghton Mifflin, 1974), 2: 553; Piers Brendon, *Ike: His Life and Times* (New York: Harper and Row, 1986), 164. See also Omar N. Bradley and Clay Blair, *A General's Life: An Autobiogra-*

phy (New York: Simon and Schuster, 1983), 328, in which Bradley observed of MARKET GARDEN: "I think in this instance Ike succumbed to Monty in part to stroke his ego and keep peace in the family." See also Max Hastings, *Armageddon: The Battle for Germany, 1944–1945* (New York: Knopf, 2004), 62: "The Supreme Commander could have made a notable contribution to ending the war in 1944 by asserting other priorities and preventing Montgomery's Arnhem adventure from taking place at all." But see Ambrose, *Supreme Commander*, 532–533, who finds it difficult to see how Eisenhower could have made any other decision than to reinforce success by taking the risk of MARKET GARDEN.

15. Eisenhower, *Crusade in Europe*, 284–285.

16. *EP*, 4: no. 2038, pp. 2222–2223; emphasis in original. See also Montgomery, *Memoirs*, 283–287, 290 292; Forrest C. Pogue, *George C. Marshall: Organizer of Victory, 1943–1945* (New York: Viking, 1973), 487; Ambrose, *Supreme Commander*, 534–535.

17. *EP*, 4: no. 2038, p. 2225n6, emphasis in original; Pogue, *Supreme Command*, 298.

18. Bryant, *Triumph in the West*, 259.

19. Ibid., 265; Arthur Tedder, *With Prejudice* (Boston: Little, Brown, 1966), 620–622. See also Crosswell, *Chief of Staff*, 264; Pogue, *Supreme Command*, 316–317; Montgomery, *Memoirs*, 270–274; Ambrose, *Supreme Commander*, 549–551.

20. Tedder, *With Prejudice*, 625. See also Eisenhower's prophecy in his order of the day: "By rushing out from his fixed defenses the enemy has given us the chance to turn his great gamble into his worst defeat"; Bryant, *Triumph in the West*, 274; Harry C. Butcher, *My Three Years with Eisenhower* (New York: Simon and Schuster, 1946), 733–734.

21. *EP*, 4: no. 2186, pp. 2363–2365. Montgomery believed that Eisenhower should have given him the command earlier in the crisis; Montgomery, *Memoirs*, 284. Bradley did not deny the logic of the move, but believed it was probably unnecessary; Bradley, *Soldier's Story*, 476–478. Eisenhower believed that it was the only applicable solution at the time; Eisenhower, *Crusade in Europe*, 353–356.

22. Brendon, *Ike*, 174; Eisenhower, *Crusade in Europe*, 360–361; Montgomery, *Memoirs*, 284.

23. Bryant, *Triumph in the West*, 280; Montgomery, *Memoirs*, 284–285.

24. Pogue, *George C. Marshall*, 487. See also Bryant, *Triumph in the West*, 280; Brendon, *Ike*, 174. Eisenhower reassured Marshall on the matter in a New Year's Day message: "You need have no fear as to my contemplating the establishment of a ground deputy"; *EP*, 4: no. 2215, p. 2390.

25. *EP*, 4: no. 2210, pp. 2386–2387; emphasis in original.

26. Montgomery, *Memoirs*, 286; Francis de Guingand, *Generals at War* (London: Hodder and Stoughton, 1964), 108–111. Montgomery's chief of staff also informed the British commander of Marshall's 30 December message to Eisenhower. "That telegram," Montgomery recalled, "finished the issue of operational control as far as I was concerned and I knew it would be useless to open it again"; Pogue, *George C. Marshall*, 511.

27. Bryant, *Triumph in the West*, 281.

28. *EP*, 4: no. 2232, p. 2413; emphasis in original. See also ibid., no. 2233, p. 2416; John Ehrman, *Grand Strategy*, vol. 6, *October 1944–August 1945* (London: HMS, 1956–1976), 87–89; Eisenhower, *Report on Operations in Northwest Europe*, 81.

29. *EP*, 4: no. 2233, pp. 2419–2420; Eisenhower, *Report on Operations in Northwest Europe*, 82.

30. Pogue, *George C. Marshall*, 516.

31. "After closing the Rhine in the north, to direct our main effort to destroy any enemy remaining west of the Rhine, both in the north and in the south"; *EP*, 4: no. 2254, p. 2453.

32. Ibid., no. 2268, 2463. See also Bryant, *Triumph in the West*, 299.

33. Bryant, *Triumph in the West*, 305; Tedder, *With Prejudice*, 663.

34. *EP*, 4: no. 2284, pp. 2480–2481.

35. Ibid., no. 2294, p. 2494 and n1.

36. Tedder, *With Prejudice*, 664; Montgomery, *Memoirs*, 326.

37. Eisenhower, *Report on Operations in Northwest Europe*, 119; Gerard Clarfield, *Security with Solvency: Dwight D. Eisenhower and the Shaping of the American Military Establishment* (Westport, Conn.: Praeger, 1999), 12–13.

38. US Congress, Senate, Committee on Military Affairs, *Hearings on S. 84 and S. 1482*, 79th Congress, first session, 1945, (Washington, DC: GPO, 1945), 421, 427–428, 430–431; JCS Special Committee for Reorganization for National Defense, *Report of the Joint Chiefs of Staff Special Committee for Reorganization of National Defense* (Washington, DC: General Services Administration, 1945), 1, 8, 17; Lawrence J. Legere Jr., "Unification of the Armed Forces," Ph.D. diss., Harvard University, 1951, 284. Eisenhower reported later that he had not met anyone who was opposed to unification until he returned to replace Marshall as chief of staff in the fall of 1945; Alfred D. Chandler Jr. and Louis Galambos, eds., *EP*, vol. 6, *Occupation, 1945* (Baltimore: Johns Hopkins University Press, 1978), no. 493, p. 555.

39. *Hearings on S. 84 and S. 1482*, 434–436; Demetrios Caraley, *The Politics of Military Unification: A Study of Conflict and the Policy Process* (New York: Columbia University Press, 1966), 35–36, 38; Edgar F. Raines and David R. Campbell, *The Army and the Joint Chiefs of Staff: Evolution of the Army Ideas in the Command, Control, and Coordination of the US Armed Forces, 1942–1985* (Washington, DC: US Army Center of Military History, 1986). 35; James F. Schnabel, *History of the Joint Chiefs of Staff*, vol. 1, *The Joint Chiefs of Staff and National Policy, 1945–1947* (Washington, DC: GPO, 1996), 110.

40. James R. Locher III, *Victory on the Potomac* (College Station: Texas A&M University Press, 2002), 23. See also Raines and Campbell, *Army and the Joint Chiefs of Staff*, 36; Larrabee, *Commander in Chief*, 24.

41. Locher, *Victory on the Potomac*, 24; Raines and Campbell, *Army and the Joint Chiefs of Staff*, 37.

42. *Hearings on S. 84 and S. 1482*, 192–193.

43. *EP*, 4: no. 2418, p. 2616.

44. Ibid., no. 2499, p. 2696.

45. Ibid., 6: no. 177, pp. 186–187.

46. Eisenhower, *Crusade in Europe*, 448.
47. Brendon, *Ike*, 161.
48. Ibid., 186.
49. Crosswell, *Chief of Staff*, 296. See also Brendon, *Ike*, 186.
50. *EP*, 6: no. 114, p. 121, emphasis in original, and no. 115, p. 123.
51. Ibid., no. 340, p. 368.

Chapter 10. Unified Command in Washington

The epigraphs to this chapter are drawn from Louis Galambos, ed., *The Papers of Dwight David Eisenhower* (hereafter *EP*), vols. 7–9, *The Chief of Staff* (Baltimore: Johns Hopkins University Press, 1978), 8: no. 1279, p. 1477; US Congress, Senate, Committee on Military Affairs, *Hearings on S. 84 and S. 1482*, 79th Congress, first session (Washington, DC: GPO, 1945), 543; Dwight D. Eisenhower, *At Ease: Stories I Tell to Friends* (Garden City, NY: Doubleday, 1967), 317.

1. Daniel Yergin, *Shattered Peace: The Origins of the Cold War and the National Security State* (Boston: Houghton Mifflin, 1977), 197.
2. Hanson Baldwin, *The Price of Power* (New York: Harper, 1947), 18; emphasis in original.
3. Yergin, *Shattered Peace*, 195.
4. Ibid., 199.
5. Ernest R. May, "National Security in American History," in *Rethinking America's National Security: Beyond Cold War to New World Order*, ed. Graham Allison and Gregory F. Treverton (New York: Norton, 1992), 99. See also Yergin, *Shattered Peace*, 196 and 199.
6. Colin S. Gray, "Strategy in the Nuclear Age: The United States, 1945–1991," in *The Making of Strategy: Rulers, States, and War*, ed. Williamson Murray, MacGregor Knox, and Alvin Bernstein (New York: Cambridge University Press, 1944), 599; emphasis in original. Despite the dominance of the perceived Soviet threat, the new approach to national security, with its linkage of that threat perception to core values, helped to produce institutional, ideological, and societal constraints that prevented the growth of a garrison state. See Aaron L. Friedberg, *In the Shadow of the Garrison State: America's Anti-Statism and Its Cold War Grand Strategy* (Princeton: Princeton University Press, 2000). For national security as a unifying "Commanding idea," see Yergin, *Shattered Peace*, 196.
7. *Hearings on S. 84 and S. 1482*, 117. See also Yergin, *Shattered Peace*, 194; Ernest R. May, "Cold War and Defense," in *The Cold War and Defense*, ed. Keith Neilson and Ronald G. Hay (New York: Praeger, 1990), 28; Arnold Wolfers, "National Security as an Ambiguous Symbol," in *Discord and Collaboration* (Baltimore: Johns Hopkins University Press, 1962), 147–166; Melvyn P. Leffler, *A Preponderance of Power: National Security, the Truman Administration, and the Cold War* (Stanford: Stanford University Press, 1992), 10–15; Melvyn P. Leffler, "National Security," in *Explaining the History of American Foreign Policy*, ed. Michael J. Hogan and Thomas G. Paterson (New York: Cambridge University Press, 2004), 123–136.

8. Yergin, *Shattered Peace,* 220. See also ibid., 200-201, 219.

9. Townsend Hoopes and Douglas Brinkley, *Driven Patriot: The Life and Times of James Forrestal* (New York: Knopf, 1992), 195.

10. Harry S. Truman, *Memoirs,* vol. 2, *Years of Trial and Hope* (Garden City, NY: Doubleday, 1956), 47. See also Stephen E. Ambrose, *Eisenhower,* vol. 1, *Soldier, General of the Army, President-Elect, 1890-1952* (New York: Simon and Schuster, 1983), 443.

11. US Congress, Senate, *Report to Hon. James Forrestal, Secretary of the Navy on Unification of the War and Navy Departments and Postwar Organization for National Security* (hereafter Eberstadt Report) (Washington, DC: GPO, 1945), 19. See also ibid., v, 1. Eberstadt and Forrestal first met in 1909 while they were attending Princeton and later worked together in Dillon, Read and Company; Jeffery M. Dorwart, *Eberstadt and Forrestal: A National Security Partnership* (College Station: Texas A&M University Press, 1991), 12, 22.

12. Eberstadt Report, 37. See also Douglas T. Stuart, *Creating the National Security State: A History of the Law That Transformed America* (Princeton: Princeton University Press, 2008), 88-90; Lawrence J. Legere Jr., "Unification of the Armed Forces," Ph.D. diss., Harvard University, 1951, 299-304; John C. Ries, *The Management of Defense: Organization and Control of the US Armed Services* (Baltimore: Johns Hopkins University Press, 1964), 55-56; Michael J. Hogan, *A Cross of Iron: Harry S. Truman and the Origins of the National Security State, 1945-1954* (Cambridge: Cambridge University Press, 1998), 31-32.

13. Alfred D. Chandler Jr. and Louis Galambos, eds., *EP,* vol. 6, *Occupation, 1945* (Baltimore: Johns Hopkins University Press, 1978), no. 393, p. 410n1.

14. Ibid., no. 369, p. 406.

15. Eisenhower, *At Ease,* 314.

16. James Forrestal, *The Forrestal Diaries,* ed. Walter Millis, with Eugene S. Duffield (New York: Viking, 1951), 118. For the texts of the two bills, see *Hearings on S. 84 and S. 1482,* 2-4.

17. Demetrios Caraley, *The Politics of Military Unification: A Study of Conflict and the Policy Process* (New York: Columbia University Press, 1966), 49. See also ibid., 44, 55; Legere, "Unification of the Armed Forces," 304.

18. *Hearings on S. 84 and S. 1482,* 50-51.

19. Ibid., 12.

20. Ibid., 170.

21. Ibid., 156. See also ibid., 162-163.

22. Ibid., 161, 158, 164-165. The Collins Plan specifically rejected the Richardson Committee recommendation that the commander (now chief of staff) of the armed forces serve also as chief of staff to the president; ibid., 179.

23. Ibid., 161, 163.

24. Ibid., 175.

25. Ibid., 451.

26. Ibid., 359-360.

27. Ibid., 360.

28. Ibid., 362-363.

29. Ibid., 365–367.

30. Ibid., 383–384.

31. Alice C. Cole, Alfred Goldberg, Samuel A. Tucker, and Rudolf A. Winnacker, eds., *The Department of Defense: Documents on Establishment and Organization, 1944–1978* (hereafter *DOD Documents*) (Washington, DC: Historical Office, Office of the Secretary of Defense, 1978), 7–9, 15–16.

32. Caraley, *Politics of Military Unification*, 56.

33. *EP*, 6: no. 493, pp. 553, emphasis in original. See also ibid., 555 and n5.

34. Caraley, *Politics of Military Unification*, 129.

35. Louis Galambos, ed., *EP*, vols. 7–9, *The Chief of Staff* (Baltimore: Johns Hopkins University Press, 1978), 7: no. 610 p. 703n1.

36. Dorwart, *Eberstadt and Forrestal*, 131.

37. *EP*, 7: no. 854, p. 1015, and no. 918, pp. 1116 and 1117n2. See also John W. Masland and Laurence I. Radway, *Soldiers and Scholars: Military Education and National Policy* (Princeton: Princeton University Press, 1957), 140–142, 307–316.

38. *EP*, 7: no. 780, pp. 928–932; James F. Schnabel, *History of the Joint Chiefs of Staff*, vol. 1, *The Joint Chiefs of Staff and National Policy, 1945–1947* (Washington, DC: GPO, 1996), 112.

39. *EP*, 7: no. 780, pp. 928–929.

40. Caraley, *Politics of Military Unification*, 131, 253–254.

41. US Congress, Senate, Committee on Naval Affairs, *Hearings on S. 2044*, 79th Congress, second session (Washington, DC: GPO, 1946), 31–32.

42. Ibid., 115, 119.

43. *EP*, 7: no. 892, pp. 1057–1058. See also ibid., no. 832, p. 997n3.

44. Forrestal, *Diaries*, 160–161. See also Caraley, *Politics of Military Unification*, 135–136; Truman, *Memoirs*, 2: 50. Patterson had apparently already been consulted on the issue in advance; Gerard Clarfield, *Security with Solvency: Dwight D. Eisenhower and the Shaping of the American Military Establishment* (Westport, Conn.: Praeger, 1999), 42–43.

45. *EP*, 7: no. 894, p. 1062.

46. *Hearings on S. 2044*, 207–209; Legere, "Unification of the Armed Forces," 328–329.

47. *EP*, 7: no. 894, p. 1063n5.

48. Hoopes and Brinkley, *Driven Patriot*, 337. See also *Hearings on S. 2044*, 211; Caraley, *Politics of Military Unification*, 139–140.

49. *Hearings on S. 2044*, 348. See also Caraley, *Politics of Military Unification*, 143; Legere, "Unification of the Armed Forces," 330–332.

Chapter 11. Creation of the National Security State

The epigraphs to this chapter are drawn from Dwight D. Eisenhower, *The Eisenhower Diaries*, ed. Robert H. Ferrell (New York: Norton, 1981), 137; and US Congress, House, Committee on Armed Services, *The National Defense Program—Unification and Strategy: Hearings*, 81st Congress, first session (Washington, DC: GPO, 1949), 562.

1. US Congress, Joint Committee on the Investigation of the Pearl Harbor Attack, *Report: Investigation of the Pearl Harbor Attack* (Washington, DC: GPO, 1946), 240, 244; emphasis in original.

2. Ibid., 245.

3. US Congress, Senate, Committee on Military Affairs, *Hearings on S. 84 and S. 1482*, 79th Congress, first session (Washington, DC: GPO, 1945), 191; US Congress, Senate, Committee on Armed Services, *Defense Organization: The Need for Change*, 99th Congress, first session (Washington, DC: GPO, 1985), 355 (hereafter Locher Report).

4. *Investigation of the Pearl Harbor Attack*, 252.

5. For Eisenhower's outline, see Louis Galambos, ed., *The Papers of Dwight David Eisenhower* (hereafter *EP*), vols. 7–9, *The Chief of Staff* (Baltimore: Johns Hopkins University Press, 1978), 7: no. 1108, pp. 1297–1299.

6. James F. Schnabel, *History of the Joint Chiefs of Staff*, vol. 1, *Joint Chiefs of Staff and National Policy, 1945–1947* (Washington, DC: GPO, 1996), 86; Ronald H. Cole, Walter S. Poole, James F. Schnabel, Robert J. Watson, and Willard J. Webb, *The History of the Unified Command Plan, 1946–1993* (Washington, DC: Office of the Joint History Office, Office of the Joint Chiefs of Staff, 1995), 12.

7. James Forrestal, *The Forrestal Diaries*, ed. Walter Millis, with Eugene S. Duffield (New York: Viking, 1951), 204–205; Demetrios Caraley, *The Politics of Military Unification: A Study of Conflict and the Policy Process* (New York: Columbia University Press, 1966), 148; Clark Clifford with Richard Holbrooke, *Counsel to the President: A Memoir* (New York: Random House, 1991), 153–154; Townsend Hoopes and Douglas Brinkley, *Driven Patriot: The Life and Times of James Forrestal* (New York: Knopf, 1992), 340.

8. Forrestal, *Diaries*, 205; emphasis in original.

9. Caraley, *Politics of Military Unification*, 148–149; Clifford, *Counsel to the President*, 154.

10. Clifford, *Counsel to the President*, 153; Gerard Clarfield, *Security with Solvency: Dwight D. Eisenhower and the Shaping of the American Military Establishment* (Westport, Conn.: Praeger, 1999), 47; US Congress, Senate, Committee on Armed Services, *Hearings on S. 758*, 80th Congress, first session (Washington, DC: GPO, 1947), 90.

11. *Hearings on S. 758*, 2.

12. Ibid., 22, 29, 53.

13. Ibid., 102, 97–98.

14. Ibid., 99; Forrestal, *Diaries*, 269.

15. Caraley, *Politics of Military Unification*, 167–168.

16. Gordon W. Keiser, *The US Marine Corps and Defense Unification: The Politics of Survival* (Washington, DC: National Defense University Press, 1982), 98–99; Caraley, *Politics of Military Unification*, 158–159.

17. US Congress, House, Committee on Expenditures in the Executive Departments, *Hearings on H.R. 2319*, 80th Congress, first session (Washington, DC: GPO, 1947), 273–275.

18. Ibid., 320–321.

19. Keiser, *US Marine Corps and Defense Unification*, 102. In an interview fourteen years after the hearings, Hoffman began a response to a general question concerning his role in settling the unification issue by mentioning what he perceived as Eisenhower's disingenuousness concerning his JCS proposals in the 1478 series; Caraley, *Politics of Military Unification*, 317.

20. *Hearings on H.R. 2319*, 297–298.

21. Ibid., 325, 315. See also ibid., 276, 282, 312, 280.

22. *EP*, 8: no. 1565, pp. 1775–1776, and no. 1575, p. 1784; Eisenhower, *Diaries*, 142.

23. Caraley, *Politics of Military Unification*, 175; *EP*, 9: no. 1675, p. 1868n4; Alice C. Cole, Alfred Goldberg, Samuel A. Tucker, and Rudolph A. Winnacker, eds., *The Department of Defense: Documents on Establishment and Organization, 1944–1978* (hereafter *DOD Documents*) (Washington, DC: Office of the Secretary of Defense Historical Office, 1978), 33.

24. *DOD Documents*, 36, 40. S. 758 had described a secretary of national security presiding over the National Security Organization. The conference committee adopted the House version of a secretary of defense presiding over the National Military Establishment, the latter not defined in the act; Steven L. Rearden, *History of the Office of the Secretary of Defense*, vol. 1, *The Formative Years, 1947–1950* (Washington, DC: Historical Office, Office of the Secretary of Defense, 1984), 23.

25. *DOD Documents*, 40–47; Rearden, *Office of the Secretary of Defense*, 1: 24–25.

26. *DOD Documents*, 45–46.

27. Hoopes and Brinkley, *Driven Patriot*, 352.

28. Ibid., 355–356.

29. *EP*, 9: no. 2055, pp. 2242–2247, 2250–2251. Eisenhower was more circumspect in his official end-of-tour report; Dwight D. Eisenhower, *Final Report of the Chief of Staff United States Army* (Washington, DC: GPO, 1948).

30. *EP*, 9: no. 1999, p. 2194.

31. Dwight D. Eisenhower, *At Ease: Stories I Tell to Friends* (Garden City, NY: Doubleday, 1967), 328.

32. Louis Galambos, ed., *EP*, vols. 10–11, *Columbia University* (Baltimore: Johns Hopkins University Press, 1984), 10: no. 42, p. 55nn3, 5, and no. 85, p. 102n5; Eisenhower, *At Ease*, 341–342.

33. *DOD Documents*, 275; Kenneth W. Condit, *History of the Joint Chiefs of Staff*, vol. 2, *The Joint Chiefs of Staff and National Policy, 1947–1949* (Washington, DC: Historical Division, Joint Chiefs of Staff, 1976), 177.

34. *DOD Documents*, 275–285. See also *EP*, 9: 2242–2256, and 10: no. 183, p. 232n3.

35. *DOD Documents*, 279; Locher Report, 141, 277, 307.

36. *DOD Documents*, 287; Condit, *Joint Chiefs of Staff*, 2: 183; Hoopes and Brinkley, *Driven Patriot*, 372; Rearden, *Office of the Secretary of Defense*, 1: 396.

37. *DOD Documents*, 282 and 289; Hoopes and Brinkley, *Driven Patriot*, 372;

Condit, *Joint Chiefs of Staff*, 2: 181–184; Paul Y. Hammond, *Organizing for Defense: The American Military Establishment in the Twentieth Century* (Princeton: Princeton University Press, 1961), 237.

38. Clifford, *Counsel to the President*, 160.

39. *EP*, 10: no. 183, p. 231, 234n4.

40. Rearden, *Office of the Secretary of Defense*, 1: 423.

41. Clifford, *Counsel to the President*, 160–161.

42. *EP*, 10: no. 189, p. 239; Forrestal, *Diaries*, 500.

43. Forrestal, *Diaries*, 497.

44. *EP*, 10: no. 223, p. 284n3.

45. Ibid.

46. Forrestal, *Diaries*, 540.

47. *EP*, 10: no. 294, p. 365.

48. Ibid., no. 336, pp. 448–449, and no. 348, p. 471n2.

49. US National Military Establishment, *First Report of the Secretary of Defense* (Washington, DC: GPO, 1948), 9; Rearden, *Office of the Secretary of Defense*, 1: 402.

50. *EP*, 10: no. 315, p. 402.

51. Eisenhower, *At Ease*, 353.

52. *EP*, 10: no. 345, pp. 461–462, and 462n1.

53. Ibid., no. 347, p. 466.

54. Ibid., no. 348, pp. 467–469; emphasis in original. Eisenhower also attached a statement for the president that he had drafted on 24 January; ibid., 471n2.

55. Ibid., no. 358, pp. 482–483.

56. Hoopes and Brinkley, *Driven Patriot*, 424–425; Rearden, *Office of the Secretary of Defense*, 1: 42; Clifford, *Counsel to the President*, 161.

57. "Separate Statement by Vice Chairman Acheson, Commissioners Mead, Pollock and Rowe," appended to US Commission on Organization of the Executive Branch of the Government, *The National Security Organization: A Report to the Congress* (Washington, DC: GPO, 1949), 28–29.

58. *EP*, 10: no. 384, p. 527, and no. 408, p. 553.

59. *DOD Documents*, 80. See also *EP*, 10: no. 327, p. 433.

60. *EP*, 10: no. 401, 546; emphasis in original. See also Rearden, *Office of the Secretary of Defense*, 1: 44, 49; Eisenhower, *At Ease*, 329.

61. Condit, *Joint Chiefs of Staff*, 2: 325.

62. *National Defense Program*, 623.

63. *EP*, 10: no. 415, p. 564. See also Rearden, *Office of the Secretary of Defense*, 1: 412–414; Condit, *Joint Chiefs of Staff*, 2: 332–334; Hammond, *Organizing for Defense*, 245–247.

64. US Congress, Senate, Committee on Armed Services, *National Security Act Amendments of 1949: Hearings on S. 1269 and S. 1843*, 81st Congress, first session (Washington, DC: GPO, 1949), 123. See also Rearden, *Office of the Secretary of Defense*, 1: 51.

65. *DOD Documents*, 87–94; John C. Ries, *The Management of Defense Organi-

zation and Control of the US Armed Services (Baltimore: Johns Hopkins University Press, 1964), 141–143; Rearden, *Office of the Secretary of Defense,* 1: 53.

66. *DOD Documents,* 86, 94–95; Rearden, *Office of the Secretary of Defense,* 1: 54.

67. *DOD Documents,* 88; Ries, *Management of Defense,* 147–149.

68. Rearden, *Office of the Secretary of Defense,* 1: 55.

69. Eisenhower, *At Ease,* 355.

70. *EP,* 10: no. 560, pp. 778, 779n2.

71. *EP,* 10: no. 574, p. 798n1.

72. *National Defense Program,* 523, 525–526.

73. Ibid., 530–531, 535–536.

74. Ibid., 562–566.

75. *EP,* 10: no. 573, p. 796n3.

76. Ibid., no. 574, pp. 797, 798n4. In a draft of a 17 November letter to Swede Hazlett, Eisenhower would write and then delete from the final version: "I can merely say that I absolve none of the parties from guilt"; ibid., no. 598, p. 835n4.

77. Ibid., no. 639, pp. 899–906.

78. Eisenhower, *At Ease,* 352.

79. Stephen E. Ambrose, *Eisenhower,* vol. 1, *Soldier, General of the Army, President-Elect, 1890–1952* (New York: Simon and Schuster, 1983), 487. See also Rearden, *Office of the Secretary of Defense,* 1: 138.

Chapter 12. The Great Debate

The epigraphs in this chapter are drawn from Dwight D. Eisenhower, *At Ease: Stories I Tell to Friends* (Garden City, NY: Doubleday, 1967), 372; Louis Galambos, ed., *The Papers of Dwight David Eisenhower* (hereafter *EP*), vols. 10–11, *Columbia University* (Baltimore: Johns Hopkins University Press, 1984), 11: no. 1109, pp. 1461–1462, emphasis in original; and Louis Galambos, ed., *EP,* vols. 12–13, *NATO and the Campaign of 1952* (Baltimore: Johns Hopkins University Press, 1989), 12: no. 51, p. 75.

1. The NAC first met in September 1949, chaired by Secretary of State Dean Acheson. The Council Deputies were created in May 1950. Lionel Hastings Ismay, *NATO: The First Five Years, 1949–1954* (The Hague: North Atlantic Treaty Organization, 1955), 68–69; Doris M. Condit, *History of the Office of the Secretary of Defense,* vol. 2, *The Test of War, 1950–1953* (Washington, DC: Historical Office, Office of the Secretary of Defense, 1988), 310. See also Thomas M. Sisk, "Forging the Weapon: Eisenhower as NATO's Supreme Allied Commander, Europe, 1950–1952," in *Eisenhower: A Centenary Assessment,* ed. Guenter Bischof and Stephen E. Ambrose (Baton Rouge: Louisiana State University Press, 1955), 65.

2. Ismay, *NATO,* 30; Walter S. Poole, *History of the Joint Chiefs of Staff,* vol. 4, *The Joint Chiefs of Staff and National Policy, 1950–1952* (Washington, DC: Office of Joint History, Office of the Chairman of the Joint Chiefs of Staff, 1998), 96.

3. *EP,* 11: no. 870, p. 1190.

4. Ibid., no. 874, p. 1200n4.

5. James Chace, *Acheson: The Secretary of State Who Created the American World* (New York: Simon and Schuster, 1998), 290.

6. For the universalist approach of NSC-68 in terms of risk minimization and the linkage to all events no matter how peripheral to the broader grand strategy of containment, see "NSC-68: United States Objectives and Programs for National Security," 14 April 1950, in *Containment: Documents on American Policy and Strategy, 1945–1950*, ed. Thomas H. Etzold and John Lewis Gaddis (New York: Columbia University Press, 1978), 383–392, and in particular, 390: "In a shrinking world, which now faces the threat of atomic warfare, it is not an adequate objective merely to seek to check the Kremlin design, for the absence of order among nations is becoming less and less tolerable." See also John Lewis Gaddis, *Strategies of Containment: A Critical Appraisal of Postwar American National Security Policy* (New York: Oxford University Press, 1982), 89–117; Frederick W. Kagan, "Back to the Future: NSC-68 and the Right Course for America Today," *SAIS Review* 19 (1999), 390.

7. Condit, *Secretary of Defense*, 2: 307, 314. "It was not very long before it became obvious that collective capacity to resist armed attack could not be effectively developed unless there were unity of command, unified planning and uniformity of military training, procedure, and, as far as possible equipment"; Ismay, *NATO,* 14.

8. Dean Acheson, *Present at the Creation: My Years in the State Department* (New York: Norton, 1969), 399.

9. US Department of State, *Foreign Relations of the United States* (hereafter *FRUS*), *1950*, vol. 3, *Western Europe* (Washington, DC: GPO, 1971), 212.

10. Poole, *Joint Chiefs of Staff*, 4: 99. See also Condit, *Secretary of Defense*, 2: 316–317.

11. Harry S. Truman, *Memoirs*, vol. 2, *Years of Trial and Hope* (Garden City, NY: Doubleday, 1956), 253.

12. *FRUS*, 3: 273.

13. For the joint reply to the president, see ibid., 273–278. Truman referred the joint communication to the National Security Council and the secretary of the treasury for consideration. On 11 September the president approved the communication, which was then circulated as NSC-82; ibid., 273n1.

14. *Public Papers of the President of the United State: Harry S. Truman, 1950* (Washington, DC: GPO, 1965), 626. See also Acheson, *Present at the Creation,* 440; Poole, *Joint Chiefs of Staff*, 4: 104.

15. *EP*, 11: no. 986, p. 1320n1.

16. Ibid., no. 982, p. 1314n2.

17. Acheson, *Present at the Creation,* 440. In the hearings, conservative Republicans such as William Jenner held Marshall responsible for the fall of Nationalist China and denounced him as "a front man for traitors" and "a living lie"; Poole, *Joint Chiefs of Staff*, 4: 256. See also *EP*, 11: no. 999, p. 1334n3.

18. Ismay, *NATO,* 185–186; *FRUS*, 3: 350–352.

19. Condit, *Secretary of Defense*, 2: 326; Timothy P. Ireland, *Creating the Entangling Alliance: The Origins of the North Atlantic Treaty Organization* (Westport,

Conn.: Greenwood, 1981), 200–204; Robert McGeehan, *The German Rearmament Question: American Diplomacy and European Defense After World War II* (Urbana: University of Illinois Press, 1971), 75–80; Poole, *Joint Chiefs of Staff*, 4: 109–110.

20. *FRUS*, 3: 404–406; Acheson, *Present at the Creation*, 459; Condit, *Secretary of Defense*, 2: 327; Poole, *Joint Chiefs of Staff*, 4: 110; and McGeehan, *German Rearmament Question*, 62–66.

21. *EP*, 11: no. 1045, p. 1390.

22. Truman, *Memoirs*, 2: 257. See also Eisenhower, *At Ease*, 361.

23. *EP*, 11: no. 1045, p. 1391, and no. 1050, pp. 1396, 1397n5.

24. *FRUS*, 3: 531–538.

25. Ibid., 548–564.

26. Ibid., 554.

27. *EP*, 11: no. 1113, pp. 1468–1469.

28. *FRUS*, 3: 578–580.

29. Ibid., 591, 595–596. See also Ismay, *NATO*, 186–187.

30. *FRUS*, 3: 559–560, 562–563.

31. Ismay, *NATO*, 17; Ireland, *Creating the Entangling Alliance*, 225.

32. *FRUS, 1951*, vol. 3, part 1, *European Security and the German Question* (Washington, DC: GPO, 1981), 14; *EP*, 12: no. 7, pp. 12–13n3. Eisenhower noted that the speech left him in a state of "waiting for our own starvation or destruction"; ibid., 11.

33. *FRUS*, 3: part 1, p. 22; US Congress, Senate, Committee on Foreign Relations and Committee on Armed Services, Hearing on S. Con. Res. 8, *Assignment of Ground Forces of the United States to Duty in the European Area* (hereafter *Assignment of Ground Forces*), 82nd Congress, first session (Washington, DC: GPO, 1951), 38.

34. *Public Papers of the Presidents of the United States: Harry S. Truman, 1951* (Washington, DC: GPO, 1965), 20.

35. *EP*, 11: no. 1134, p. 1498n2. Eisenhower had announced his intention of making the trip on 19 December; *FRUS*, 3: part 1, p. 392n1.

36. *FRUS*, 3: part 1, p. 403n2.

37. Eisenhower, *At Ease*, 366.

38. Stephen E. Ambrose, *Americans at War* (Jackson: University Press of Mississippi, 1977), 178–179; Stephen E. Ambrose and Morris Honick, "Eisenhower: Rekindling the Spirit of the West," in *Generals in International Politics: NATO's Supreme Allied Commanders, Europe*, ed. Robert S. Jordan (Lexington: University Press of Kentucky, 1987), 12; emphasis in original.

39. Ambrose and Honick, "Eisenhower," 13; Ambrose, *Americans at War*, 139; Stephen E. Ambrose, *Eisenhower*, vol. 1, *Soldier, General of the Army, President-Elect, 1890–1952* (New York: Simon and Schuster, 1983), 502.

40. *FRUS*, 3: part 1, pp. 402–449. See also *EP*, 12: no. 15, pp. 21–24, and no. 16, pp. 24–32.

41. Eisenhower, *At Ease*, 368.

42. *EP*, 12: no. 388, p. 568. See also Eisenhower, *At Ease*, 368; Ambrose, *Americans at War*, 180; and Ambrose and Honick, "Eisenhower," 13–14.

43. *FRUS*, 3: part 1, p. 454.

44. *Assignment of Ground Forces,* 15, 31–32.

45. Ibid., 15–16, 25, 31; Eisenhower, *At Ease,* 369.

46. Robert A. Taft, *A Foreign Policy for Americans* (Garden City, NY: Doubleday, 1951), 100.

47. *Assignment of Ground Forces,* 30.

48. Ibid., 45, 50.

49. Ibid., 740.

50. Ibid., 118. See also ibid., 608–612, 615, 683–684, 695, 709.

51. Ibid., 80.

52. Ibid., 82.

53. Robert J. Donovan, *Tumultuous Years: The Presidency of Harry S. Truman, 1949–1953* (New York: Norton, 324; *Truman Papers, 1951,* 215.

54. Eisenhower, *At Ease,* 363.

Chapter 13. The European Command Test

The epigraphs to this chapter are drawn from Louis Galambos, ed., *The Papers of Dwight David Eisenhower* (hereafter *EP*), vols. 12–13, *NATO and the Campaign of 1952* (Baltimore: Johns Hopkins University Press, 1989), 12: no. 365, p. 532, and no. 561, pp. 817–818.

1. *EP,* 12: no. 142, p. 222.

2. Ibid., no. 77, pp. 118–119.

3. Lionel Hastings Ismay, *NATO: The First Five Years, 1949–1954* (The Hague: North Atlantic Treaty Organization, 1955), 72–73; Doris M. Condit, *History of the Office of the Secretary of Defense,* vol. 2, *The Test of War, 1950–1953* (Washington, DC: Historical Office, Office of the Secretary of Defense, 1988), 362–363.

4. Stephen E. Ambrose and Morris Honick, "Eisenhower: Rekindling the Spirit of the West," in *Generals in International Politics: NATO's Supreme Allied Commanders, Europe,* ed. Robert S. Jordan (Lexington: University Press of Kentucky, 1987), 13. For Eisenhower's litany of the problems he faced, see Dwight D. Eisenhower, *Annual Report to the Standing Group, North Atlantic Treaty Organization* (Paris: SHAPE, 1952), 13. See also Andrew J. Goodpaster, "Introduction: The Development of SHAPE: 1950–1953," in Jordan, *Generals in International Politics,* 4, who described Eisenhower's task in spring 1951 as "a staggering one"; Ismay, *NATO,* 70, 72.

5. *EP,* 12: no. 101, p. 154; no. 45, pp. 64–65; no. 52, p. 81; no. 58, p. 91; no. 118, p. 168; and no. 111, p. 160.

6. Ibid., no. 81, p. 127.

7. Ibid., no. 77, p. 118; emphasis in original. See also ibid., no. 111, p. 169, and no. 115, p. 180. "The sooner I can get rid of all these questions that are outside the military scope," Eisenhower wrote Marshall in 1942, "the happier I will be"; Alfred D. Chandler Jr., ed., *EP,* vols. 1–5, *The War Years* (Baltimore: Johns Hopkins University Press, 1970), 2: no. 673, p. 781.

8. Walter S. Poole, *History of the Joint Chiefs of Staff,* vol. 4, *The Joint Chiefs of Staff and National Policy, 1950–1952* (Washington, DC: Office of Joint History, Office

of the Chairman of the Joint Chiefs of Staff, 1998), 118; US Department of State, *Foreign Relations of the United States* (hereafter *FRUS*), *1951*, vol. 3, part 1, *European Security and the German Question* (Washington, DC: GPO, 1981), 68.

9. *FRUS*, 3: part 1, p. 68.

10. *EP*, 12: no. 81, p. 128, and no. 215, p. 341. See also ibid., no. 77, p. 118, and no. 167, p. 263.

11. Ibid., no. 218, pp. 345–346. See also *FRUS*, 3: part 1, p. 183.

12. *EP*, 12: no. 238, p. 380, emphasis in original; *FRUS*, 3: part 1, p. 189.

13. *EP*, 12: no. 230, p. 365.

14. John Gunther, *Eisenhower: The Man and the Symbol* (New York: Harper, 1957), 3; emphasis in original. See also Robert S. Jordan, "Conclusions: What Can We Learn from the NATO Experience in Multinational Military Leadership?" in Jordan, *Generals in International Politics*, 189.

15. Stephen E. Ambrose, *Americans at War* (Jackson: University Press of Mississippi, 1997), 181–182. See also *EP*, 12: no. 208, pp. 332–333n3.

16. *EP*, 12: no. 250, p. 396. In mid-July, Marshall informed Eisenhower of the results of a recent visit of key House committee members to SHAPE. "The men," he wrote, "were very favorable impressed. . . . They have a very clear idea of the magnitude of the problems facing you and are very laudatory in their description of the way you are going about things"; ibid., no. 281, p. 434n2. See also ibid., no. 209, p. 333; Ambrose, *Americans at War*, 181; Ambrose and Honick, "Eisenhower," 23.

17. Cited in *EP*, 12: no. 273, p. 426n2.

18. Ibid., no., 53, p. 83, and no. 77, p. 120; *FRUS*, 3: part 1, pp. 485–486. In subsequent years, Juin would take over as commander in chief of the Central Region (CINCENT).

19. *EP*, 12: no. 52, p. 83; no. 57, pp. 90–91n3; and no. 429, p. 636n2. "I think we are hurling the adjective 'Supreme' around rather carelessly these days," Eisenhower wrote Marshall. "It was invented, as I understand it, to designate an Allied Commander who would necessarily control troops of *all* services. Soon we'll have to use 'Colossal Supreme'"; ibid., no. 77, p. 119; emphasis in original. See also Poole, *Joint Chiefs of Staff*, 4: 121.

20. *EP*, 12: no. 236, p. 376. After finishing this last step in establishing the SHAPE command structure, Eisenhower reported, "We began to see definite improvements in the morale and readiness of the troops"; Eisenhower, *Annual Report to the Standing Group*, 16. See also Ismay, *NATO*, 73; Condit, *Secretary of Defense*, 2: 362–363.

21. Poole, *Joint Chiefs of Staff*, 4: 145–146.

22. Dean Acheson, *Present at the Creation: My Years in the State Department* (New York: Norton, 1969), 601–603.

23. Louis Galambos, ed., *EP*, vols. 10–11, *Columbia University* (Baltimore: Johns Hopkins University Press, 1984), 10: no. 380, pp. 515–519nn1–4; Poole, *Joint Chiefs of Staff*, 4: 83–84; Steven L. Rearden, *History of the Office of the Secretary of Defense*, vol. 1, *The Formative Years, 1947–1950* (Washington, DC: Historical Office, Office of the Secretary of Defense, 1984), 65; Thomas M. Sisk, "Forging the Weapon: Eisenhower as NATO's Supreme Allied Commander, Europe, 1950–1952," in *Eisenhower: A*

Centenary Assessment, ed. Guenter Bischof and Stephen E. Ambrose (Baton Rouge: Louisiana State University Press, 1995), 67, 72.

24. Condit, *Secretary of Defense,* 2: 372; *EP,* 12: no. 364, p. 531n4.

25. There were also evacuation provisions for US and Allied forces in Austria, Trieste, Iran, Turkey, and Greece; *EP,* 12: no. 405, p. 594n3.

26. Ibid., 592–593.

27. Ibid., no. 553, p. 805n2; Poole, *Joint Chiefs of Staff,* 4: 159.

28. *EP,* 13: no. 777, p. 1147.

29. Acheson, *Present at the Creation,* 558; *FRUS,* 3: part 1, p. 851.

30. *EP,* 12: no. 365, pp. 531–532.

31. Ismay, *NATO* 43.

32. Ibid., 187; *FRUS,* 3: part 1, p. 692.

33. *FRUS,* 3: part 1, p. 315.

34. *EP,* 12: no. 424, p. 629.

35. *FRUS,* 3: part 1, pp. 733–734. See also ibid., 357–363; Ismay, *NATO,* 45; Condit, *Secretary of Defense,* 2: 373.

36. *EP,* 12: no. 583, p. 856n2.

37. *FRUS, 1952–1954,* vol. 5, part 1, *Western European Security* (Washington, DC: GPO, 1983), 178; Ismay, *NATO,* 47.

38. On 15 January, Eisenhower had informed the Standing Group that the Paris conference had produced an adequate plan for a European Army. All other alternatives for obtaining a German military contribution, he reported, appeared "undesirable if not unacceptable." All NATO agencies, he concluded, should work for the early establishment of the EDC. The US representative to the Standing Group endorsed Eisenhower's conclusions; Poole, *Joint Chiefs of Staff,* 4: 149.

39. Acheson, *Present at the Creation,* 626. See also *FRUS,* 5: part 1, pp. 177–179, 226–254; Ismay, *NATO,* 190–192.

40. Eisenhower, *Annual Report to the Standing Group,* 36.

41. Ibid., 8–11, 21–26, 33.

42. Ibid., 5. See also Ismay, *NATO,* 102.

43. Ismay, *NATO,* 50–51; Acheson, *Present at the Creation,* 647–650; *FRUS,* 5: part 1, pp. 298–301, 684–686.

44. *FRUS,* 5: part 1, pp. 298–299; Sisk, "Forging the Weapons," 71, 82; and Galambos, Introduction to *EP,* 12: xvii.

Chapter 14. Executive Reform and the New Look

The epigraphs to this chapter are drawn from Alice C. Cole, Alfred Goldberg, Samuel A. Tucker, and Rudolph A. Winnacker, eds., *The Department of Defense: Documents on Establishment and Organization, 1944–1978* (hereafter *DOD Documents*) (Washington, DC: Office of the Secretary of Defense, Historical Office, 1978), 149; and *Public Papers of the President: Dwight D. Eisenhower, 1953* (Washington, DC: GPO, 1960), 250.

1. Dwight D. Eisenhower, *The White House Years,* vol. 1, *Mandate for Change,*

1952–1956 (Garden City, NY: Doubleday, 1963), 486; Robert J. Watson, *History of the Office of the Secretary of Defense,* vol. 4, *Into the Missile Age, 1956–1960* (Washington, DC: Historical Office, Office of the Secretary of Defense, 1977), 6.

2. For the cost-risk patterns throughout the Cold War, see John Lewis Gaddis, "Containment and the Logic of Strategy," *National Interest,* no. 10 (1987–1988), 27–38.

3. John Lewis Gaddis, *Strategies of Containment: A Critical Appraisal of Postwar American National Security Policy* (New York: Oxford University Press, 1982), 352–353.

4. Ibid., 91–92.

5. "NSC-68: United States Objectives and Programs for National Security," 14 April 1950, in *Containment: Documents on American Policy and Strategy, 1945–1950,* ed. Thomas H. Etzold and John Lewis Gaddis (New York: Columbia University Press, 1978), 401.

6. Dwight D. Eisenhower, "The Chance for Peace," address delivered before the American Society of Newspaper Editors, 16 April, 1953, *Eisenhower Papers, 1953,* 182. As early as April 1949, Eisenhower wrote Swede Hazlett that "since a democracy must always retain a waiting, strategically defensive, attitude it is mandatory that some middle line be determined between desirable strength and unbearable cost." Louis Galambos, ed., *The Papers of Dwight David Eisenhower* (hereafter *EP*), vols. 10–11, *Columbia University* (Baltimore: Johns Hopkins University Press, 1984), 10: no. 415, p. 564.

7. Watson, *Secretary of Defense,* 4: 20.

8. Richard M. Leighton, *History of the Office of the Secretary of Defense,* vol. 3, *Strategy, Money, and the New Look, 1953–1956* (Washington, DC: Historical Office, Office of the Secretary of Defense, 2001), 21; *Organizational Development of the Joint Chiefs of Staff, 1942–1989* (Washington, DC: Historical Division, Joint Secretariat, Joint Chiefs of Staff, November 1989), 29.

9. Doris M. Condit, *History of the Office of the Secretary of Defense,* vol. 2, *The Test of War, 1950–1953* (Washington, DC: Historical Office, Office of the Secretary of Defense, 1988), 526.

10. *DOD Documents,* 124, 118–119.

11. Louis Galambos, ed., *EP,* vols. 12–13, *NATO and the Campaign of 1952* (Baltimore: Johns Hopkins University Press, 1989), 13: no. 995, p. 1436.

12. Louis Galambos and Daun Van Ee, eds., *EP,* vols. 14–17, *The Presidency: The Middle Way* (Baltimore: Johns Hopkins University Press, 1996), 14: no. 1, p. 5. See also Eisenhower, *White House Years,* 1: 102; Piers Brendon, *Ike: His Life and Times* (New York: Harper and Row, 1986), 238.

13. Condit, *Secretary of Defense,* 2: 529.

14. Ann C. Whitman File, Administration Series, box 11, Eisenhower Library. For an example of Eisenhower's interest and involvement in proposing members for the Rockefeller Committee, see *EP,* 14: no. 85, p. 104.

15. US Congress, House, Committee on Government Operations, *Reorganization Plan No. 6 of 1953: Department of Defense, Hearings on H.R. Res. 264, 83rd Congress,*

first session (Washington DC: GPO, 1953), 140. For the list of witnesses, see Ann C. Whitman File, Administration Series, box 40, Eisenhower Library; Annex B, *Report of the Rockefeller Committee on Department of Defense Reorganization* (Washington, DC: GPO, 1953), 22.

16. Rockefeller's and Wilson's cover memoranda, White House Central Files, Official File, OF 3, box 23, Eisenhower Library. See also *Hearings on H.R. 264,* 140–141.

17. Undated "Notes on Defense Department Reorganization Plan and Report," Bryce Harlow File, Series I: Pre-Accession, box 19, Eisenhower Library; Gerard Clarfield, *Security with Solvency: Dwight D. Eisenhower and the Shaping of the American Military Establishment* (Westport, Conn.: Praeger, 1999), 101; *DOD Documents,* 157; *EP,* 14: no. 26, p. 36n2.

18. All quotations from the 30 April message in *DOD Documents,* 149–156.

19. *DOD Documents,* 152.

20. Eisenhower, *White House Years,* 1: 448; *DOD Documents,* 154, 150, 155. See also Robert J. Watson, *History of the Joint Chiefs of Staff,* vol. 5, *The Joint Chiefs of Staff and National Policy, 1953–1954* (Washington, DC: Historical Division, Joint Chiefs of Staff, 1986), 107.

21. *DOD Documents,* 155–156.

22. *Hearings on H.R. 264,* 252–253.

23. Cited ibid., 255–258, 260.

24. Ibid., 9, 186.

25. *DOD Documents,* 158.

26. *Eisenhower Papers, 1953,* 249–250.

27. *Hearings on H.R. 264,* 68. In their last working session, the Rockefeller Committee members had agreed to "an important proviso," reflecting the concern of the JCS voiced by General Bradley that the Joint Chiefs might be hampered operationally in dealing under the new arrangements with emergency or wartime conditions; *DOD Documents,* 136.

28. Hammond, *Organizing for Defense,* 289–290, 348–349.

29. Leighton, *Secretary of Defense,* 3: 6; Eisenhower, *White House Years,* 1: 86, 110–112; Douglas Kinnard, "Civil-Military Relations: The President and the General," in *The National Security: Its Theory and Practice, 1945–1960,* ed. Norman A. Graebner (New York: Oxford University Press, 1986), 208–209. For Eisenhower's analysis of Wilson, see his 14 May 1953 diary entry, *EP,* 14: no. 188, p. 225. For his chief of staff's analysis, see Sherman Adams, *Firsthand Report: The Story of the Eisenhower Administration* (New York: Harper, 1961), 402–403. In 1978 General Andrew Goodpaster pointed out that Eisenhower recognized in Wilson and his successor, Neil McElroy, that "he had people who were essentially managers but were not deeply grounded in matters of military policy or strategic direction. He recognized that and would have been the first to object to any attempt on their part to fulfill or to perform this strategic function." Oral History Interview with Andrew Goodpaster, 16 January 1978, OH 378, no. 4 of 4, Dr. Thomas Soapes, Eisenhower Library, 103.

30. Watson, *Joint Chiefs of Staff*, 5: 14–15; Glen H. Snyder, "The 'New Look' of 1953," in *Strategy, Politics, and Defense Budgets*, ed. Warner R. Schilling, Paul Y. Hammond, Glen H. Snyder (New York: Columbia University Press, 1962), 410–412.

31. *Eisenhower Papers, 1953*, 293–294.

32. Snyder, "New Look," 413.

33. Paul Y. Hammond, "Super Carriers and B-36 Bombers: Appropriations, Strategy, and Politics," in *American Civil-Military Decisions: A Book of Case Studies*, ed. Harold Stein (Birmingham: University of Alabama Press, 1963), 517, 515.

34. Adams, *Firsthand Report*, 404. See also Snyder, "New Look," 391, 393; Robert J. Donovan, *Eisenhower: The Inside Story* (New York: Harper, 1956), 18–19.

35. Watson, *Secretary of Defense*, 4: 21.

36. James M. Gavin, *War and Peace in the Space Age* (New York: Harper, 1958), 168.

37. Maxwell D. Taylor, *The Uncertain Trumpet* (New York: Harper, 1960), 110; Snyder, "New Look," 518.

38. Dwight D. Eisenhower, *The White House Years*, vol. 2, *Waging Peace, 1956–1961* (Garden City, NY: Doubleday, 1965), 255. See also Watson, *Secretary of Defense*, 4: 21.

39. Samuel P. Huntington, *The Common Defense: Strategic Programs in National Politics* (New York: Columbia University Press, 1961), 114.

40. Watson, *Secretary of Defense*, 4: 21.

41. US Department of State, *Foreign Relations of the United States* (hereafter *FRUS*), *1955–1957*, vol. 19, *National Security Policy* (Washington, DC: GPO, 1990), 281–282.

42. Oral History Interview with Andrew Goodpaster, OH 477, 10 April 1982, Malcolm S. McDonald, Eisenhower Library, 42.

43. Kinnard, "Civil-Military Relations," 218; I. M. Destler, "The Presidency and National Security Organization," in Graebner, *National Security*, 231.

44. Destler, "Presidency and National Security Organization," 233. On the entire National Security Council system instituted by Eisenhower, even as he addressed Defense Department reorganization, see Robert R. Bowie and Richard H. Immerman, *Waging Peace: How Eisenhower Shaped an Enduring Cold War Strategy* (New York: Oxford University Press, 1998), chapter 5; Robert Cutler, *No Time for Rest* (Boston: Little, Brown, 1965), chapter 18.

45. Stephen E. Ambrose, *Eisenhower*, vol. 2, *The President* (New York: Simon and Schuster, 1984), 676. See also Watson, *Secretary of Defense*, 4: 9, 801.

46. *FRUS, 1952–1954*, vol. 2, part 1, *National Security Affairs* (Washington, DC: GPO, 1984), 236.

47. *Eisenhower Papers, 1953*, 312.

48. Ibid., 293, 546–549. See also Leighton, *Secretary of Defense*, 3: 161–164.

49. *FRUS*, 2: part 1, p. 544.

50. Ibid., 571; Leighton, *Secretary of Defense*, 3: 198–199.

51. *FRUS*, 2: part 1, p. 582; Leighton, *Secretary of Defense*, 3: 189.

52. *FRUS*, 2: part 1, pp. 572–574.

53. Watson, *Joint Chiefs of Staff*, 5: 32, 67–68; Snyder, "New Look," 450; Clarfield, *Security with Solvency*, 139; Leighton, *Secretary of Defense*, 3: 213.

54. Watson, *Joint Chiefs of Staff*, 5: 68. See also Leighton, *Secretary of Defense*, 3: 213–214; Clarfield, *Security with Solvency*, 142.

55. Matthew B. Ridgway, *Soldier: The Memoirs of Matthew B. Ridgway* (New York: Harper, 1956), 267.

56. A. J. Bacevich, "The Paradox of Professionalism: Eisenhower, Ridgway, and the Challenge to Civilian Control, 1953–1955," *Journal of Military History* 61 (1997), 303–333.

57. *FRUS*, 2: part 1, p. 595.

Chapter 15. The Strains Deepen

The epigraphs to this chapter are drawn from Matthew B. Ridgway, *Soldier: The Memoirs of Matthew B. Ridgway* (New York: Harper, 1956), 332; and *Public Papers of the President: Dwight D. Eisenhower, 1956* (Washington, DC: GPO, 1958), 516.

1. Robert J. Watson, *History of the Joint Chiefs of Staff*, vol. 5, *The Joint Chiefs of Staff and National Policy, 1953–1954* (Washington, DC: Historical Division, Joint Chiefs of Staff, 1986), 39.

2. Ibid., 71; Richard M. Leighton, *History of the Office of the Secretary of Defense*, vol. 3, *Strategy, Money and the New Look, 1953–1956* (Washington, DC: Historical Office, Office of the Secretary of Defense, 2001), 261.

3. Watson, *Joint Chiefs of Staff*, 5: 42; Leighton, *Secretary of Defense*, 3: 261–262, 265–267.

4. Watson, *Joint Chiefs of Staff*, 5: 74.

5. Leighton, *Secretary of Defense*, 3: 327–328; Watson, *Joint Chiefs of Staff*, 5: 75.

6. Leighton, *Secretary of Defense*, 3: 344; US Department of State, *Foreign Relations of the United States* (hereafter *FRUS*), *1952–1954*, vol. 2, part 1, *National Security Affairs* (Washington, DC: GPO, 1984), 804–806.

7. *FRUS*, 2: part 1, p. 805.

8. Douglas Kinnard, "Civil-Military Relations: The President and the General," *The National Security: Its Theory and Practice, 1945–1960*, ed. Norman A. Graebner (New York: Oxford University Press, 1986), 204; Leighton, *Secretary of Defense*, 3: 329–330.

9. *FRUS, 1955–1957*, vol. 19, *National Security Policy* (Washington, DC: GPO, 1990), 9–24, 32–33. See also Leighton, *Secretary of Defense*, 3: 353–354; Watson, *Joint Chiefs of Staff*, 5: 53, 57.

10. Watson, *Joint Chiefs of Staff*, 5: 57. This may explain why Eisenhower agreed in November and December to proposals not only by the secretary of defense and the JCS but by the secretary of state to revise basic national security policy by including, in effect, the strategy of "flexible response"; Campbell Craig, *Destroying the Village:*

Eisenhower and Thermonuclear War (New York: Columbia University Press, 1998), 50–52.

11. Leighton, *Secretary of Defense*, 3: 367.

12. *Public Papers of the President: Dwight D. Eisenhower, 1954* (Washington, DC: GPO, 1960), 225–226.

13. *FRUS*, 19: 39–40. Presidential Press Secretary James Haggerty noted that as Eisenhower was talking, "you could hear a pin drop in the room"; ibid., 40.

14. Kinnard, "Civil-Military Relations," 204.

15. Maxwell D. Taylor, *The Uncertain Trumpet* (New York: Harper, 1959), 28–29. The official memorandum of the conversation with the president noted that Taylor "indicated complete understanding and acceptance" of Eisenhower's viewpoints; Kinnard, "Civil-Military Relations," 204.

16. On 4 January 1955 the *New York Times* published a detailed analysis of the field manual and of the fundamental Army–Air Force discord demonstrated by the manual over funding, manpower, and roles and missions; Leighton, *Secretary of Defense*, 3: 332–333; Taylor, *Uncertain Trumpet*, 23–26.

17. Taylor, *Uncertain Trumpet*, 27. Taylor returned to Asia, where he was promoted to commander in chief, Far East, a position he would hold until replacing Ridgway on 1 July.

18. Leighton, *Secretary of Defense*, 3: 373. See also Watson, *Joint Chiefs of Staff*, 5: 87.

19. James C. Hagerty, *The Diary of James C. Hagerty: Eisenhower in Mid-Course, 1954–1955*, ed. Robert H. Ferrell (Bloomington: Indiana University Press, 1983), 218–219.

20. Louis Galambos and Daun Van Ee, eds., *The Papers of Dwight David Eisenhower* (hereafter *EP*), vols. 14–17, *The Presidency: The Middle Way* (Baltimore: Johns Hopkins University Press, 1996), 14: no. 1430, p. 1705.

21. Gerard Clarfield, *Security with Solvency: Dwight D. Eisenhower and the Shaping of the American Military Establishment* (Westport, Conn.: Praeger, 1999), 162.

22. Watson, *Joint Chiefs of Staff*, 5: 80, 82.

23. Kenneth W. Condit, *History of the Joint Chiefs of Staff*, vol. 6, *The Joint Chiefs of Staff and National Policy, 1955–1956* (Washington, DC: Historical Office Joint Staff, 1992), 47; Leighton, *Secretary of Defense*, 3: 378.

24. Dwight D. Eisenhower, *The White House Years*, vol. 1, *Mandate for Change, 1952–1956* (Garden City, NY: Doubleday, 1963), 545.

25. *EP*, 16: no. 159, p. 1864n1; emphasis in original.

26. Leighton, *Secretary of Defense*, 3: 610–611; Clarfield, *Security with Solvency*, 170.

27. *Eisenhower Papers, 1956*, 168–169.

28. *EP*, 16: no. 1766, p. 2041.

29. *Eisenhower Papers, 1956*, 263–279.

30. *FRUS*, 19: 235–236.

31. Ibid., 238–241. See also Leighton, *Secretary of Defense*, 3: 656–657.

32. Taylor, *Uncertain Trumpet*, 115.

33. Robert J. Watson, *History of the Secretary of Defense*, vol. 4, *Into the Missile Age, 1956–1960* (Washington, DC: Historical Office, Office of the Secretary of Defense, 1997), 76; Condit, *Joint Chiefs of Staff*, 6: 52; Leighton, *Secretary of Defense*, 3: 658.

34. Taylor, *Uncertain Trumpet*, 37.

35. Leighton, *Secretary of Defense*, 3: 641. See also David Halberstam, *The Best and the Brightest* (New York: Random House, 1972), 473; Clarfield, *Security with Solvency*, 185; Kinnard, "Civil-Military Relations," 221–222. At a meeting of the chairman with the president on 18 April, Radford referred to some of the problems of Army morale. In reply, Eisenhower recalled a recent conversation with his son, in which John had commented that the lack of a doctrine assigning the Army a definite and permanent mission had left Army officers "unsatisfied and even bewildered" with a role that was "rather hazy to many of them." *FRUS*, 19: 298.

36. Halberstam, *Best and the Brightest*, 476.

37. Kinnard, "Civil-Military Relations," 222; E. Bruce Geelhold, *Charles E. Wilson and Controversy at the Pentagon* (Detroit: Wayne State University Press, 1979), 136–138.

38. John M. Taylor, *General Maxwell Taylor: The Sword and the Pen* (New York: Doubleday, 1989), 209–210; Leighton, *Secretary of Defense*, 3: 643.

39. *Eisenhower Papers, 1956*, 513–515.

40. *FRUS*, 19: 312–313.

41. Ibid., 314.

42. Ibid., 305.

43. *EP*, 17: no. 1963, p. 2256n4.

44. Ibid., no. 1898, p. 291; Piers Brendon, *Ike: His Life and Times* (Harper and Row, 1986), 321. See also *EP*, 17: no. 1894, p. 2188n1, and no. 1911, p. 2201.

45. Sherman Adams, *Firsthand Report: The Story of the Eisenhower Administration* (New York: Harper, 1961), 404–405; Watson, *Secretary of Defense*, 4: 77.

46. Dwight D. Eisenhower, *The White House Years*, vol. 2, *Waging Peace, 1956–1961* (Garden City, NY: Doubleday, 1965), 58.

47. Watson, *Secretary of Defense*, 4: 79.

48. Condit, *Joint Chiefs of Staff*, 6: 52.

49. Brendon, *Ike*, 334.

50. *EP*, 17: no. 2094, p. 2392n1, and no. 2155, p. 2410n1.

51. *FRUS*, 19: 389. See also ibid., 386–390; Andrew J. Goodpaster, 20 December 1956 memorandum of conference, 19 December 1956 White House meeting, Ann C. Whitman File, Dwight D. Eisenhower Diary Series, box 20, Eisenhower Library.

52. *FRUS*, 19: 391, 394, 393.

53. Leighton, *Secretary of Defense*, 3: 84; Clarfield, *Security with Solvency*, 195; Andrew J. Goodpaster, 12 January 1957 memorandum for record, White House Office, Office of the Staff Secretary Subject Series: Department of Defense Subseries, box 2, Eisenhower Library.

54. *FRUS,* 19: 393–394n6; 31 December 1956 White House memorandum, Ann C. Whitman File, Administration Series, box 41, Eisenhower Library.

55. *EP,* 17: no. 2152, p. 2471.

56. Andrew J. Goodpaster, 1 January 1957 memorandum for record, White House Office, Office of the Staff Secretariat Subject Series: Department of Defense Subseries, box 2, Eisenhower Library; *FRUS* 19: 395–396.

57. Eisenhower, *White House Years,* 1: 455. See also Leighton, *Secretary of Defense,* 3: 36–43.

Chapter 16. Impetus from Space

The epigraphs to this chapter are drawn from James R. Killian Jr., *Sputnik, Scientists, and Eisenhower: A Memoir of the First Special Assistant to the President for Science and Technology* (Cambridge: MIT Press, 1977), 8; and Dwight D. Eisenhower, *The White House Years,* vol. 2, *Waging Peace, 1956–1960* (Garden City, NY: Doubleday, 1965), 226.

1. Ann C. Whitman File, Eisenhower Library: 3 January 1958 Cabinet meeting, Cabinet Series, box 10, and Dwight D. Eisenhower Diary Series, box 30.

2. Robert J. Watson, *History of the Office of the Secretary of Defense,* vol. 4, *Into the Missile Age, 1956–1960* (Washington, DC: Historical Office, Office of the Secretary of Defense, 1997), 111.

3. Ibid., 113. See also ibid., 110–112.

4. Interview of Neil H. McElroy by Ed Edwin (hereafter McElroy interview), 8–9 May 1967, Eisenhower Administration Project, Oral History Research Office, Columbia University Columbia University, 7; *Public Papers of the Presidents: Dwight D. Eisenhower, 1957* (Washington, DC: GPO, 1958), 590, 703; Watson, *Secretary of Defense,* 4: 126–127, 129–131. "He picked up things very quickly . . ."; interview of Charles Coolidge by Ed Erwin, 7 June 1967, Eisenhower Administration Project, Oral History Research Office, Columbia University, 26.

5. Watson, *Secretary of Defense,* 4: 30. See also Gerard Clarfield, *Security with Solvency: Dwight Eisenhower and the Shaping of the American Military Establishment* (Westport, Conn.: Praeger, 1999), 208; Bryon R. Fairchild and Walter S. Poole, *History of the Joint Chiefs of Staff,* vol. 7, *The Joint Chiefs of Staff and National Policy, 1957–1960* (Washington, DC: Office of Joint History, Office of the Chairman of the Joint Chiefs of Staff, 2000), 2.

6. Piers Brendon, *Ike: His Life and Times* (New York: Harper and Row, 1986), 347. See also Robert A. Divine, *The Sputnik Challenge: Eisenhower's Response to the Soviet Satellite* (New York: Oxford University Press, 1993), 64–65.

7. John Emmett Hughes, *The Ordeal of Power: A Political Memoir of the Eisenhower Years* (New York: Atheneum, 1963), 247. See also Watson, *Secretary of Defense,* 4: 123–124.

8. Killian, *Sputnik, Scientists, and Eisenhower,* 347.

9. *Eisenhower Papers, 1957,* 723, 728, 730.

10. Watson, *Secretary of Defense*, 4: 126; *Eisenhower Papers, 1957*, 735–736.

11. Hughes, *Ordeal of Power*, 248.

12. Ibid., 249; Clarfield, *Security with Solvency*, 208.

13. "Reorganization of the Department of Defense," 14 October 1957 Budget Bureau memorandum, Ann C. Whitman File, Miscellaneous Series, box 1, Eisenhower Library. A handwritten notation on the document reads: "President informed."

14. 14 October 1957 Budget Bureau memorandum, Ann C. Whitman File, Miscellaneous Series, box 1, Eisenhower Library. The 1956 Unified Command Plan provided that unless authorized specifically, "no unified commander was to exercise direct command of any of the Service components or of a subordinate force"; Ronald H. Cole, Walter S. Poole, James F. Schnabel, Robert J. Watson, and Willard J. Webb, eds., *The History of the Unified Command Plan 1946–1999* (Washington, DC: Joint History Office, Office of the Joint Chiefs of Staff, 2003), 24. For Eisenhower's interaction with the 1956 UCP, see Arthur W. Radford to Andrew J. Goodpaster, 22 June memorandum, White House Office, Office of the Staff Secretary Subject Series: Department of Defense Subseries, box 4, Eisenhower Library.

15. 14 October 1957 Budget Bureau memorandum, Ann C. Whitman File, Miscellaneous Series, box 1, Eisenhower Library.

16. Undated Rockefeller "Reorganization of the Department of Defense" document attached to Andrew J. Goodpaster, 28 October 1957 memorandum for record, White House Office, Office of the Staff Secretary Subject Series: White House Subseries, box 5, and Ann C. Whitman File, Miscellaneous Series, box 1, Eisenhower Library; emphasis in original.

17. Divine, *Sputnik Challenge*, 43–44; Watson, *Secretary of Defense*, 4: 135–136.

18. Andrew J. Goodpaster, 4 November 1957 memorandum of conversation, 4 November 1957 White House meeting, Ann C. Whitman File, Dwight D. Eisenhower Diary Series, box 28, Eisenhower Library. See also Watson, *Secretary of Defense*, 4: 247; Divine, *Sputnik Challenge*, 86; Clarfield, *Security with Solvency*, 209–210.

19. Divine, *Sputnik Challenge*, 35–37; Paul H. Nitze with Ann M. Smith and Steven L. Reardon, *From Hiroshima to Glasnost: At the Center of Decision* (New York: Grove Weidenfeld, 1989), 167; Fred Kaplan, *The Wizards of Armageddon* (New York: Simon and Shuster, 1983), 136–141. The twenty-nine-page Gaither report was much shorter than NSC 68, but as Fred Kaplan notes, "nearly as gripping"; Kaplan, *Wizards of Armageddon*, 141. For the entire Gaither report, see US Department of State, *Foreign Relations of the United States* (hereafter *FRUS*), *1955–1957*, vol. 19, *National Security Policy* (Washington, DC: GPO, 1990), 638–661.

20. *FRUS*, 19: 621.

21. Dwight D. Eisenhower, letter to Swede Hazlett, 18 November 1957 Ann C. Whitman File, Dwight D. Eisenhower Diary Series, box 28, Eisenhower Library; Dwight D. Eisenhower, *Ike's Letters to a Friend*, ed. Robert Griffith (Lawrence: University Press of Kansas, 1984), 190.

22. Barry M. Goldwater, *With No Apologies: The Personal and Political Memoirs of United States Senator Barry M. Goldwater* (New York: William Morrow, 1970), 79.

See also Divine, *Sputnik Challenge*, 41, 47; Killian, *Sputnik, Scientists, and Eisenhower*, 11.

23. *FRUS*, 19: 648.

24. Ibid., 622.

25. Ibid., 645. Eisenhower later acknowledged the usefulness of the Gaither report, which "acted as a gadfly on any in the administration given to complacency, and . . . elicited a number of facts, conclusions and opinions that provided a checklist for searching examination"; Eisenhower, *White House Years*, 2: 223.

26. *FRUS*, 19: 622-623.

27. Andrew J. Goodpaster, 6 November 1957 memorandum for record, 4 November 1957 White House meeting, White House Office, Office of the Staff Secretary, Subject Series: Department of Defense Subseries, box 1, and Ann C. Whitman File, Dwight D. Eisenhower Dairy Series, box 28, Eisenhower Library.

28. Ibid.

29. Ibid.

30. Ibid.; emphasis in original.

31. *FRUS*, 19: 635. The national security adviser specifically called on McCloy; ibid., 632. See also ibid., 632-634; Divine, *Sputnik Challenge*, 39; Kaplan, *Wizards of Armageddon*, 149.

32. *Eisenhower Papers, 1957*, 230.

33. Nelson Rockefeller and Percy Brundage, 15 November 1957 memorandum, with attached 12 November 1957 draft report, "Reorganization of the Department of Defense," Ann C. Whitman File, Administration Series, box 25, and Miscellaneous Series, box 1, Eisenhower Library.

34. Andrew J. Goodpaster, 27 November 1957 memorandum for record, Ann C. Whitman File, Miscellaneous Series, box 1, and White House Office, Office of the Staff Secretary Subject Series: White House Subseries, box 5, Eisenhower Library.

35. 2 December 1957 entry, Ann C. Whitman File, Diary Series, box 9, Eisenhower Library.

36. Eisenhower, *Ike's Letters to a Friend*, 198.

37. *FRUS*, 19: 699.

38. Divine, *Sputnik Challenge*, 73. At the first NAC meeting at the Palais de Challot, Eisenhower sat "erect and attentive" for more than three hours in what his special assistant for national security affairs described as "a remarkable demonstration of courageous, complete recovery"; Robert Cutler, *No Time for Rest* (Boston: Little, Brown, 1965), 359.

39. Divine, *Sputnik Challenge*, 87. See also ibid., 48-50.

40. Ibid., 64, 66.

41. Eisenhower, *White House Years*, 2: 245.

42. Ann C. Whitman File, Eisenhower Library: 31 December 1957 Ann Whitman note to Eisenhower, Diary Series, box 9; Andrew J. Goodpaster, 10 January 1958 memorandum of conversation, 9 January 1958 White House meeting, Dwight D. Eisenhower Diary Series, box 30.

43. McElroy interview, 74. On 27 November, McElroy testified before the John-

son subcommittee that he would devote "considerable attention" to defense reorganization, but that it was an area of "such really major importance" that it would require
careful study; Watson, *Secretary of Defense,* 4: 249.

44. Watson, *Secretary of Defense,* 4: 250.

45. William Bragg Ewald Jr., *Eisenhower the President: Crucial Days, 1951–1960*
(Englewood Cliffs, NJ: Prentice-Hall, 1981), 321.

46. Killian, *Sputnik, Scientists, and Eisenhower,* 98. See also Kaplan, *Wizards of
Armageddon,* 153; Divine, *Sputnik Challenge,* 72.

47. Rockefeller Brothers Fund, *Prospects for America: The Rockefeller Panel Reports* (Garden City, NY: Doubleday, 1961), 108.

48. Divine, *Sputnik Challenge,* 77–78.

49. *Prospects for America,* 122–125.

50. Watson, *Secretary of Defense,* 4: 251.

51. Bob Burke and Ralph G. Thompson, *Bryce Harlow: Mr. Integrity* (Oklahoma
City: Oklahoma Heritage Association Publications, 2000), 59–60.

52. Ewald, *Eisenhower the President,* 145.

53. *Public Papers of the Presidents: Dwight D. Eisenhower, 1958* (Washington, DC:
GPO, 1959), 8.

54. 9 January 1958 entry, Ann C. Whitman File, Diary Series, box 9, Eisenhower
Library.

55. *Eisenhower Papers, 1958,* 92.

56. Ibid.

Chapter 17. Reform Proposals and Congressional Gauntlet

The epigraphs to this chapter are drawn from Dwight D. Eisenhower, *The White
House Years,* vol. 2, *Waging Peace, 1956–1961* (Garden City, NY: Doubleday, 1965), 244,
246; and deleted portion of 6 May 1958 Republican dinner speech, Bryce Harlow
Papers, Series I, box 3, Eisenhower Library.

1. 17 January 1958 Cabinet meeting, Ann C. Whitman File, Cabinet Series, box
10, Eisenhower Library.

2. Eisenhower, *White House Years,* 2: 244.

3. Eisenhower, *White House Years,* 2: 245; Eisenhower Library: Andrew J. Good-
paster, 30 January 1958 memorandum for record, 25 January 1958 Pentagon meeting,
White House Office, Office of the Staff Secretary Subject Series: Department of De-
fense Subseries, box 1; Bryce Harlow, 30 January 1958 memorandum for record, 25
January 1958 Pentagon meeting, Ann C. Whitman File, Dwight D. Eisenhower Diary
Series, box 30; 25 January 1958 entry, Ann C. Whitman File, Diary Series, box 9.

4. Goodpaster 30 January 1958 memorandum for record; Harlow 30 January
1958 memorandum for record; Eisenhower, *White House Years,* 2: 245. According to
Harlow's memorandum, Eisenhower calls the executive agent system "crazy." According to Goodpaster's memorandum, the president considers it to be "most unwise."

5. Interview of Charles Coolidge by Ed Edwin (hereafter Coolidge interview),

7 June 1967, Eisenhower Administration Project, Oral History Research Office, Columbia University, 5–7.

6. Ibid., 7, 25.

7. Andrew J. Goodpaster, 28 February 1958 memorandum of conference, 27 February 1958 White House meeting, White House Office, Office of the Staff Secretary Subject Series: Department of Defense Subseries, box 1, Eisenhower Library.

8. 30 March 1958 entry, Ann C. Whitman File, Diary Series, box 9, Eisenhower Library.

9. Ann C. Whitman File, Eisenhower Library: Dwight D. Eisenhower to Henry Cabot Lodge, Dwight D. Eisenhower Diary Series, box 32, and Administrative Series, box 24; 2 April 1958 entry, Diary Series, box 10.

10. Ann C. Whitman File, Eisenhower Library: 1 April 1958 legislative meeting, Legislative Meeting Series, box 3, and Dwight D. Eisenhower Diary Series, box 32.

11. This and all subsequent references to the president's 3 April reorganization message to Congress are contained in Alice C. Cole, Alfred Goldberg, Samuel A. Tucker, and Rudolph A. Winnacker, eds., *The Department of Defense: Documents on Establishment and Organization, 1944–1978* (hereafter *DOD Documents*) (Washington, DC: Office of the Secretary of Defense Historical Office, 1978), 175–186.

12. *Public Papers of the Presidents: Dwight D. Eisenhower, 1958* (Washington, DC: GPO, 1959), 320; US Congress, House, Committee on Armed Services, *Hearings on Reorganization of the Department of Defense,* 85th Congress, second session (Washington, DC: GPO, 1958), 6710–6711; Robert J. Watson, *History of the Office of the Secretary of Defense,* vol. 4, *Into the Missile Age, 1956–1960* (Washington, DC: Historical Office, Office of the Secretary of Defense, 1997), 263. At a press conference the same day, the president was less than candid when queried about the funding issue. "Never in all the years I have been in the military, or since," he responded, "have I advocated the making of appropriations in one lump sum to the Secretary of Defense or to any other individual"; *Eisenhower Papers, 1958,* 312–313.

13. US Congress, House, Committee on Armed Services, *Department of Defense Reorganization Bill of 1958,* 85th Congress, second session, H. Doc. 371 (Washington, DC: GPO, 1958); Eisenhower, *White House Years,* 2: 249; Richard M. Leighton, *History of the Office of the Secretary of Defense,* vol. 3, *Strategy, Money, and the New Look, 1953–1956* (Washington, DC: Historical Office, Office of the Secretary of Defense, 2001), 42; Watson, *Secretary of Defense,* 4: 38–40, 244–245.

14. 16 April 1958 Address of Hon. Carl Vinson, M.C., Chairman, Committee on Armed Services, undated press release, Bryce Harlow File, Series I, box 3, Eisenhower Library. See also Watson, *Secretary of Defense,* 4: 264; Robert A. Divine, *The Sputnik Challenge: Eisenhower's Response to the Soviet Satellite* (New York: Oxford University Press, 1993), 133.

15. Gerard Clarfield, *Security with Solvency: Dwight D. Eisenhower and the Shaping of the American Military Establishment* (Westport, Conn.: Praeger, 1999), 219.

16. *House Reorganization Hearings,* 5974–5975.

17. Ibid., 5998–5999.

18. *Eisenhower Papers, 1958,* 343.

19. *House Reorganization Hearings,* 6041, 6043, 6048, 6098. At one point during discussion on the proposed repeal of the congressional testimony provision, McElroy told the committee: "I don't think it is the most important thing one way or the other, to be perfectly honest with you"; ibid., 6041.

20. Ibid., 6020, 6022, 6129, 6011, 6109.

21. Ibid., 6110–6113.

22. Undated, unsigned memorandum of record, 26 April 1958 Eisenhower-McElroy telephone conversation, Ann C. Whitman File, Miscellaneous Series, box 1, Eisenhower Library.

23. Final presidential statement attached to 26 April 1958 Bryce Harlow rework of a draft presidential statement, Bryce Harlow File, Series I, box 3, Eisenhower Library.

24. Bob Burke and Ralph G. Thompson, *Bryce Harlow: Mr. Integrity* (Oklahoma City: Oklahoma Heritage Association Publications, 2000), 135.

25. Eisenhower, *White House Years,* 2: 251; Watson, *Secretary of Defense,* 4: 269.

26. Eisenhower, *White House Years,* 2: 251.

27. Dwight D. Eisenhower to Arthur K. Atkinson, Wabash Railroad Company, St. Louis, 5 May 1958 letter, Bryce Harlow File, Series I, Pre-Accession, box 2, Eisenhower Library. For the gestation of the letter writing campaign, see 21 April 1958 entry, Ann C. Whitman File, Diary Series, box 10, Eisenhower Library.

28. Eisenhower, *White House Years,* 2: 251. "I guess I must have sent out around 450 letters," Eisenhower recalled later to his White House Chief of Staff; Sherman Adams, *Firsthand Report: The Story of the Eisenhower Administration* (New York: Harper, 1961), 419. Harlow considered it to be a "tour de force" effort, in which "for the first time Dwight Eisenhower used all his powers as President; it was sheer muscle all the way"; William Bragg Ewald Jr., *Eisenhower the President: Crucial Days, 1951–1960* (Englewood Cliffs, NJ: Prentice-Hall, 1981), 247.

29. *House Reorganization Hearings,* 6427–6428, 6345, 6353.

30. Ibid., 6355–6357, 6366–6367, 6384–6385, 6377.

31. Ibid., 6797–6806, 6791–6797, 6701; Watson, *Secretary of Defense,* 4: 268.

32. Ibid., 6524, 6472, 6487, 6541, 6526, 6474.

33. US Congress, Senate, Armed Services Committee, *Hearings, Department of Defense Reorganization Act of 1958,* 85th Congress, second session (Washington, DC: GPO, 1958), 1–7; Watson, *Secretary of Defense,* 4: 269.

34. Bryce Harlow, 26 May 1958 memorandum for record, 12 May 1958 White House meeting, Ann C. Whitman File, Dwight D. Eisenhower Diary Series, box 32, Eisenhower Library.

35. *House Reorganization Hearings,* 6810–6811, 6815; 14 and 16 May entries, Ann C. Whitman, Diary Series, box 10, Eisenhower Library.

36. Dwight D. Eisenhower to Arthur Krock, 30 May 1958, Ann C. Whitman File, Dwight D. Eisenhower Diary Series, box 33, Eisenhower Library.

37. *Eisenhower Papers, 1958,* 107.

38. *House Reorganization Hearings,* 6850, 6853–6855.

39. Bryce Harlow to Robert Stevens, 20 May 1958, Bryce Harlow File, Series I: Pre-Accession, box 2, Eisenhower Library.

40. L. A. Minnich Jr., 19 May 1958 notes, White House Office, Office of the Staff Secretary, Legislative Meetings Series, box 5; L. A. Minnich Jr., 19 May 1958 memorandum for Maurice Stans, Ann C. Whitman File, Legislative Meetings Series, box 33, Eisenhower Library.

41. L. A. Minnich Jr., 27 May 1958 notes, White House Office, Office of the Staff Secretary, Legislative Meetings Series, box 5, Eisenhower Library. See also *DOD Documents*, 187; *House Reorganization Hearings*, 6857; Divine, *Sputnik Challenge*, 138; Watson, *Secretary of Defense*, 4: 270; Eisenhower, *White House Years*, 2: 252; Bryce Harlow, 28 May memorandum for record, 27 May 1958 White House meeting, Ann C. Whitman File, Dwight D. Eisenhower Diary Series, box 32, Eisenhower Library.

42. *Eisenhower Papers, 1958,* 439–443; emphasis in original.

43. *New York Times,* 2 June 1958.

44. Dwight D. Eisenhower to Arthur Krock, 30 May 1958, Ann C. Whitman File, Dwight D. Eisenhower Diary Series, box 33, Eisenhower Library.

45. Clarfield, *Security with Solvency,* 227.

46. Charles Coolidge, 17 June 1958 memorandum to Oliver Gale, Bryce Harlow File, Series I: Pre-Accession, box 1, Eisenhower Library; *Senate Reorganization Hearings*, 2.

47. Dwight D. Eisenhower, letter to Representative Francis F. Bolton, 17 June 1958, White House Central Files 1953–61, Official File OF 3-vv, Eisenhower Library. Fifteen Republicans and twenty Democrats crossed party lines; *DOD Documents*, 187.

Chapter 18. Executive-Legislative Reform

The epigraph to this chapter is drawn from *Public Papers of the Presidents: Dwight D. Eisenhower, 1958* (Washington, DC: GPO, 1959), 332.

1. *Eisenhower Papers, 1958,* 177. That day, Eisenhower sent Harlow two bottles of Chivas Regal; William Bragg Ewald Jr., *Eisenhower the President: Crucial Days, 1951–1960* (Englewood Cliffs NJ: Prentice-Hall, 1981), 247.

2. *Eisenhower Papers, 1958,* 200.

3. Clinton Rossiter, *The American Presidency* (New York: Harcourt, Brace, 1960), 161.

4. Alice C. Cole, Alfred Goldberg, Samuel A. Tucker, and Rudolph A. Winnacker, eds., *The Department of Defense: Documents on Establishment and Organization, 1944–1978* (hereafter *DOD Documents*) (Washington, DC: Office of the Secretary of Defense Historical Office, 1978), 281.

5. Ibid., 207, 210, 213.

6. US Congress, House, Investigations Subcommittee, Committee on Armed Services, *Hearings, Reorganization Proposals for the Joint Chiefs of Staff,* 97th Congress, second session (Washington, DC: GPO, 1982), 462.

7. *DOD Documents,* 218; William J. Lynn, "The War Within: The Joint Military Structure and Its Critics," in *Reorganizing America's Defense: Leadership in War and Peace,* ed. Robert J. Art, Vincent Davis, and Samuel P. Huntington (New York: Pergamon-Brassey, 1985), 177–178.

8. *DOD Documents,* 204–205, 198.

9. Ibid., 200; Robert J. Watson, *History of the Office of the Secretary of Defense,* vol. 6, *Into the Missile Age, 1956–1960* (Washington, DC: Historical Office, Office of the Secretary of Defense, 1997), 78.

10. US Congress, Senate, Committee on Armed Services, *Hearings, Department of Defense Reorganization Act of 1958,* 85th Congress, second session (Washington, DC: GPO, 1958), 1; *DOD Documents,* 185.

11. Dwight D. Eisenhower, *The White House Years,* vol. 2, *Waging Peace, 1956–1961* (Garden City, NY: Doubleday, 1965), 252. See also *DOD Documents,* 199.

12. *DOD Documents,* 197–198.

13. Ibid., 199, 198.

14. Eisenhower, *White House Years,* 2: 252.

15. Andrew J. Goodpaster, 30 August 1958 memorandum of conversation, 28 August 1958 White House meeting, White House Office, Office of the Staff Secretary Subject Series: Department of Defense Subseries, box 1, Eisenhower Library. The new UCP was approved by the president and issued by the secretary of defense on 4 September 1958.

16. Andrew J. Goodpaster, 30 September 1958 memorandum of conversation, 29 September 1958 White House meeting, Ann C. Whitman File, Dwight D. Eisenhower Diary Series, box 36, Eisenhower Library; Robert A. Divine, *The Sputnik Challenge: Eisenhower's Response to the Soviet Satellite* (New York: Oxford University Press, 1993), 200, 202–203, 185, 196, 198.

17. Watson, *Secretary of Defense,* 4: 279–280.

18. Unsigned 18 November 1958 "Comments on Draft Department of Defense Directive 5100.1," Bryce Harlow File, Series I: Pre-Accession, box 3, Eisenhower Library.

19. *DOD Documents,* 317–318.

20. Major John S. D. Eisenhower, 23 December 1958 memorandum of conversation, 22 December 1958 White House meeting, White House Office, Office of the Staff Secretary Subject Series: Department of Defense Subseries, box 4, Eisenhower Library.

21. Ibid.

22. Ibid.

23. Ibid.

24. Donald A. Quarles, 26 December 1958 memorandum to Bryce Harlow, Bryce Harlow File, Series I, Pre-Accession, box 3, Eisenhower Library; *DOD Documents,* 316.

25. Douglas T. Stuart, *Creating the National Security State: A History of the Law That Transformed America* (Princeton: Princeton University Press, 2008), 275.

26. Eisenhower, *White House Years*, 2: 247. Amy Zegart, on the other hand, focuses on the "largely unchanging state of JCS design and operations," particularly when compared with the evolution of the NSC system, and concludes that "the Eisenhower reforms of 1953 and 1958 were more far-reaching on paper than in practice. The president's efforts failed to get at the root problem: service power and interests"; Amy Zegart, *Flawed by Design: The Evolution of the CIA, JCS, and NSC* (Stanford: Stanford University Press, 1999), 132, 138.

27. Eisenhower, *White House Years*, 2: 253.

28. US Congress, House, Committee on Armed Services, *Hearings, The National Defense Program—Unification and Strategy*, 81st Congress, first session (Washington, DC: GPO, 1949), 563–564.

Epilogue

The epigraphs to this chapter are drawn from US Congress, Senate, Committee on Armed Services, *Hearings, Department of Defense Reorganization of 1958*, 85th Congress, second session (Washington, DC: GPO, 1958), 417–418; 131 *Congressional Record* (2 October 1985) S. 12403, 99th Congress, first session, 25539–25541; James R. Locher III, *Victory on the Potomac: The Goldwater-Nichols Act Unifies the Pentagon* (College Station: Texas A&M University Press, 2002), 352.

1. US Congress, House, Armed Services Committee, Investigations Subcommittees, *Hearings, Reorganization Proposals for the Joint Chiefs of Staff*, 97th Congress, second session, HASC no. 97-47 (Washington, DC: GPO, 1982), 462.

2. Committee on the Defense Establishment, *Report to President Kennedy* (hereafter Symington Report) (Washington, DC: GPO, 1960); Blue Ribbon Defense Panel, *Report to the President and the Secretary of Defense on the Department of Defense* (hereafter Blue Ribbon Report) (Washington, DC: GPO, 1970); Richard C. Steadman, *Report to the Secretary of Defense on the National Military Command Structure* (hereafter Steadman Report) (Washington, DC: GPO, 1978).

3. Locher, *Victory on the Potomac*, 29; William J. Lynn and Barry R. Posen, "The Case for JCS Reform," *International Security* 16 (1985–1986), 97; Daniel J. Kaufman, "National Security: Organizing the Armed Forces," *Armed Forces and Society* 14 (1987), 100.

4. Symington Report, 6; Amy B. Zegart, *Flawed by Design: The Evolution of the CIA, JCS, and NSC* (Stanford: Stanford University Press, 1999), 148.

5. Samuel P. Huntington, "Organization and Strategy," in *Reorganizing America's Defense: Leadership in War and Peace*, ed. Robert J. Art, Vincent Davis, and Samuel P. Huntington (New York: Pergamon-Brassey, 1985), 237.

6. Peter J. Roman and David W. Tarr, "The Joint Chiefs of Staff: From Service Parochialism to Jointness," *Political Science Quarterly* 113 (1998), 94.

7. Ibid.; Steadman Report, 57. The 1970 Blue Ribbon Defense Panel characterized the JCS staffing system as one "based not only on coordination with the Services, but on their concurrence"; appendix N, Blue Ribbon Report, 14.

8. Steadman Report, 53.

9. Huntington, "Organization and Strategy," 241; Kaufman, "National Security," 103–104.

10. Blue Ribbon Report, 27, and appendix N, 8. See also Lynn and Posen, "Case for JCS Reform," 83; Kaufman, "National Security," 99; William J. Lynn, "The Wars Within: The Joint Military Structure and Its Critics," in Art, Davis, and Huntington, *Reorganizing America's Defense*, 183. For the distinction between "chain" and "channel" of command, see US Congress, Senate, Committee on Armed Services, *Hearings, Reorganization of the Department of Defense*, 99th Congress, first session, S. Hrg. 99-1083 (Washington, DC: GPO, 1987), 393; Archie D. Barrett, *Reappraising Defense Organization* (Washington, DC: National Defense University Press, 1983), 79–80.

11. Colin Powell, with Joseph E. Perscis, *My American Journey* (New York: Random House, 1995), 576. See also Huntington, "Organization and Strategy," 249; Locher, *Victory on the Potomac*, 29–30; David C. Jones, "What's Wrong with Our Defense Establishment," *New York Times Magazine*, 7 November 1982, 70.

12. Huntington, "Organization and Strategy," 248.

13. Locher, *Victory on the Potomac*, 44.

14. Joint Chiefs of Staff Publication 2, *Unified Action Armed Forces*, with changes (Washington, DC: Office of the Joint Chiefs of Staff, 1959); Lynn and Posen, "Case for JCS Reform," 93.

15. Lynn and Posen, "Case for JCS Reform," 84; Kaufman, "National Security," 109; C. Kenneth Allard, *Command, Control, and the Common Defense* (New Haven: Yale University Press, 1990), 129.

16. Blue Ribbon Report, 50. See also US Congress, Senate, Committee on Armed Services, *Defense Organization: The Need for Change*, 99th Congress, first session (Washington, DC: GPO, 1985), 307–309 (hereafter Locher Report); Kaufman, "National Security," 99; Lynn, "Wars Within," 183.

17. Steadman Report, 16.

18. Alice C. Cole, Alfred Goldberg, Samuel A. Tucker, and Rudolph A. Winnacker, eds., *The Department of Defense Documents on Establishment and Organization, 1944–1978* (hereafter *DOD Documents*) (Washington, DC: Office of the Secretary of Defense Historical Office, 1978), 121. See also Lynn, "Wars Within," 195.

19. Locher, *Victory on the Potomac*, 264.

20. *DOD Documents*, 218.

21. David C. Jones, "Why the Joint Chiefs of Staff Must Change," *Armed Forces Journal International*, March 1982, 64.

22. *1982 House Hearings, Reorganization Proposals*, 46–97; Lynn, "Wars Within," 186–187.

23. Gerard Clarfield, *Security with Solvency: Dwight D. Eisenhower and the Shaping of the American Military Establishment* (Westport, Conn.: Praeger, 1999), 240.

24. Edward C. Meyer, "The JCS: How Much Reform Is Needed?" *Armed Forces Journal International*, April 1982, 89; Lynn, "Wars Within," 193; Maxwell D. Taylor, *The Uncertain Trumpet* (New York: Harper, 1960), 176–177. "He had a reputation for knowing what he was talking about," JCS Chairman Admiral William Crowe recalled

of Meyer almost a decade later. "No one concerned with the military was likely to dismiss his opinions outright"; William J. Crowe Jr., with David Chanoff, *The Line of Fire* (New York: Simon and Schuster, 1993), 147.

25. *1982 House Hearings, Reorganization Proposals*, 3, 5.

26. Ibid., 461, 458, 444.

27. US Congress, Senate, Committee on Armed Services, *Hearings, Organization, Structure, and Decisionmaking Procedures of the Department of Defense*, 98th Congress, first session, S. Hrg. 98-375, part 5, 2 November 1983, 182.

28. 131 *Congressional Record* (2 October 1985) S. 12402, 99th Congress, first session, 25539-25541; emphasis added.

29. Locher, *Victory on the Potomac*, 330. See also Locher Report, 240. For Locher's briefing, see *1985 SASC Hearings, Reorganization of the Defense Department*, 13-40.

30. Locher, *Victory on the Potomac*, 352.

31. Ibid., 397.

32. Center of Strategic and International Studies, *Toward a More Effective Defense: The Final Report of the Defense Organization Project* (Washington, DC: CSIS, Georgetown University, 1985), 8.

33. Locher, *Victory on the Potomac*, 396. For Goodpaster's 4 December 1985 testimony before the Senate committee, see *1985 SASC Hearings, Reorganization of the Department of Defense*, 355-361.

34. Locher, *Victory on the Potomac*, 397.

35. *Public Papers of the Presidents of the United States: Ronald Reagan, 1986*, book 2 (Washington, DC: GPO, 1989), 1312.

36. Kaufman, "National Security," 89-92; Archie D. Barrett, "Empowering Eisenhower's Concept," *Joint Force Quarterly*, no. 13 (Autumn 1996), 13.

37. For this and the following provisions of the 1986 legislation, see Public Law 99-433, 1 October 1986, *Goldwater-Nichols Department of Defense Reorganization Act of 1986*, Titles I-VI; Douglas C. Lovelace, "The DOD Reorganization Act of 1986: Improving the Department Through Centralization and Integration," in *Organizing for National Security*, ed. Douglas T. Stuart (Carlisle, PA: Strategic Studies Institute, 2000), 65-100; Roman and Tarr, "Joint Chiefs of Staff," 100-102.

38. Richard H. Kohn, "The Crisis in Military-Civilian Relations," *National Interest*, Spring 1994, 3-17; Roman and Tarr, "Joint Chiefs of Staff," 110-111.

39. Carl E. Mundy, "Cautions on Goldwater-Nichols," *Joint Force Quarterly*, no. 13 (Autumn 1996), 21.

40. Locher, *Victory on the Potomac*, 440.

41. "The Chairman as Principal Military Adviser: An Interview with Colin L. Powell," *Joint Force Quarterly*, no. 13 (Autumn 1996), 30.

42. Sam Nunn, "Future Trends in Defense Organization," *Joint Force Quarterly*, no. 13 (Autumn 1996), 63, 65.

43. National Defense Panel, *Transforming Defense: National Security in the 21st Century* (Arlington, VA: National Defense Panel, 1997); Center for Strategic and International Studies, *Beyond Goldwater-Nichols: US Government and Defense Reform for a New Strategic Era, Phases I and II Reports* (Washington, DC: CSIS, 2004,

2005); US Commission on National Security/21st Century, Phase III Report, *Road Map for National Security: Imperative for Change* (Washington, DC: GPO, 2001).

44. The focus has turned to "unified action" as the "synchronization, coordination, and/or integration of the activities of governmental and nongovernmental entities with military operations to achieve unity of effort"; Joint Chiefs of Staff, *Joint Publication 1: Doctrine for the Armed Forces of the United States* (Washington, DC: GPO, 2007), GL-11.

45. Stephen E. Ambrose, *Eisenhower,* vol. 1, *Soldier, General of the Army, President-Elect, 1890–1952* (New York: Simon and Schuster, 1983), 308.

Index

160-161; at the Arcadia Conference, 38-39; at the Army War College, 19; as assistant to General MacArthur, 24, 26-27; as assistant to General Moseley, 22-23; on the Battle Monuments Commission, 18-19; and the British military leadership, 57-58, 106, 110-111, 113-114, 123, 130-131; at Camp Colt, 13-14; as candidate for president, 213; and Churchill, 66, 81, 96, 114-115, 132; and the Combined Chiefs of Staff, 52-53, 66-67, 70, 81, 96, 98-99, 110, 111-112, 117-118; as consultant to Forrestal, 172, 173-174; European admiration for, 206, 216; football as influence on, 13; and Forrestal, 171-172; health problems of, 175-176, 249, 253, 269-270; and the Joint Chiefs of Staff, 3, 163, 172, 175, 181, 237; as liaison between Roosevelt and Churchill, 51, 52; Marshall as adviser to, 49-50, 67-68, 82, 83, 91, 107, 118-119, 127, 130; and negotiations for unification bill, 156-157; personal attributes of, 137; promotions of, 13, 55, 88; as staff officer for General Marshall, 36-37; at West Point, 7; White House staff reorganized by, 235-236; on working with Allies, 40-41, 54
—and implementation of unity of command in World War II, 3, 101-102, 104-105, 136-138: in execution of OVERLORD, 122-138; in Italy, 95-100; and miscommunications with Montgomery, 125-131; in planning for OVERLORD, 106-121; strategic air forces as challenge for, 112-115
—leadership roles of: as Army chief of staff, 145-146, 151; as chairman of the Joint Chiefs, 174; as chief of War Plans Division, 48-49; as commander in chief, U.S. Forces of Occupation, Germany, 138; as commander of the European Theater of Operations, 59, 63-74; as head of the Operations Division (OPD), 49-51, 53; named commander of OVERLORD, 104-105; named supreme commander, Allied Expeditionary Force (SCAEF), 111-112; as president of Columbia University, 165, 169, 171; as supreme Allied commander, Europe (SACEUR) for NATO, 192-198, 200, 201-217; as Third Army chief of staff, 31-32
—and North African invasion: at the Casablanca Conference, 84-86, 92; and new Allied command structure, 86-89, 90, 92; problems with unity of command, 76-85; unity of command tested on the battlefield, 89-93
—as president of the United States: defense budget as ongoing issue for, 241-243, 247, 250-251, 253-254, 255-256, 259, 265, 266, 271; inauguration of, 225; international crises faced by, 241, 242, 245, 247, 249, 301;

and the Joint Chiefs, 224, 252-253, 256-257; national security as concern of, 221-223; New Look strategy of, 223-224, 238-240, 241-243, 258; and nuclear weapons strategy, 243-245, 246; and reorganization of Defense Department, 3, 224-235, 259-274, 275-294, 295-305; scientific research supported by, 269, 270, 280; second term sought by, 250, 254; and tensions with military advisers, 243-248
—See also North Atlantic Treaty Organization (NATO); unified command
Eisenhower, John Doud, 17, 116, 250, 259
Eisenhower, Mamie Doud, 13, 16, 21
Eisenhower, Milton, 226, 250
Europe. See Eastern Europe; Western Europe
European Army, 213, 215-216
European Defense Community (EDC), 211, 242
European Defense Force (EDF), 211
European Theater of Operations (ETO): Eisenhower as commander of, 63-74, 106-121; Eisenhower's recommendations for, 56. See also Eisenhower, Dwight David; OVERLORD

Faircloth, Jean, 27
Faulkner, William, 4
First Allied Airborne Army, 125
Foch, Ferdinand, 14, 17, 41, 68, 73
Forrestal, James V.: as advocate of unified command, 143-144, 146-147, 155, 170-171; death of, 176; as opponent of Eisenhower's approach to unification, 144, 160-161; relationship with Eisenhower, 152-153, 171-172; as secretary of defense, 165, 170-171, 173-174, 175; as secretary of the Navy, 143-144, 152-153, 157
Foster, William, 275
France: as member of NATO, 191-192, 196
Fredendall, Lloyd, 75, 90
French military leadership: Eisenhower's problems with, 77-78

Gaddis, John Lewis, 222
Gaither, H. Rowan, 265
Gaither report, 265-266, 269, 272
German Air Force, 114
German Army: in North Africa, 76-77. See also OVERLORD; World War II
Germany: as member of NATO, 193, 200; rearmament of, 211; surrender of, 136
Gerow, Leonard (Gee), 18, 30, 48
Goldwater, Barry, 266, 314; and reorganization of the armed services, 317-318
Goldwater-Nichols Act, 3, 321-324
Goodpaster, Andrew, 235-236, 255-256, 269, 276, 277, 286-287, 296, 301, 307-308, 313, 316

384 INDEX